DAISUKE
ASHIHARA

When two deadlines pile up, I get a little overwhelmed. When three pile up, it turns out I get fat. Here's *World Trigger* volume 2.

—Daisuke Ashihara, 2013

Daisuke Ashihara began his manga career at the age of 27 when his manga *Room 303* won second place in the 75th Tezuka Awards. His first series, *Super Dog Rilienthal*, began serialization in *Weekly Shonen Jump* in 2009. *World Trigger* is his second serialized work in *Weekly Shonen Jump*. He is also the author of several shorter works, including the one-shots *Super Dog Rilienthal*, *Trigger Keeper* and *Elite Agent Jin*.

# WORLD TRIGGER VOL. 2
## SHONEN JUMP Manga Edition

### STORY AND ART BY DAISUKE ASHIHARA

Translation/Lillian Olsen
Touch-Up Art & Lettering/Annaliese Christman
Design/Sam Elzway
Editor/Hope Donovan

Printed in the U.S.A.

Published by VIZ Media, LLC
P.O. Box 77010
San Francisco, CA 94107

10 9 8 7 6 5 4 3 2 1
First printing, October 2014

SHONEN JUMP MANGA EDITION

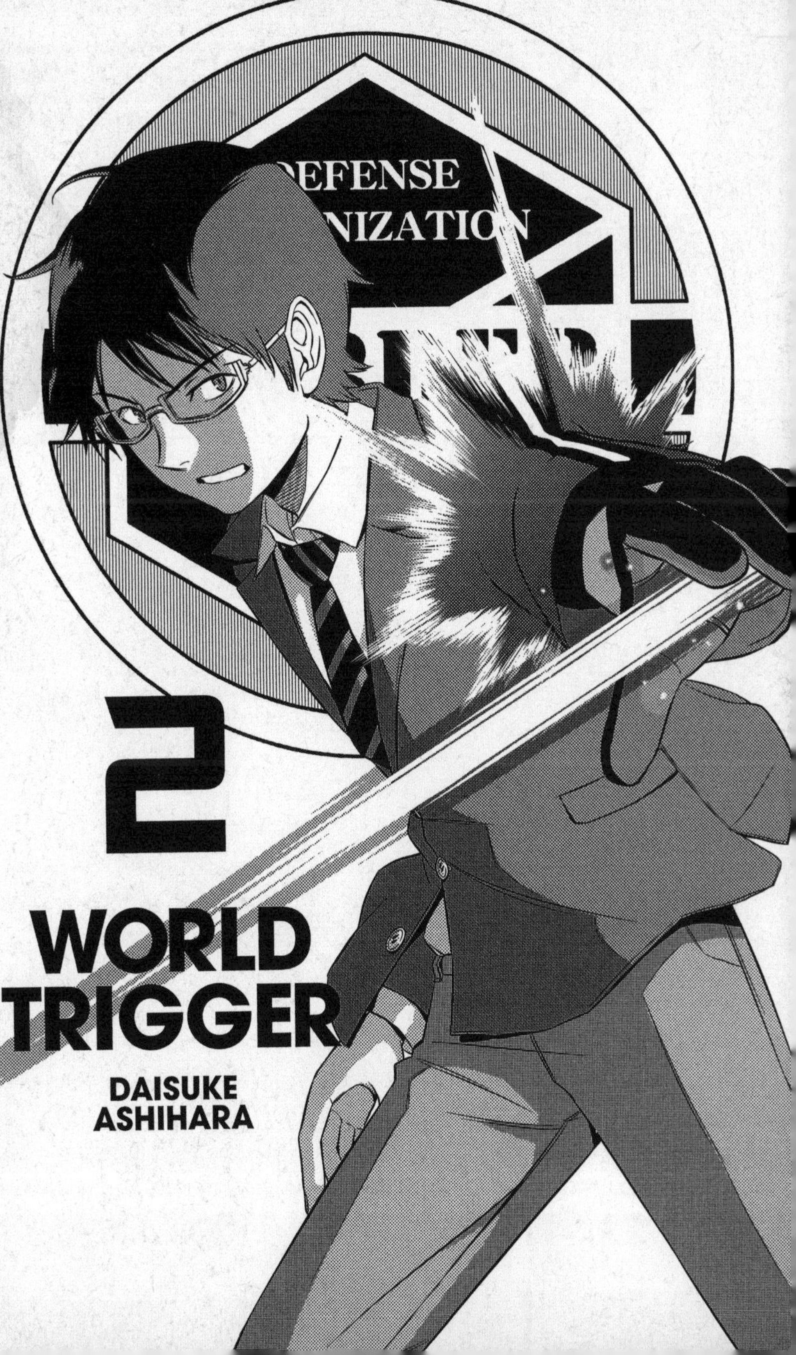
DEFENSE
NIZATION

2

# WORLD TRIGGER

DAISUKE ASHIHARA

# CHARACTERS

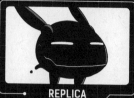

REPLICA

Yuma's chaperone.

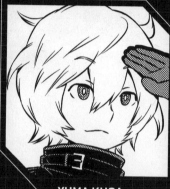

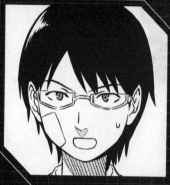

OSAMU MIKUMO

Ninth-grader who's compelled to help those in trouble. Border agent.

YUMA KUGA

Short, but same grade as Osamu. Since he's a Neighbor, he lacks common sense.

## What are Neighbors?

Invaders from another dimension that enter Mikado City through Gates. Most "Neighbors" here are Trion soldiers built for war. The Neighbors who actually live on the other side of the Gates are human, like Yuma.

H-HEY, IT'S COMING THIS WAY!!
WHOA...
WAAAAH!
ZK
GATE DETECTED.
ZZAK
ZAP
COORDINATES MARGIN OF ERROR: 7.66.

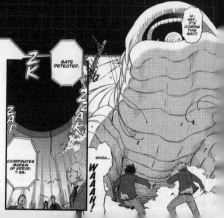

## ARASHIYAMA SQUAD: HQ's A-Rank Squad

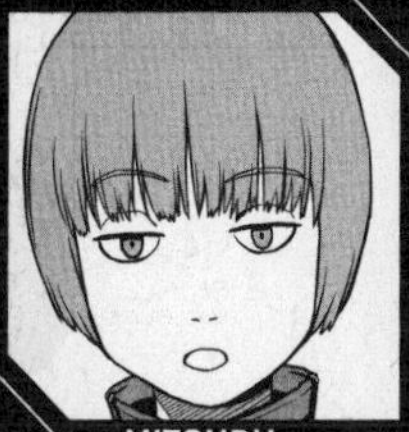

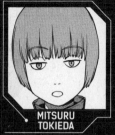

MITSURU TOKIEDA

Always calm.

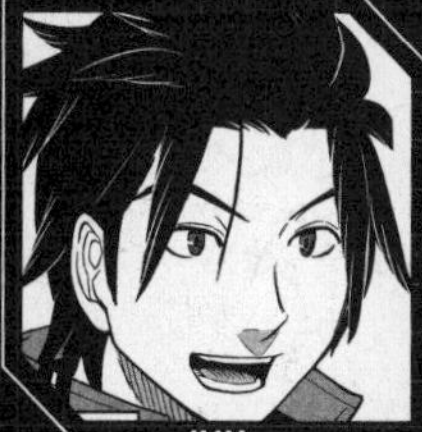

JUN ARASHIYAMA

Captain. Loves his siblings.

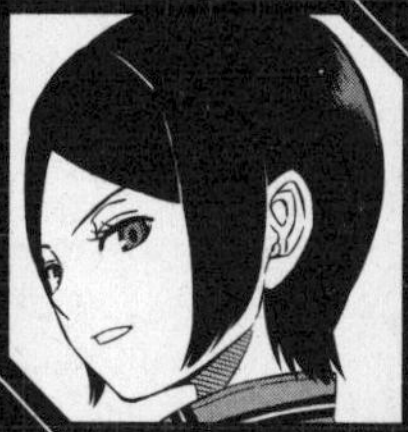

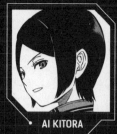

AI KITORA

Strong-willed and hates to lose.

### What is Border?

Its official name is Border Defense Agency, or "Border" for short. Its purpose is to research Neighbor technology and protect the city from Neighbors. Agent classification is as follows: C-Rank for trainees, B-Rank for main forces and A-Rank for elites. Citizens idolize Border agents, and A-Rank agents can even be celebrities.

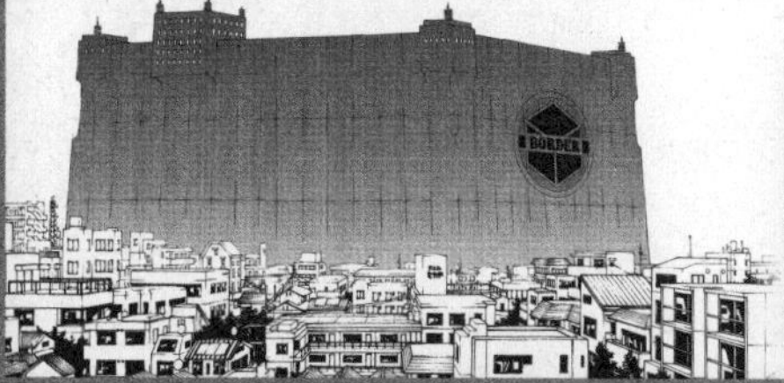
BORDER

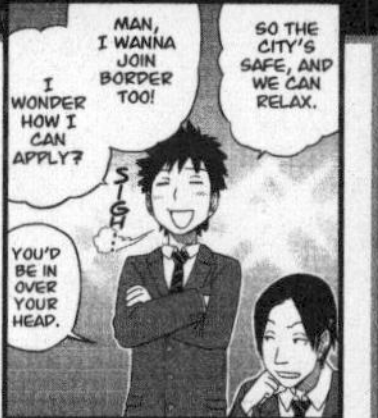
SO THE CITY'S SAFE, AND WE CAN RELAX.
MAN, I WANNA JOIN BORDER TOO!
I WONDER HOW I CAN APPLY?
SIGH
YOU'D BE IN OVER YOUR HEAD.

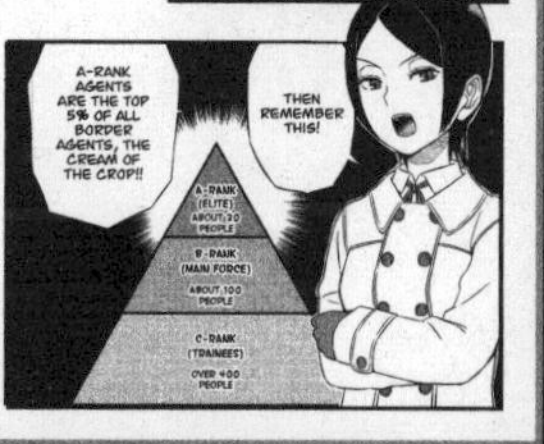
THEN REMEMBER THIS!
A-RANK AGENTS ARE THE TOP 5% OF ALL BORDER AGENTS, THE CREAM OF THE CROP!!
A-RANK (ELITE) ABOUT 20 PEOPLE
B-RANK (MAIN FORCE) ABOUT 100 PEOPLE
C-RANK (TRAINEES) OVER 400 PEOPLE

# STORY

About four years ago, a Gate connecting to another dimension opened in Mikado City, leading to the appearance of invaders called Neighbors. After the establishment of the Border Defense Agency, people were able to return to their normal lives.

Osamu Mikumo is a C-Rank Border trainee and junior high student living in Mikado City. One day, transfer student Yuma Kuga confesses that he's a Neighbor, but Osamu decides to remain his friend. Just then, a Gate opens outside the Emergence Area and Osamu's school is attacked. Yuma fights back, but Osamu takes credit to hide the fact that Yuma's a Neighbor. Since Osamu wasn't permitted to use his Trigger outside the base, he's summoned to HQ and escorted there by Ai Kitora. Another abnormal Gate opens on the way, and the city is under attack! Prideful A-Rank agent Ai Kitora decides to fight solo...!

# WORLD TRIGGER
## CONTENTS

2

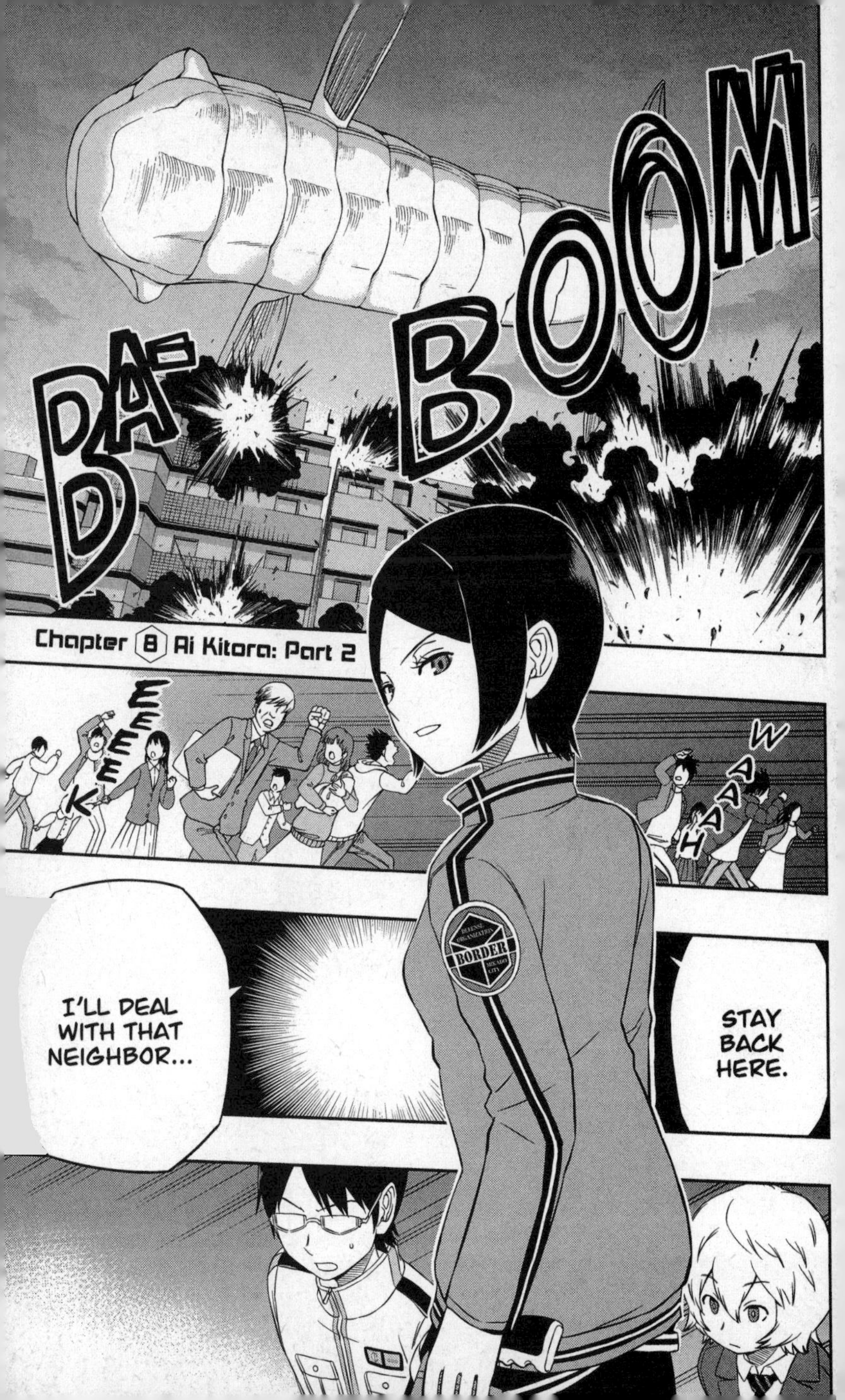
BA BOOOM
Chapter 8 Ai Kitora: Part 2
WAAAH
EEEEK
BORDER
STAY BACK HERE.
I'LL DEAL WITH THAT NEIGHBOR...

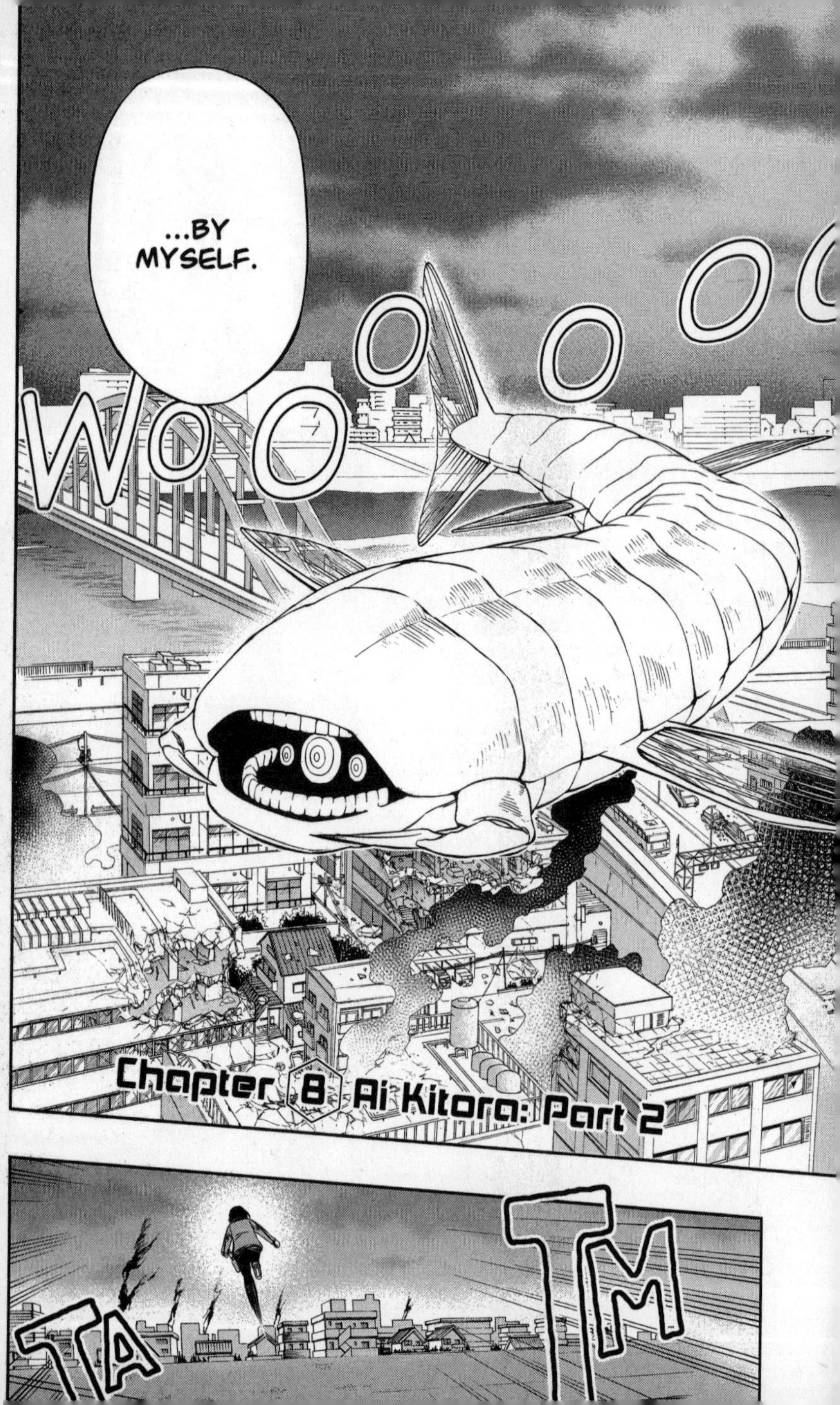
...BY MYSELF.
WOOOOOOO
Chapter 8 Ai Kitora: Part 2
TM
TA

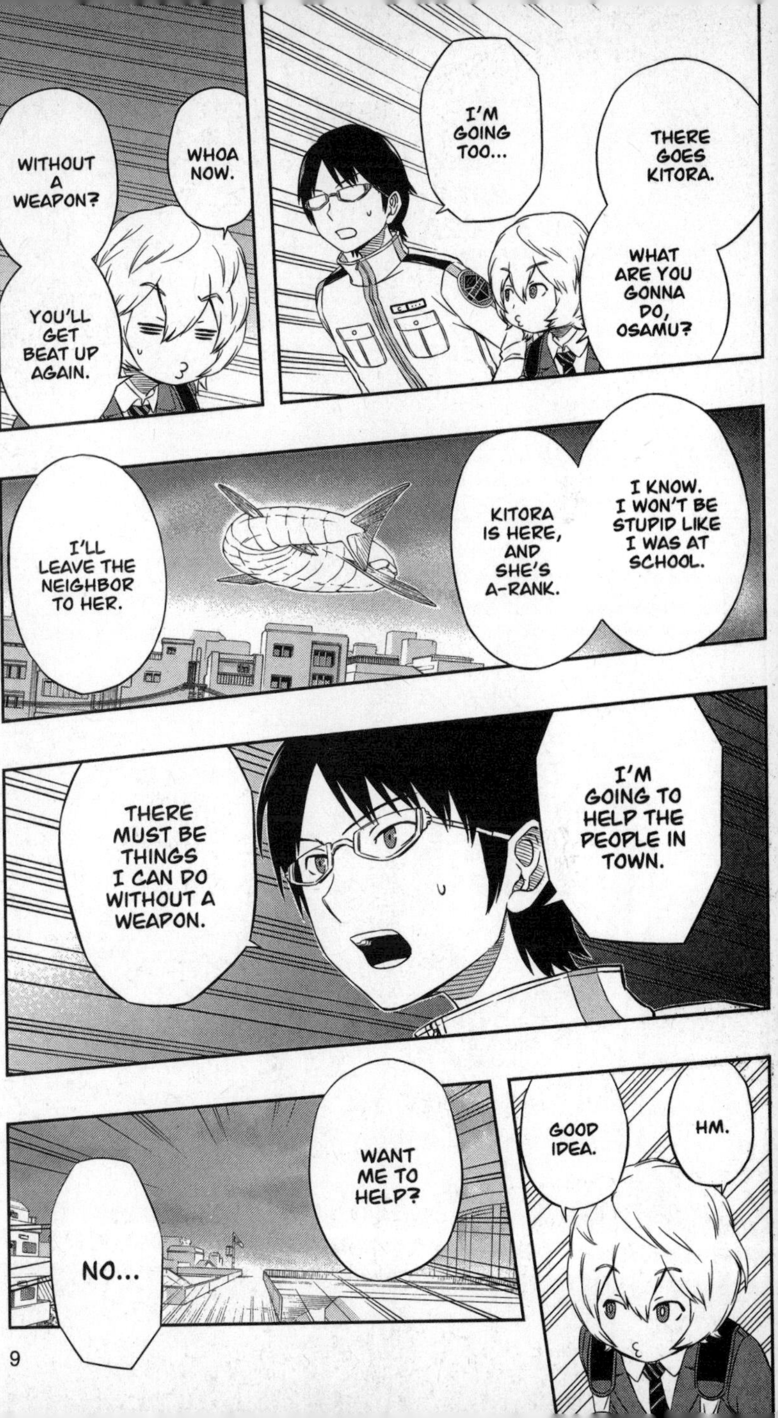
THERE GOES KITORA.
WHAT ARE YOU GONNA DO, OSAMU?
I'M GOING TOO...
WHOA NOW.
WITHOUT A WEAPON?
YOU'LL GET BEAT UP AGAIN.
I KNOW. I WON'T BE STUPID LIKE I WAS AT SCHOOL.
KITORA IS HERE, AND SHE'S A-RANK.
I'LL LEAVE THE NEIGHBOR TO HER.
I'M GOING TO HELP THE PEOPLE IN TOWN.
THERE MUST BE THINGS I CAN DO WITHOUT A WEAPON.
HM.
GOOD IDEA.
WANT ME TO HELP?
NO...

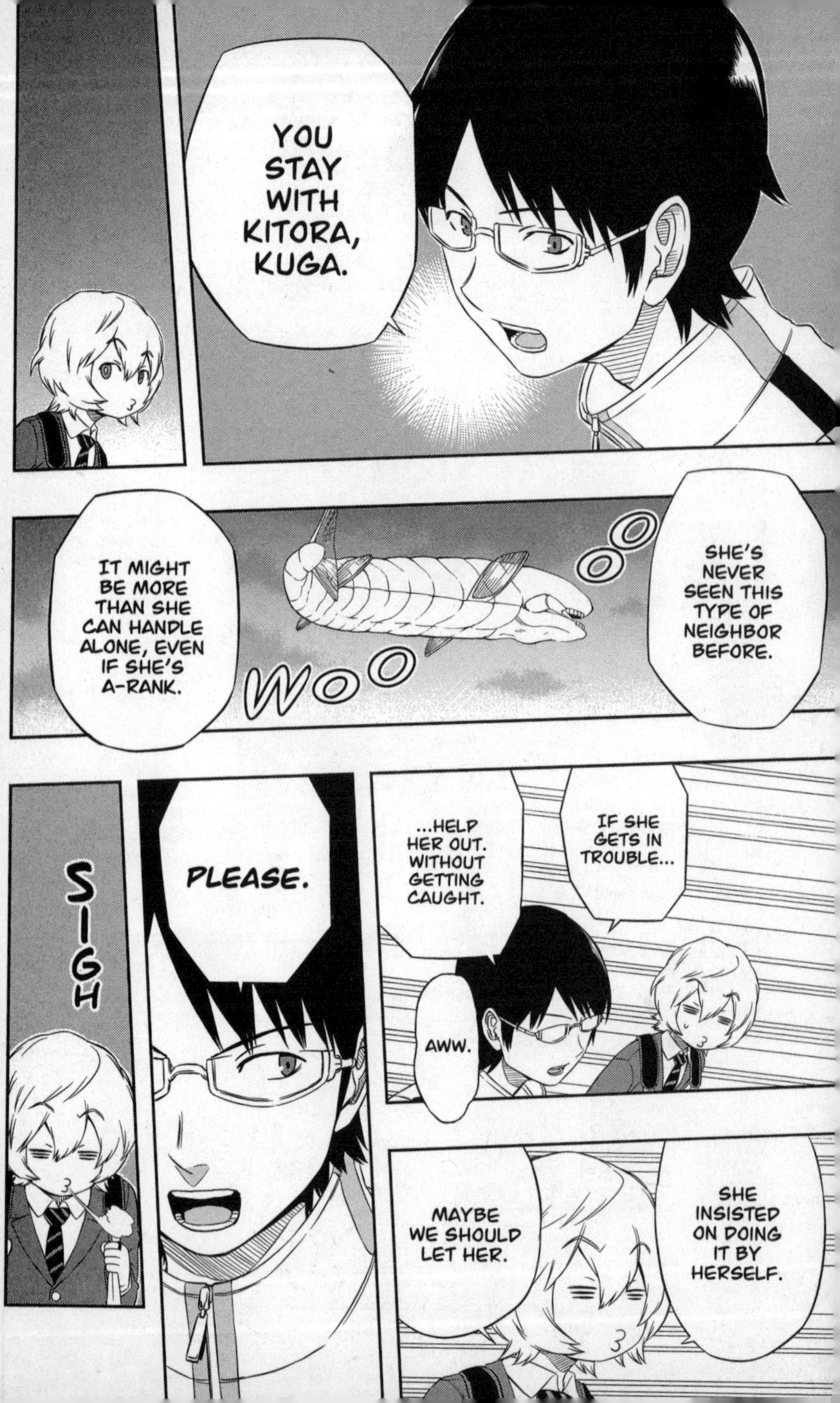
YOU STAY WITH KITORA, KUGA.
SHE'S NEVER SEEN THIS TYPE OF NEIGHBOR BEFORE.
WOOOO
IT MIGHT BE MORE THAN SHE CAN HANDLE ALONE, EVEN IF SHE'S A-RANK.
IF SHE GETS IN TROUBLE...
...HELP HER OUT. WITHOUT GETTING CAUGHT.
AWW.
SHE INSISTED ON DOING IT BY HERSELF.
MAYBE WE SHOULD LET HER.
PLEASE.
SIGH

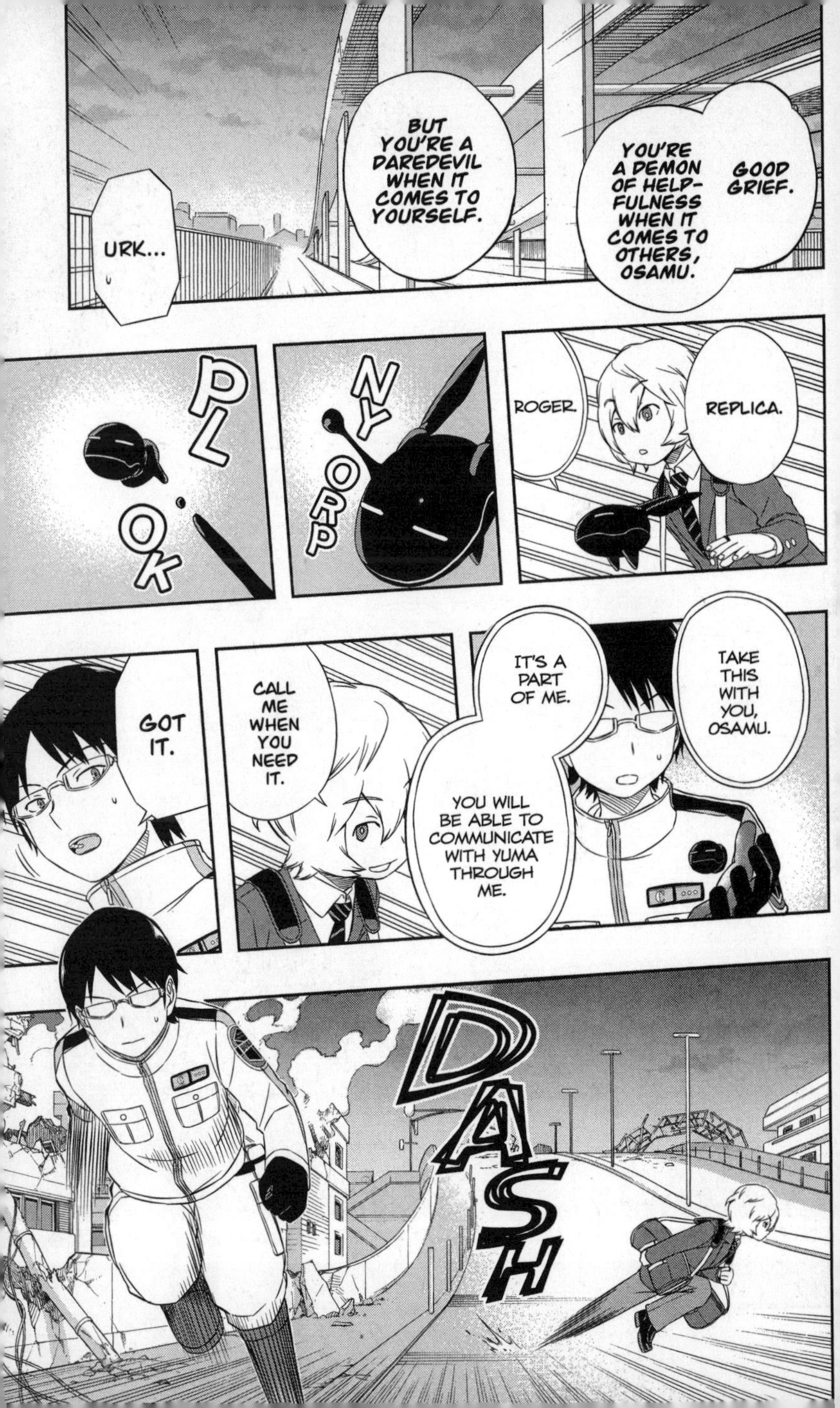
GOOD GRIEF.
YOU'RE A DEMON OF HELP-FULNESS WHEN IT COMES TO OTHERS, OSAMU.
BUT YOU'RE A DAREDEVIL WHEN IT COMES TO YOURSELF.
URK...
REPLICA.
ROGER.
NYORP
PLOK
TAKE THIS WITH YOU, OSAMU.
IT'S A PART OF ME.
YOU WILL BE ABLE TO COMMUNICATE WITH YUMA THROUGH ME.
CALL ME WHEN YOU NEED IT.
GOT IT.
DASH

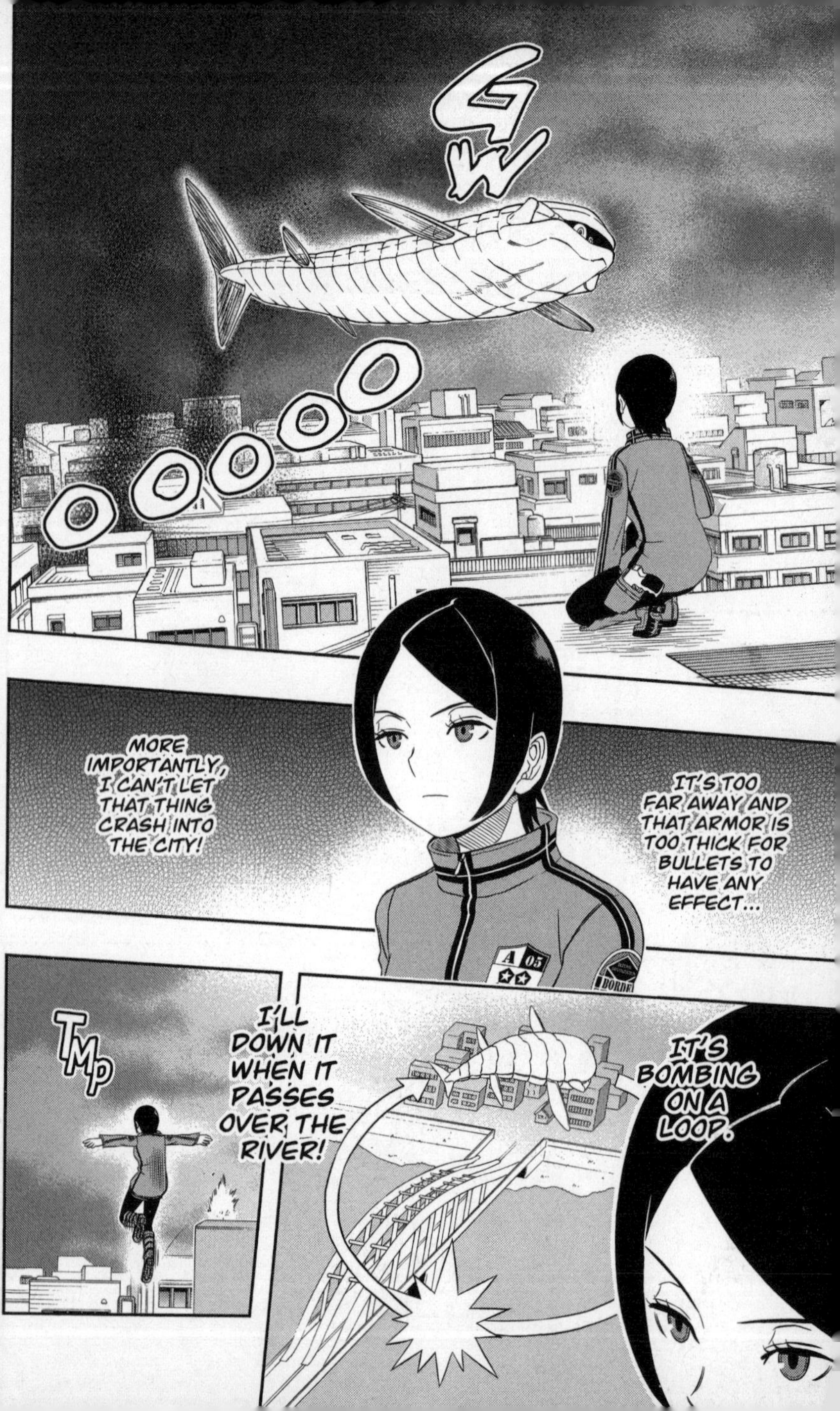
GWOOOOOO
IT'S TOO FAR AWAY AND THAT ARMOR IS TOO THICK FOR BULLETS TO HAVE ANY EFFECT...
MORE IMPORTANTLY, I CAN'T LET THAT THING CRASH INTO THE CITY!
A 05
BORDE
IT'S BOMBING ON A LOOP.
I'LL DOWN IT WHEN IT PASSES OVER THE RIVER!
TMP

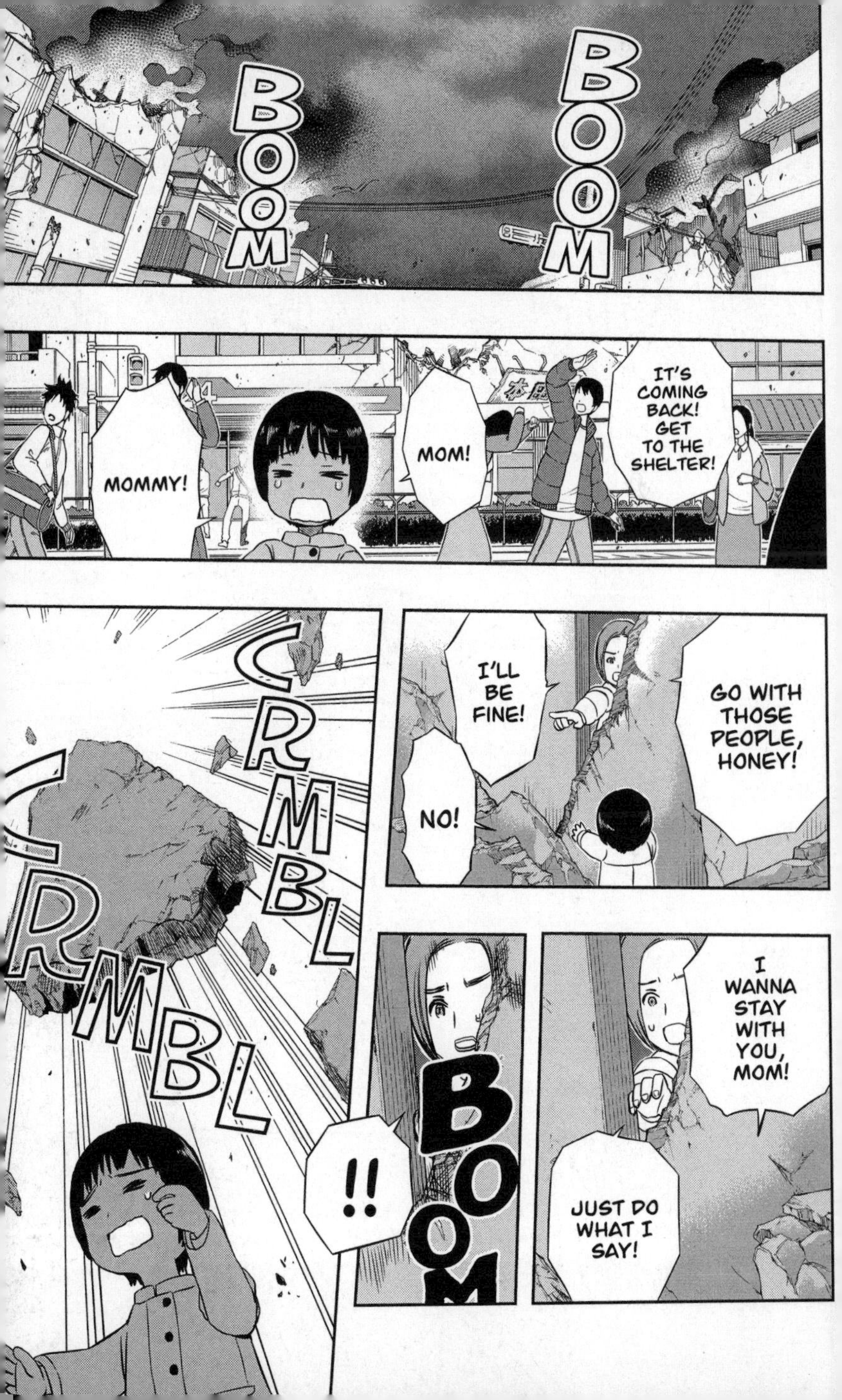
BOOM
BOOM
IT'S COMING BACK! GET TO THE SHELTER!
MOM!
MOMMY!
GO WITH THOSE PEOPLE, HONEY!
I'LL BE FINE!
NO!
I WANNA STAY WITH YOU, MOM!
JUST DO WHAT I SAY!
BOOM
!!
CRMBL
CRMBL

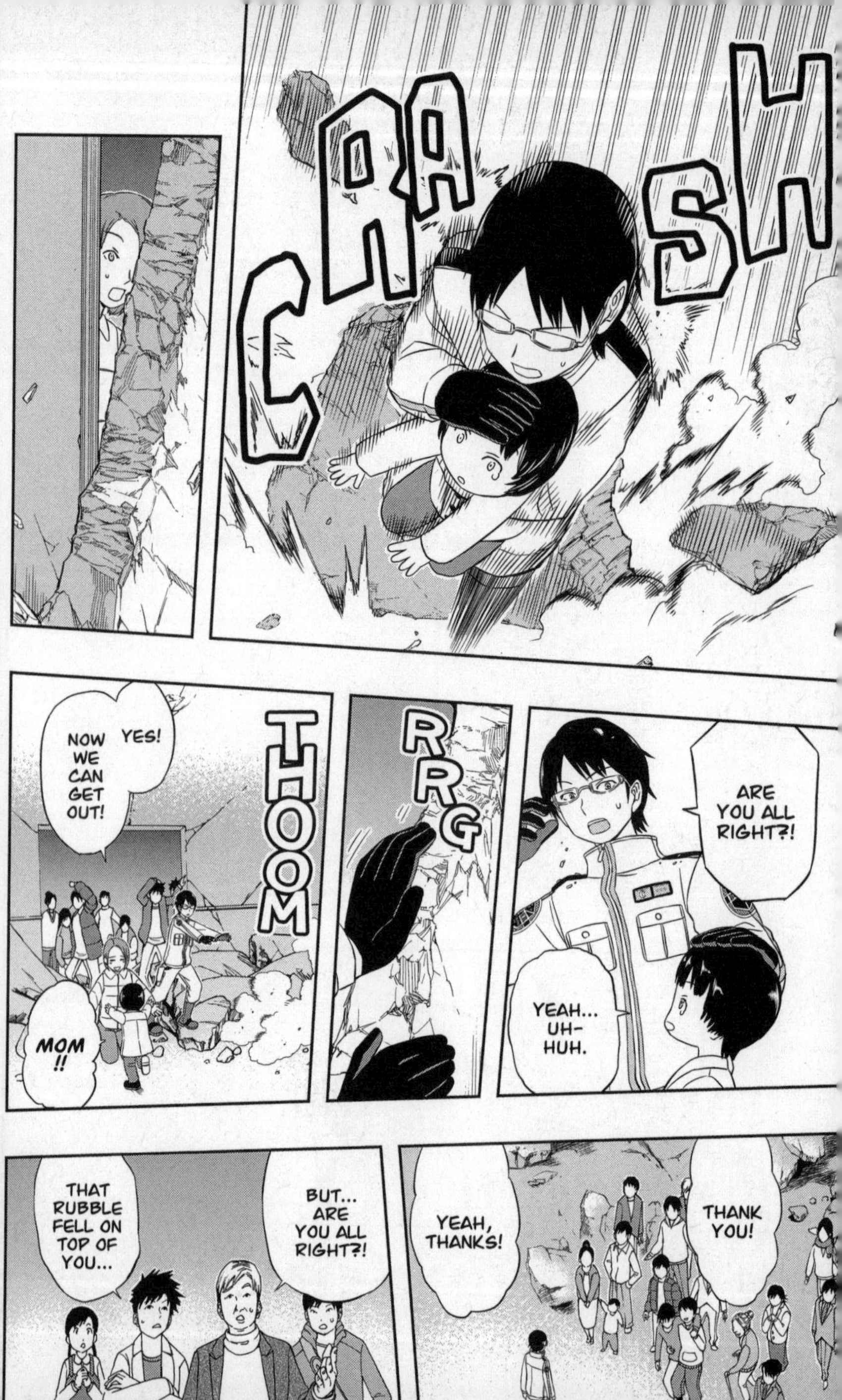
CRASH
ARE YOU ALL RIGHT?!
YEAH... UH-HUH.
RRG
THOOM
YES!
NOW WE CAN GET OUT!
MOM!!
THANK YOU!
YEAH, THANKS!
BUT... ARE YOU ALL RIGHT?!
THAT RUBBLE FELL ON TOP OF YOU...

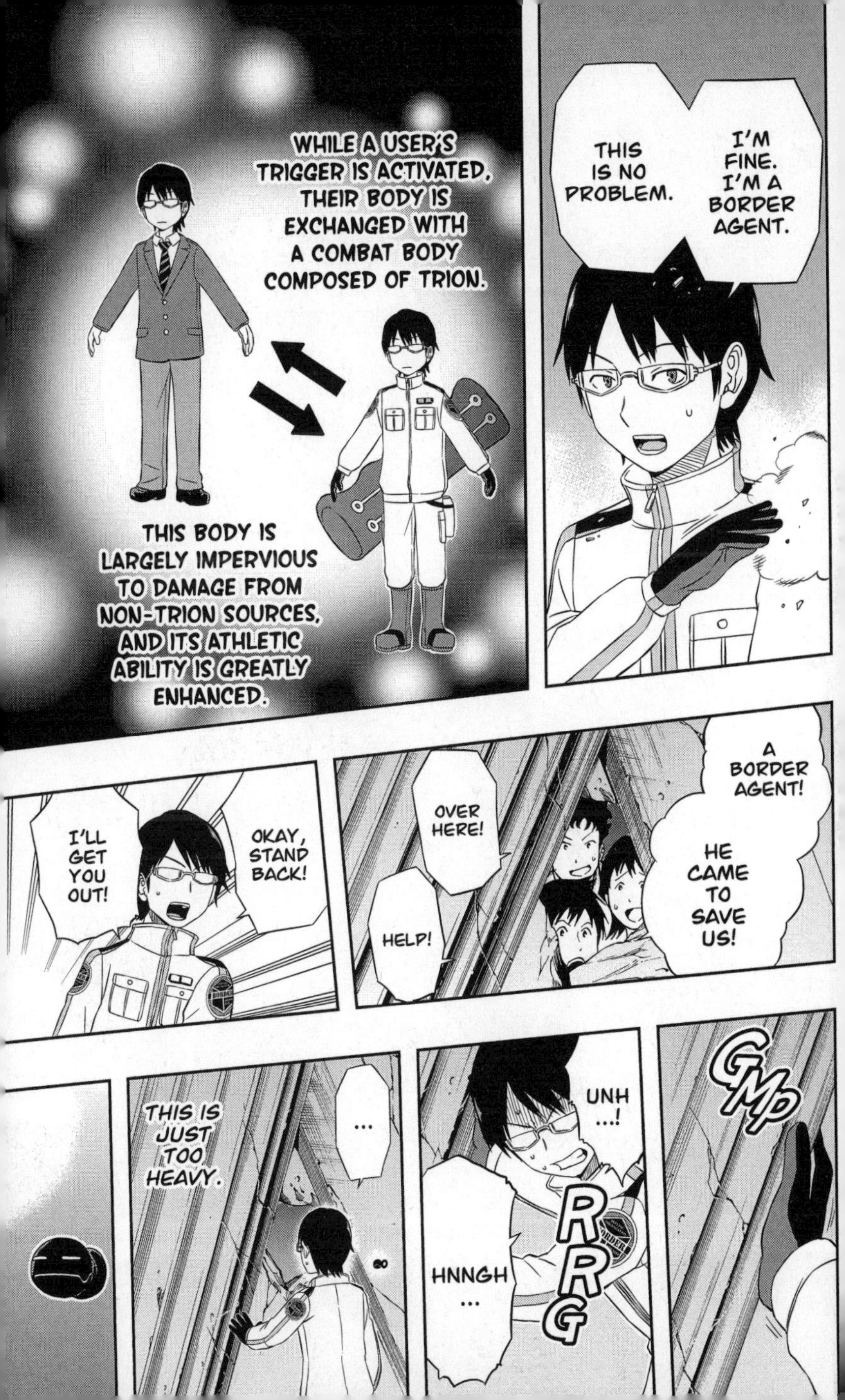
I'M FINE. I'M A BORDER AGENT.
THIS IS NO PROBLEM.
WHILE A USER'S TRIGGER IS ACTIVATED, THEIR BODY IS EXCHANGED WITH A COMBAT BODY COMPOSED OF TRION.
THIS BODY IS LARGELY IMPERVIOUS TO DAMAGE FROM NON-TRION SOURCES, AND ITS ATHLETIC ABILITY IS GREATLY ENHANCED.
A BORDER AGENT!
HE CAME TO SAVE US!
OVER HERE!
HELP!
OKAY, STAND BACK!
I'LL GET YOU OUT!
GMP
UNH ...!
RRRG
HNNGH ...
...
THIS IS JUST TOO HEAVY.

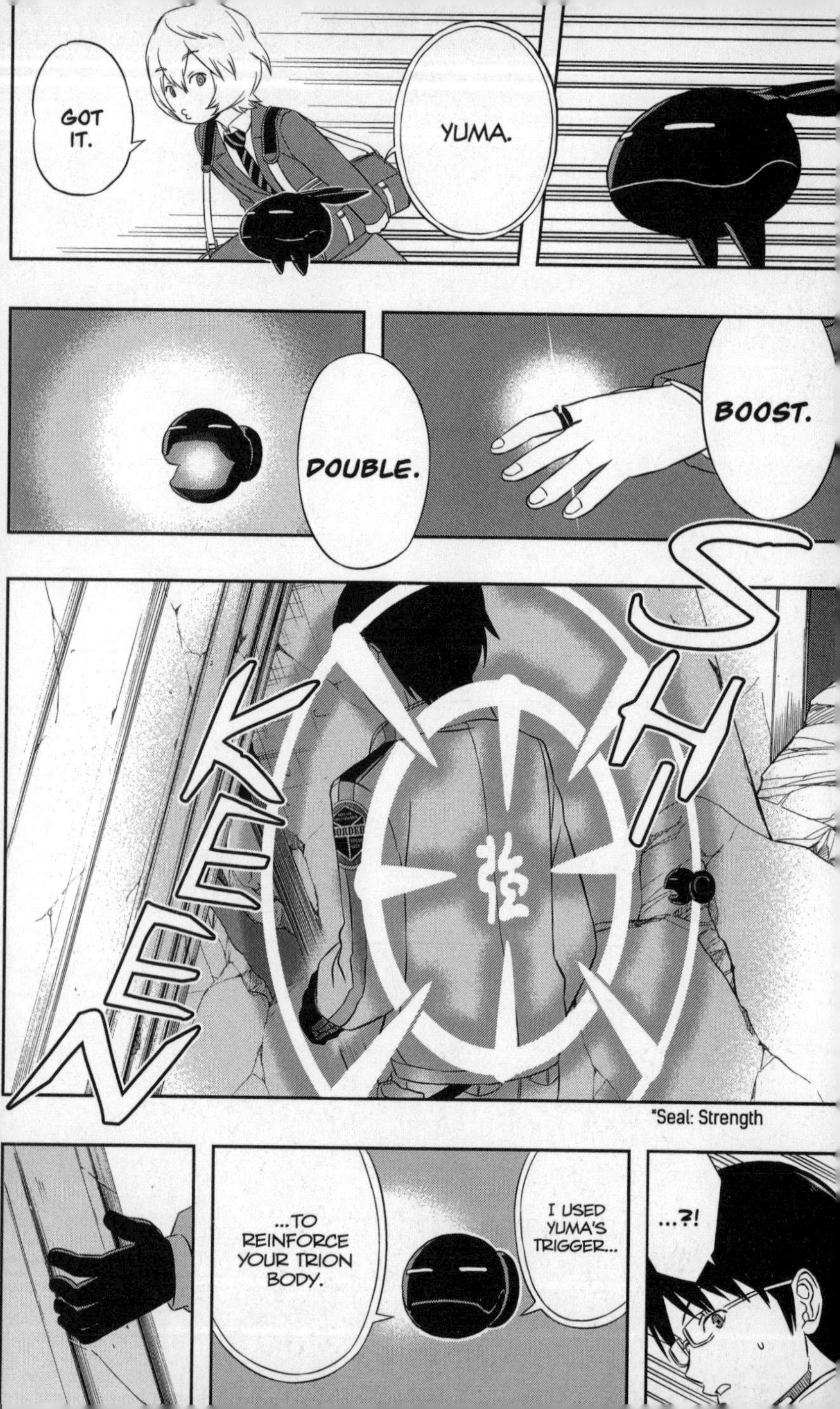
YUMA.
GOT IT.
BOOST.
DOUBLE.
ZEEKSH
強
*Seal: Strength
...?!
I USED YUMA'S TRIGGER...
...TO REINFORCE YOUR TRION BODY.

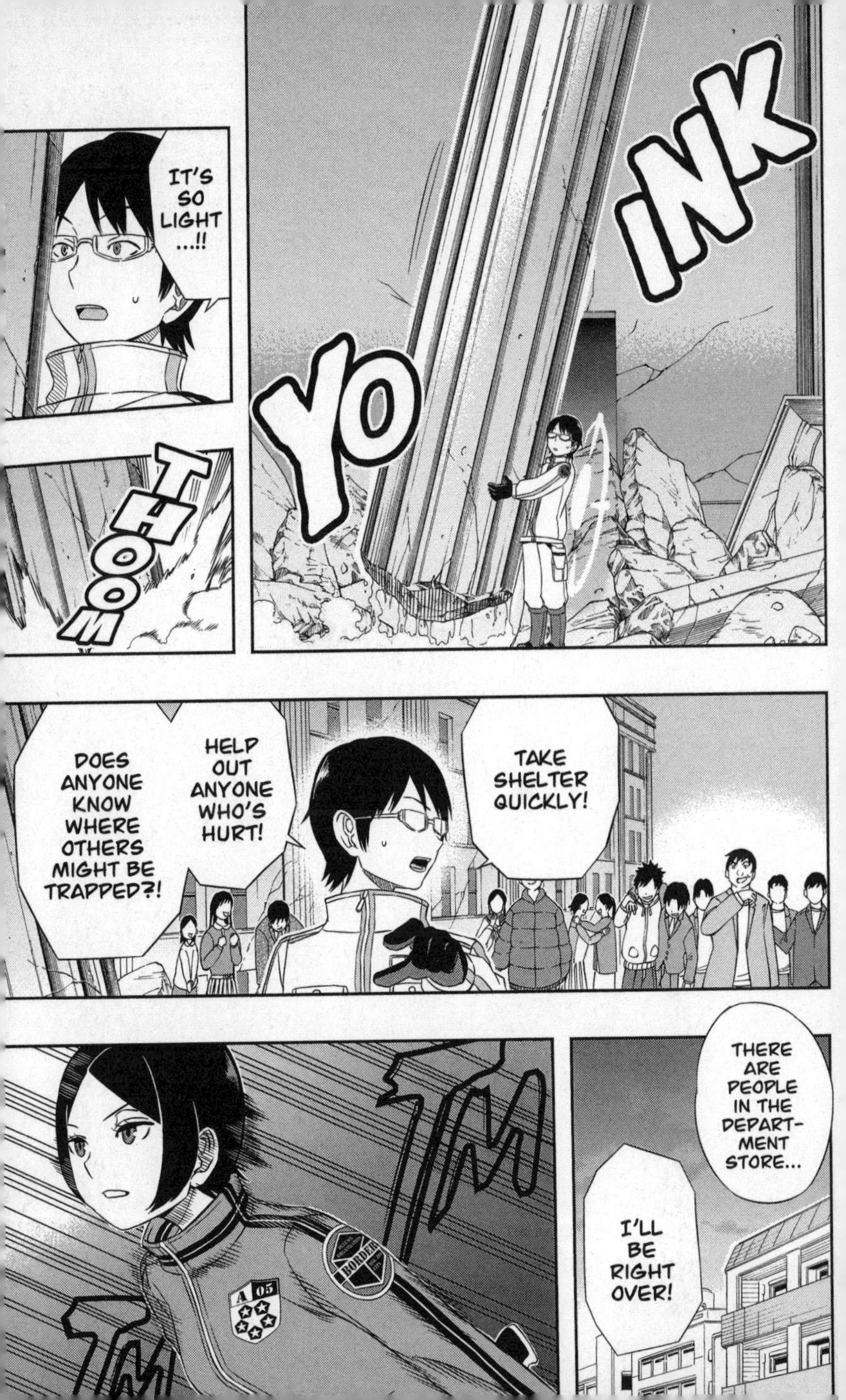
YO
INK
IT'S SO LIGHT...!!
THOOM
TAKE SHELTER QUICKLY!
HELP OUT ANYONE WHO'S HURT!
DOES ANYONE KNOW WHERE OTHERS MIGHT BE TRAPPED?!
THERE ARE PEOPLE IN THE DEPART-MENT STORE...
I'LL BE RIGHT OVER!
TM
TM

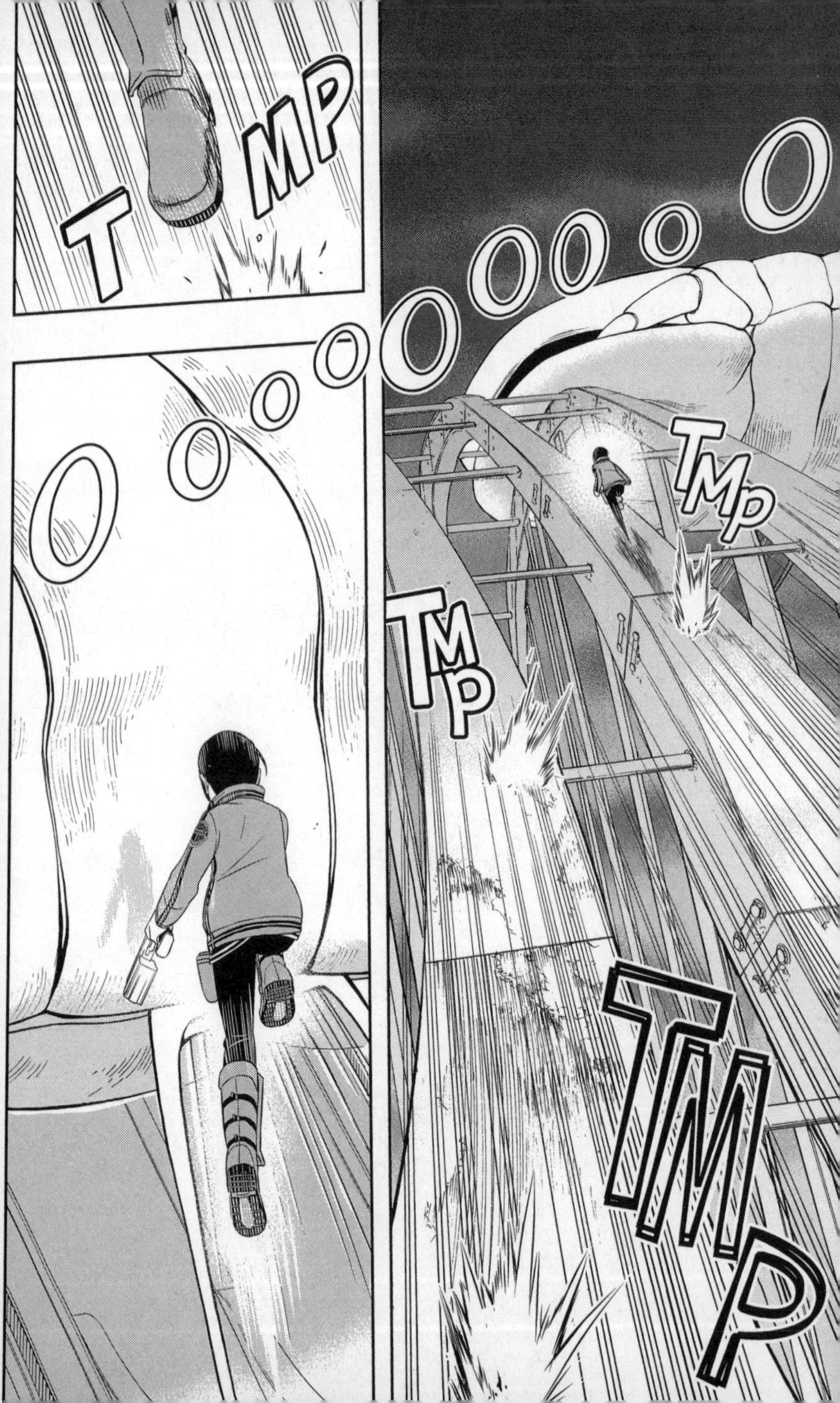

TMp
TMp
TMP
TOMP
OOOOOOOOOOO

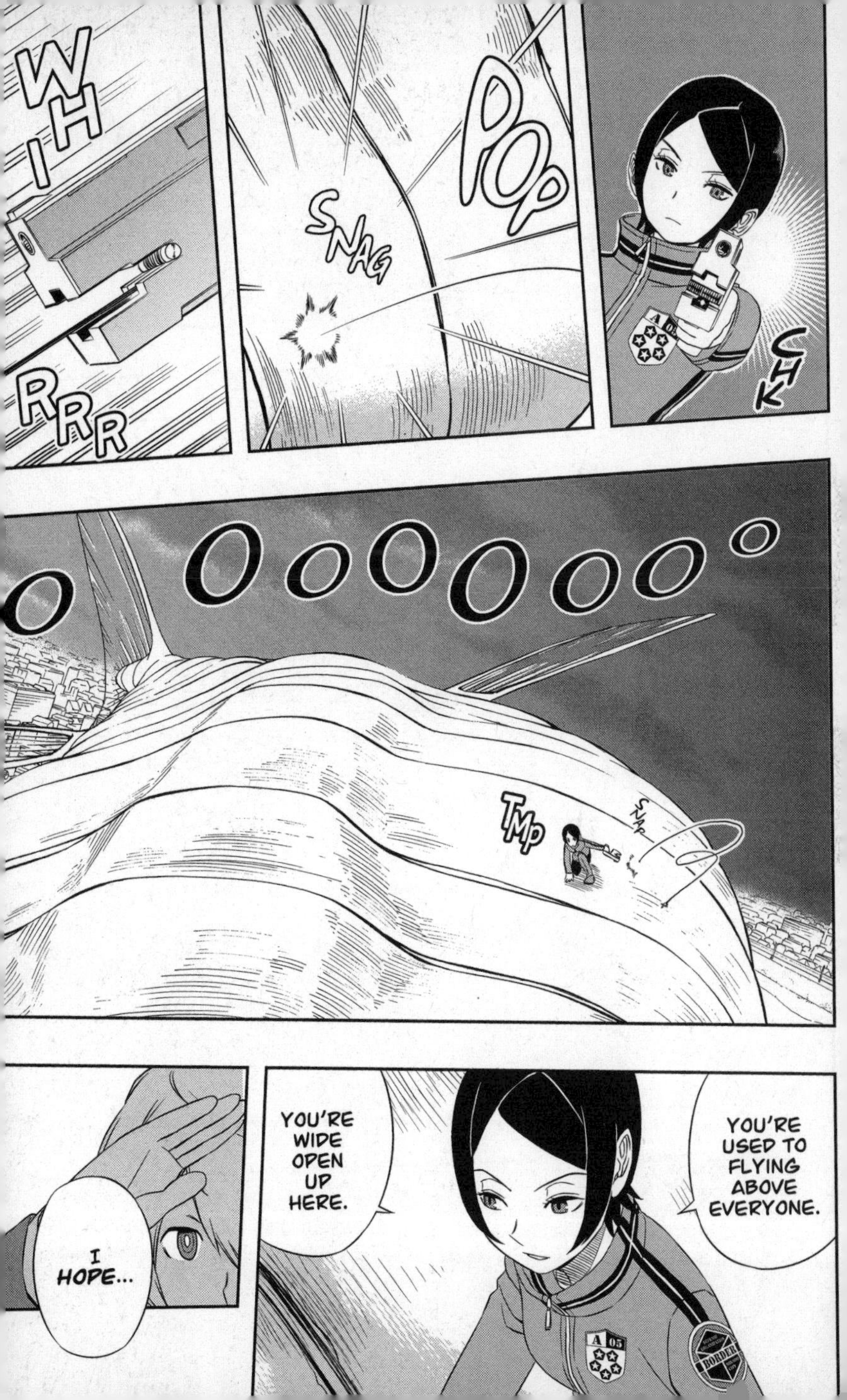
CHK
POP
SNAG
WHIRRR
OOOOOOOO
SNAP
TMP
YOU'RE USED TO FLYING ABOVE EVERYONE.
YOU'RE WIDE OPEN UP HERE.
I HOPE...

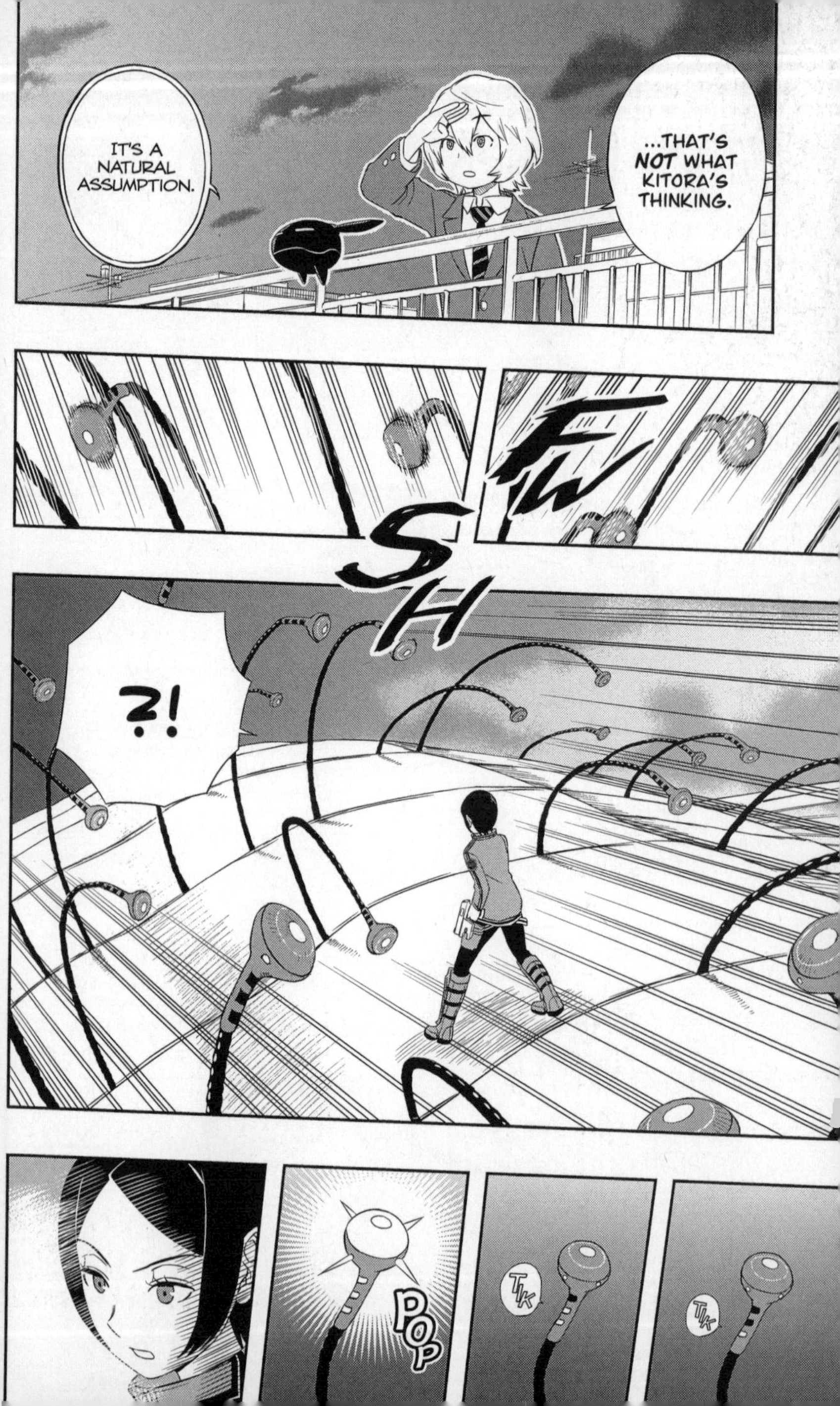
...THAT'S **NOT** WHAT KITORA'S THINKING.
IT'S A NATURAL ASSUMPTION.
FWSSH
?!
TIK
TIK
POP

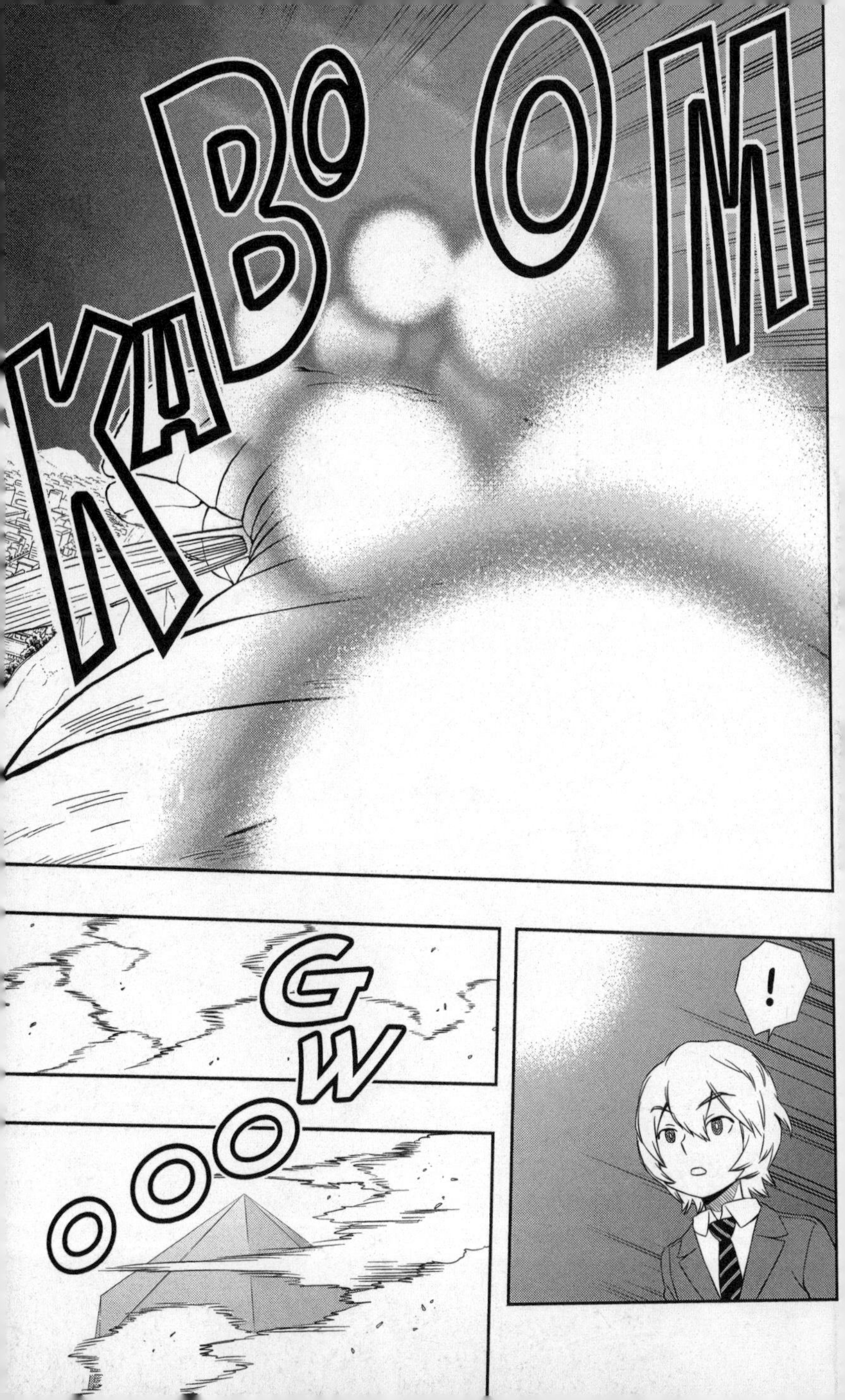
KABOOM
!
GWOOOO

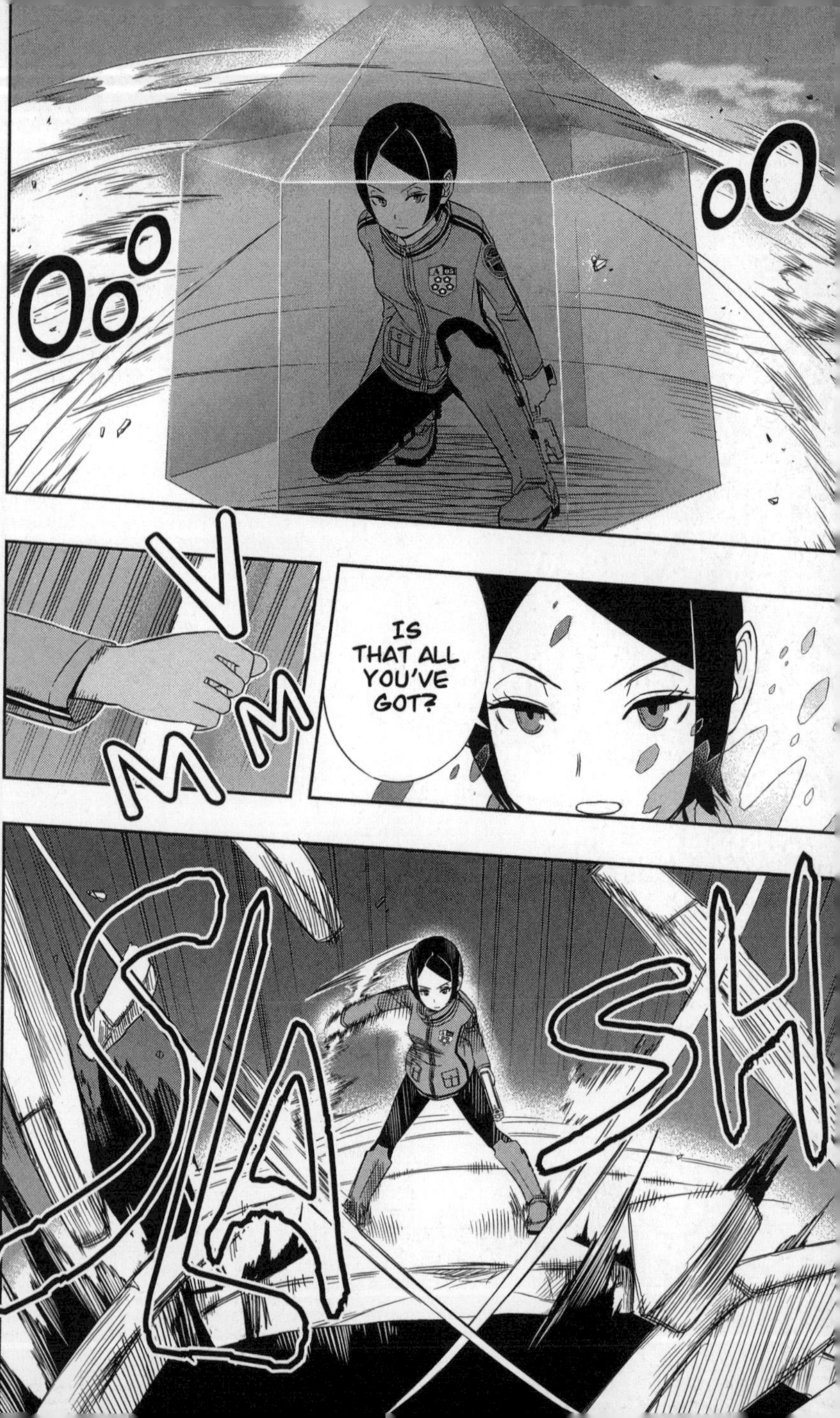
oO
Ooo
IS THAT ALL YOU'VE GOT?
VMM
SLASH

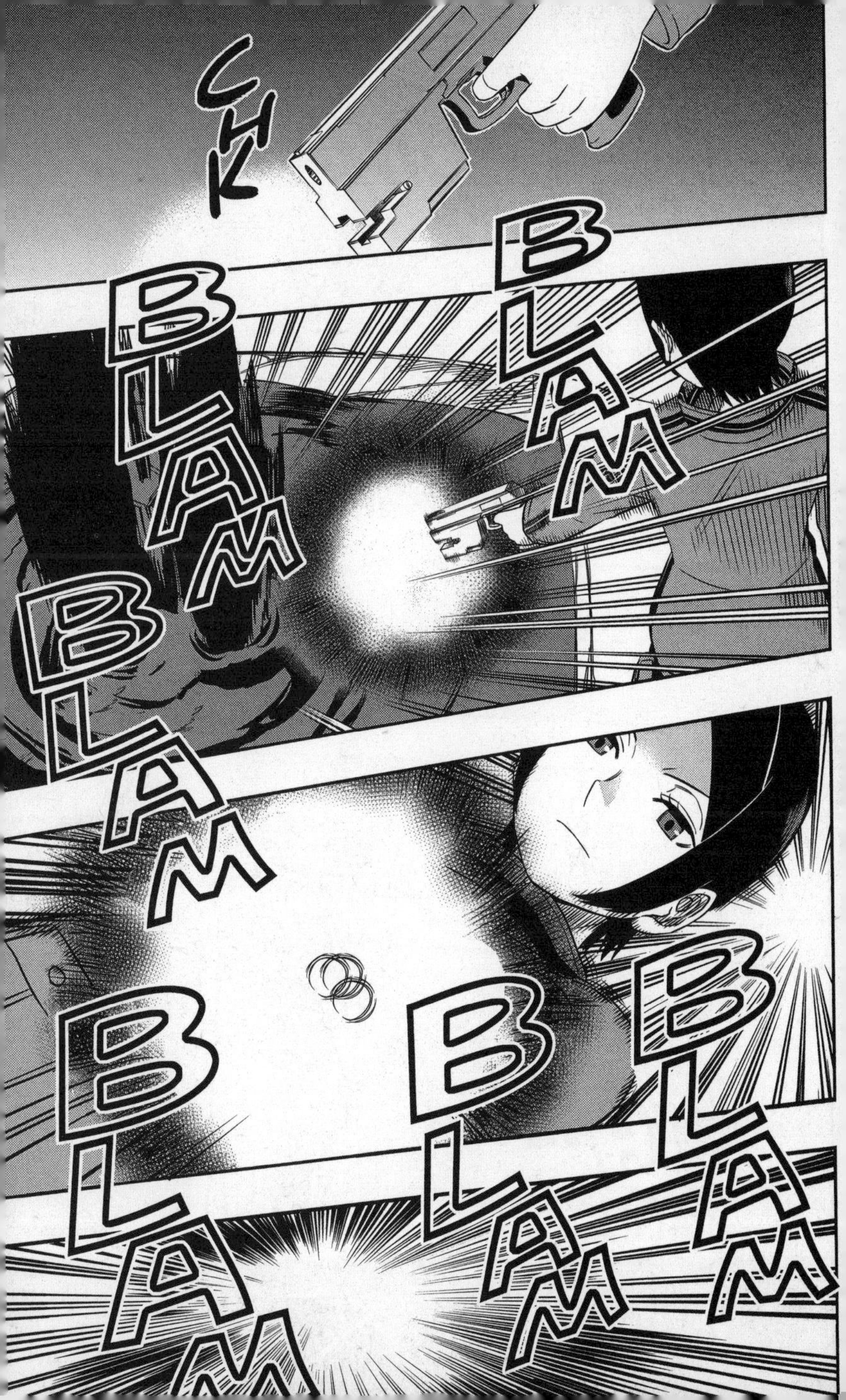
CHK
BLAM
BLAM
BLAM
BLAM
BLAM
BLAM

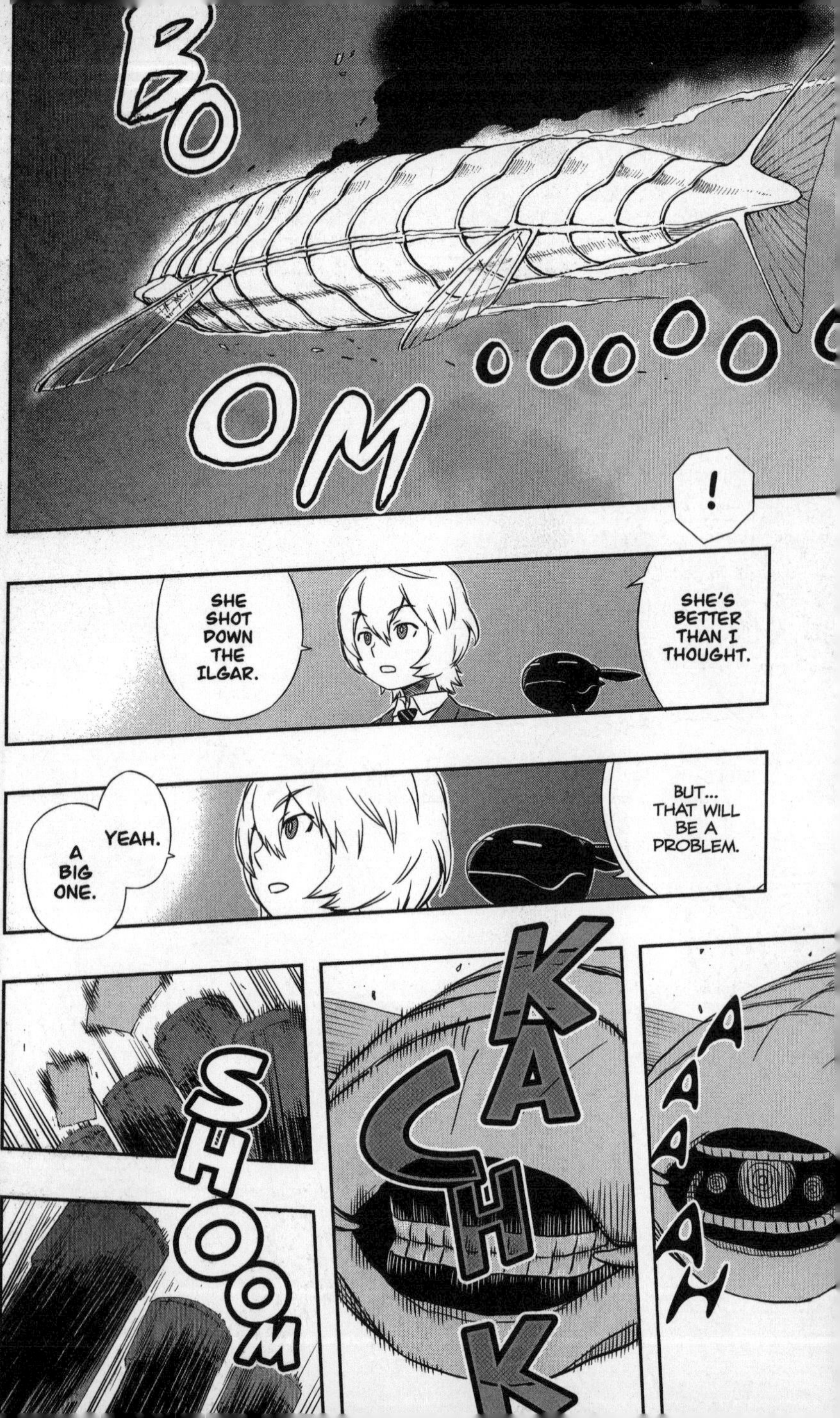
BOOOOOOOOOM
!
SHE'S BETTER THAN I THOUGHT.
SHE SHOT DOWN THE ILGAR.
BUT... THAT WILL BE A PROBLEM.
YEAH. A BIG ONE.
AAAAAAH
KACHK
SHOOOM

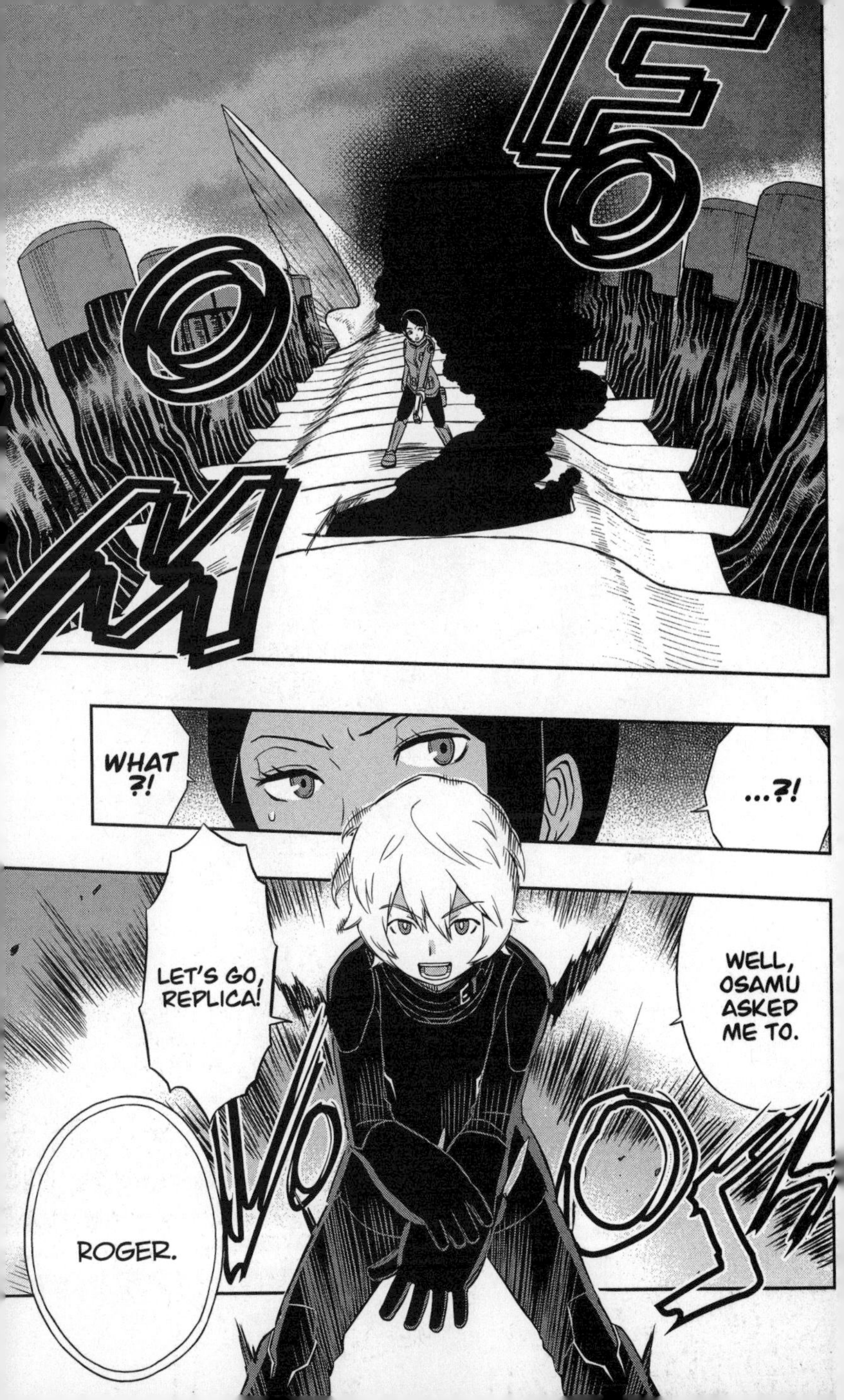
...?!
WHAT ?!
WELL, OSAMU ASKED ME TO.
LET'S GO, REPLICA!
ROGER.

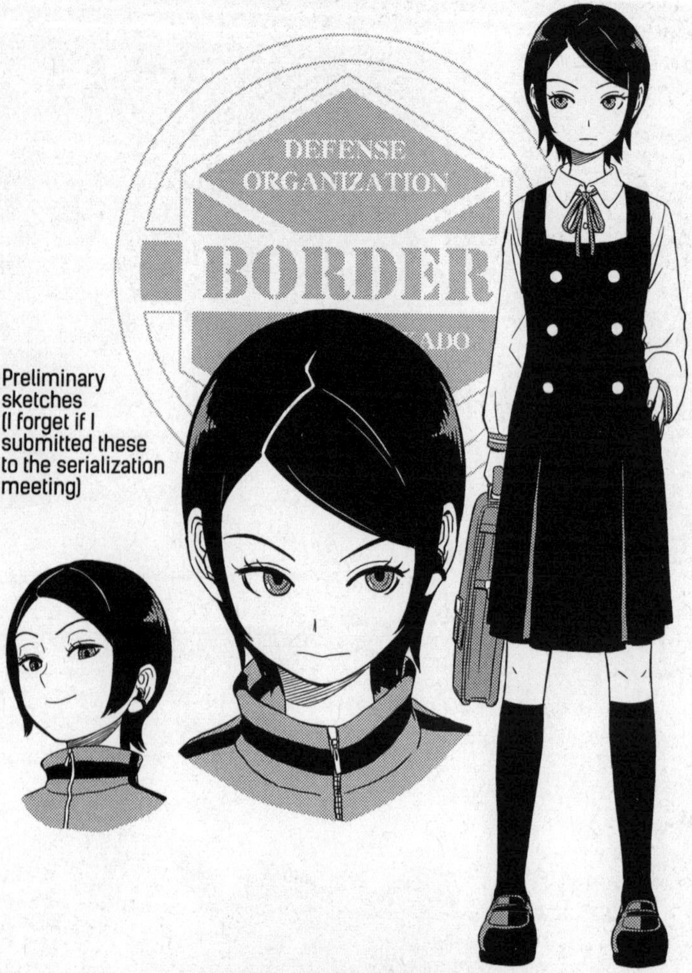
DEFENSE
ORGANIZATION
BORDER

■Preliminary sketches (I forget if I submitted these to the serialization meeting)

## Ai Kitora

This is before her bust was enlarged. Since an initial sketch existed even though she's not a main character, I imagine I liked her a lot. She doesn't have many lines, so she's easy to draw. Her face is easier than even Osamu's.

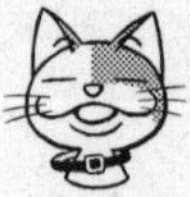

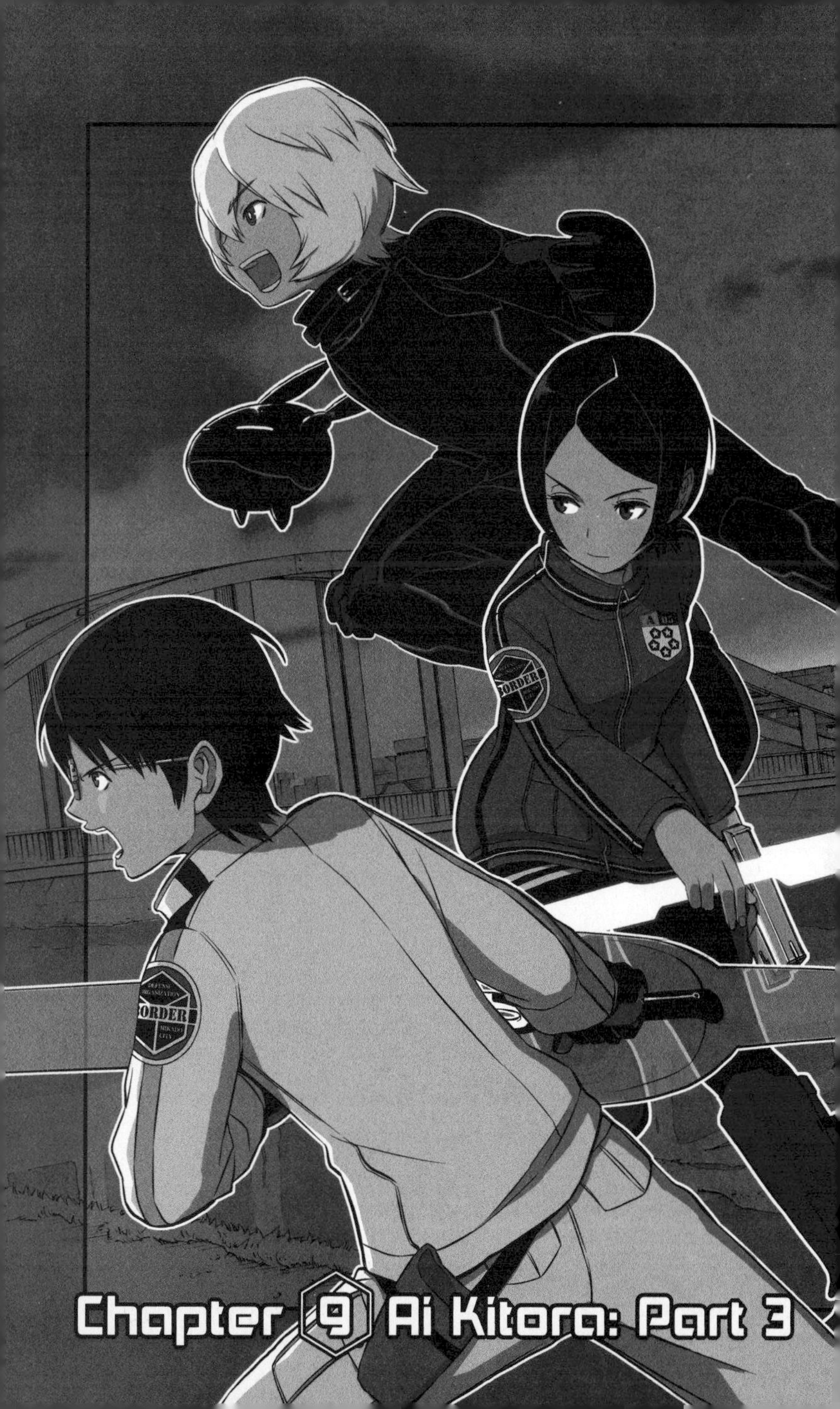
BORDER
DEFENSE ORGANIZATION
BORDER
MIKADO CITY

# Chapter 9 Ai Kitora: Part 3

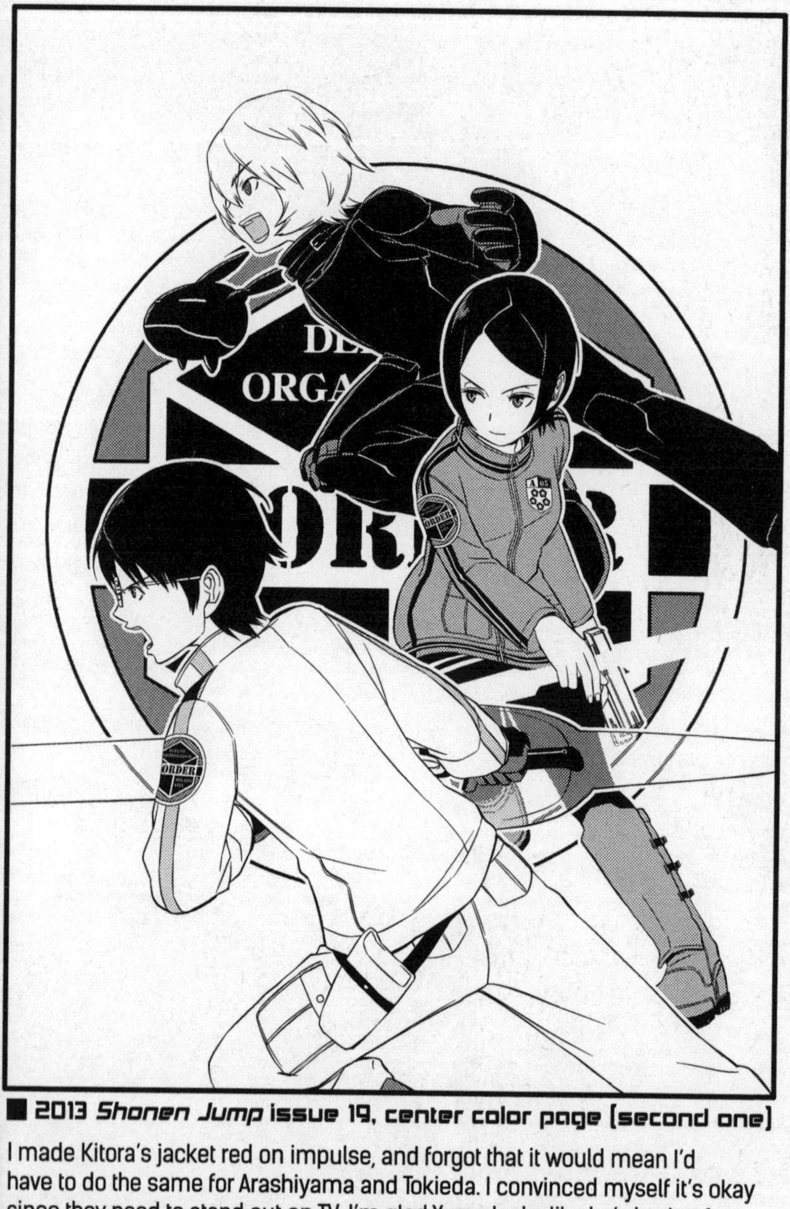
ORDER
ORDER

■ 2013 *Shonen Jump* issue 19, center color page [second one]

I made Kitora's jacket red on impulse, and forgot that it would mean I'd have to do the same for Arashiyama and Tokieda. I convinced myself it's okay since they need to stand out on TV. I'm glad Yuma looks like he's having fun.

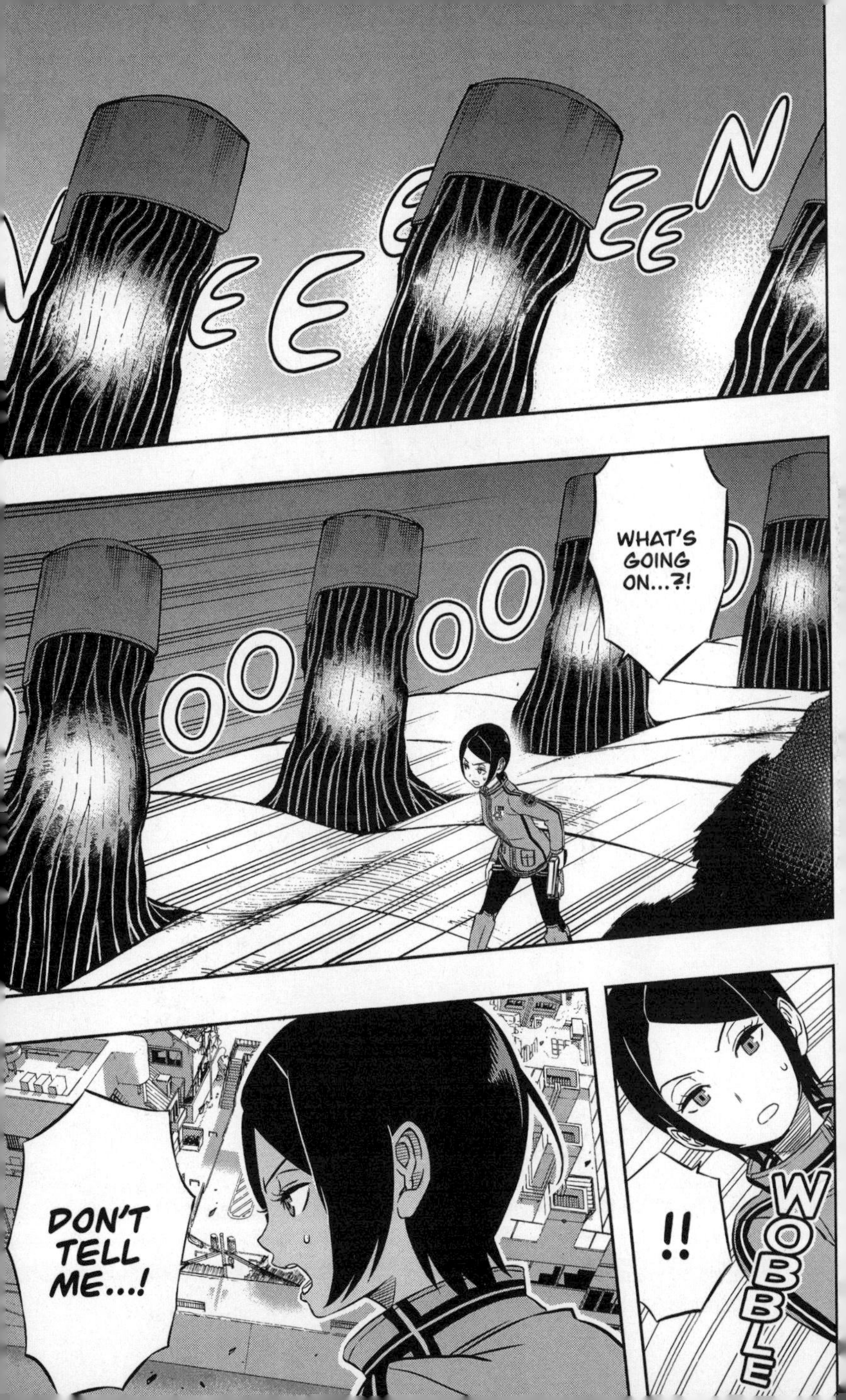
VEEEEEEEN
OOOOOOO
WHAT'S GOING ON...?!
!!
WOBBLE
DON'T TELL ME...!

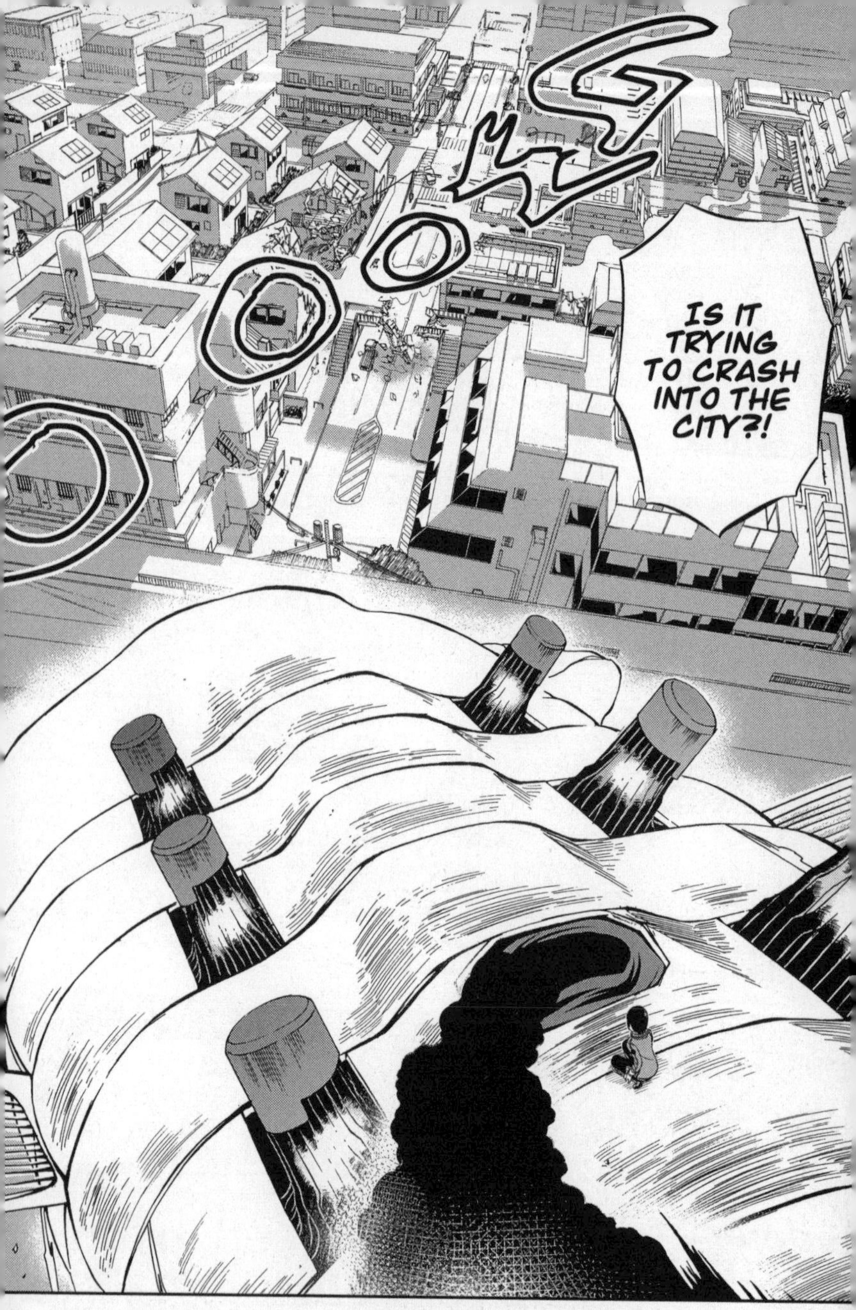
GOOOO
IS IT TRYING TO CRASH INTO THE CITY?!

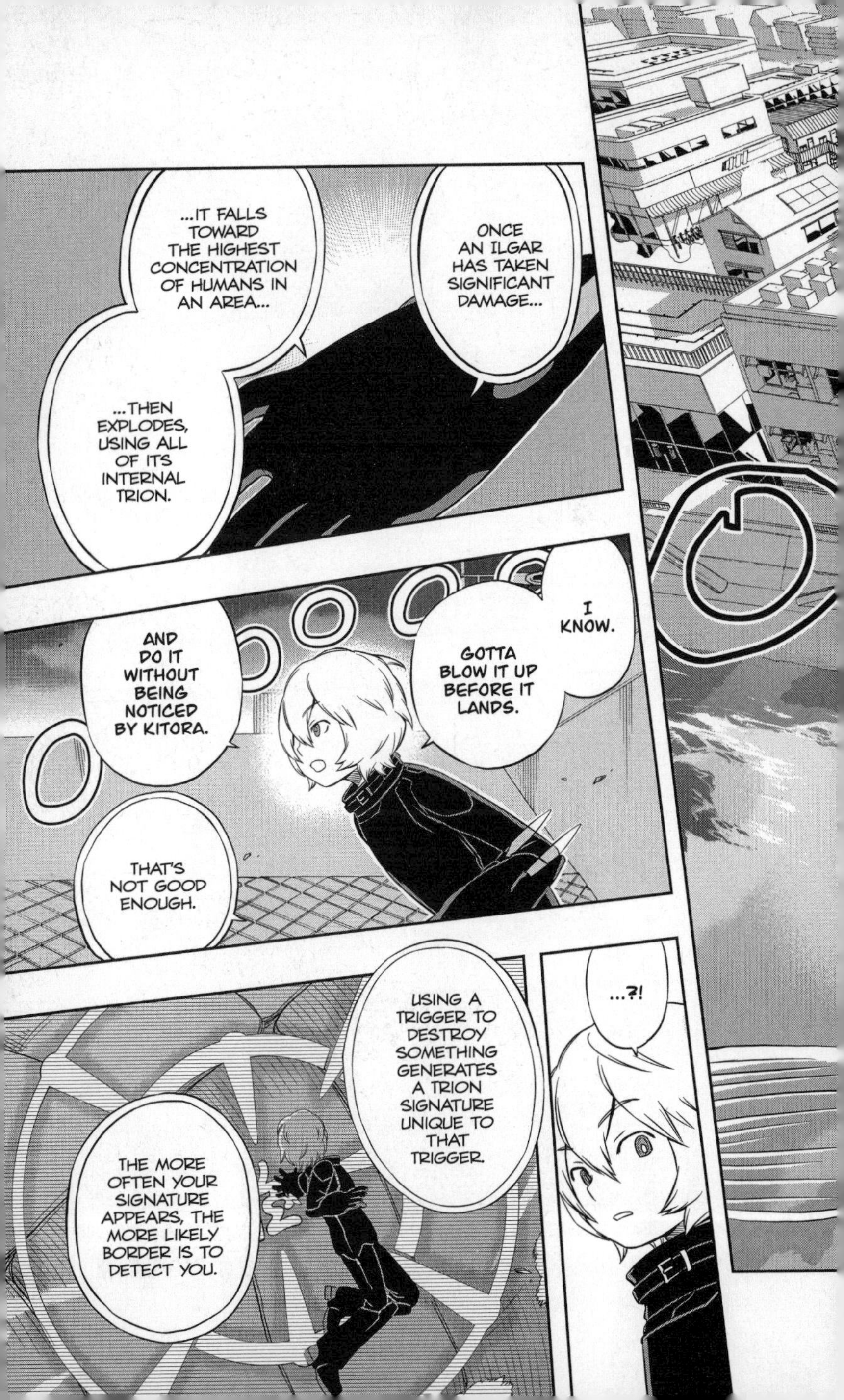

ONCE AN ILGAR HAS TAKEN SIGNIFICANT DAMAGE...
...IT FALLS TOWARD THE HIGHEST CONCENTRATION OF HUMANS IN AN AREA...
...THEN EXPLODES, USING ALL OF ITS INTERNAL TRION.
I KNOW.
GOTTA BLOW IT UP BEFORE IT LANDS.
AND DO IT WITHOUT BEING NOTICED BY KITORA.
THAT'S NOT GOOD ENOUGH.
...?!
USING A TRIGGER TO DESTROY SOMETHING GENERATES A TRION SIGNATURE UNIQUE TO THAT TRIGGER.
THE MORE OFTEN YOUR SIGNATURE APPEARS, THE MORE LIKELY BORDER IS TO DETECT YOU.

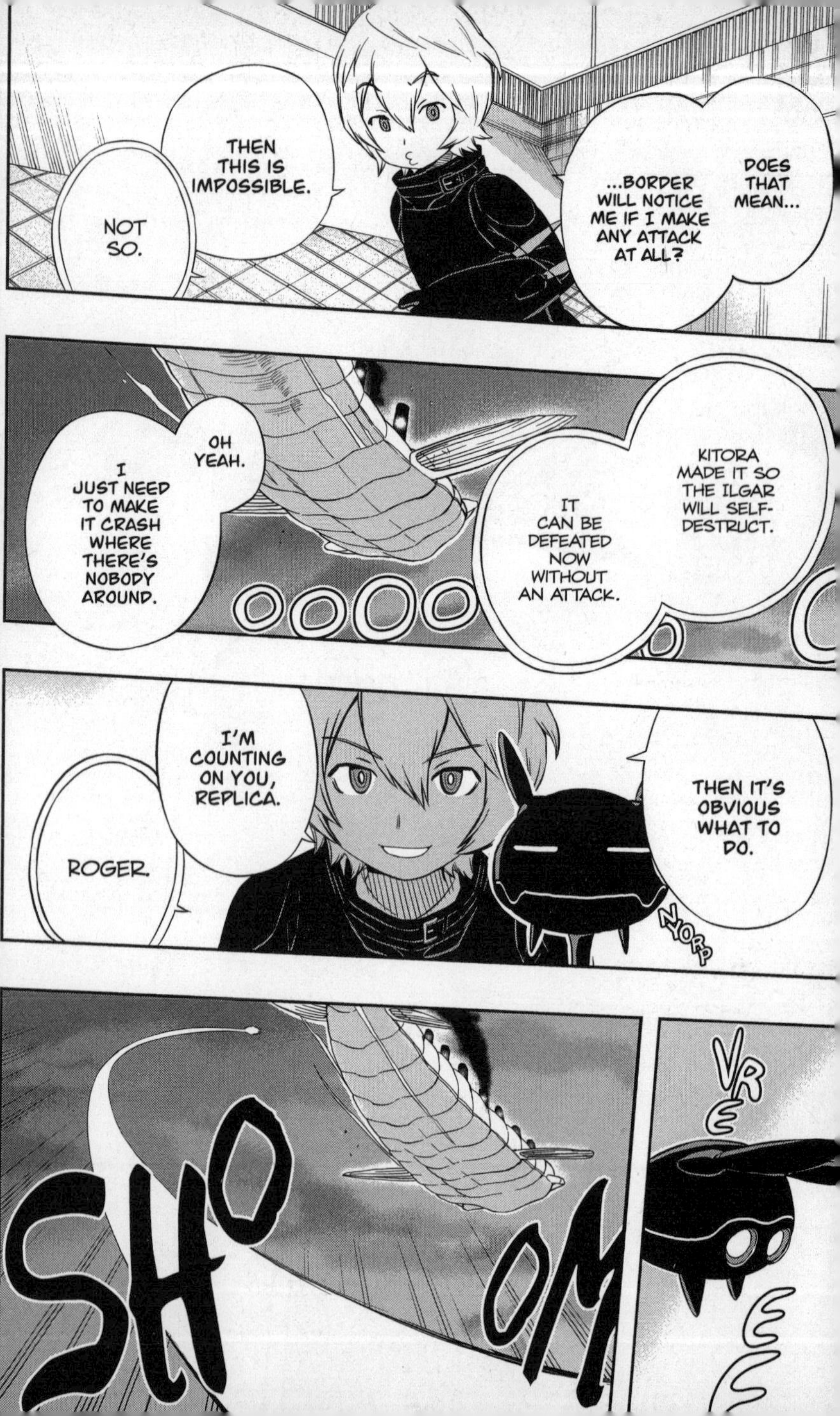
DOES THAT MEAN...
...BORDER WILL NOTICE ME IF I MAKE ANY ATTACK AT ALL?
THEN THIS IS IMPOSSIBLE.
NOT SO.
KITORA MADE IT SO THE ILGAR WILL SELF-DESTRUCT.
IT CAN BE DEFEATED NOW WITHOUT AN ATTACK.
OH YEAH.
I JUST NEED TO MAKE IT CRASH WHERE THERE'S NOBODY AROUND.
THEN IT'S OBVIOUS WHAT TO DO.
NYORP
I'M COUNTING ON YOU, REPLICA.
ROGER.
VREEE
SHOOM

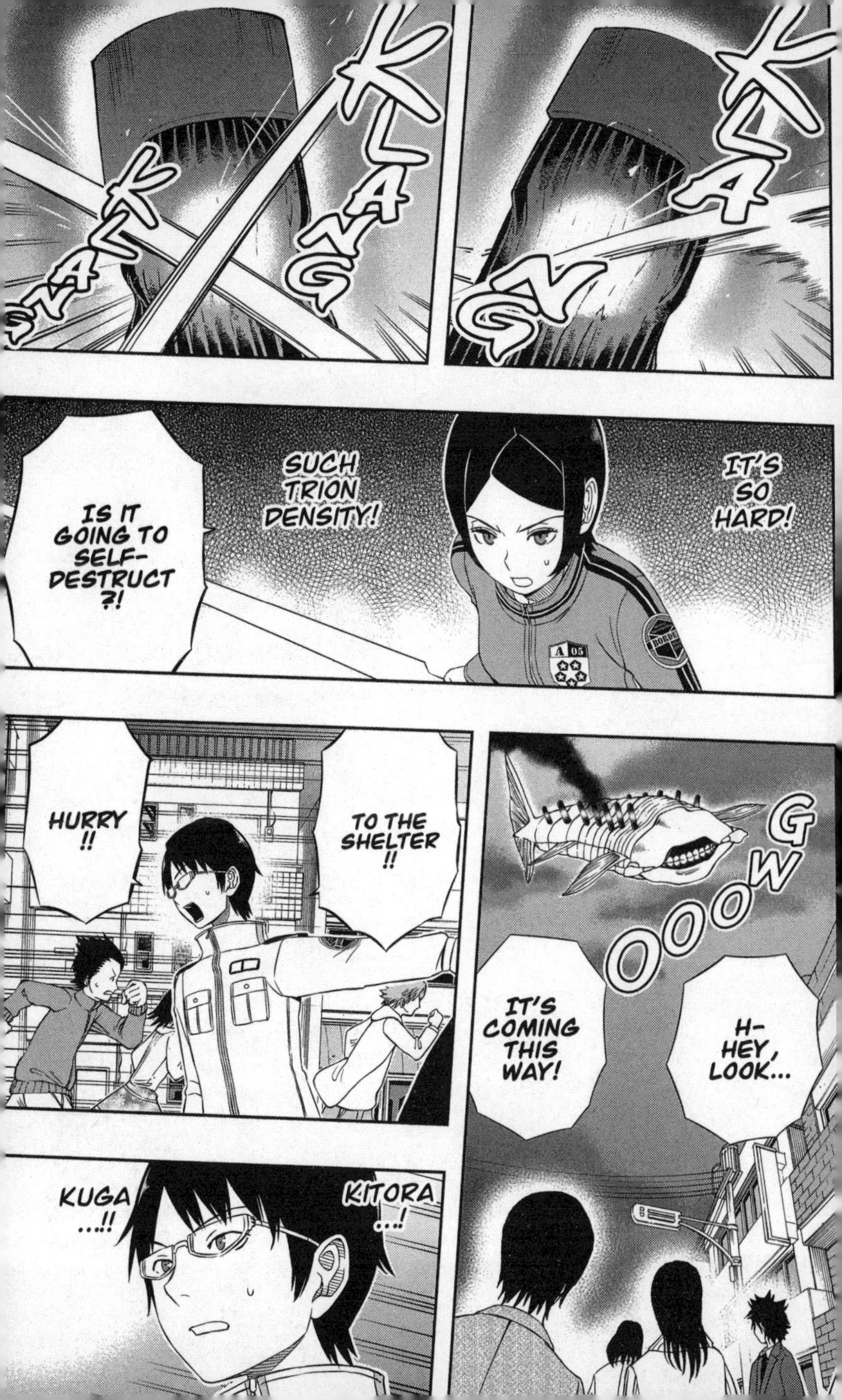
KLANG
KLANG
KLAN
IT'S SO HARD!
SUCH TRION DENSITY!
IS IT GOING TO SELF-DESTRUCT?!
GWOOOO
H-HEY, LOOK...
IT'S COMING THIS WAY!
TO THE SHELTER!!
HURRY!!
KITORA...!
KUGA...!!

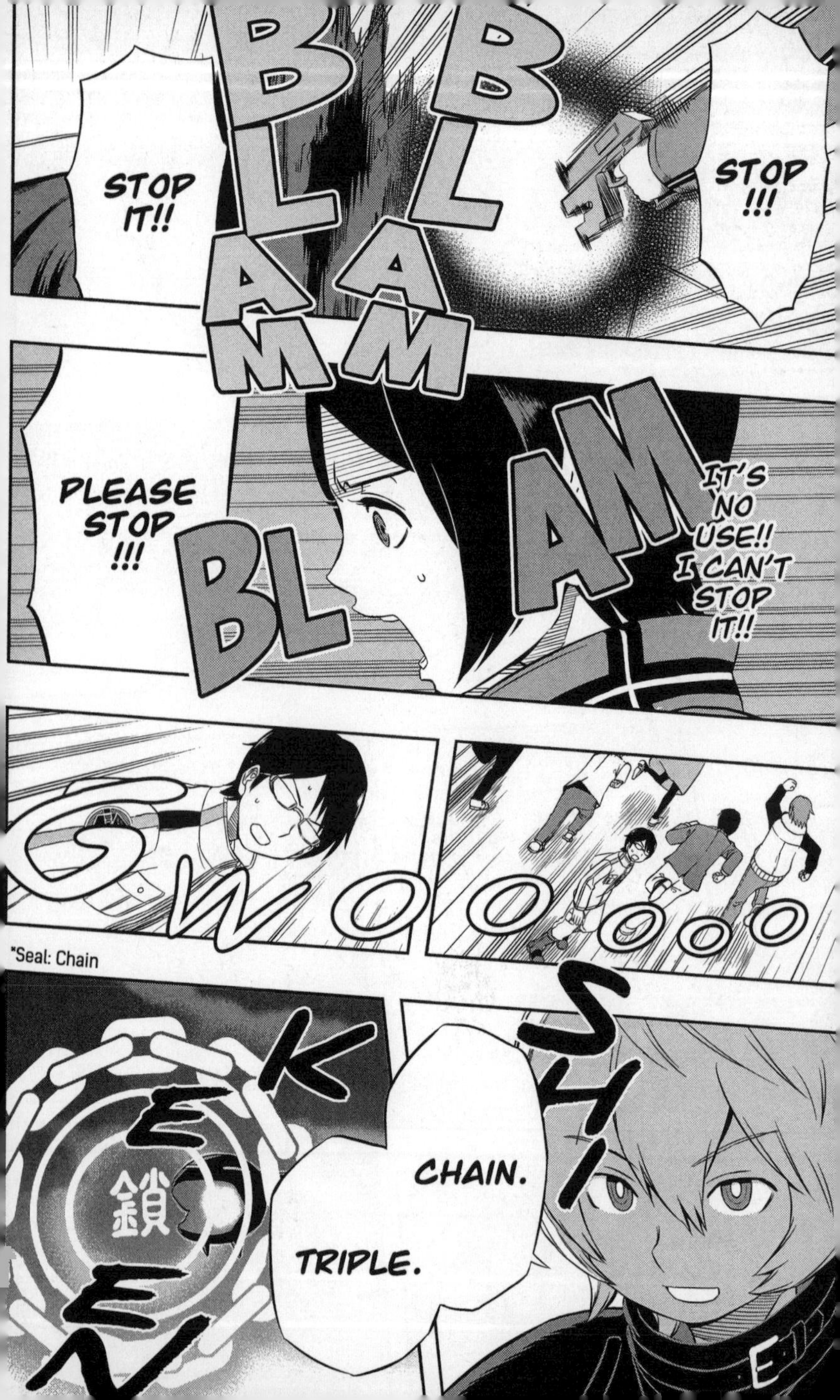
STOP !!!
BLAMM
BLAMM
STOP IT!!
IT'S NO USE!! I CAN'T STOP IT!!
BLAM
PLEASE STOP !!!
SWOOOOOOO
SHII
CHAIN.
TRIPLE.
KEEN
鎖
*Seal: Chain

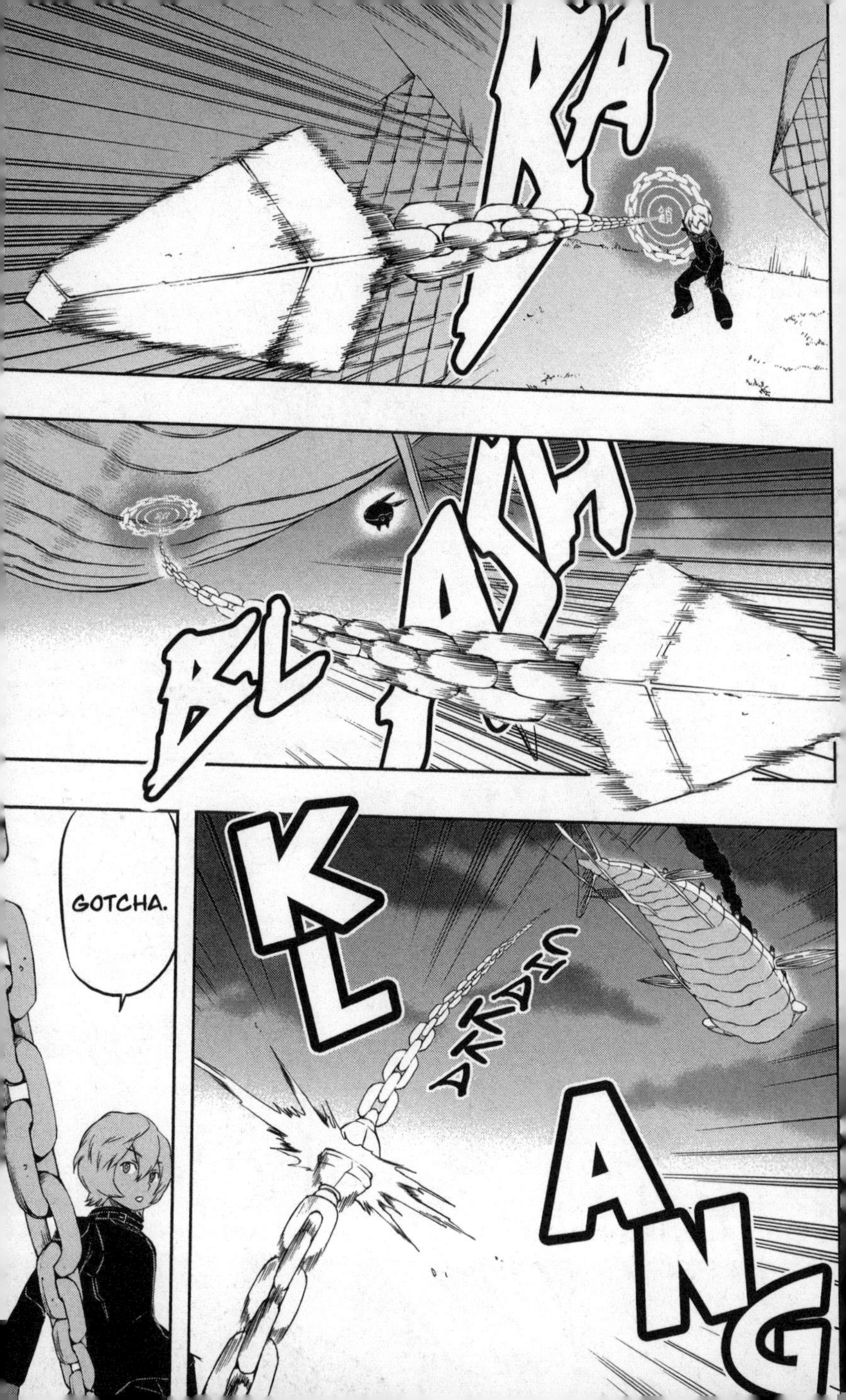
KLANG
GOTCHA.

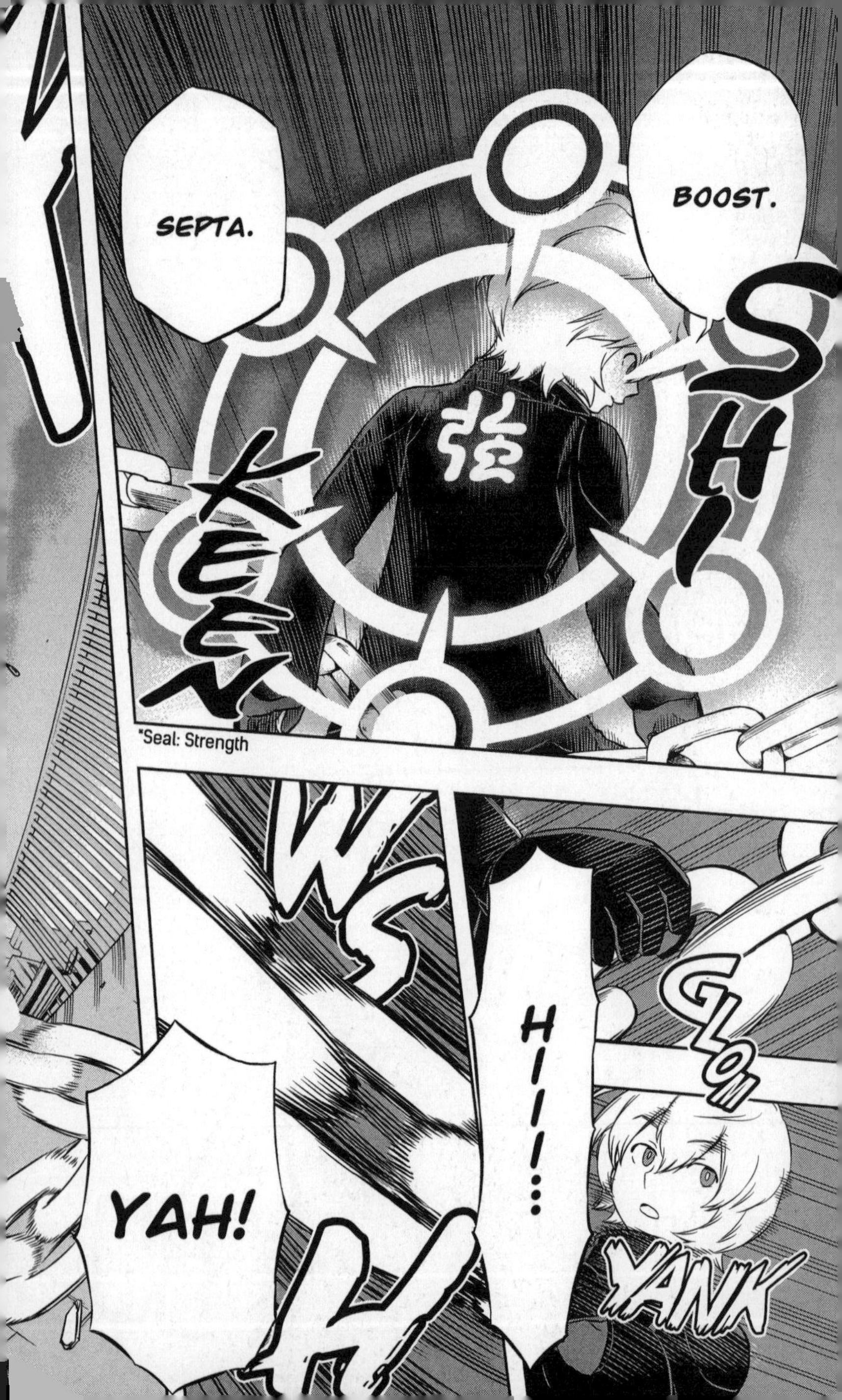
BOOST.
SEPTA.
SHI
強
KEEN
*Seal: Strength
GLOW
HIIII...!
YANK
YAH!

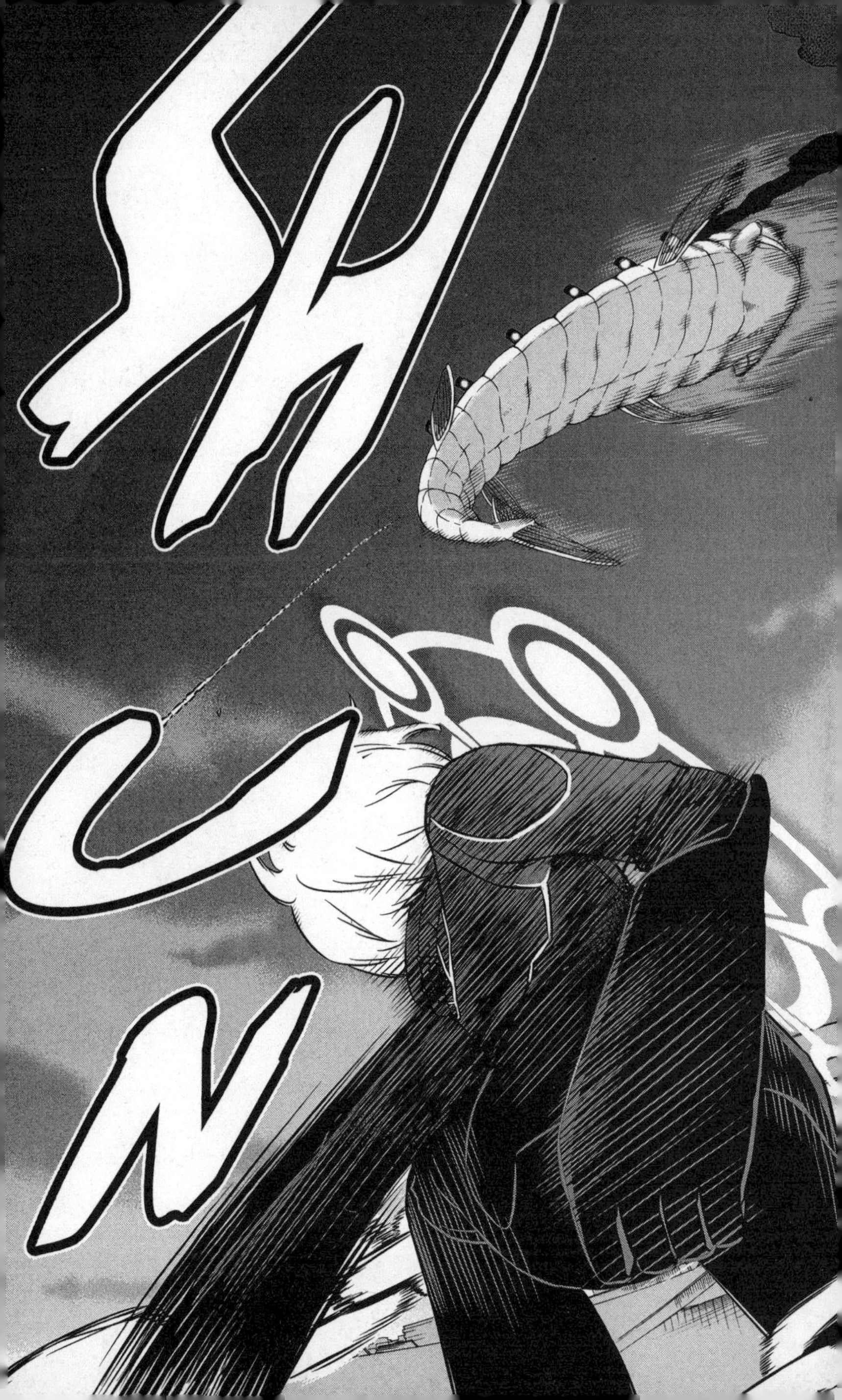
SHUN

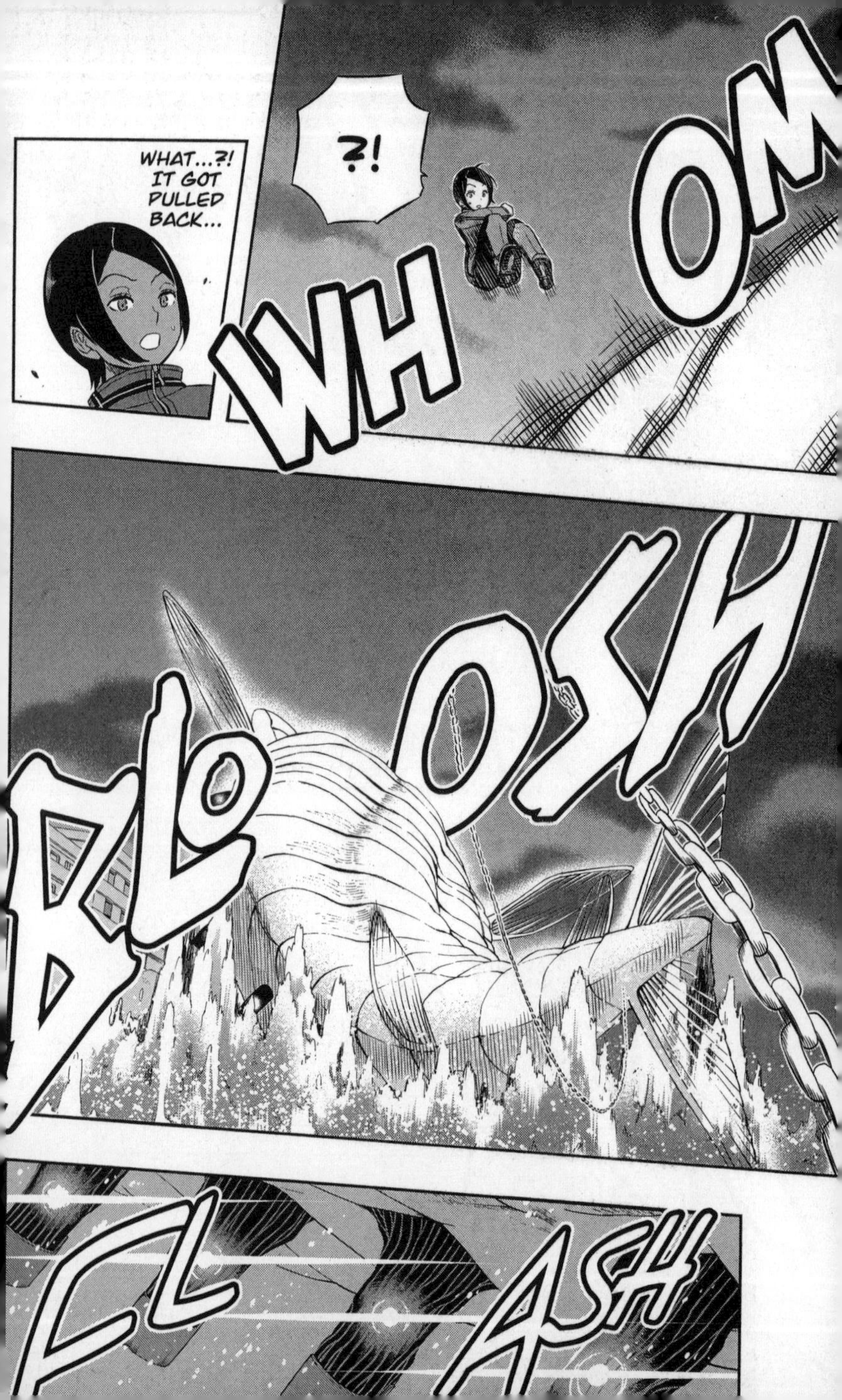
?!
WHOOM
WHAT...?! IT GOT PULLED BACK...
BLOOSH
CLASH

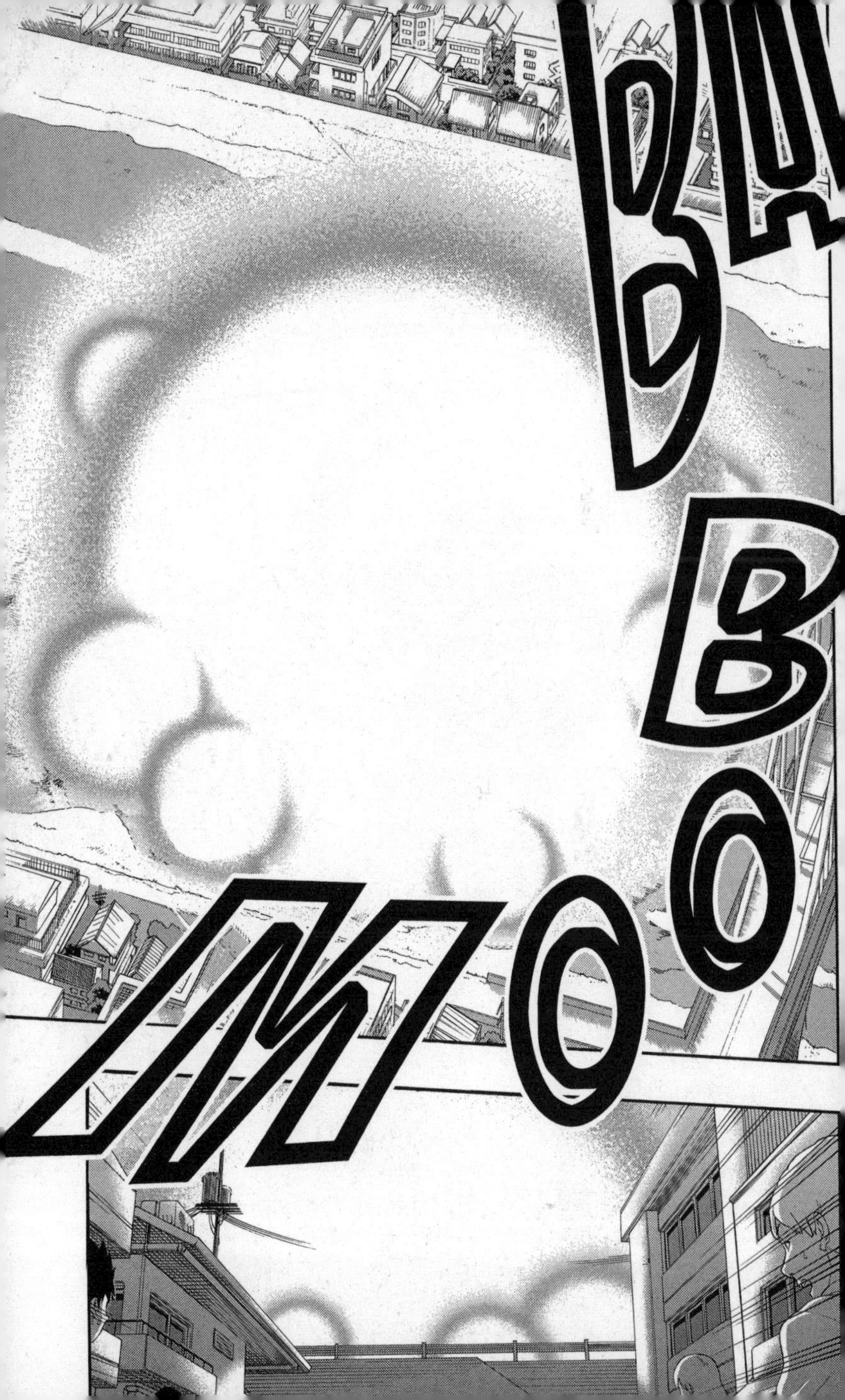
BOOM

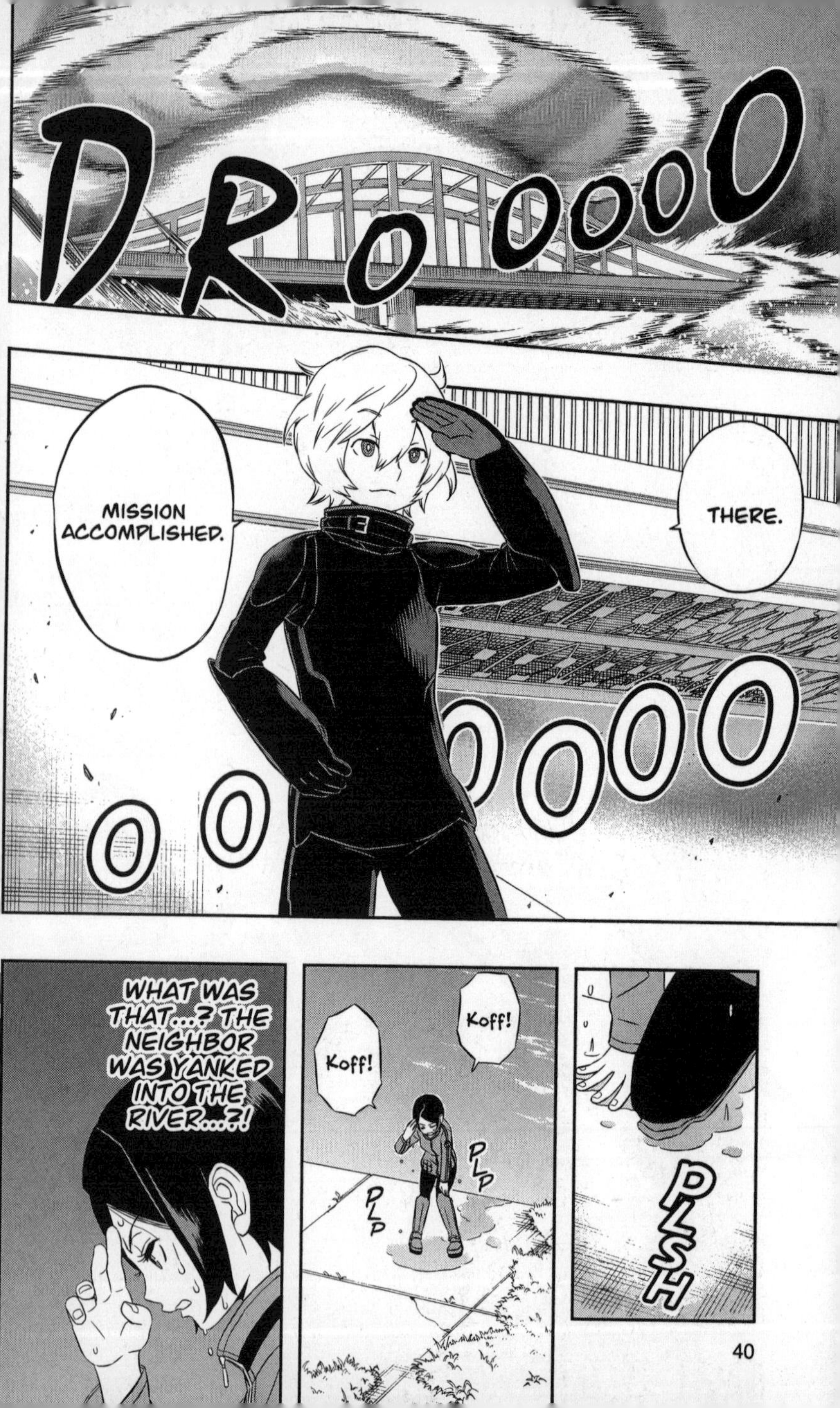
DROOOOOO
THERE.
MISSION ACCOMPLISHED.
OOOOOOO
PLSH
Koff!
Koff!
PLP
PLP
WHAT WAS THAT...? THE NEIGHBOR WAS YANKED INTO THE RIVER...?!

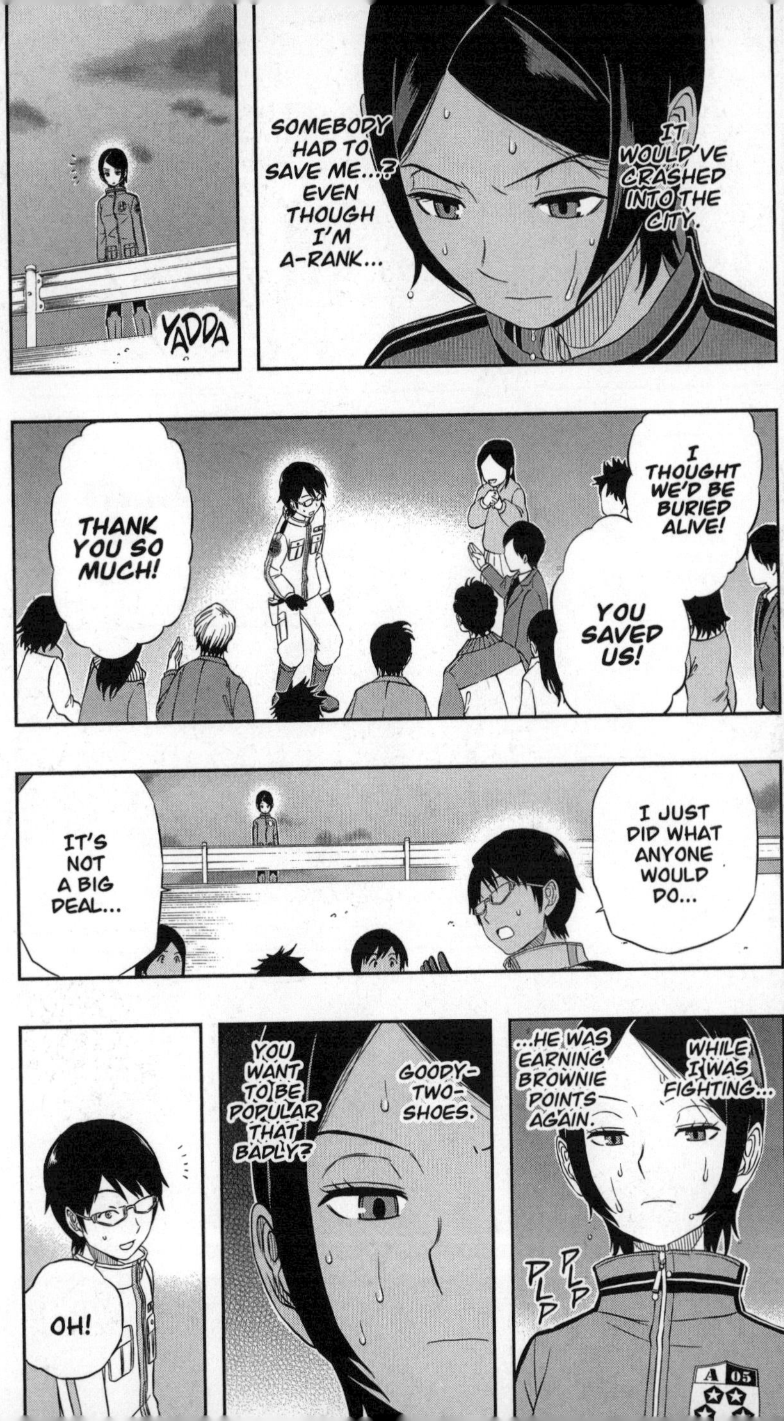
IT WOULD'VE CRASHED INTO THE CITY.
SOMEBODY HAD TO SAVE ME...? EVEN THOUGH I'M A-RANK...
YADDA
I THOUGHT WE'D BE BURIED ALIVE!
YOU SAVED US!
THANK YOU SO MUCH!
I JUST DID WHAT ANYONE WOULD DO...
IT'S NOT A BIG DEAL...
WHILE I WAS FIGHTING...
...HE WAS EARNING BROWNIE POINTS AGAIN.
PLP PLP
A 05
GOODY-TWO-SHOES.
YOU WANT TO BE POPULAR THAT BADLY?
OH!

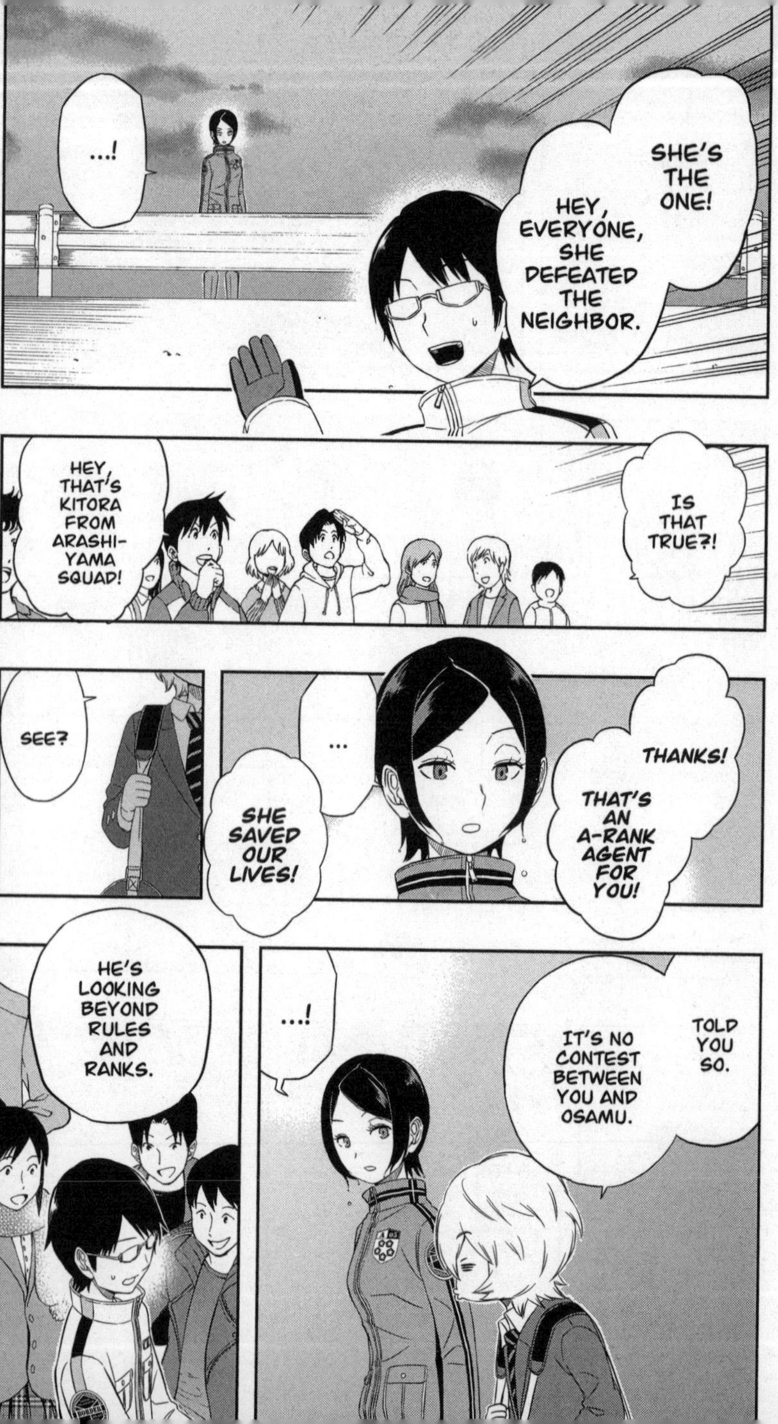
SHE'S THE ONE!
HEY, EVERYONE, SHE DEFEATED THE NEIGHBOR.
...!
IS THAT TRUE?!
HEY, THAT'S KITORA FROM ARASHI-YAMA SQUAD!
THANKS!
THAT'S AN A-RANK AGENT FOR YOU!
...
SHE SAVED OUR LIVES!
SEE?
TOLD YOU SO.
IT'S NO CONTEST BETWEEN YOU AND OSAMU.
...!
HE'S LOOKING BEYOND RULES AND RANKS.

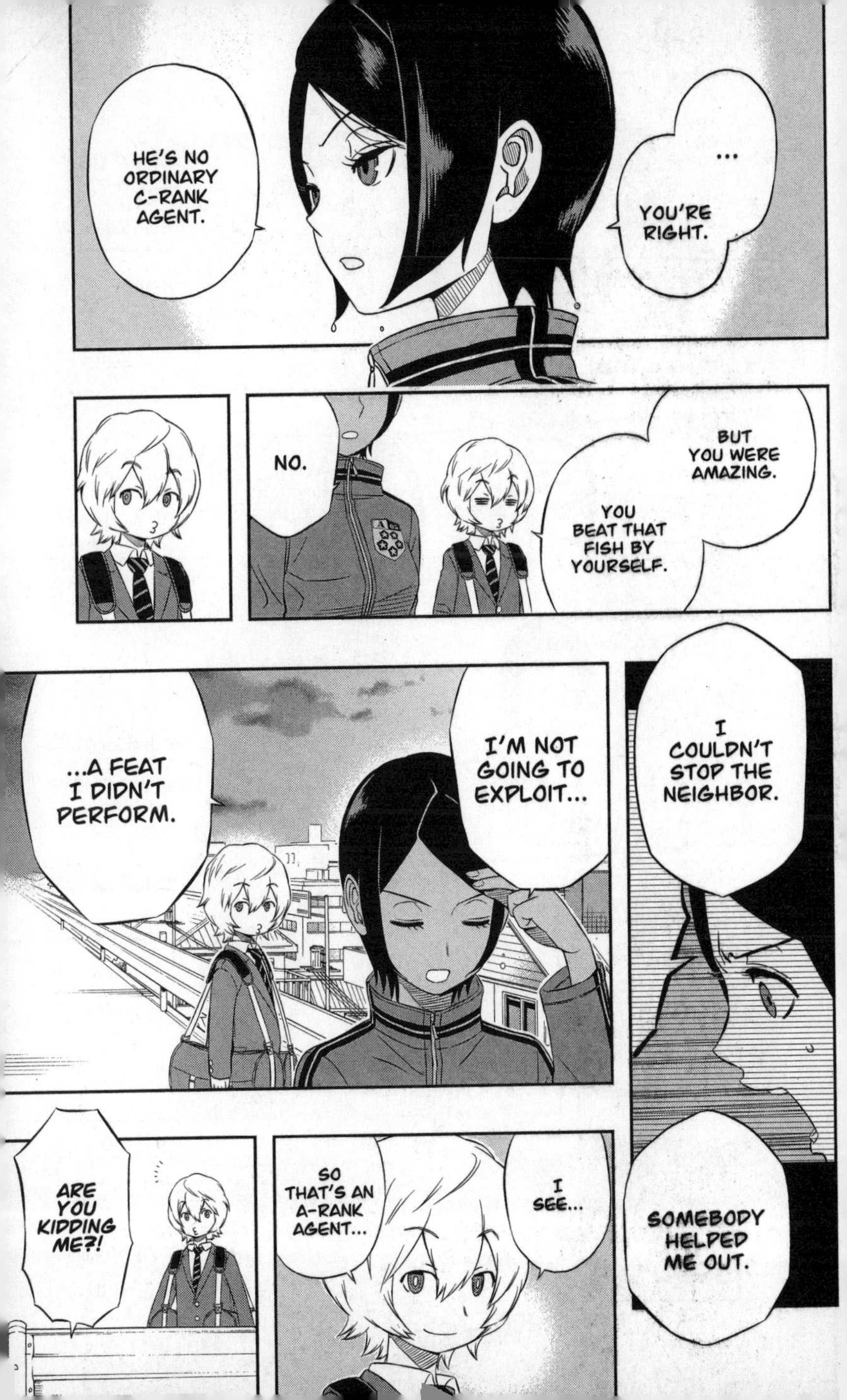
...
YOU'RE RIGHT.
HE'S NO ORDINARY C-RANK AGENT.
BUT YOU WERE AMAZING.
YOU BEAT THAT FISH BY YOURSELF.
NO.
I COULDN'T STOP THE NEIGHBOR.
SOMEBODY HELPED ME OUT.
I'M NOT GOING TO EXPLOIT...
...A FEAT I DIDN'T PERFORM.
I SEE...
SO THAT'S AN A-RANK AGENT...
ARE YOU KIDDING ME?!

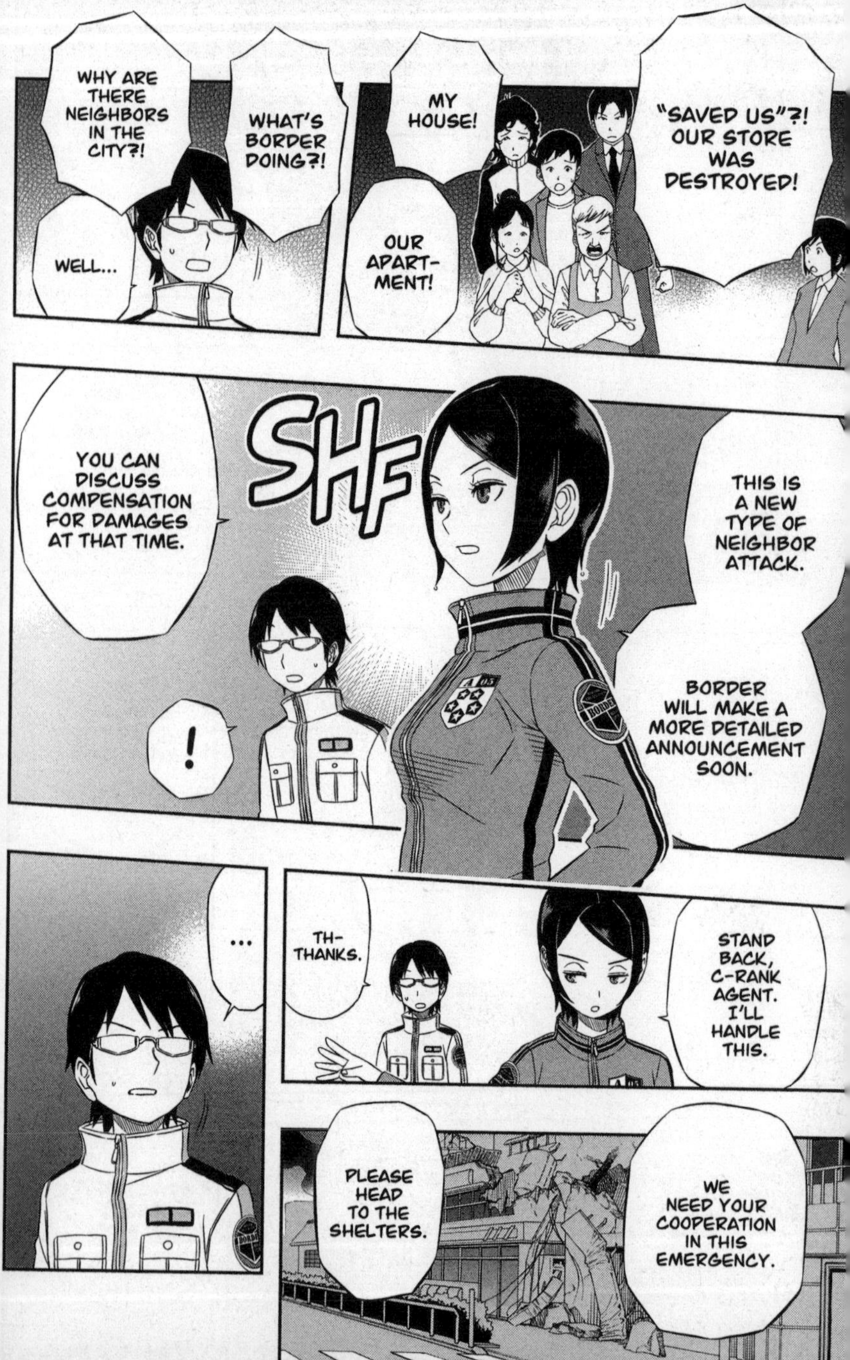
"SAVED US"?! OUR STORE WAS DESTROYED!
MY HOUSE!
OUR APART-MENT!
WHAT'S BORDER DOING?!
WHY ARE THERE NEIGHBORS IN THE CITY?!
WELL...
THIS IS A NEW TYPE OF NEIGHBOR ATTACK.
SHF
BORDER WILL MAKE A MORE DETAILED ANNOUNCEMENT SOON.
YOU CAN DISCUSS COMPENSATION FOR DAMAGES AT THAT TIME.
!
STAND BACK, C-RANK AGENT. I'LL HANDLE THIS.
TH- THANKS.
WE NEED YOUR COOPERATION IN THIS EMERGENCY.
PLEASE HEAD TO THE SHELTERS.
...

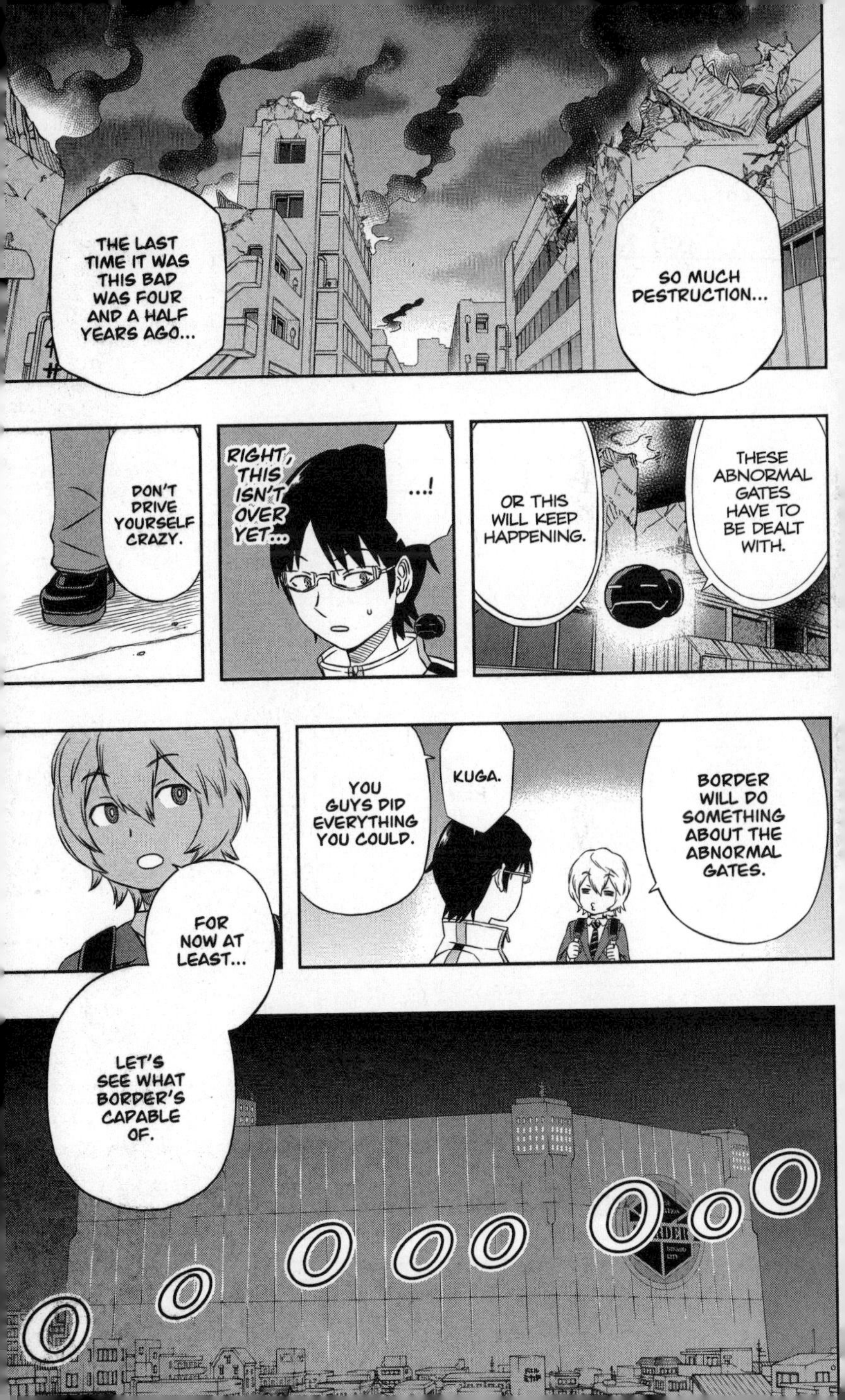
SO MUCH DESTRUCTION...
THE LAST TIME IT WAS THIS BAD WAS FOUR AND A HALF YEARS AGO...
THESE ABNORMAL GATES HAVE TO BE DEALT WITH.
OR THIS WILL KEEP HAPPENING.
...!
RIGHT, THIS ISN'T OVER YET...
DON'T DRIVE YOURSELF CRAZY.
BORDER WILL DO SOMETHING ABOUT THE ABNORMAL GATES.
KUGA.
YOU GUYS DID EVERYTHING YOU COULD.
FOR NOW AT LEAST...
LET'S SEE WHAT BORDER'S CAPABLE OF.

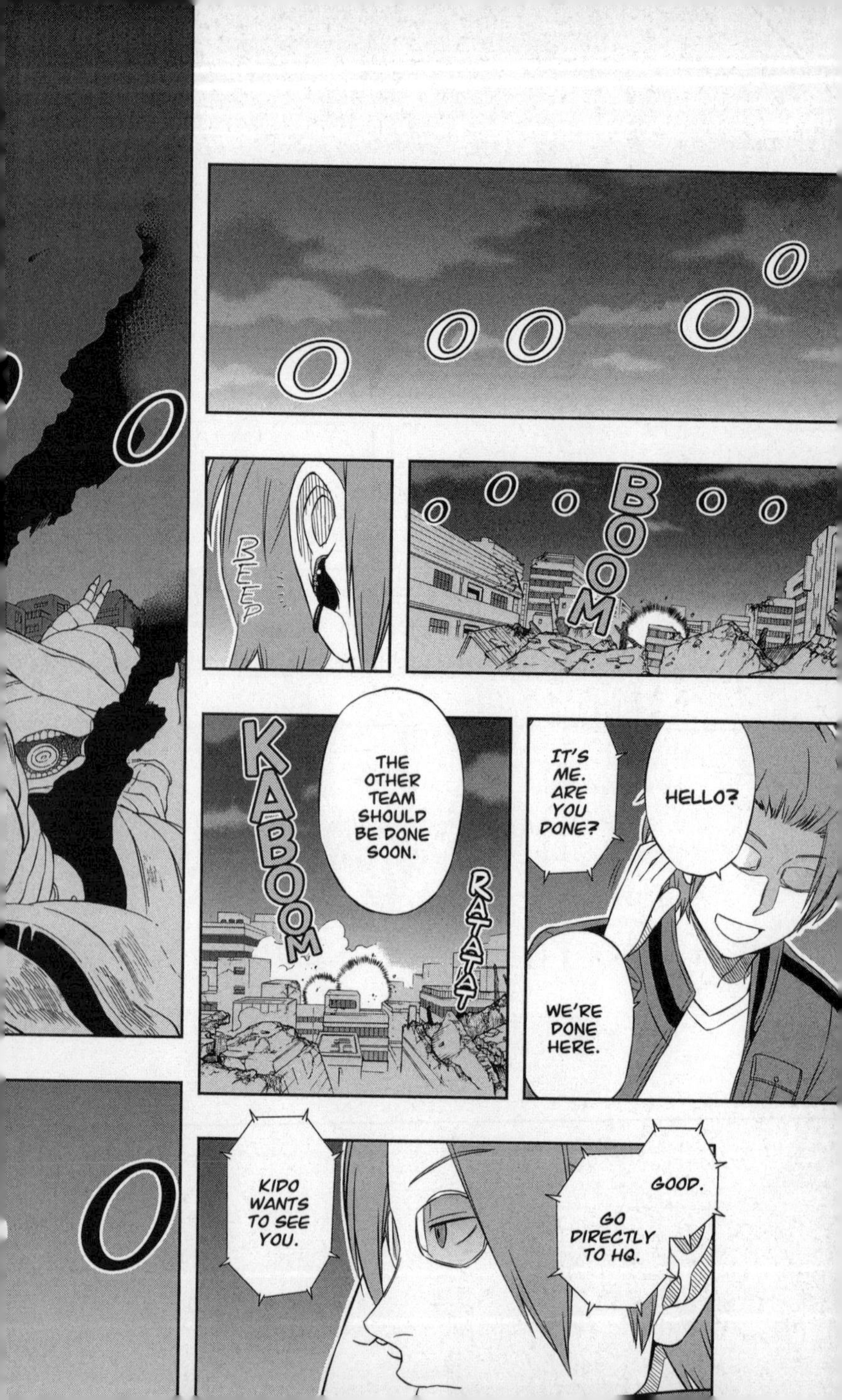
BOOM
BEEP
HELLO?
IT'S ME. ARE YOU DONE?
WE'RE DONE HERE.
THE OTHER TEAM SHOULD BE DONE SOON.
KABOOM
RATATAT
GOOD.
GO DIRECTLY TO HQ.
KIDO WANTS TO SEE YOU.

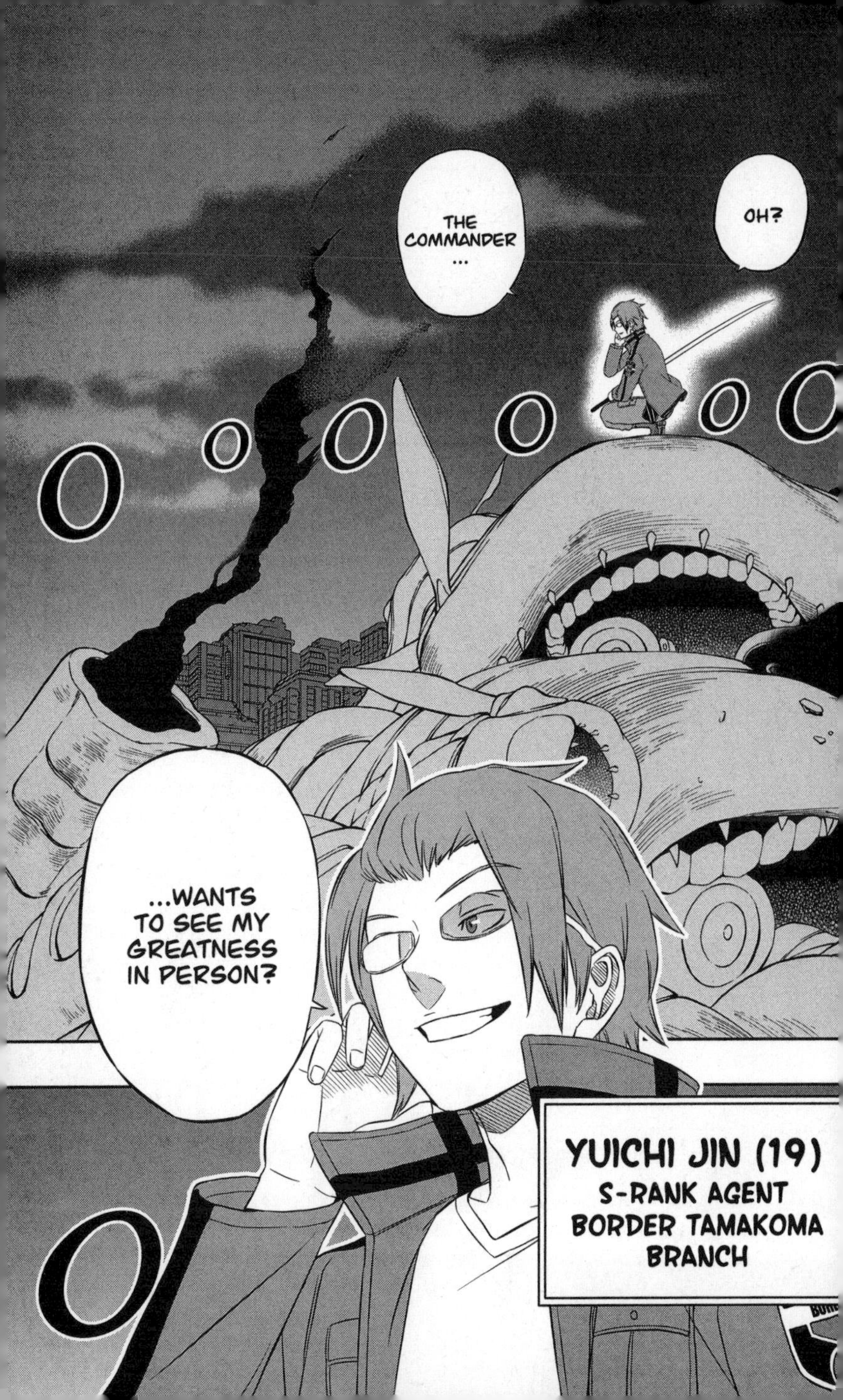
OH?
THE COMMANDER ...
OOOOOOO
...WANTS TO SEE MY GREATNESS IN PERSON?
YUICHI JIN (19)
S-RANK AGENT
BORDER TAMAKOMA BRANCH

WORLD TRIGGER

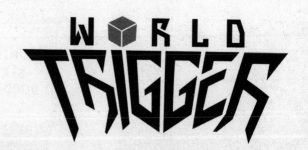

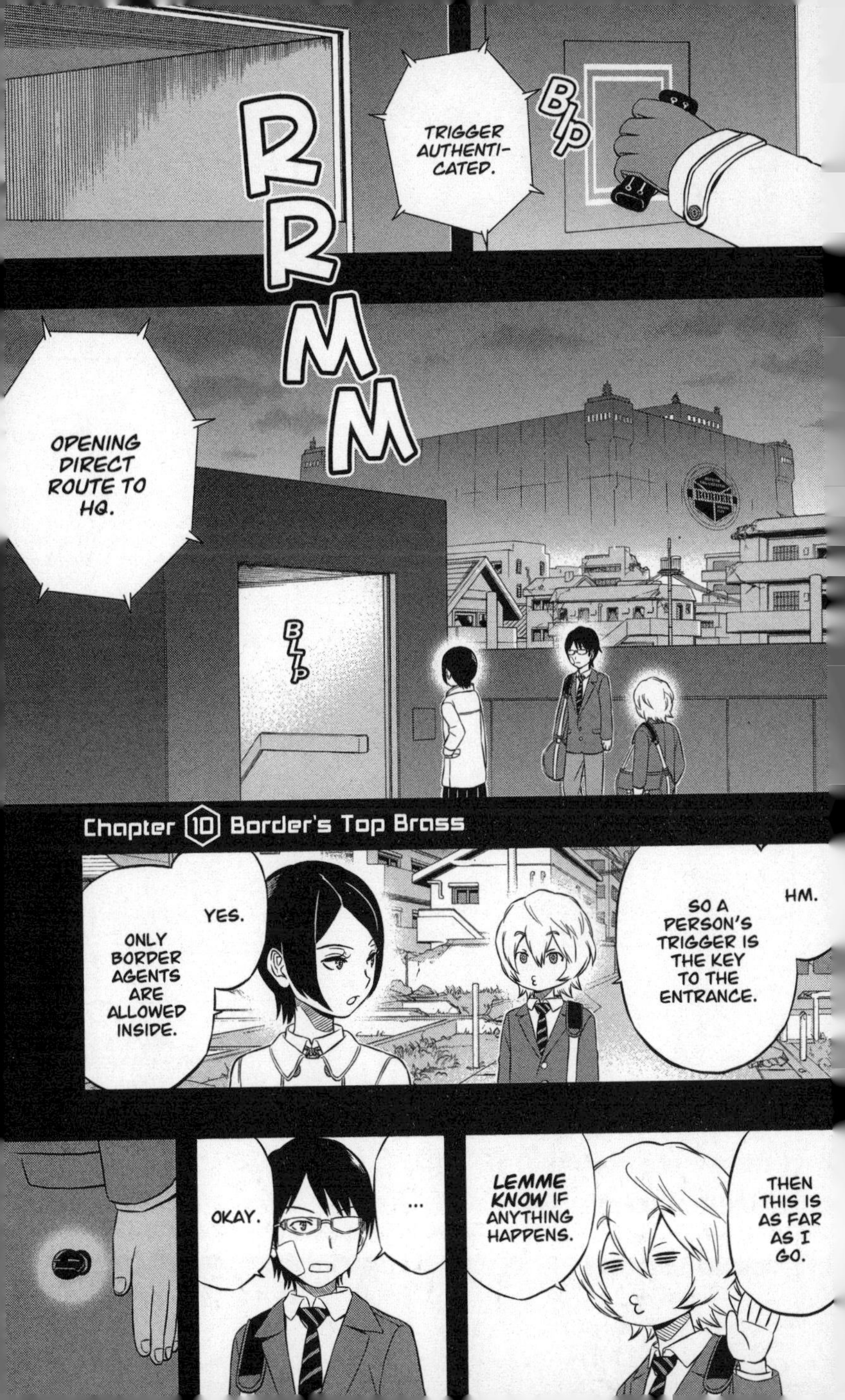
BLIP
TRIGGER AUTHENTICATED.
RRMM
OPENING DIRECT ROUTE TO HQ.
BLIP
Chapter 10 Border's Top Brass
HM.
SO A PERSON'S TRIGGER IS THE KEY TO THE ENTRANCE.
YES.
ONLY BORDER AGENTS ARE ALLOWED INSIDE.
THEN THIS IS AS FAR AS I GO.
LEMME KNOW IF ANYTHING HAPPENS.
...
OKAY.

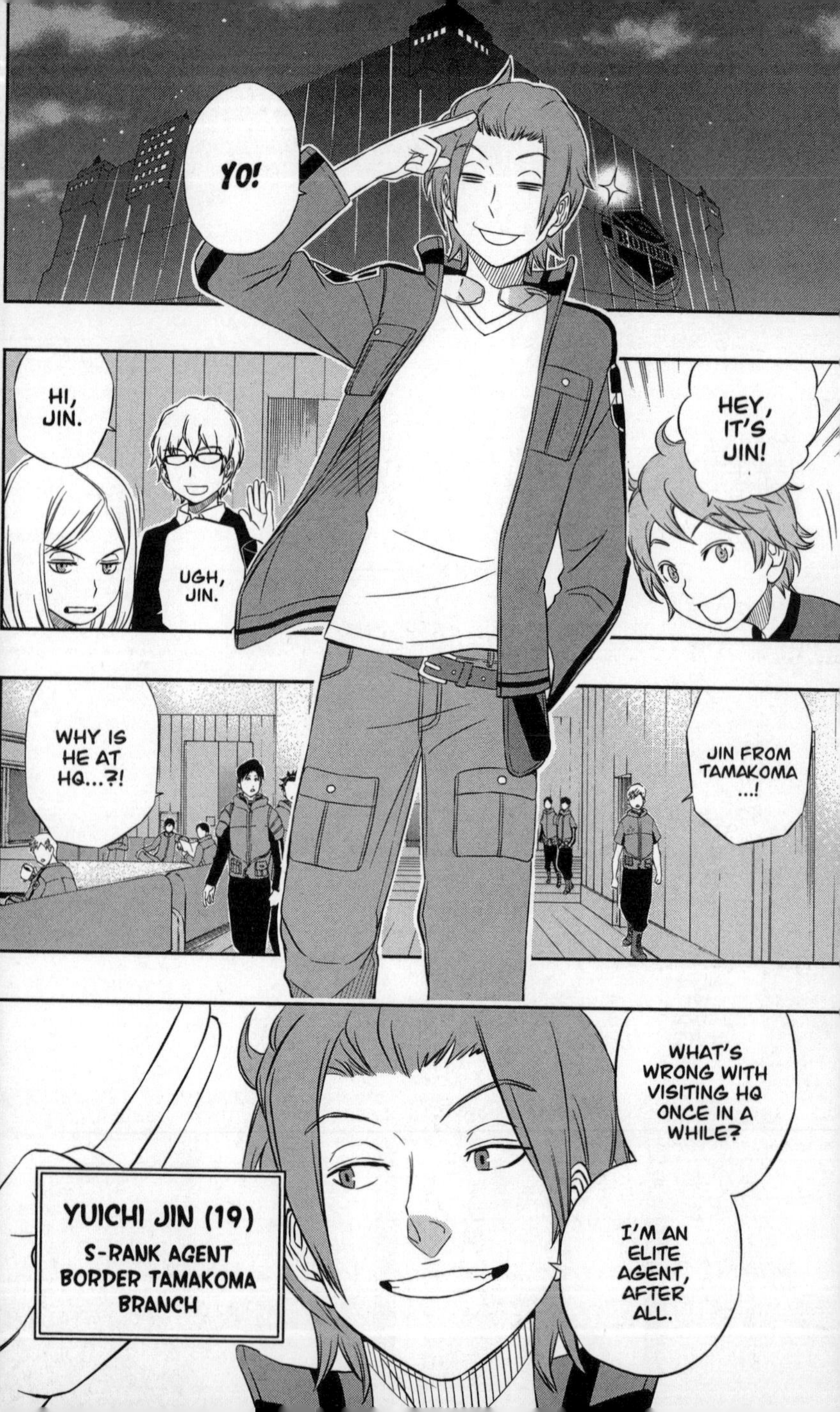
YO!
HEY, IT'S JIN!
HI, JIN.
UGH, JIN.
JIN FROM TAMAKOMA ...!
WHY IS HE AT HQ...?!
WHAT'S WRONG WITH VISITING HQ ONCE IN A WHILE?
I'M AN ELITE AGENT, AFTER ALL.
YUICHI JIN (19)
S-RANK AGENT
BORDER TAMAKOMA BRANCH

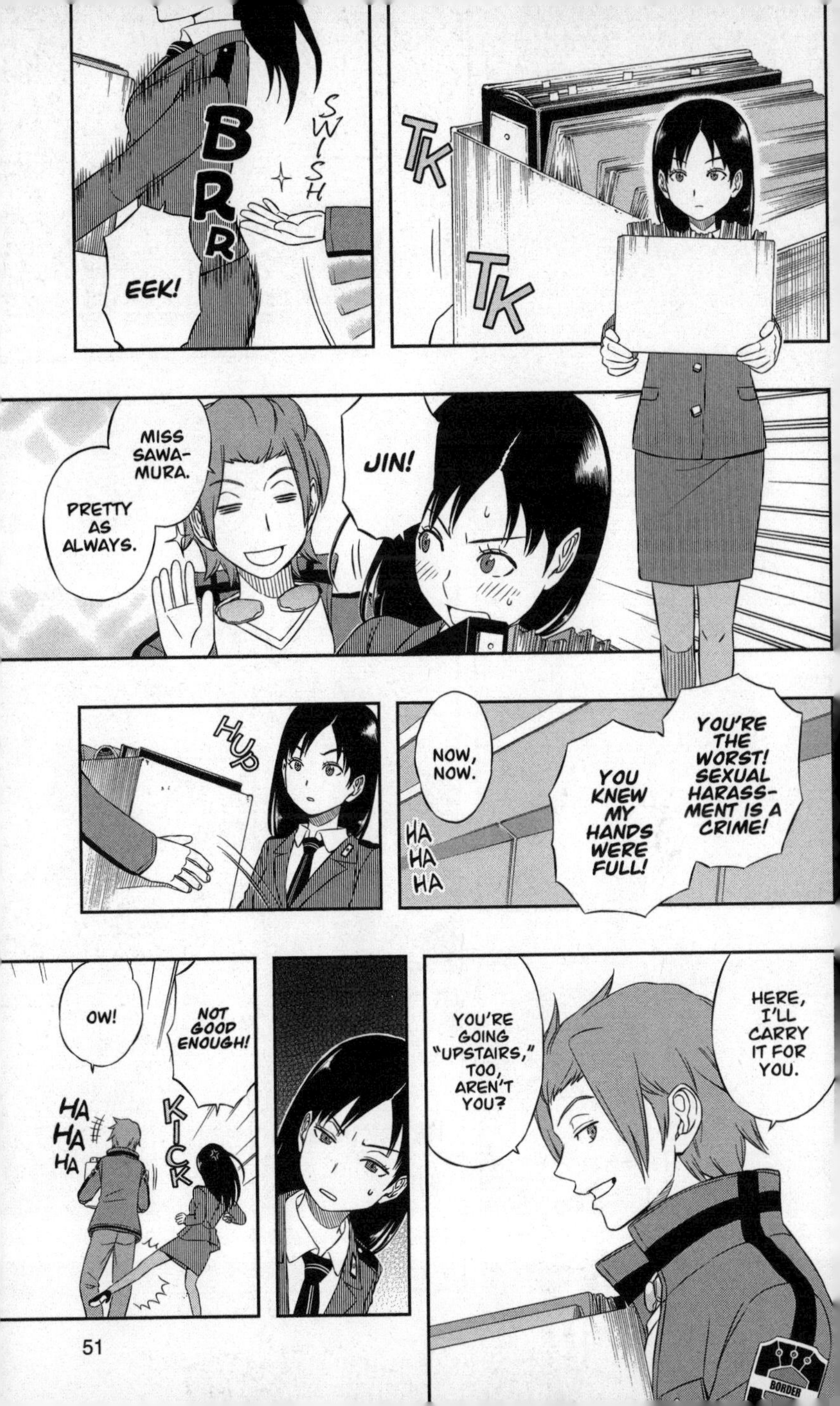
TK
TK
SWISH
BRR
EEK!
JIN!
MISS SAWAMURA.
PRETTY AS ALWAYS.
YOU'RE THE WORST! SEXUAL HARASSMENT IS A CRIME!
YOU KNEW MY HANDS WERE FULL!
NOW, NOW.
HA HA HA
HUP
HERE, I'LL CARRY IT FOR YOU.
YOU'RE GOING "UPSTAIRS," TOO, AREN'T YOU?
NOT GOOD ENOUGH!
KICK
OW!
HA HA HA
BORDER

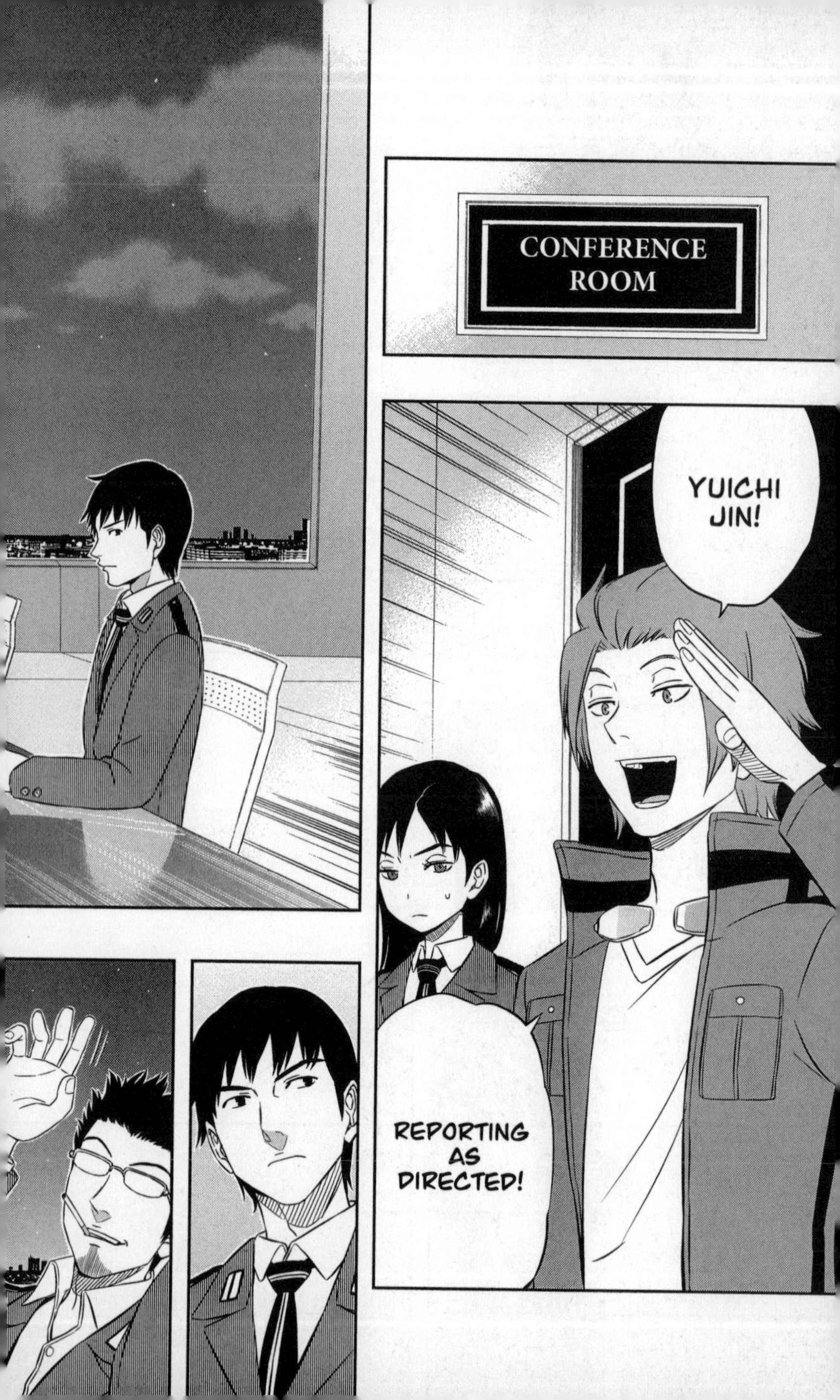
CONFERENCE ROOM
YUICHI JIN!
REPORTING AS DIRECTED!

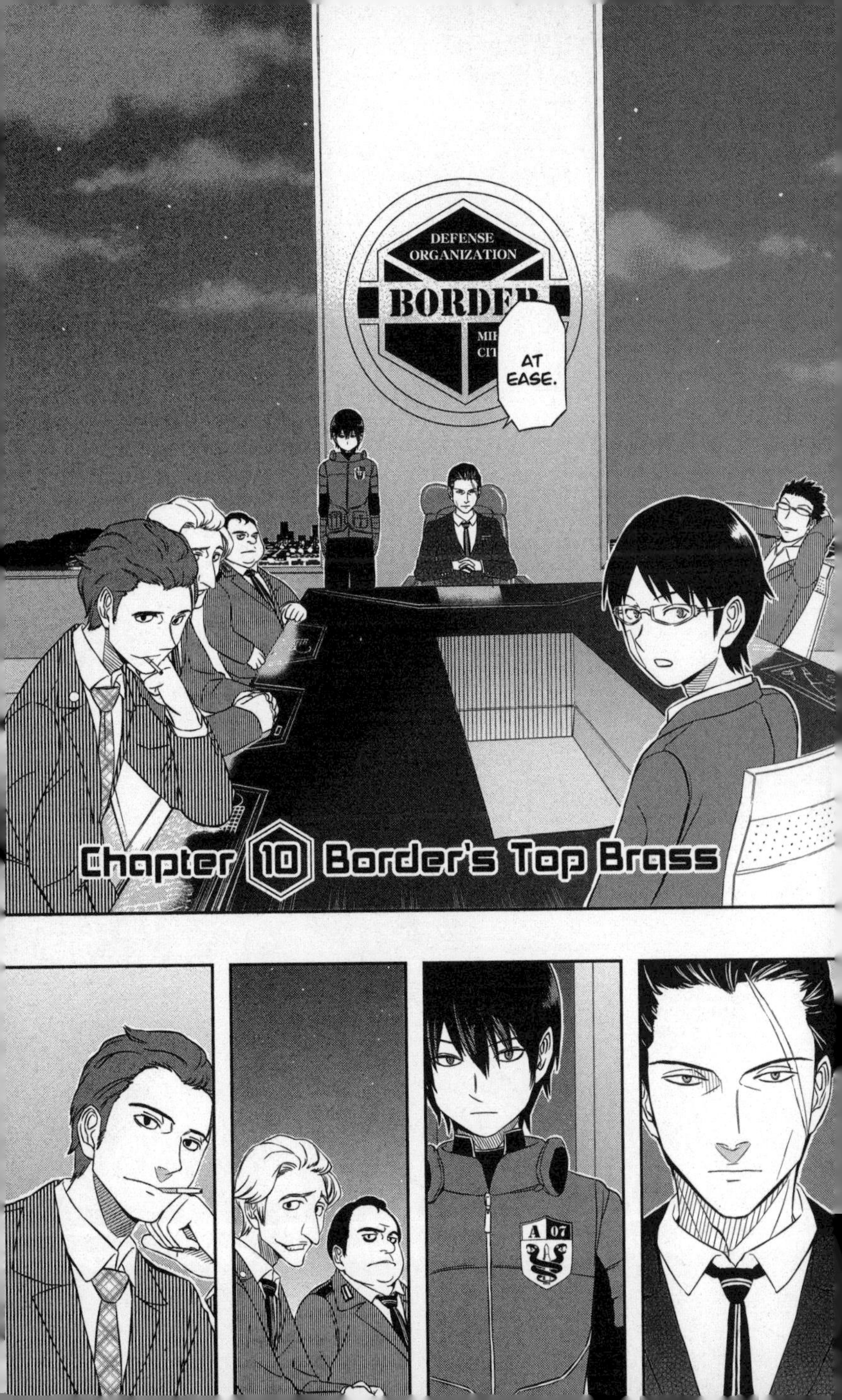
DEFENSE ORGANIZATION
BORDER
AT EASE.
Chapter 10 Border's Top Brass
A 07

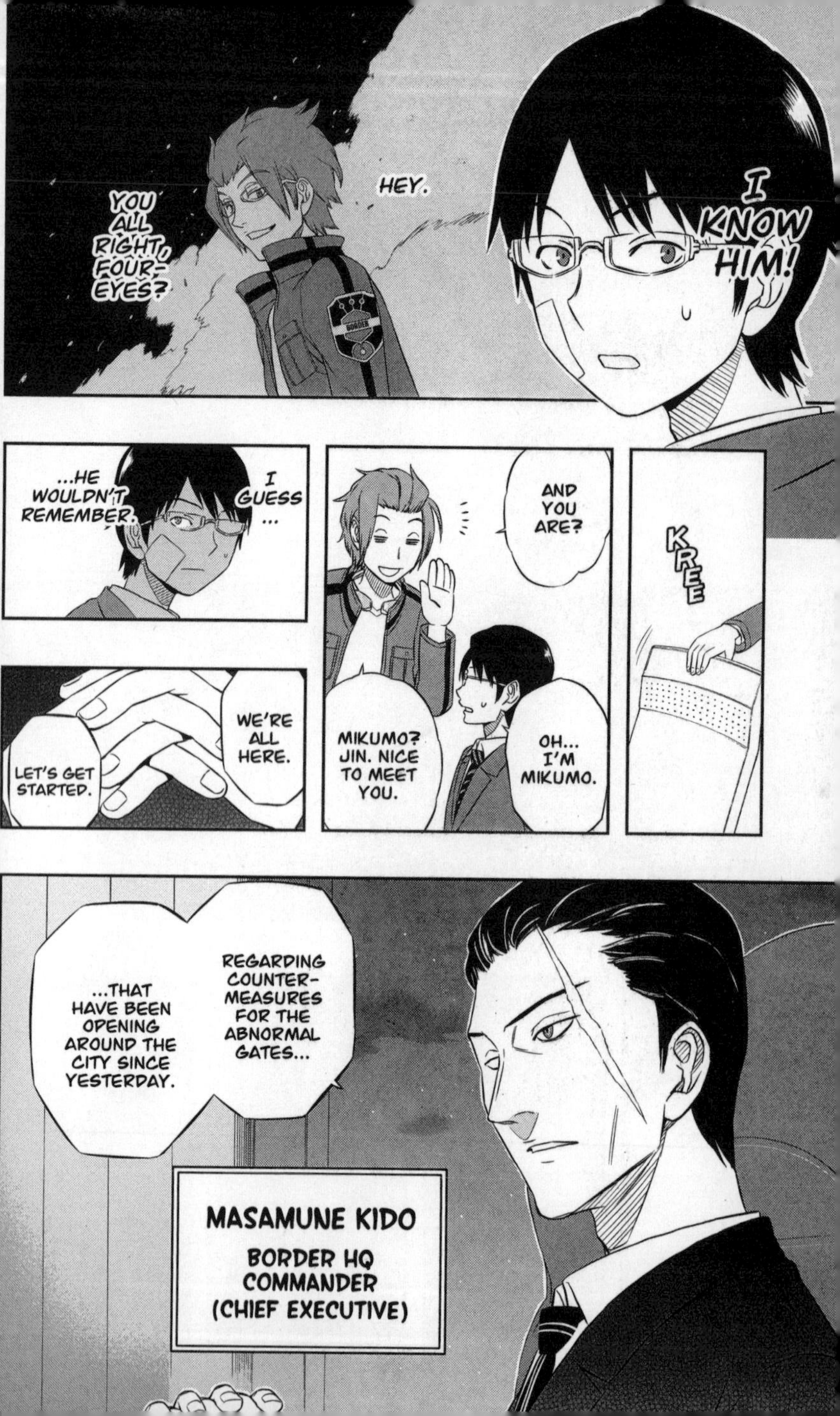
I KNOW HIM!
HEY.
YOU ALL RIGHT, FOUR-EYES?
KREE
AND YOU ARE?
OH... I'M MIKUMO.
MIKUMO? JIN. NICE TO MEET YOU.
I GUESS...
...HE WOULDN'T REMEMBER.
WE'RE ALL HERE.
LET'S GET STARTED.
REGARDING COUNTER-MEASURES FOR THE ABNORMAL GATES...
...THAT HAVE BEEN OPENING AROUND THE CITY SINCE YESTERDAY.
MASAMUNE KIDO
BORDER HQ COMMANDER (CHIEF EXECUTIVE)

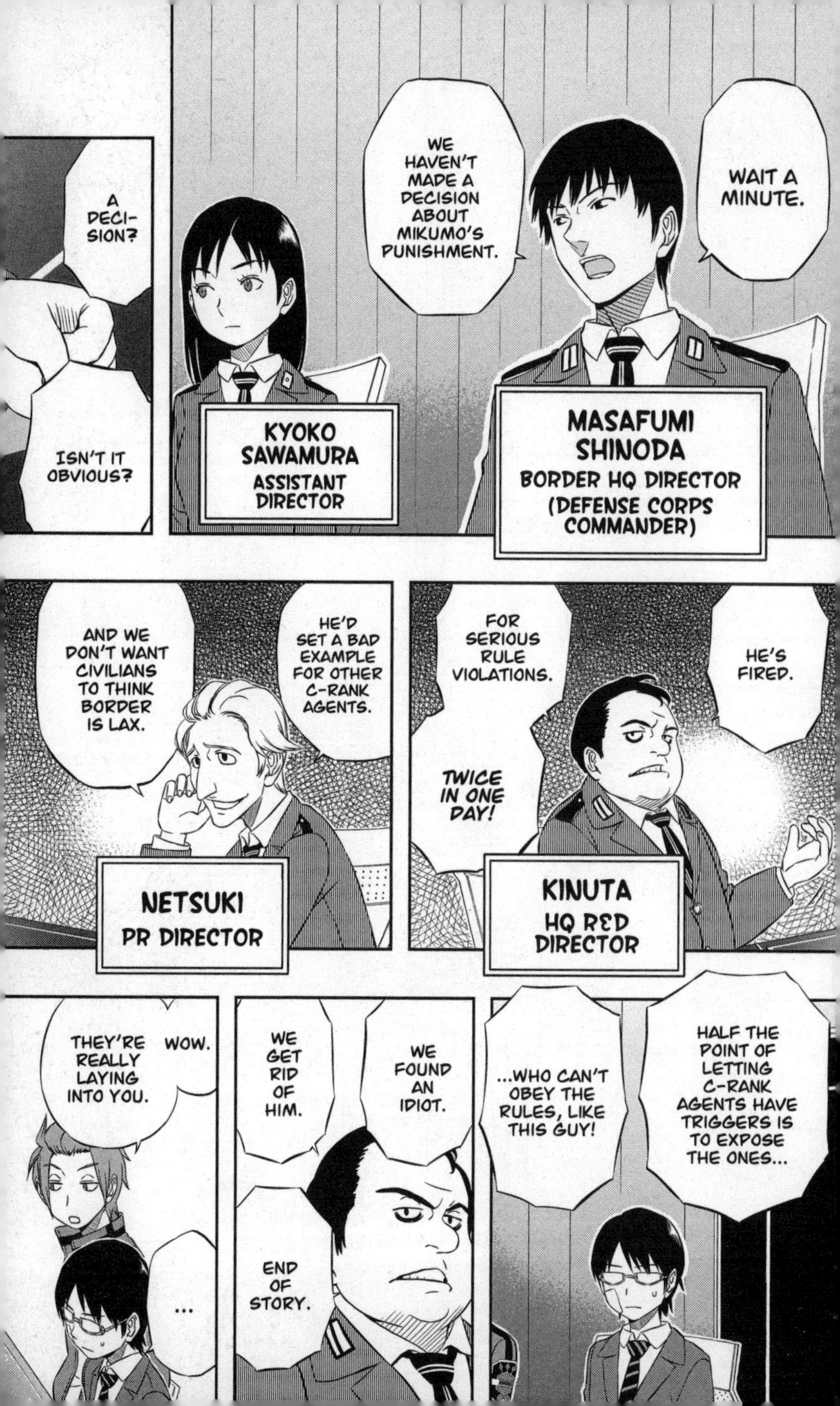
WAIT A MINUTE.
WE HAVEN'T MADE A DECISION ABOUT MIKUMO'S PUNISHMENT.
MASAFUMI SHINODA BORDER HQ DIRECTOR (DEFENSE CORPS COMMANDER)
KYOKO SAWAMURA ASSISTANT DIRECTOR
A DECI-SION?
ISN'T IT OBVIOUS?
HE'S FIRED.
FOR SERIOUS RULE VIOLATIONS.
TWICE IN ONE DAY!
KINUTA HQ R&D DIRECTOR
HE'D SET A BAD EXAMPLE FOR OTHER C-RANK AGENTS.
AND WE DON'T WANT CIVILIANS TO THINK BORDER IS LAX.
NETSUKI PR DIRECTOR
HALF THE POINT OF LETTING C-RANK AGENTS HAVE TRIGGERS IS TO EXPOSE THE ONES...
...WHO CAN'T OBEY THE RULES, LIKE THIS GUY!
WE FOUND AN IDIOT.
WE GET RID OF HIM.
END OF STORY.
WOW.
THEY'RE REALLY LAYING INTO YOU.
...

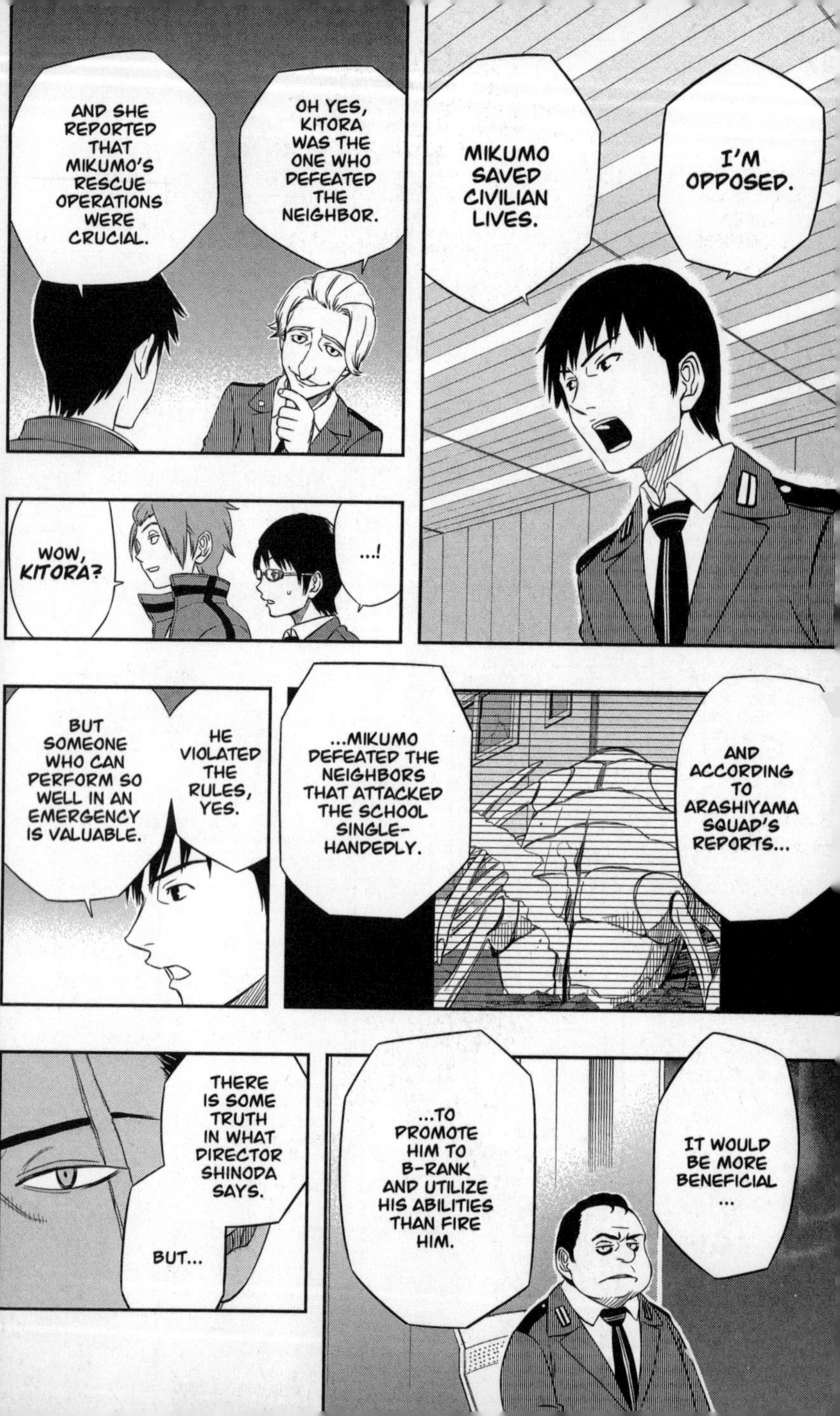
I'M OPPOSED.
MIKUMO SAVED CIVILIAN LIVES.
OH YES, KITORA WAS THE ONE WHO DEFEATED THE NEIGHBOR.
AND SHE REPORTED THAT MIKUMO'S RESCUE OPERATIONS WERE CRUCIAL.
...!
WOW, KITORA?
AND ACCORDING TO ARASHIYAMA SQUAD'S REPORTS...
...MIKUMO DEFEATED THE NEIGHBORS THAT ATTACKED THE SCHOOL SINGLE-HANDEDLY.
HE VIOLATED THE RULES, YES.
BUT SOMEONE WHO CAN PERFORM SO WELL IN AN EMERGENCY IS VALUABLE.
IT WOULD BE MORE BENEFICIAL...
...TO PROMOTE HIM TO B-RANK AND UTILIZE HIS ABILITIES THAN FIRE HIM.
THERE IS SOME TRUTH IN WHAT DIRECTOR SHINODA SAYS.
BUT...

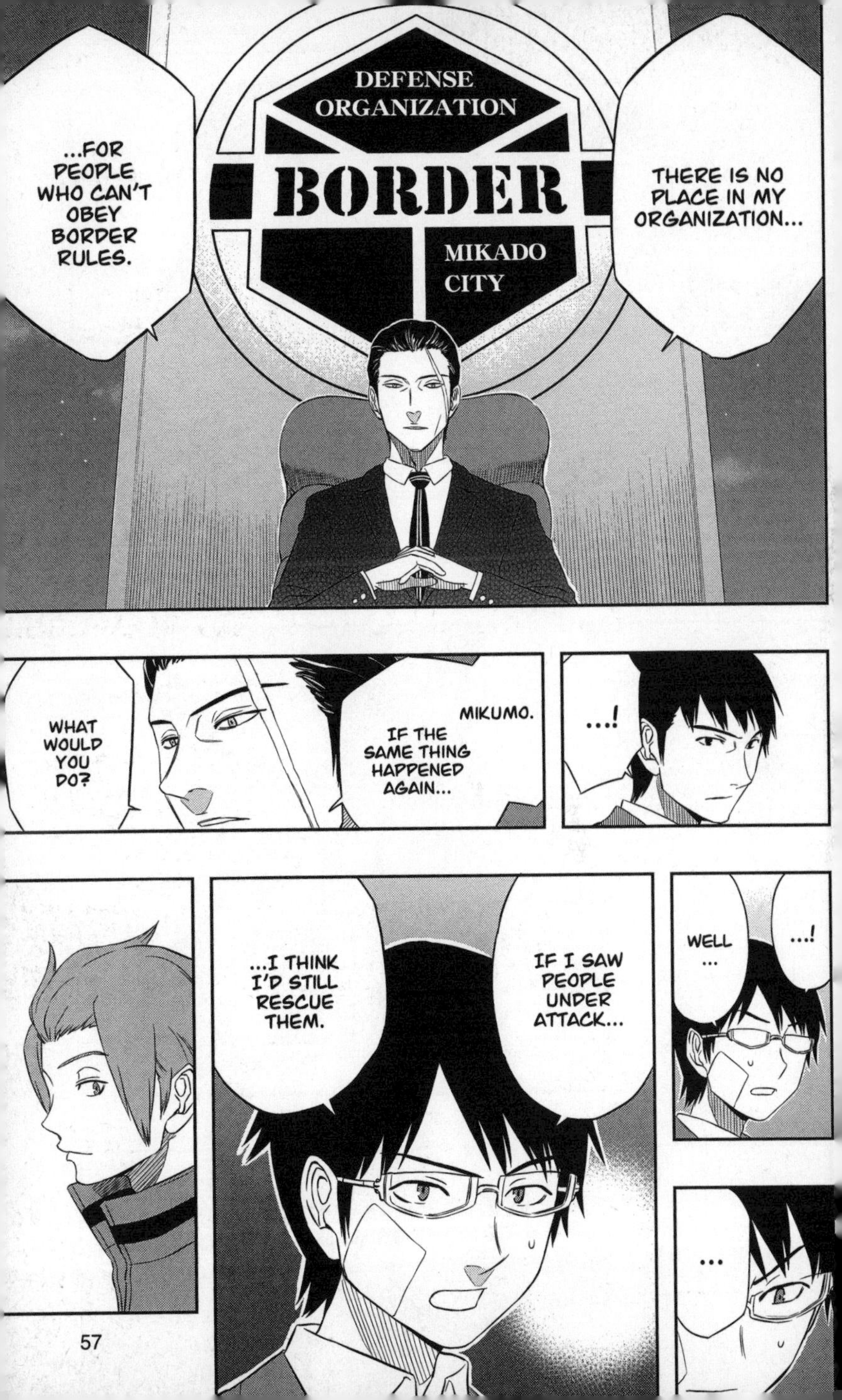
DEFENSE ORGANIZATION
BORDER
MIKADO CITY
THERE IS NO PLACE IN MY ORGANIZATION...
...FOR PEOPLE WHO CAN'T OBEY BORDER RULES.
...!
MIKUMO.
IF THE SAME THING HAPPENED AGAIN...
WHAT WOULD YOU DO?
...!
WELL ...
...
IF I SAW PEOPLE UNDER ATTACK...
...I THINK I'D STILL RESCUE THEM.

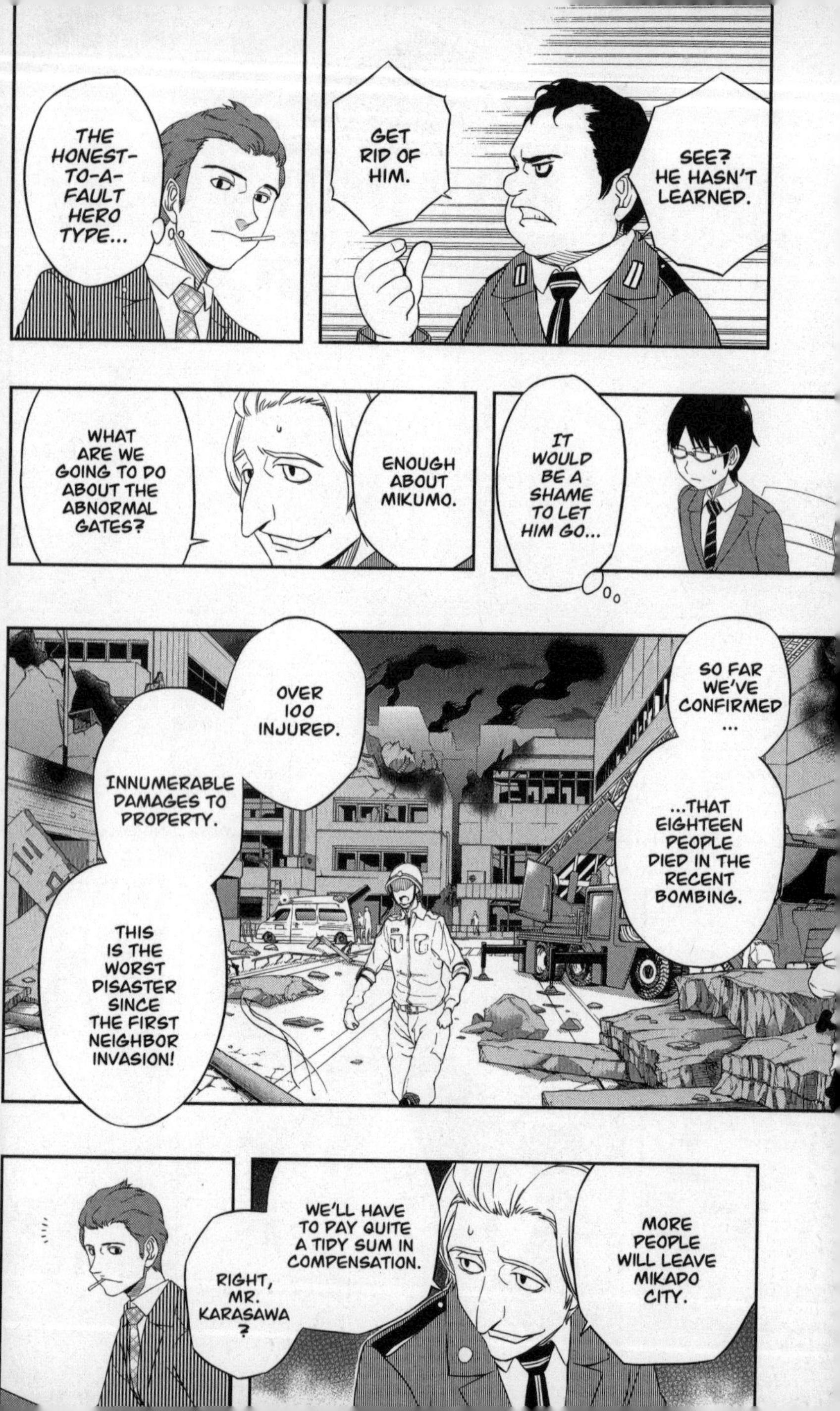
SEE? HE HASN'T LEARNED.
GET RID OF HIM.
THE HONEST-TO-A-FAULT HERO TYPE...
IT WOULD BE A SHAME TO LET HIM GO...
ENOUGH ABOUT MIKUMO.
WHAT ARE WE GOING TO DO ABOUT THE ABNORMAL GATES?
SO FAR WE'VE CONFIRMED...
...THAT EIGHTEEN PEOPLE DIED IN THE RECENT BOMBING.
OVER 100 INJURED.
INNUMERABLE DAMAGES TO PROPERTY.
THIS IS THE WORST DISASTER SINCE THE FIRST NEIGHBOR INVASION!
MORE PEOPLE WILL LEAVE MIKADO CITY.
WE'LL HAVE TO PAY QUITE A TIDY SUM IN COMPENSATION.
RIGHT, MR. KARASAWA?

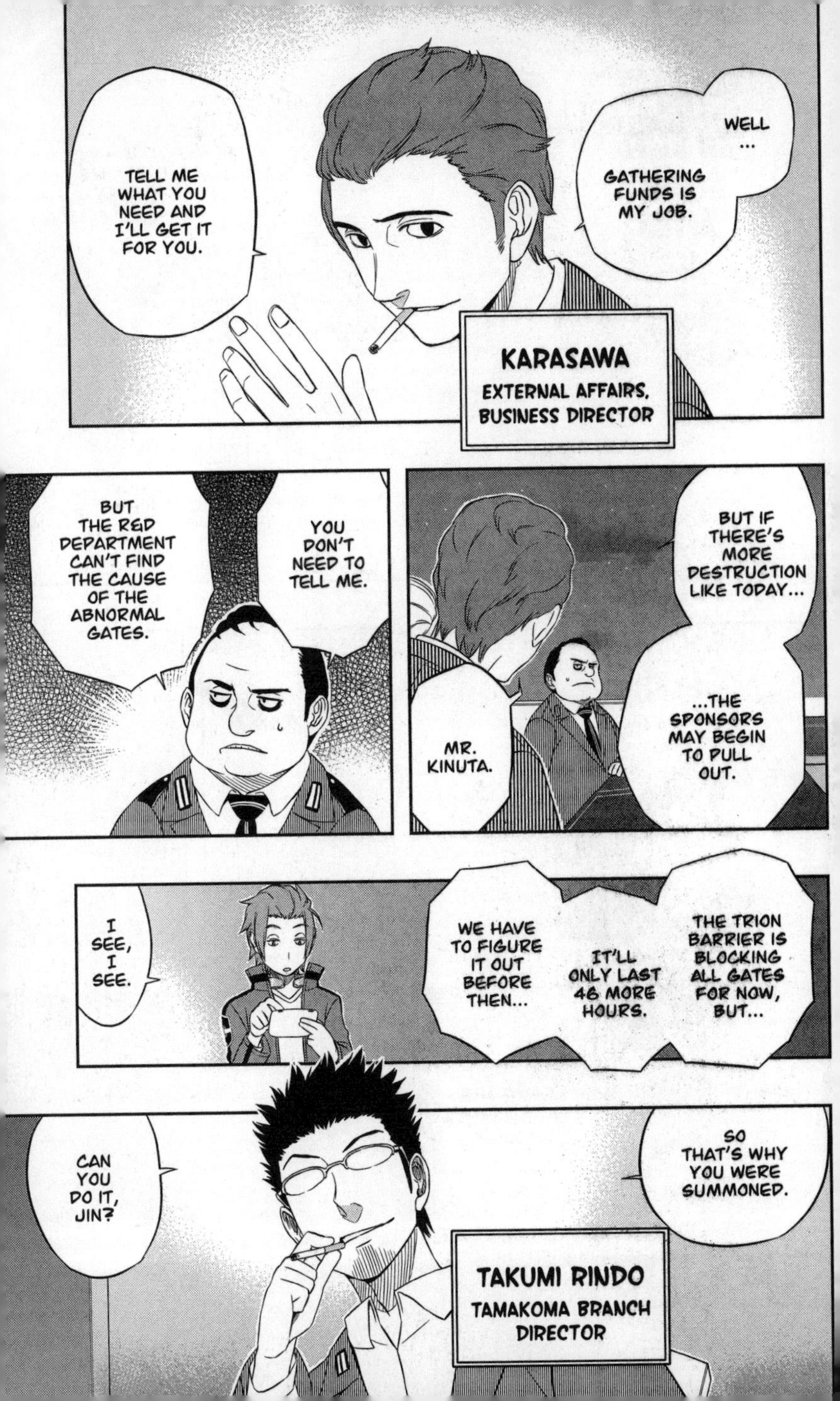
WELL...
GATHERING FUNDS IS MY JOB.
TELL ME WHAT YOU NEED AND I'LL GET IT FOR YOU.
KARASAWA
EXTERNAL AFFAIRS, BUSINESS DIRECTOR
BUT IF THERE'S MORE DESTRUCTION LIKE TODAY...
...THE SPONSORS MAY BEGIN TO PULL OUT.
MR. KINUTA.
YOU DON'T NEED TO TELL ME.
BUT THE R&D DEPARTMENT CAN'T FIND THE CAUSE OF THE ABNORMAL GATES.
THE TRION BARRIER IS BLOCKING ALL GATES FOR NOW, BUT...
IT'LL ONLY LAST 46 MORE HOURS.
WE HAVE TO FIGURE IT OUT BEFORE THEN...
I SEE, I SEE.
SO THAT'S WHY YOU WERE SUMMONED.
CAN YOU DO IT, JIN?
TAKUMI RINDO
TAMAKOMA BRANCH DIRECTOR

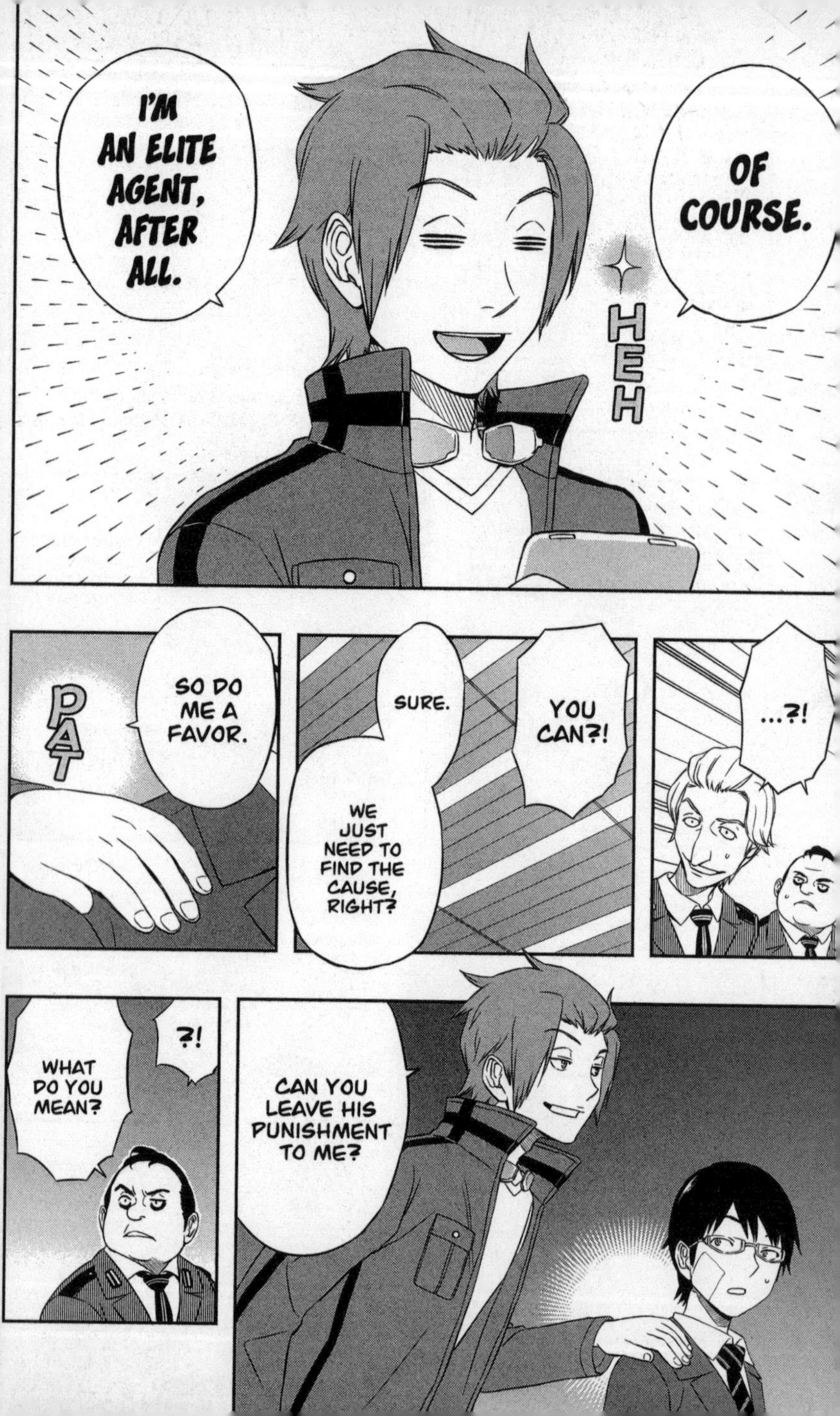
OF COURSE.
HEH
I'M AN ELITE AGENT, AFTER ALL.
...?!
YOU CAN?!
SURE.
WE JUST NEED TO FIND THE CAUSE, RIGHT?
SO DO ME A FAVOR.
PAT
CAN YOU LEAVE HIS PUNISHMENT TO ME?
?!
WHAT DO YOU MEAN?

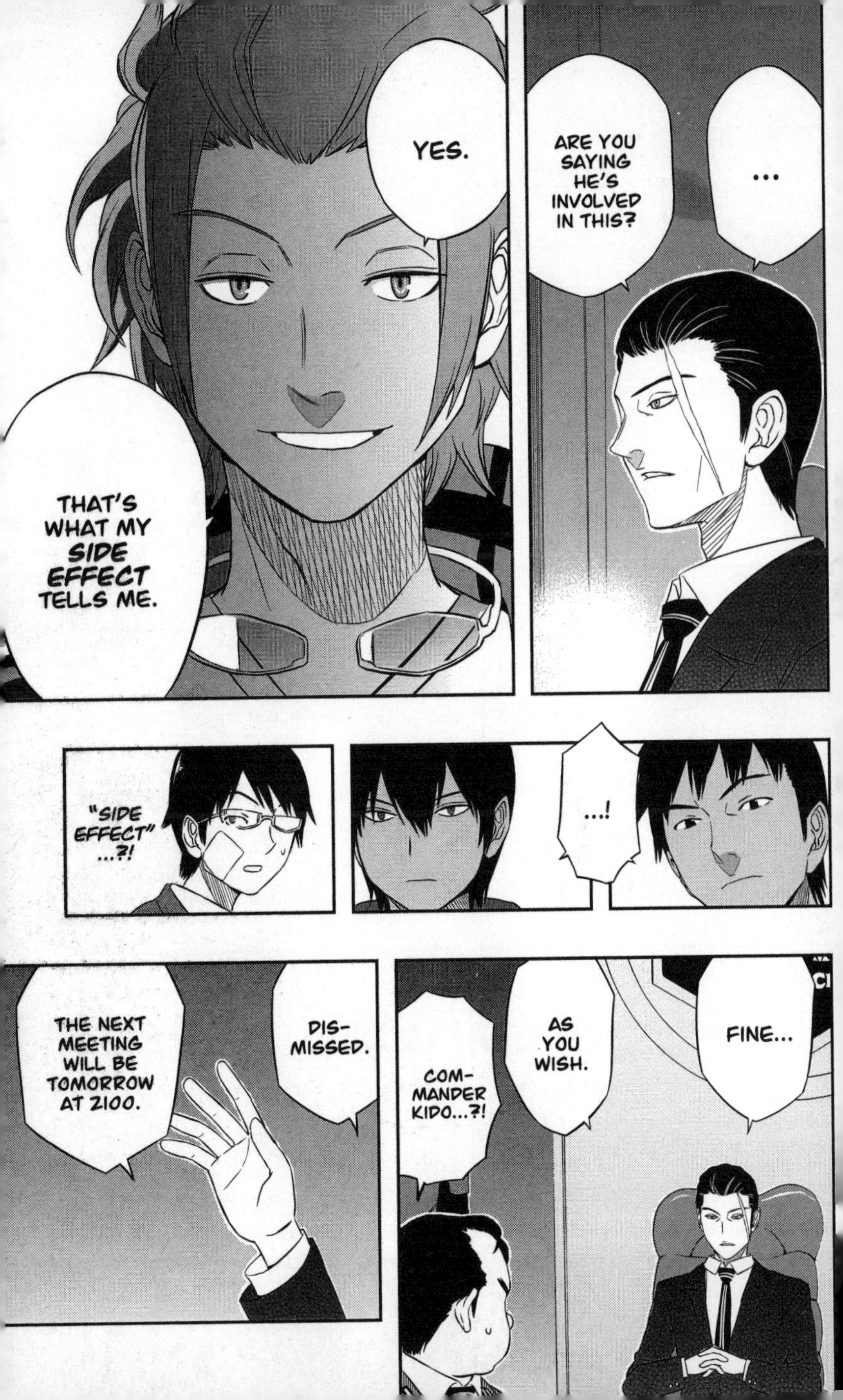
...
ARE YOU SAYING HE'S INVOLVED IN THIS?
YES.
THAT'S WHAT MY SIDE EFFECT TELLS ME.
...!
"SIDE EFFECT" ...?!
FINE...
AS YOU WISH.
COM-MANDER KIDO...?!
DIS-MISSED.
THE NEXT MEETING WILL BE TOMORROW AT 2100.

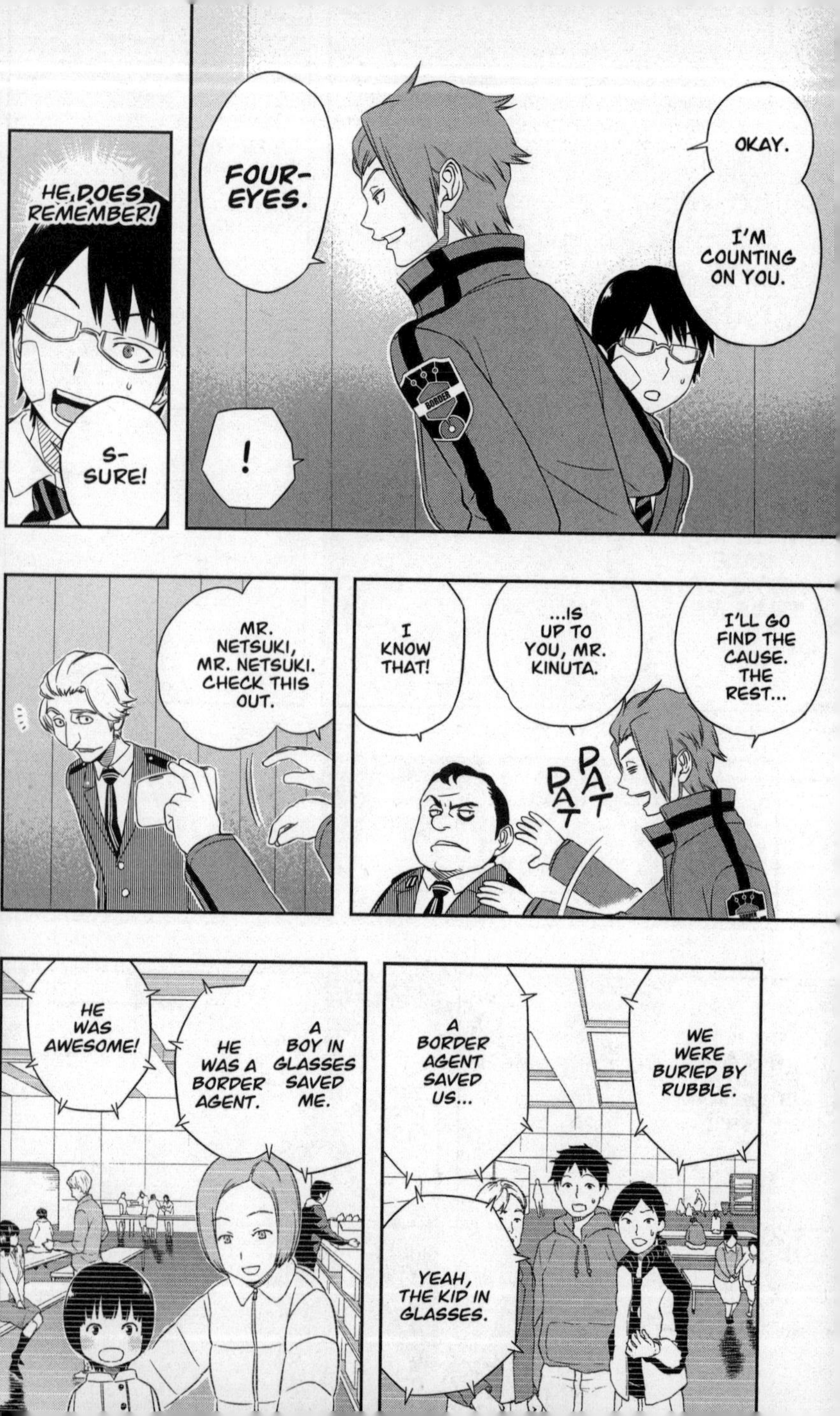
OKAY.
I'M COUNTING ON YOU.
FOUR-EYES.
!
HE DOES REMEMBER!
S-SURE!
I'LL GO FIND THE CAUSE. THE REST...
...IS UP TO YOU, MR. KINUTA.
I KNOW THAT!
PAT PAT
MR. NETSUKI, MR. NETSUKI. CHECK THIS OUT.
WE WERE BURIED BY RUBBLE.
A BORDER AGENT SAVED US...
YEAH, THE KID IN GLASSES.
A BOY IN GLASSES SAVED ME.
HE WAS A BORDER AGENT.
HE WAS AWESOME!

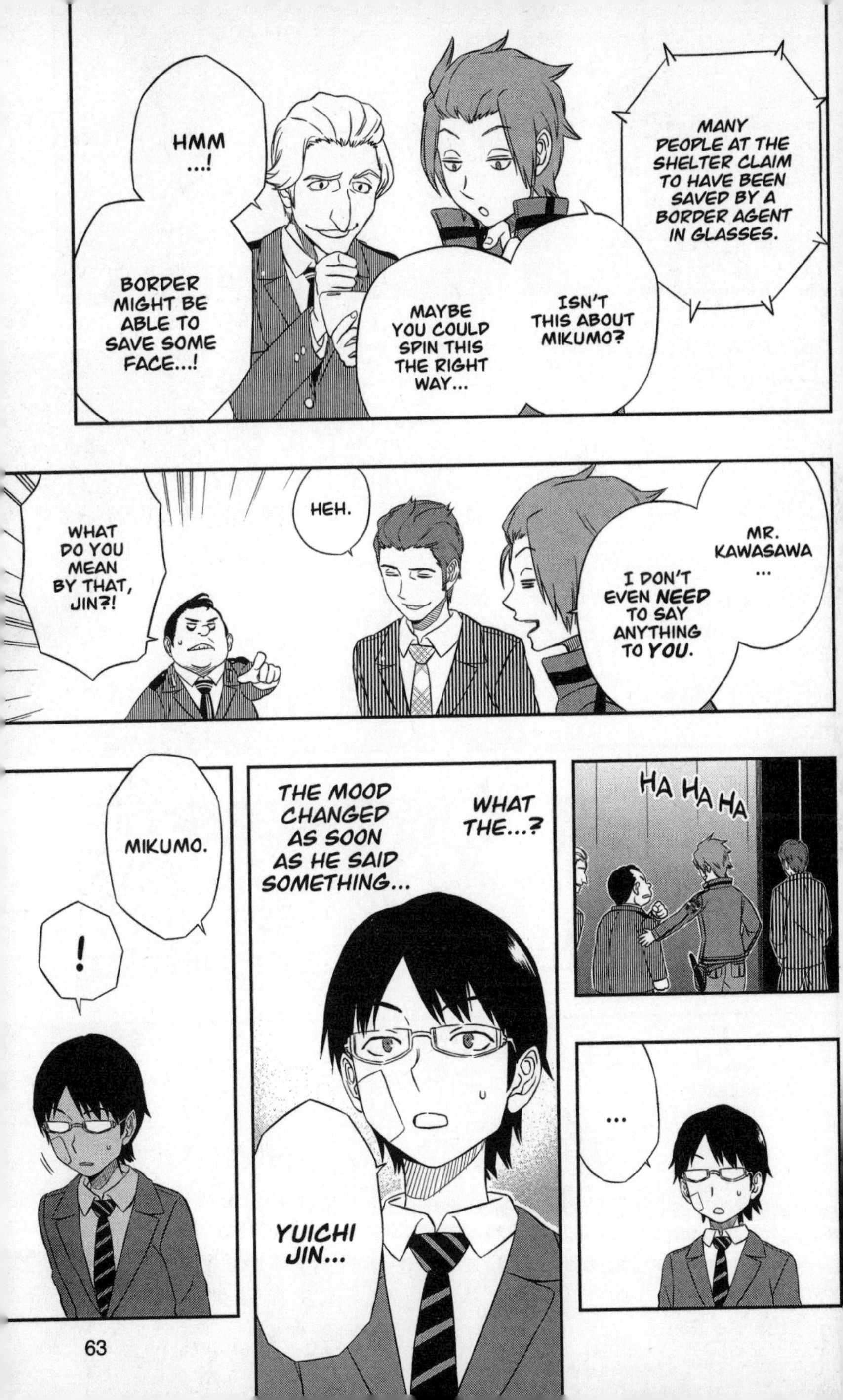
MANY PEOPLE AT THE SHELTER CLAIM TO HAVE BEEN SAVED BY A BORDER AGENT IN GLASSES.
ISN'T THIS ABOUT MIKUMO?
MAYBE YOU COULD SPIN THIS THE RIGHT WAY...
HMM ...!
BORDER MIGHT BE ABLE TO SAVE SOME FACE...!
MR. KAWASAWA ...
I DON'T EVEN NEED TO SAY ANYTHING TO YOU.
HEH.
WHAT DO YOU MEAN BY THAT, JIN?!
HA HA HA
...
WHAT THE...?
THE MOOD CHANGED AS SOON AS HE SAID SOMETHING...
YUICHI JIN...
MIKUMO.
!

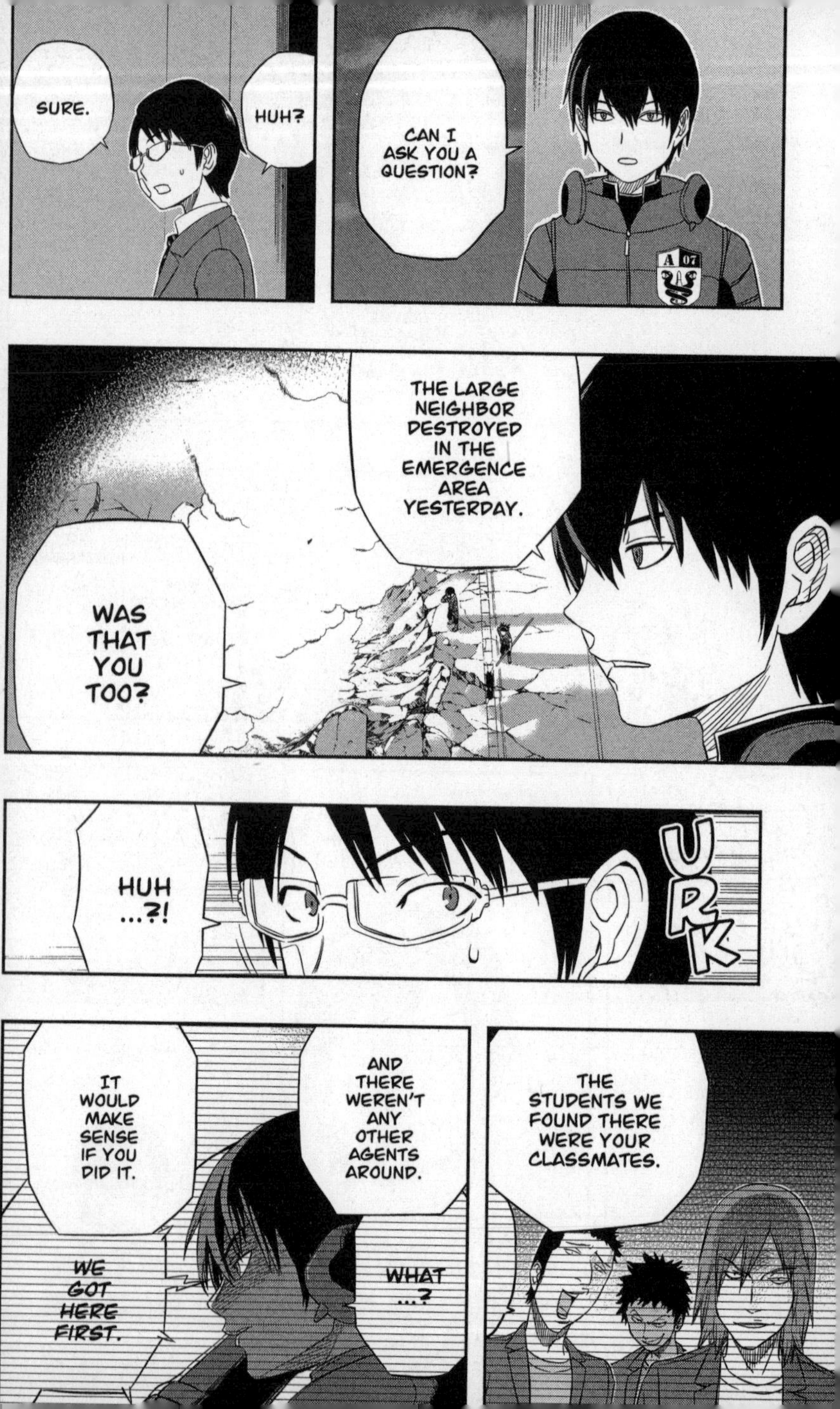
CAN I ASK YOU A QUESTION?
HUH?
SURE.
THE LARGE NEIGHBOR DESTROYED IN THE EMERGENCE AREA YESTERDAY.
WAS THAT YOU TOO?
URK
HUH ...?!
THE STUDENTS WE FOUND THERE WERE YOUR CLASSMATES.
AND THERE WEREN'T ANY OTHER AGENTS AROUND.
IT WOULD MAKE SENSE IF YOU DID IT.
WHAT ...?
WE GOT HERE FIRST.

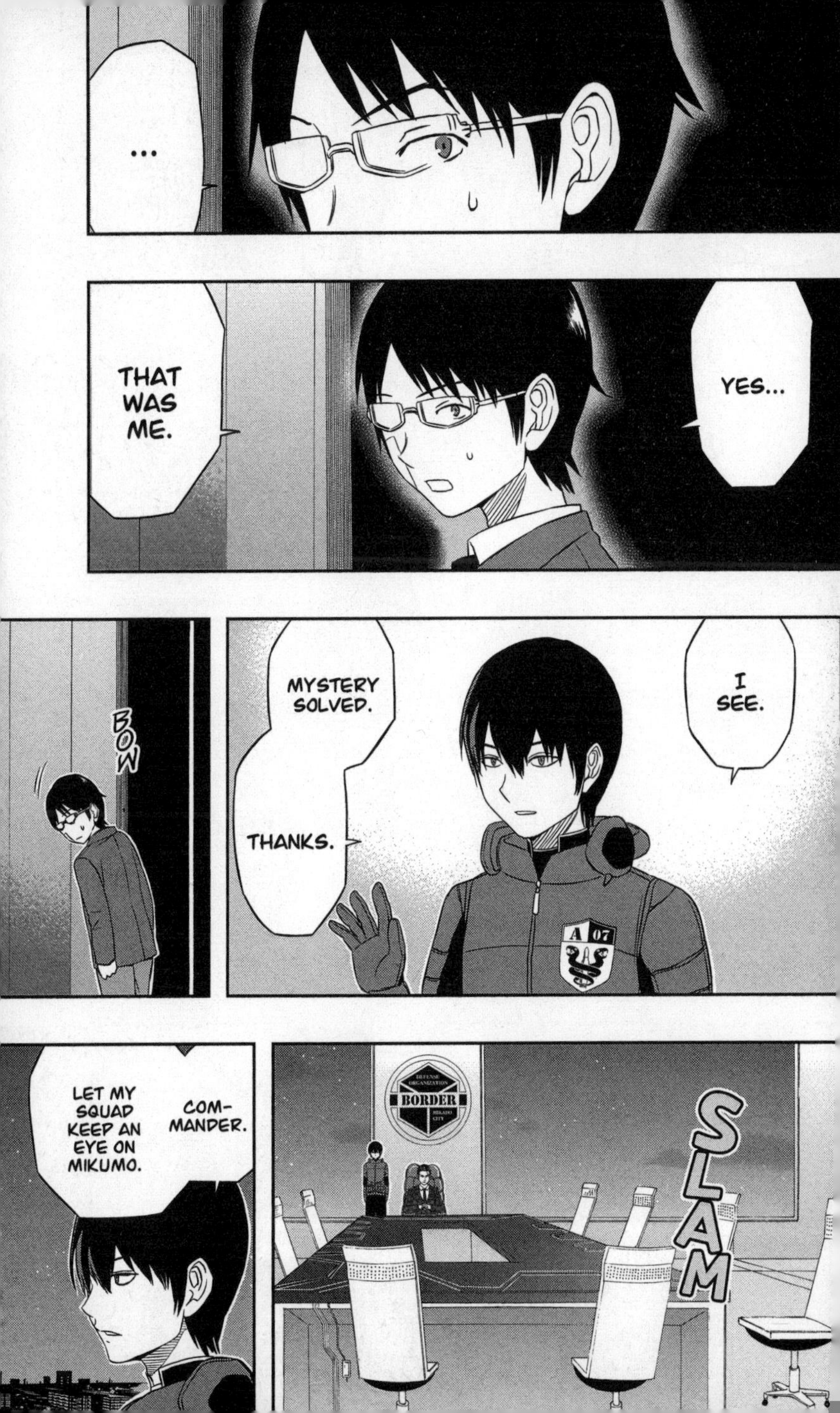
...
YES...
THAT WAS ME.
I SEE.
MYSTERY SOLVED.
THANKS.
BOW
SLAM
COM-MANDER.
LET MY SQUAD KEEP AN EYE ON MIKUMO.

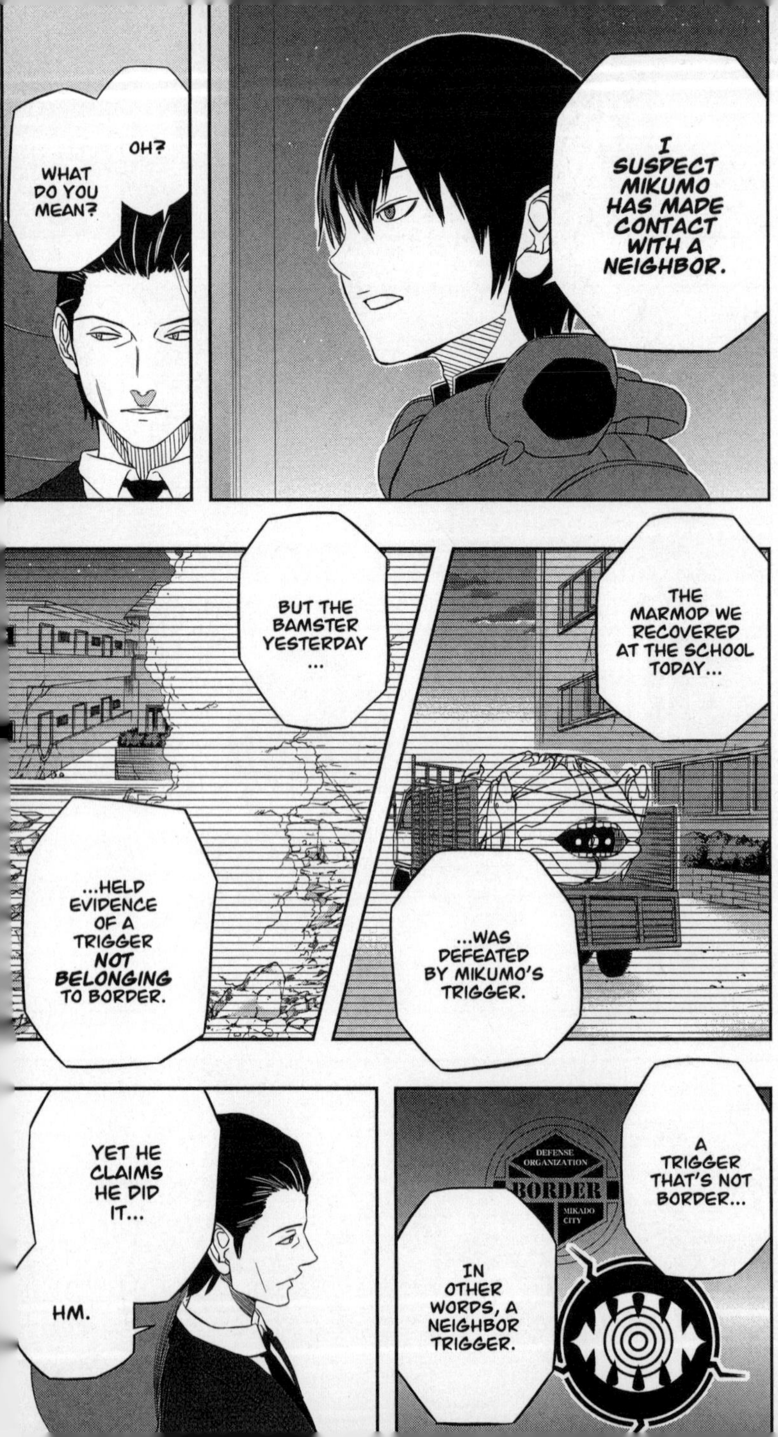
I SUSPECT MIKUMO HAS MADE CONTACT WITH A NEIGHBOR.
OH?
WHAT DO YOU MEAN?
THE MARMOD WE RECOVERED AT THE SCHOOL TODAY...
...WAS DEFEATED BY MIKUMO'S TRIGGER.
BUT THE BAMSTER YESTERDAY ...
...HELD EVIDENCE OF A TRIGGER NOT BELONGING TO BORDER.
A TRIGGER THAT'S NOT BORDER...
IN OTHER WORDS, A NEIGHBOR TRIGGER.
DEFENSE ORGANIZATION
BORDER
MIKADO CITY
YET HE CLAIMS HE DID IT...
HM.

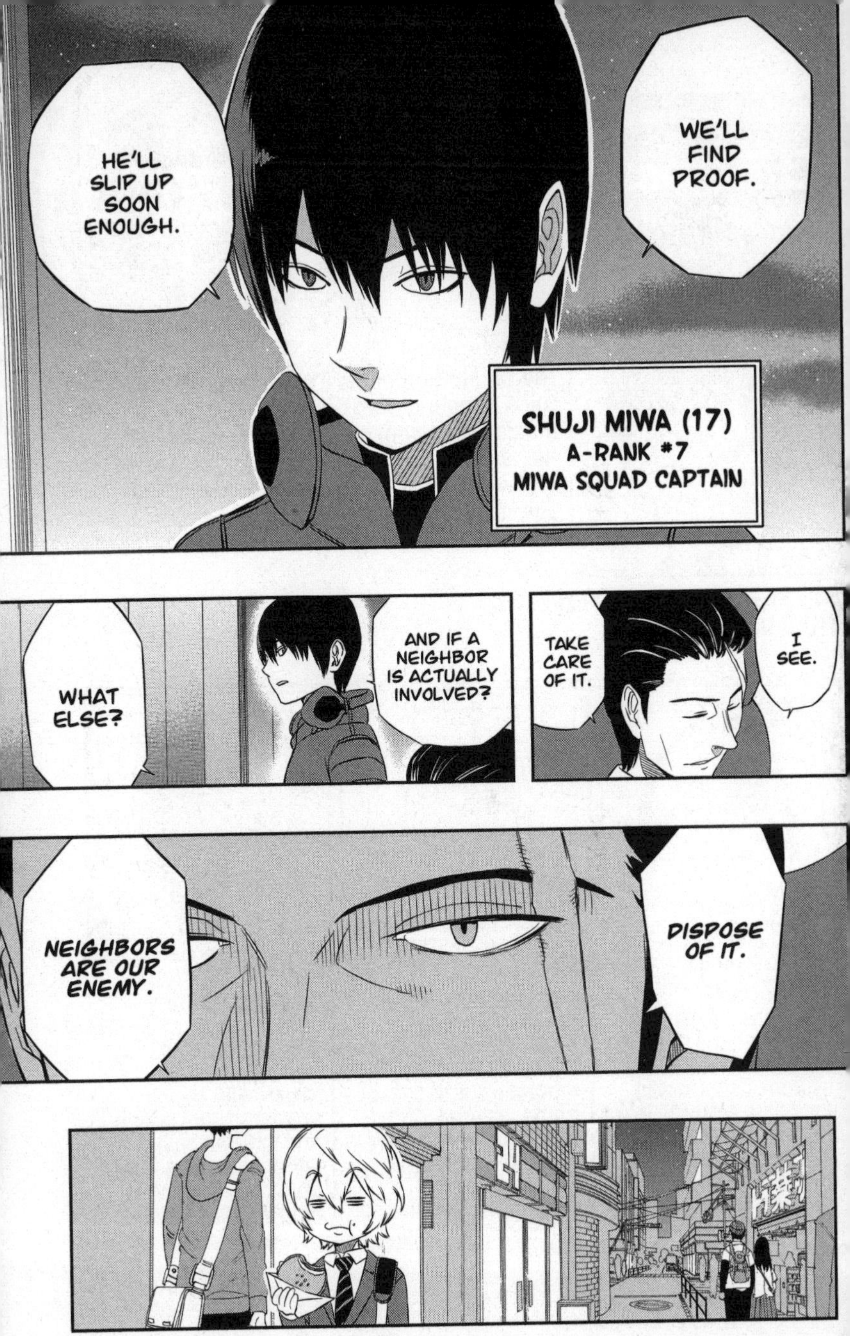
WE'LL FIND PROOF.
HE'LL SLIP UP SOON ENOUGH.
SHUJI MIWA (17)
A-RANK #7
MIWA SQUAD CAPTAIN
I SEE.
TAKE CARE OF IT.
AND IF A NEIGHBOR IS ACTUALLY INVOLVED?
WHAT ELSE?
DISPOSE OF IT.
NEIGHBORS ARE OUR ENEMY.

# HQ Senior Officers
come to the land of middle-aged dudes

DEFENSE
ORGANIZATION

**BORDER**

MIKADO
CITY

The CEO of Border. He's strict about Border rules. Creating Gate Guidance Beacons and building the giant base were his initiatives. He hates Neighbors, and so he pours his heart and soul into building Border into a larger agency. Kido himself scouted the three officers below. Single.

**Masamune Kido (42)**
**HQ Commander**

**Motokichi Kinuta (48)**
**HQ R&D Director**

An extremely competent man who developed the Gate Guidance Beacon system, constructed the basic systems in HQ, and succeeded in mass-producing Triggers. He acts arrogant, but he's earned it. Divorced.

**Eizo Netsuki (39)**
**PR Director**

A competent spokesman who deals with the press, improves Border's reputation, and manages and covers up problems. It's thanks to him that there is little anti-Border sentiment in Mikado City. Single.

**Katsumi Karasawa (33)**
**Business Director**

A go-getter who secures most of Border's funding. He negotiates with Mikado City, the prefecture, the country and internationally. Border would be in big trouble without him. Single.

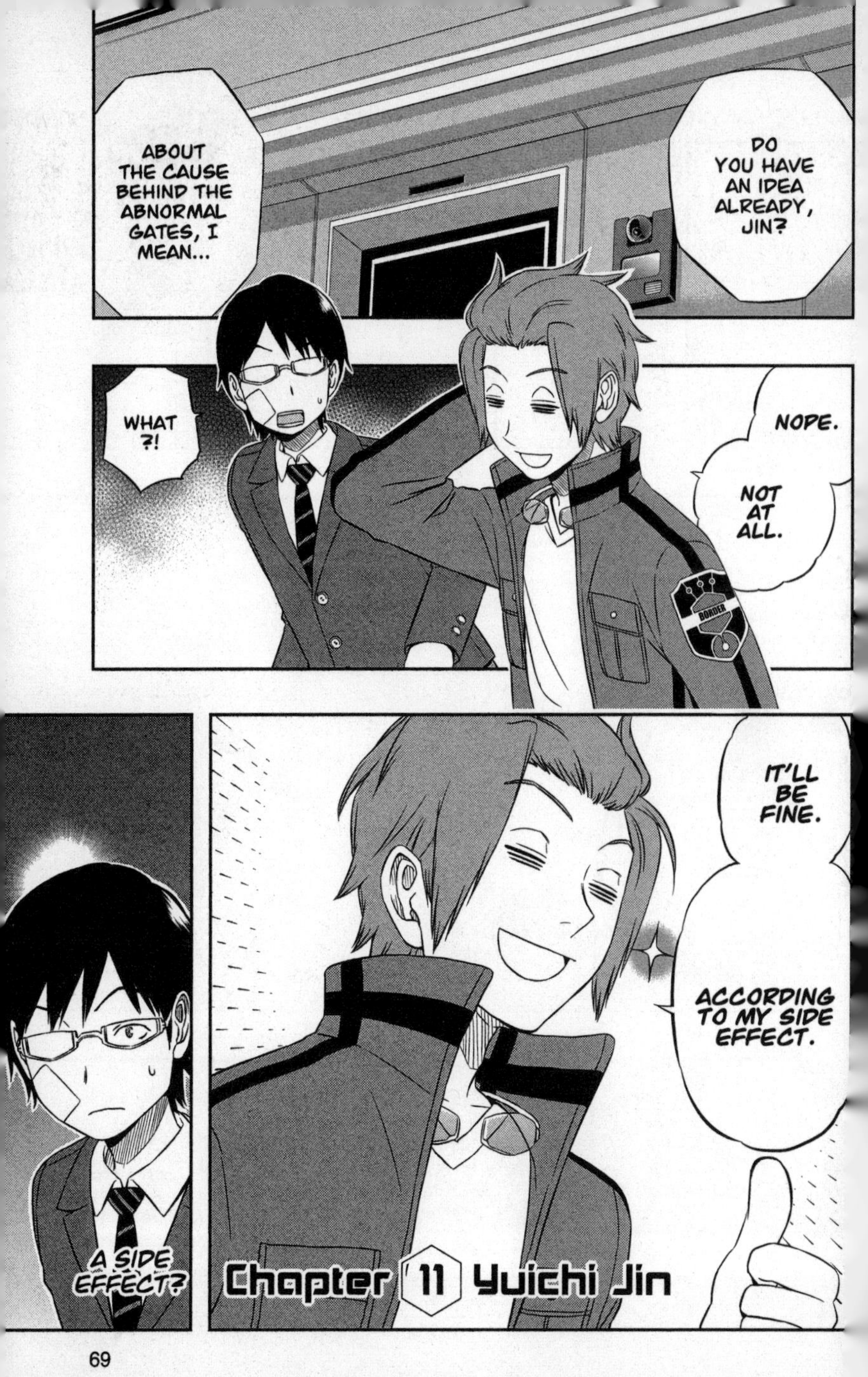
DO YOU HAVE AN IDEA ALREADY, JIN?
ABOUT THE CAUSE BEHIND THE ABNORMAL GATES, I MEAN...
NOPE.
NOT AT ALL.
WHAT?!
BORDER
IT'LL BE FINE.
ACCORDING TO MY SIDE EFFECT.
Chapter 11 Yuichi Jin
A SIDE EFFECT?

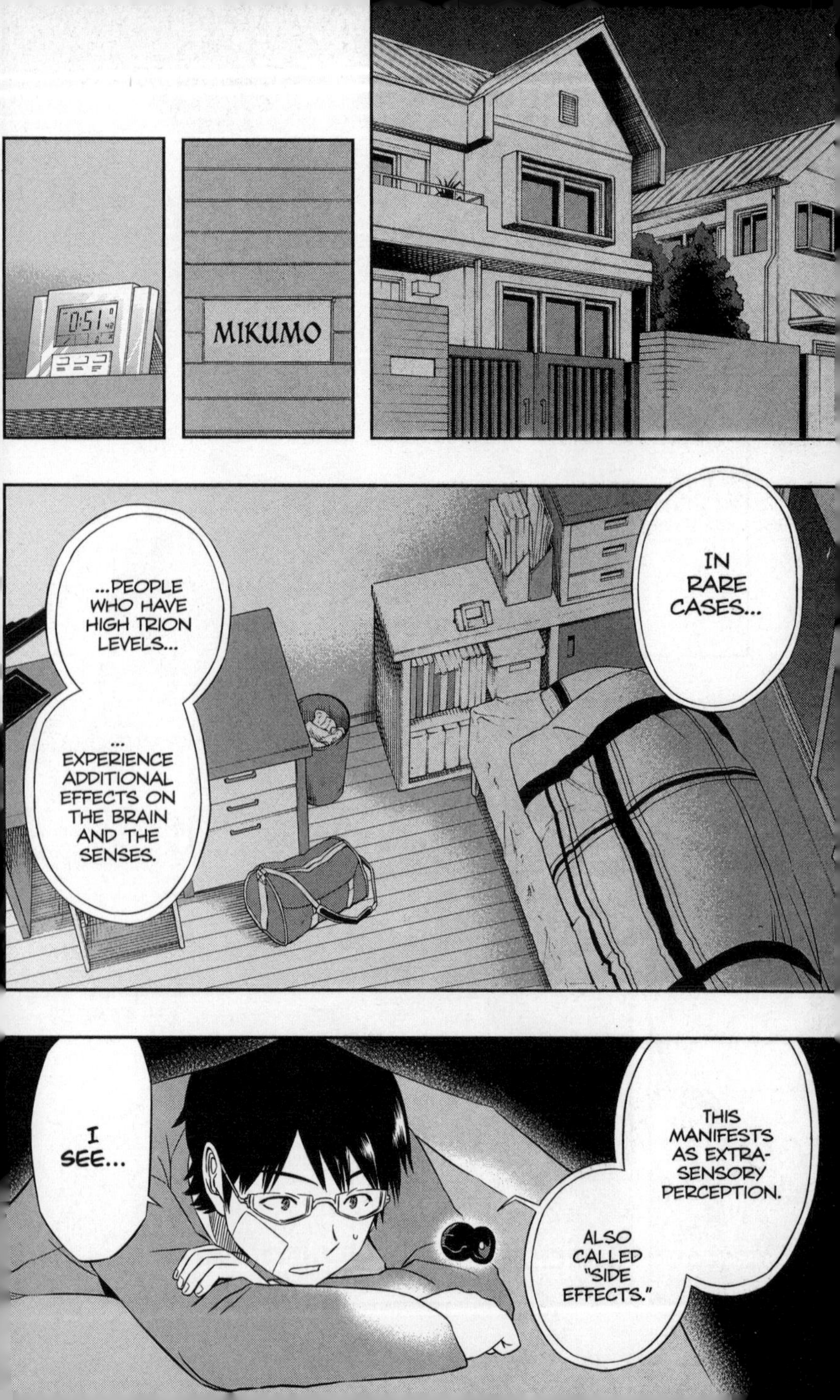
MIKUMO
0:51
IN RARE CASES...
...PEOPLE WHO HAVE HIGH TRION LEVELS...
... EXPERIENCE ADDITIONAL EFFECTS ON THE BRAIN AND THE SENSES.
THIS MANIFESTS AS EXTRA-SENSORY PERCEPTION.
ALSO CALLED "SIDE EFFECTS."
I SEE...

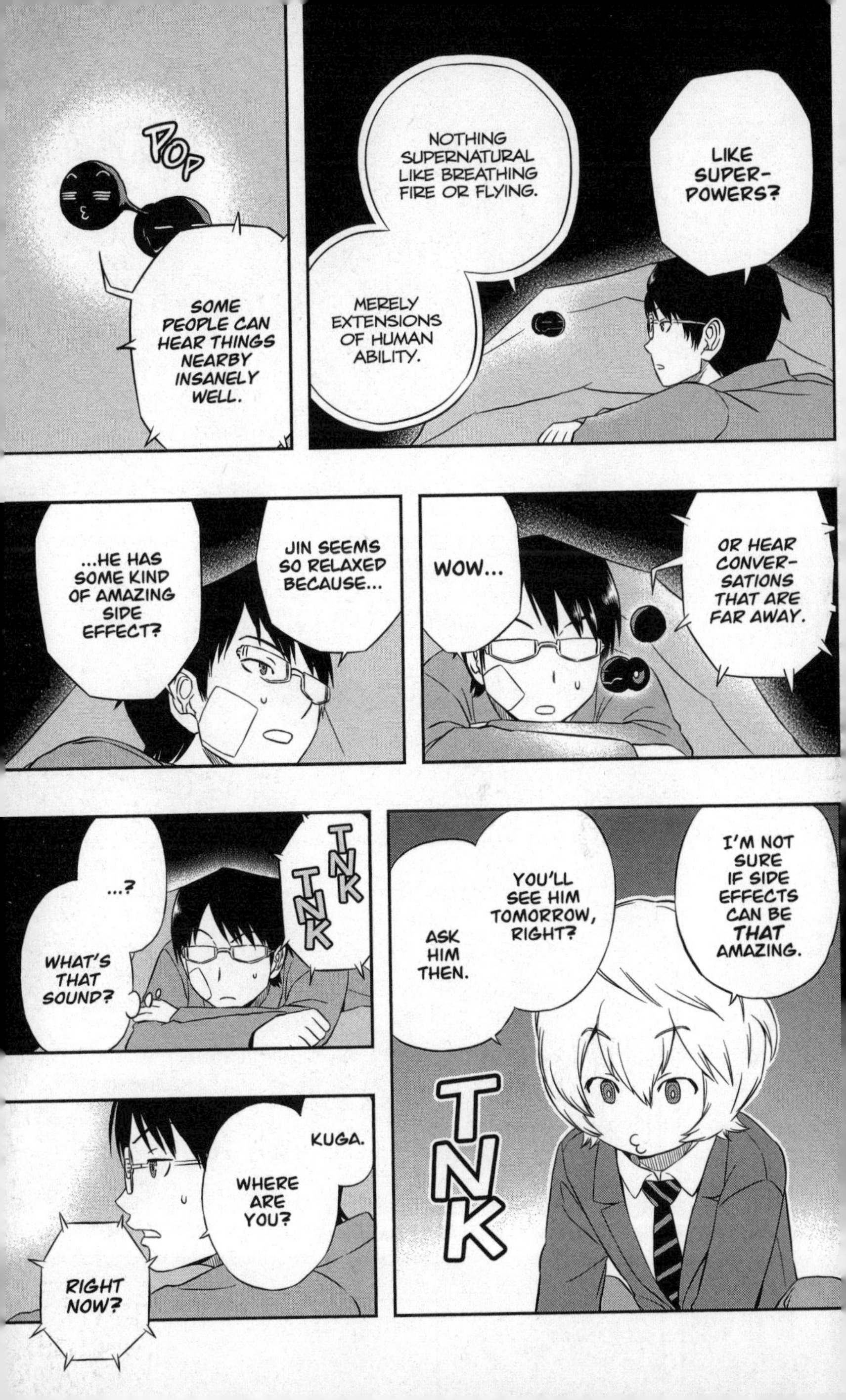
LIKE SUPER-POWERS?
NOTHING SUPERNATURAL LIKE BREATHING FIRE OR FLYING.
MERELY EXTENSIONS OF HUMAN ABILITY.
POP
SOME PEOPLE CAN HEAR THINGS NEARBY INSANELY WELL.
OR HEAR CONVERSATIONS THAT ARE FAR AWAY.
WOW...
JIN SEEMS SO RELAXED BECAUSE...
...HE HAS SOME KIND OF AMAZING SIDE EFFECT?
I'M NOT SURE IF SIDE EFFECTS CAN BE THAT AMAZING.
YOU'LL SEE HIM TOMORROW, RIGHT?
ASK HIM THEN.
TNK
TNK
TNK
...?
WHAT'S THAT SOUND?
KUGA.
WHERE ARE YOU?
RIGHT NOW?

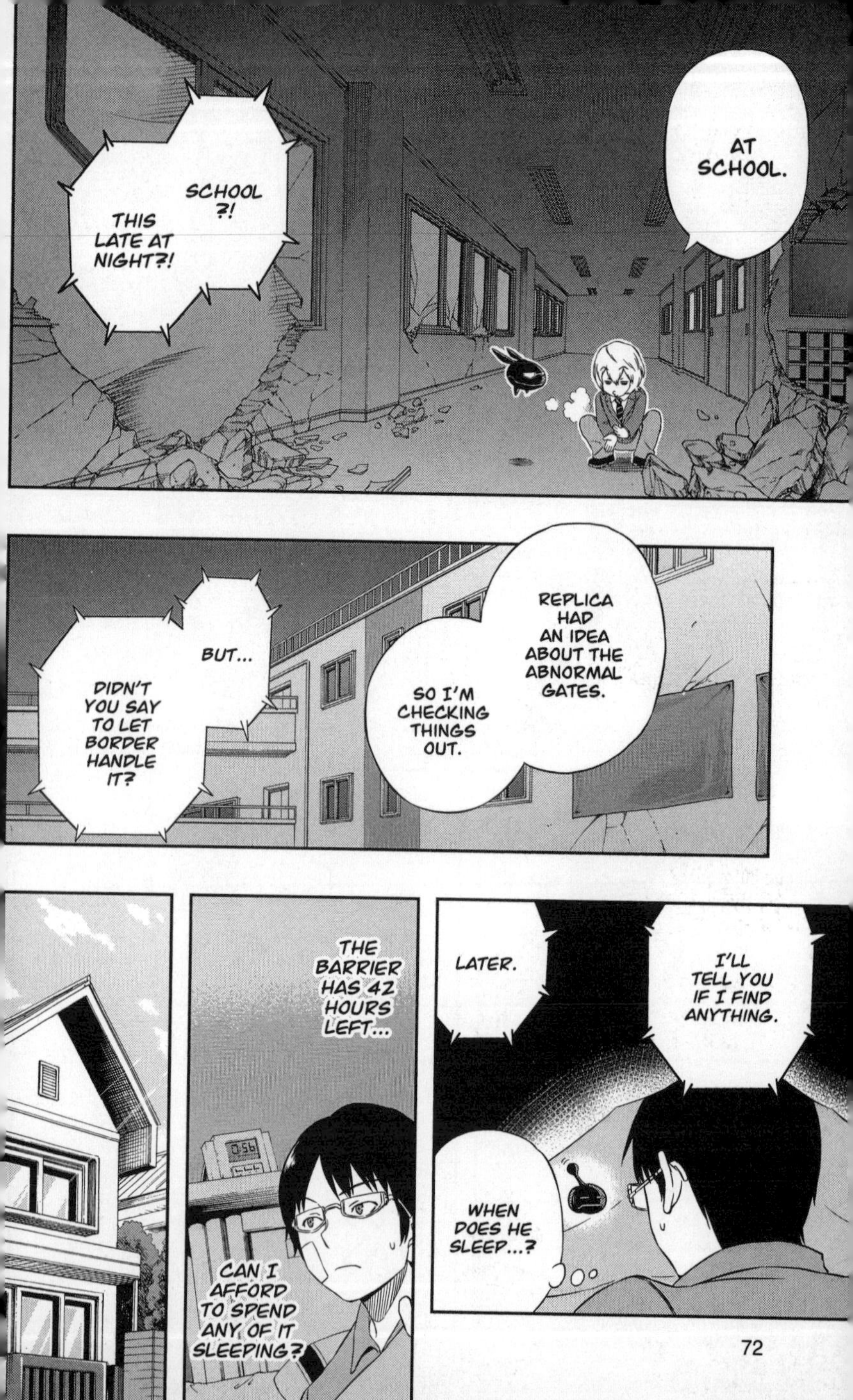
AT SCHOOL.
SCHOOL?! THIS LATE AT NIGHT?!
REPLICA HAD AN IDEA ABOUT THE ABNORMAL GATES.
SO I'M CHECKING THINGS OUT.
BUT...
DIDN'T YOU SAY TO LET BORDER HANDLE IT?
I'LL TELL YOU IF I FIND ANYTHING.
LATER.
WHEN DOES HE SLEEP...?
THE BARRIER HAS 42 HOURS LEFT...
CAN I AFFORD TO SPEND ANY OF IT SLEEPING?

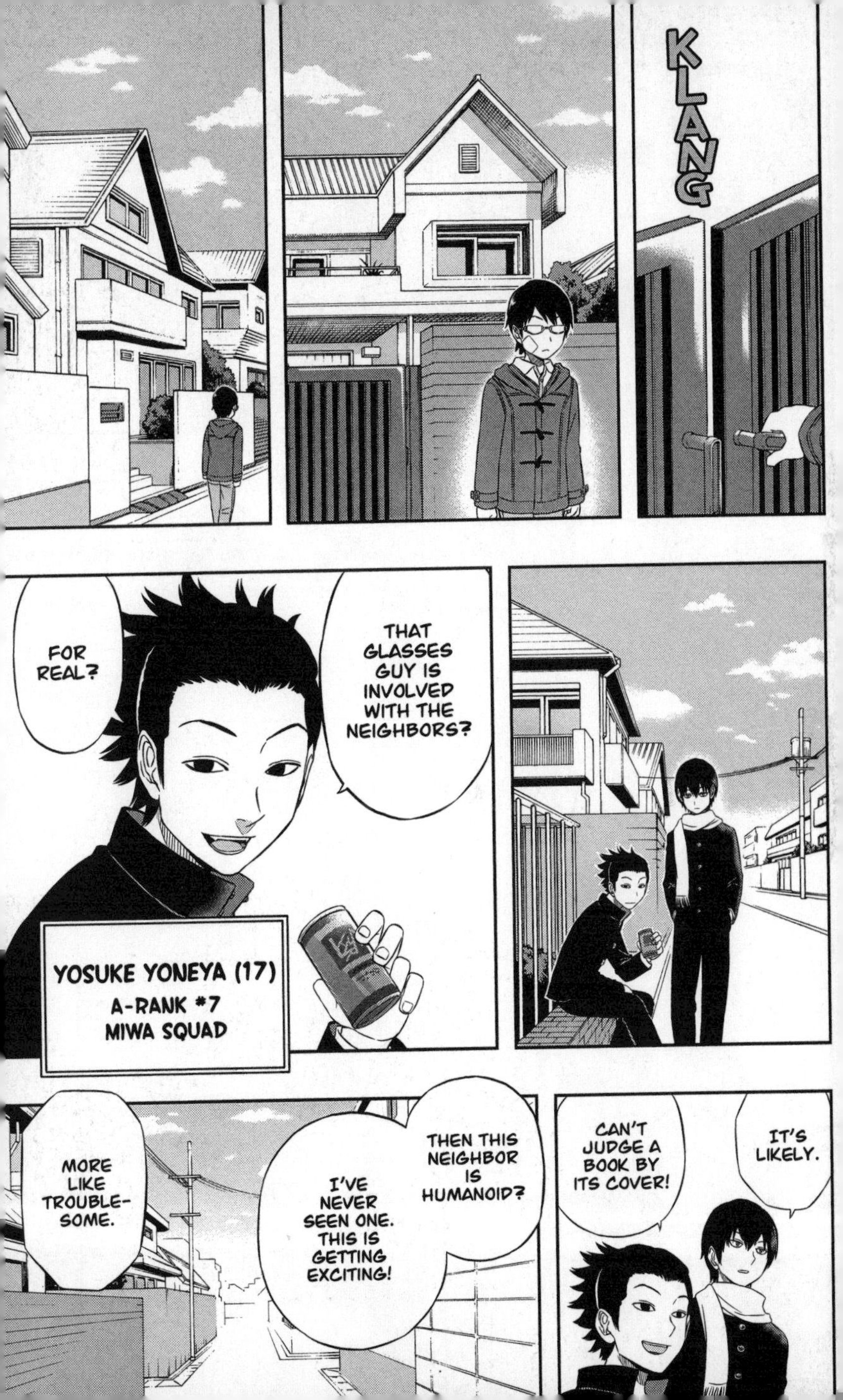
KLANG
THAT GLASSES GUY IS INVOLVED WITH THE NEIGHBORS?
FOR REAL?
YOSUKE YONEYA (17)
A-RANK #7
MIWA SQUAD
IT'S LIKELY.
CAN'T JUDGE A BOOK BY ITS COVER!
THEN THIS NEIGHBOR IS HUMANOID?
I'VE NEVER SEEN ONE. THIS IS GETTING EXCITING!
MORE LIKE TROUBLE-SOME.

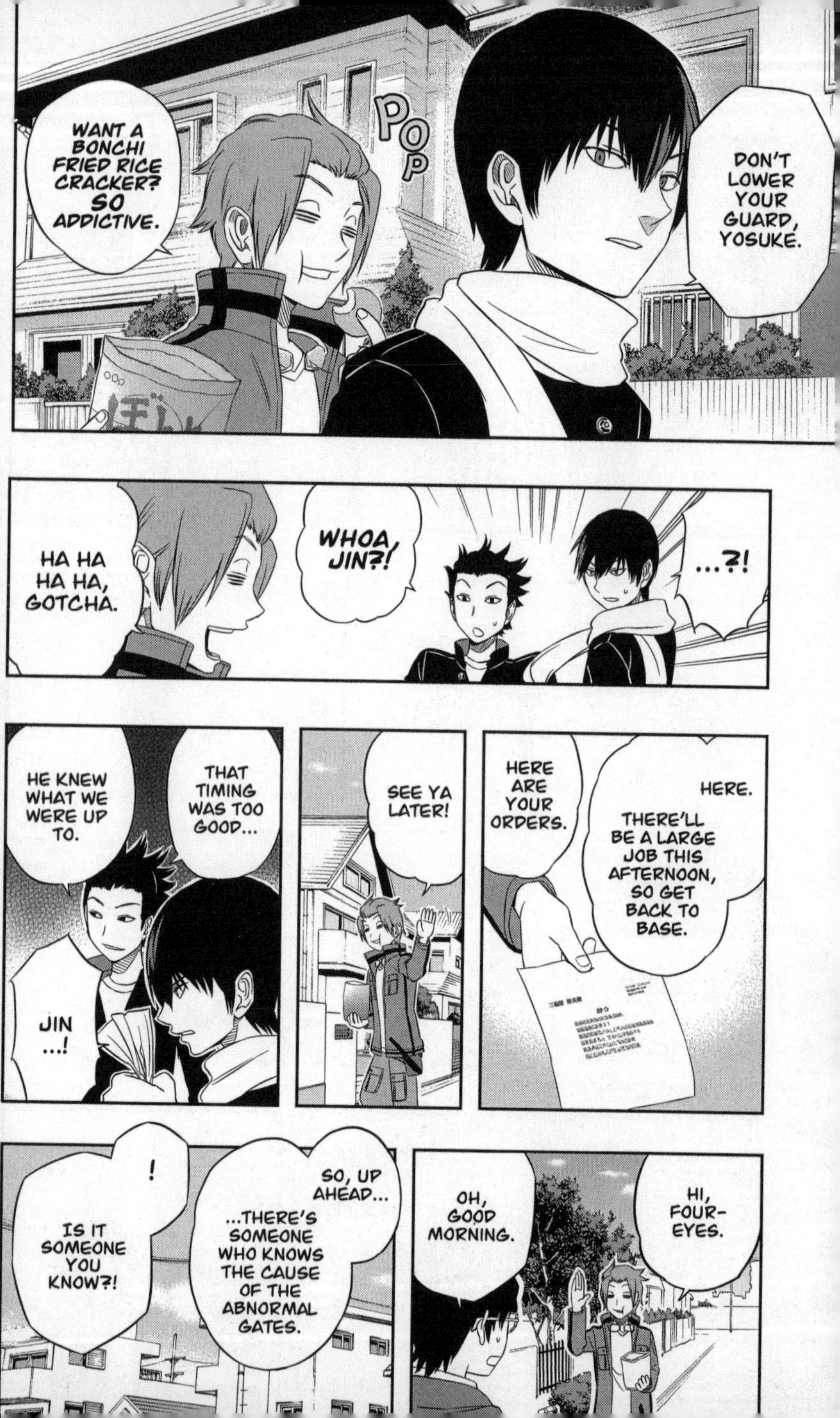
DON'T LOWER YOUR GUARD, YOSUKE.
POP
WANT A BONCHI FRIED RICE CRACKER? SO ADDICTIVE.
...?!
WHOA, JIN?!
HA HA HA HA, GOTCHA.
HERE.
THERE'LL BE A LARGE JOB THIS AFTERNOON, SO GET BACK TO BASE.
HERE ARE YOUR ORDERS.
SEE YA LATER!
THAT TIMING WAS TOO GOOD...
HE KNEW WHAT WE WERE UP TO.
JIN ...!
HI, FOUR-EYES.
OH, GOOD MORNING.
SO, UP AHEAD...
...THERE'S SOMEONE WHO KNOWS THE CAUSE OF THE ABNORMAL GATES.
!
IS IT SOMEONE YOU KNOW?!

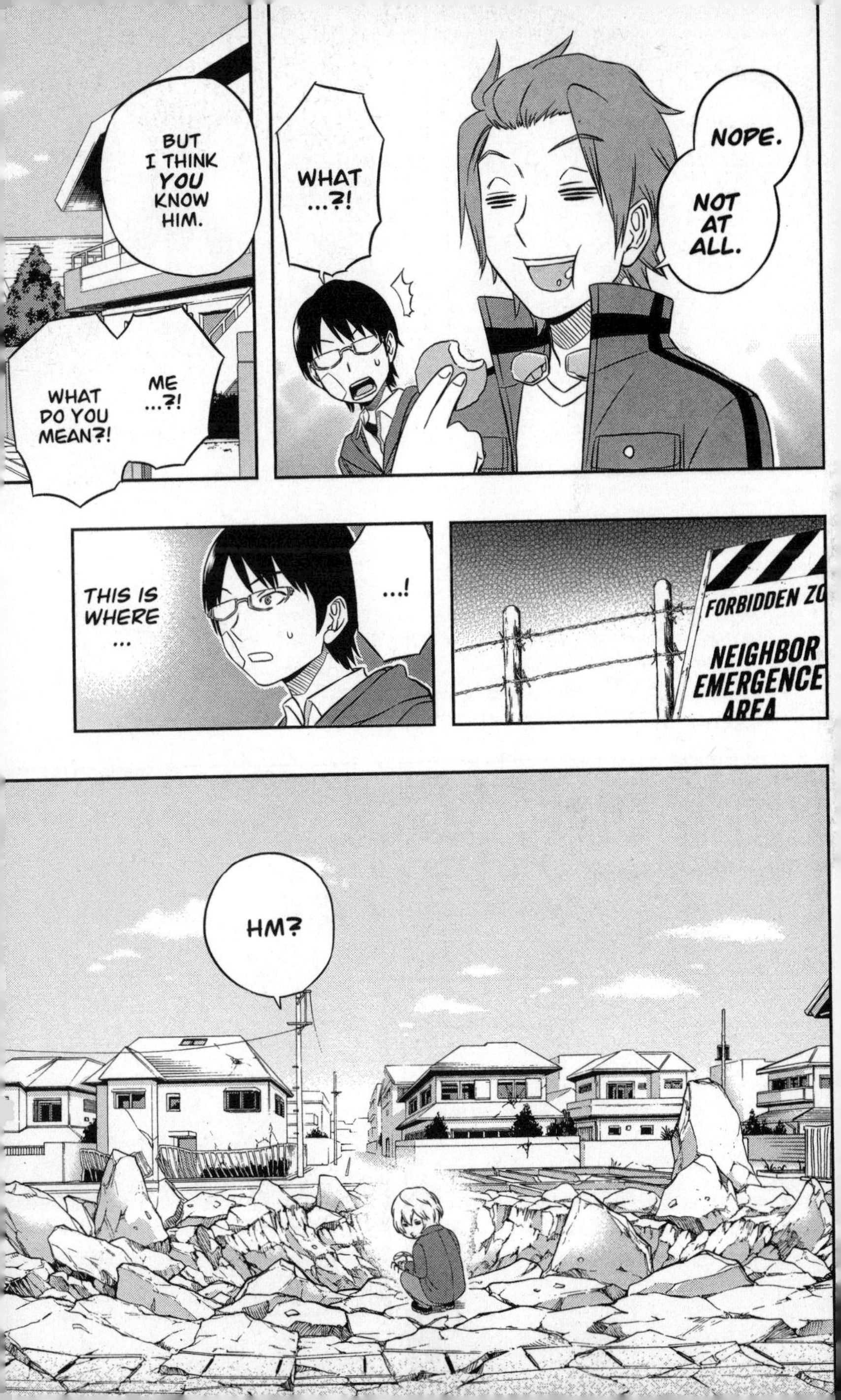
NOPE.
NOT AT ALL.
WHAT ...?!
BUT I THINK YOU KNOW HIM.
ME ...?!
WHAT DO YOU MEAN?!
FORBIDDEN ZO
NEIGHBOR EMERGENCE AREA
...!
THIS IS WHERE ...
HM?

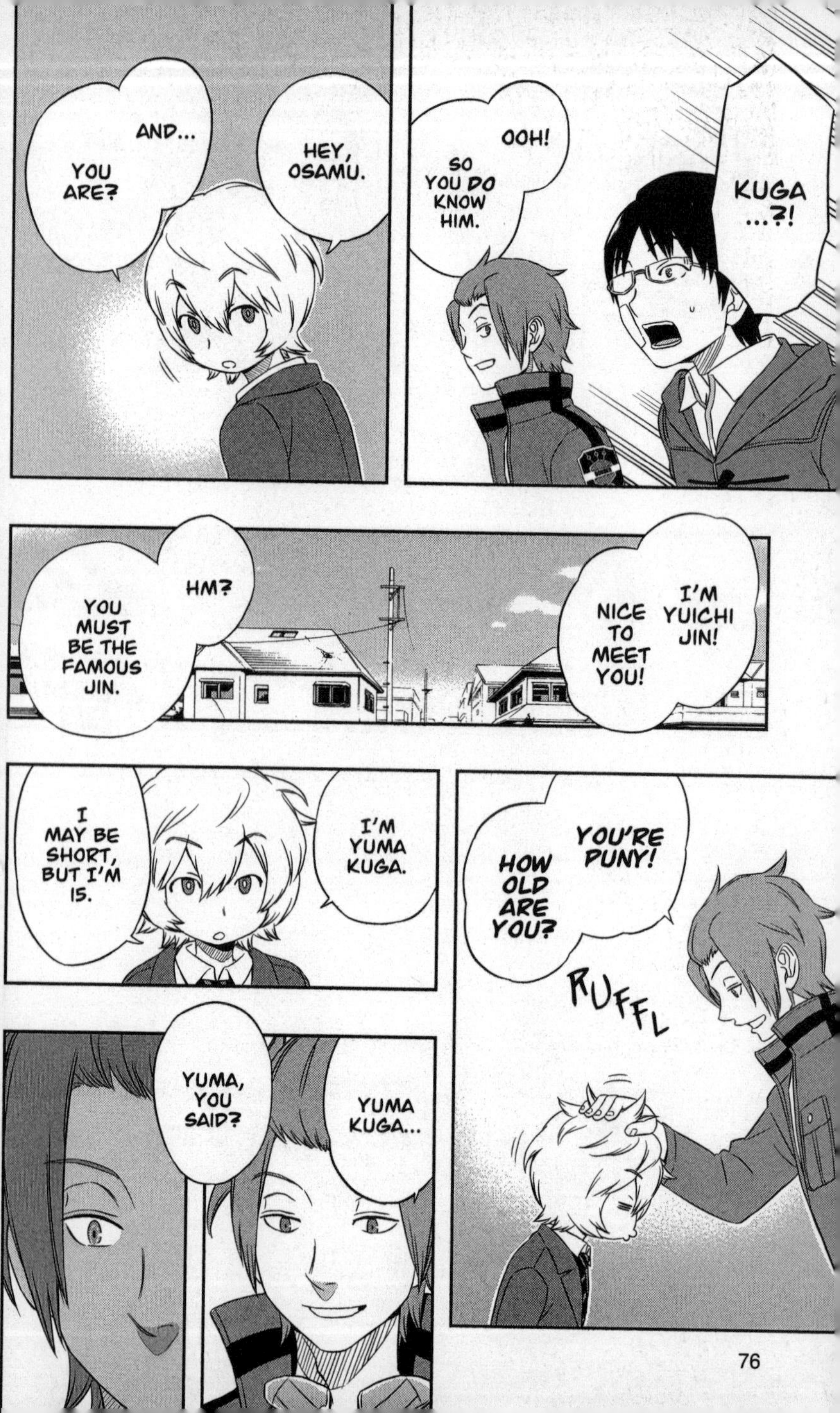
KUGA ...?!
OOH!
SO YOU DO KNOW HIM.
HEY, OSAMU.
AND...
YOU ARE?
I'M YUICHI JIN!
NICE TO MEET YOU!
HM?
YOU MUST BE THE FAMOUS JIN.
YOU'RE PUNY!
HOW OLD ARE YOU?
RUFFL
I'M YUMA KUGA.
I MAY BE SHORT, BUT I'M 15.
YUMA KUGA...
YUMA, YOU SAID?

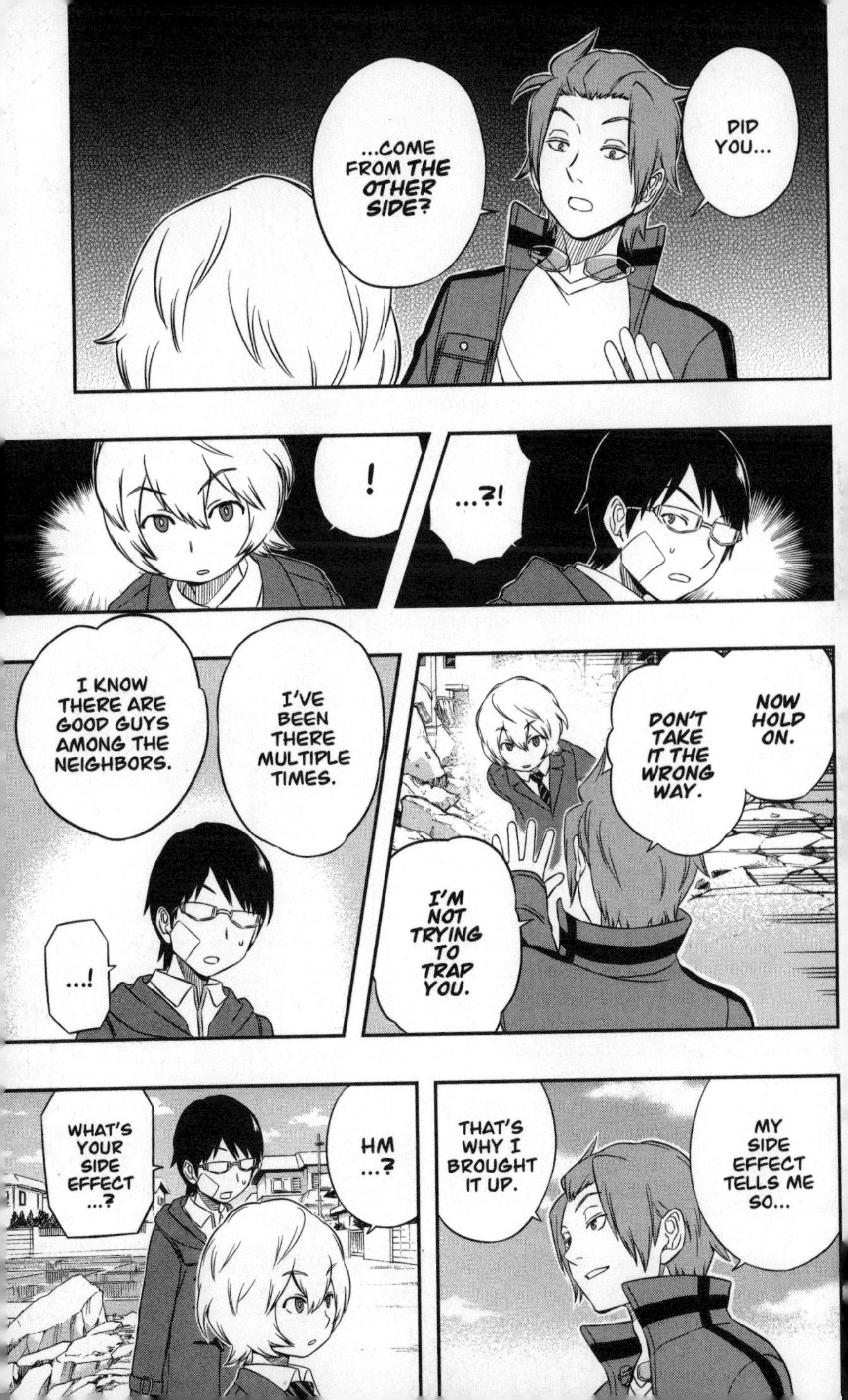
DID YOU...
...COME FROM THE OTHER SIDE?
...?!
!
NOW HOLD ON.
DON'T TAKE IT THE WRONG WAY.
I'M NOT TRYING TO TRAP YOU.
I'VE BEEN THERE MULTIPLE TIMES.
I KNOW THERE ARE GOOD GUYS AMONG THE NEIGHBORS.
...!
MY SIDE EFFECT TELLS ME SO...
THAT'S WHY I BROUGHT IT UP.
HM ...?
WHAT'S YOUR SIDE EFFECT ...?

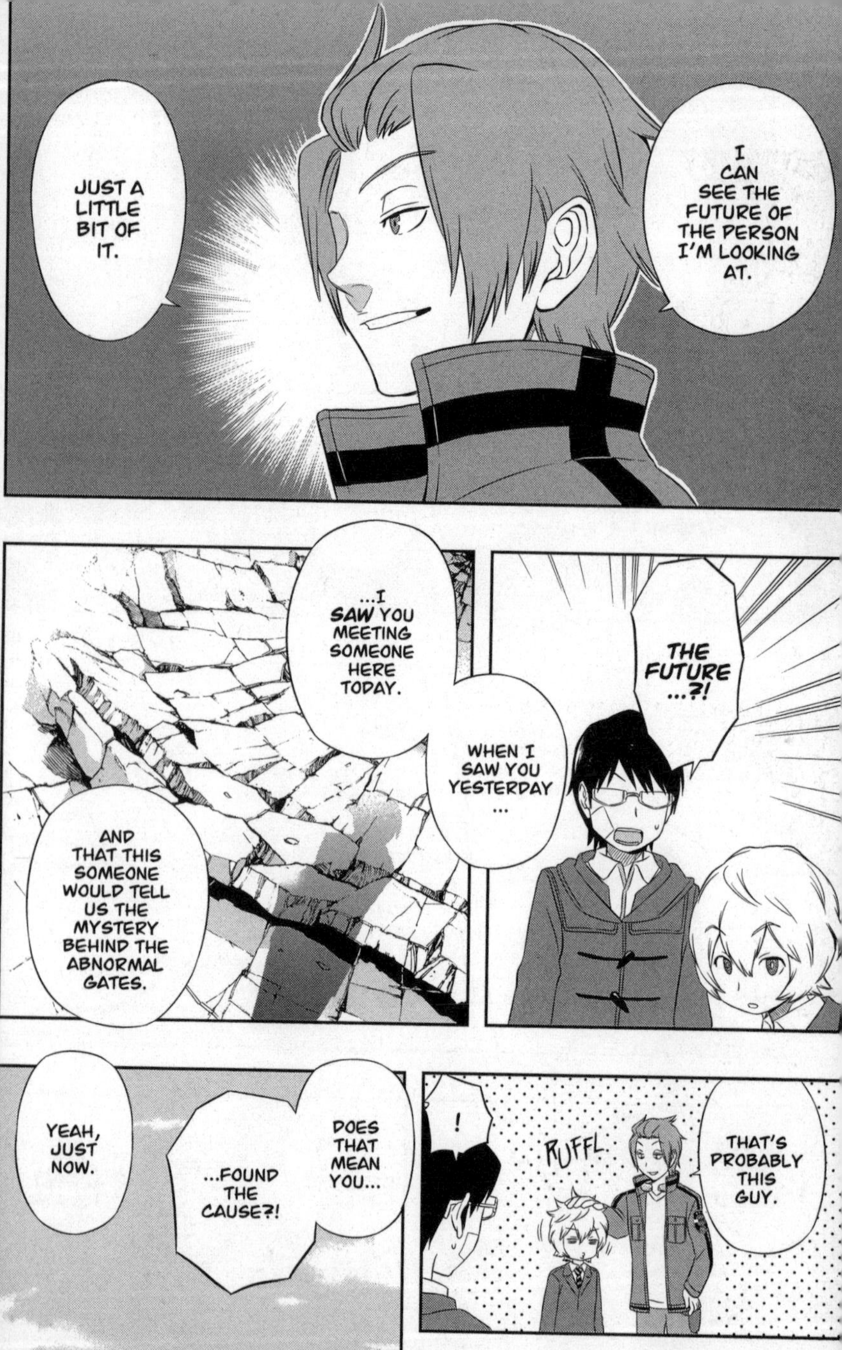
I CAN SEE THE FUTURE OF THE PERSON I'M LOOKING AT.
JUST A LITTLE BIT OF IT.
THE FUTURE ...?!
WHEN I SAW YOU YESTERDAY ...
...I SAW YOU MEETING SOMEONE HERE TODAY.
AND THAT THIS SOMEONE WOULD TELL US THE MYSTERY BEHIND THE ABNORMAL GATES.
THAT'S PROBABLY THIS GUY.
RUFFL
!
DOES THAT MEAN YOU...
...FOUND THE CAUSE?!
YEAH, JUST NOW.

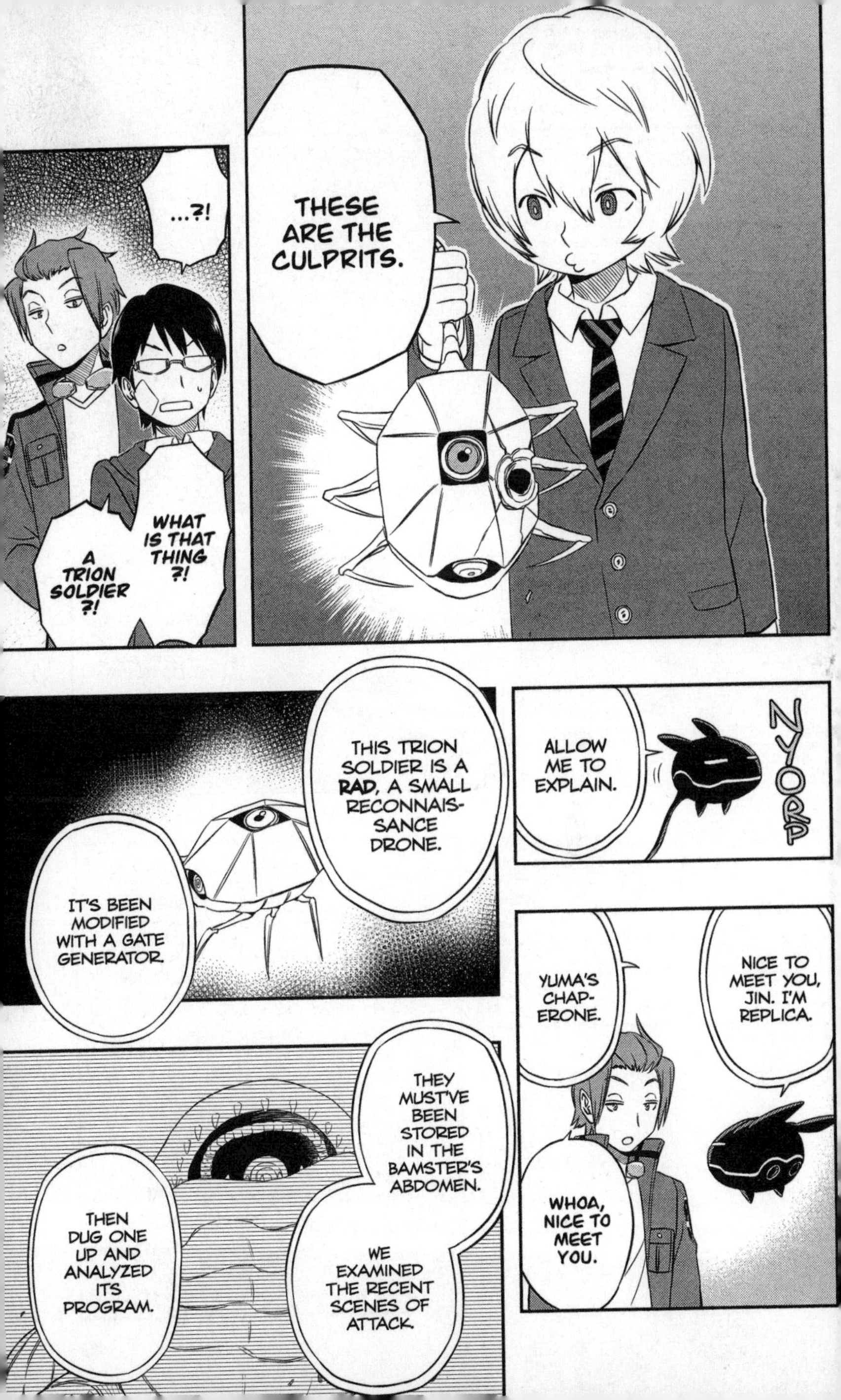
THESE ARE THE CULPRITS.
...?!
WHAT IS THAT THING ?!
A TRION SOLDIER ?!
NYORO
ALLOW ME TO EXPLAIN.
THIS TRION SOLDIER IS A RAD, A SMALL RECONNAIS-SANCE DRONE.
IT'S BEEN MODIFIED WITH A GATE GENERATOR.
NICE TO MEET YOU, JIN. I'M REPLICA.
YUMA'S CHAP-ERONE.
WHOA, NICE TO MEET YOU.
THEY MUST'VE BEEN STORED IN THE BAMSTER'S ABDOMEN.
WE EXAMINED THE RECENT SCENES OF ATTACK.
THEN DUG ONE UP AND ANALYZED ITS PROGRAM.

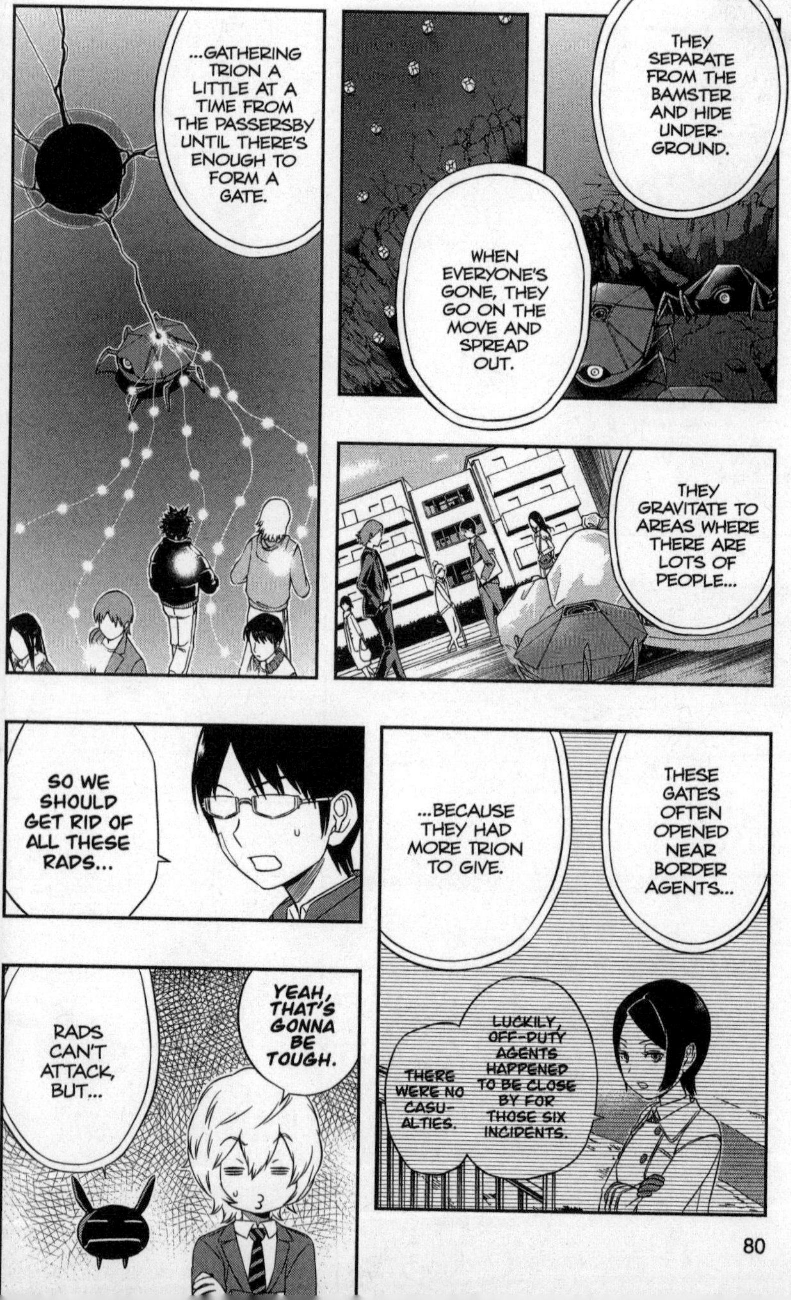
THEY SEPARATE FROM THE BAMSTER AND HIDE UNDER-GROUND.
WHEN EVERYONE'S GONE, THEY GO ON THE MOVE AND SPREAD OUT.
THEY GRAVITATE TO AREAS WHERE THERE ARE LOTS OF PEOPLE...
...GATHERING TRION A LITTLE AT A TIME FROM THE PASSERSBY UNTIL THERE'S ENOUGH TO FORM A GATE.
THESE GATES OFTEN OPENED NEAR BORDER AGENTS...
...BECAUSE THEY HAD MORE TRION TO GIVE.
LUCKILY, OFF-DUTY AGENTS HAPPENED TO BE CLOSE BY FOR THOSE SIX INCIDENTS.
THERE WERE NO CASU-ALTIES.
SO WE SHOULD GET RID OF ALL THESE RADS...
RADS CAN'T ATTACK, BUT...
YEAH, THAT'S GONNA BE TOUGH.

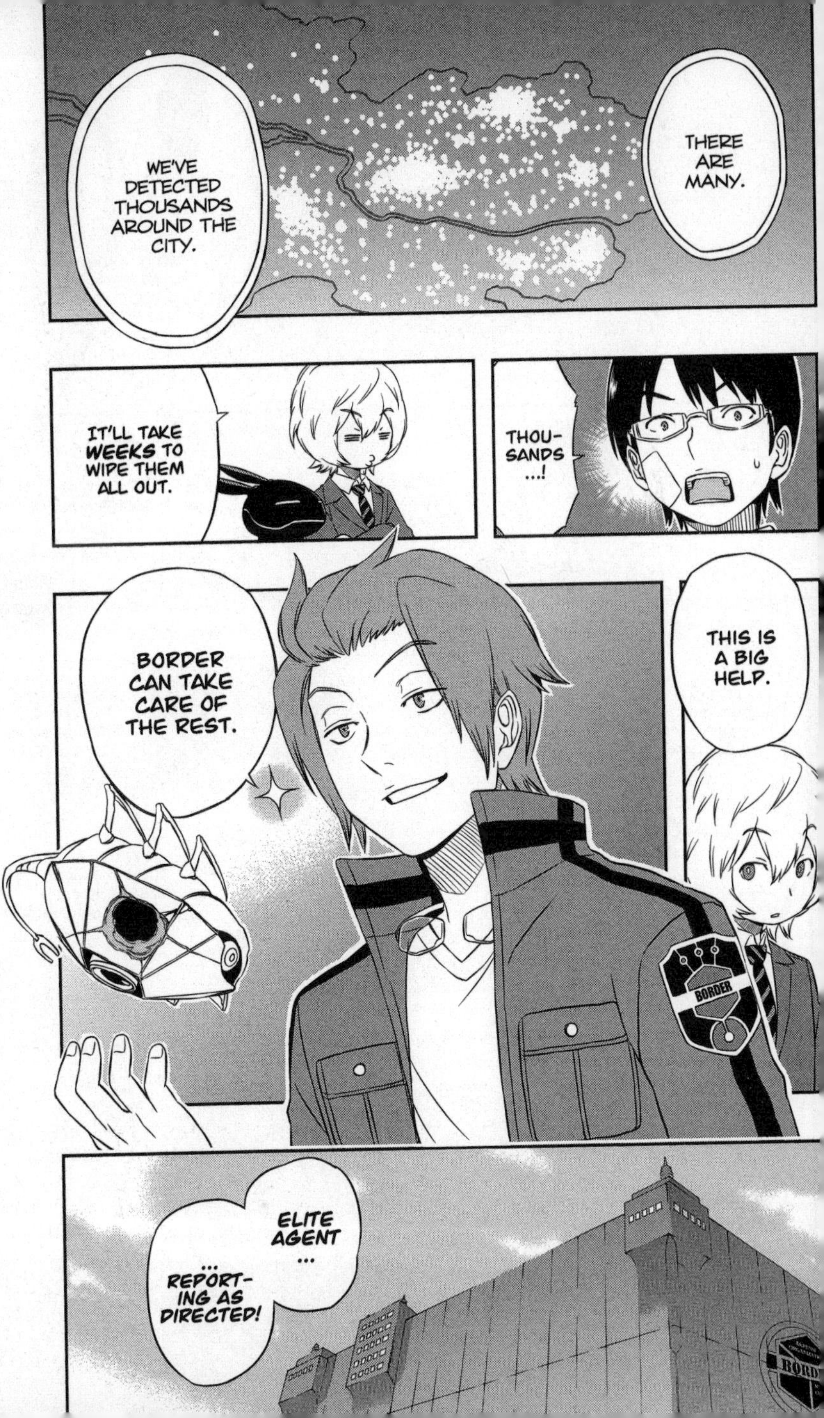
THERE ARE MANY.
WE'VE DETECTED THOUSANDS AROUND THE CITY.
THOU-SANDS ...!
IT'LL TAKE **WEEKS** TO WIPE THEM ALL OUT.
THIS IS A BIG HELP.
BORDER CAN TAKE CARE OF THE REST.
BORDER
ELITE AGENT ...
... REPORT-ING AS DIRECTED!

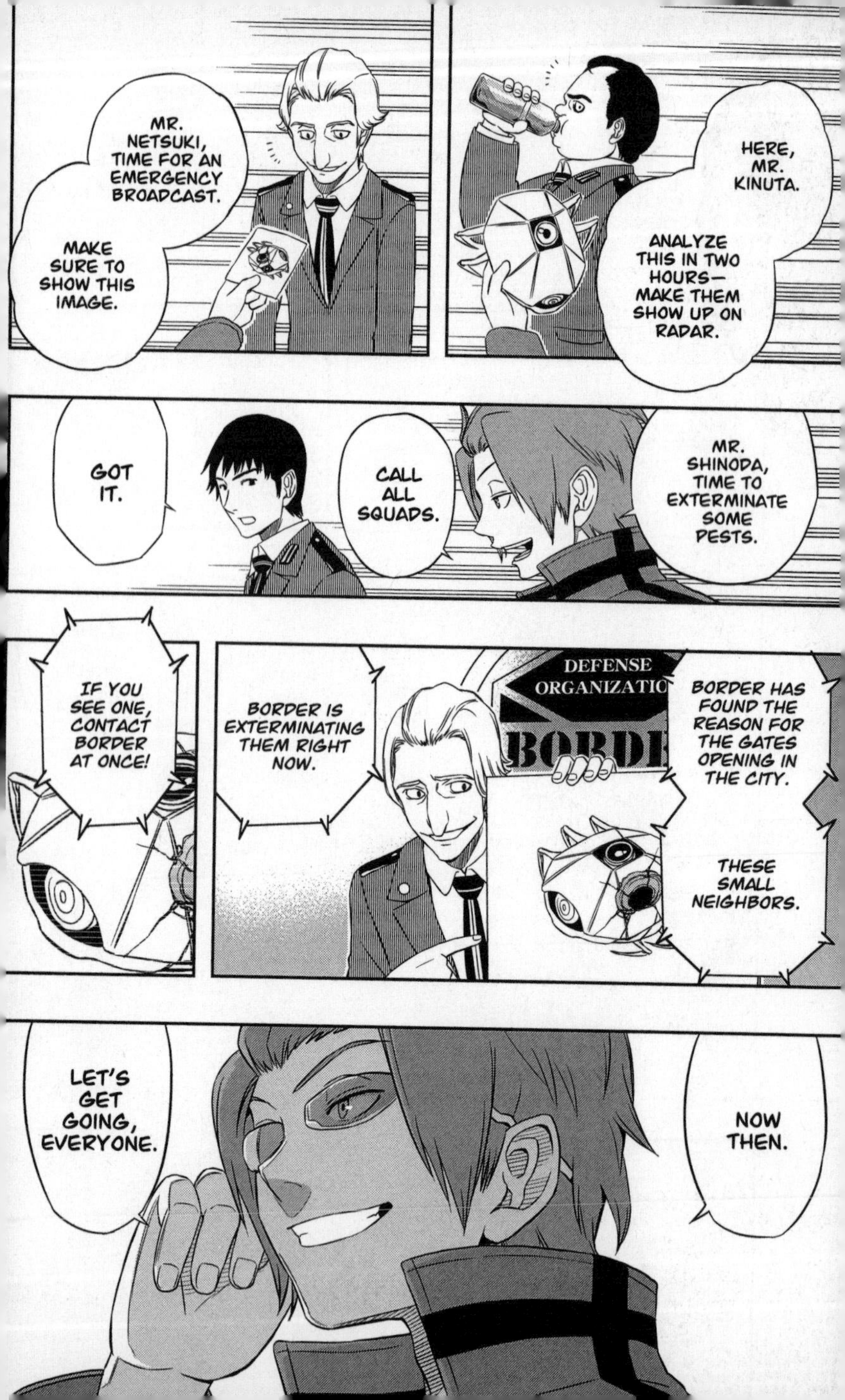
HERE, MR. KINUTA.
ANALYZE THIS IN TWO HOURS—MAKE THEM SHOW UP ON RADAR.
MR. NETSUKI, TIME FOR AN EMERGENCY BROADCAST.
MAKE SURE TO SHOW THIS IMAGE.
MR. SHINODA, TIME TO EXTERMINATE SOME PESTS.
CALL ALL SQUADS.
GOT IT.
DEFENSE ORGANIZATIO
BORDER HAS FOUND THE REASON FOR THE GATES OPENING IN THE CITY.
THESE SMALL NEIGHBORS.
BORDER IS EXTERMINATING THEM RIGHT NOW.
IF YOU SEE ONE, CONTACT BORDER AT ONCE!
NOW THEN.
LET'S GET GOING, EVERYONE.

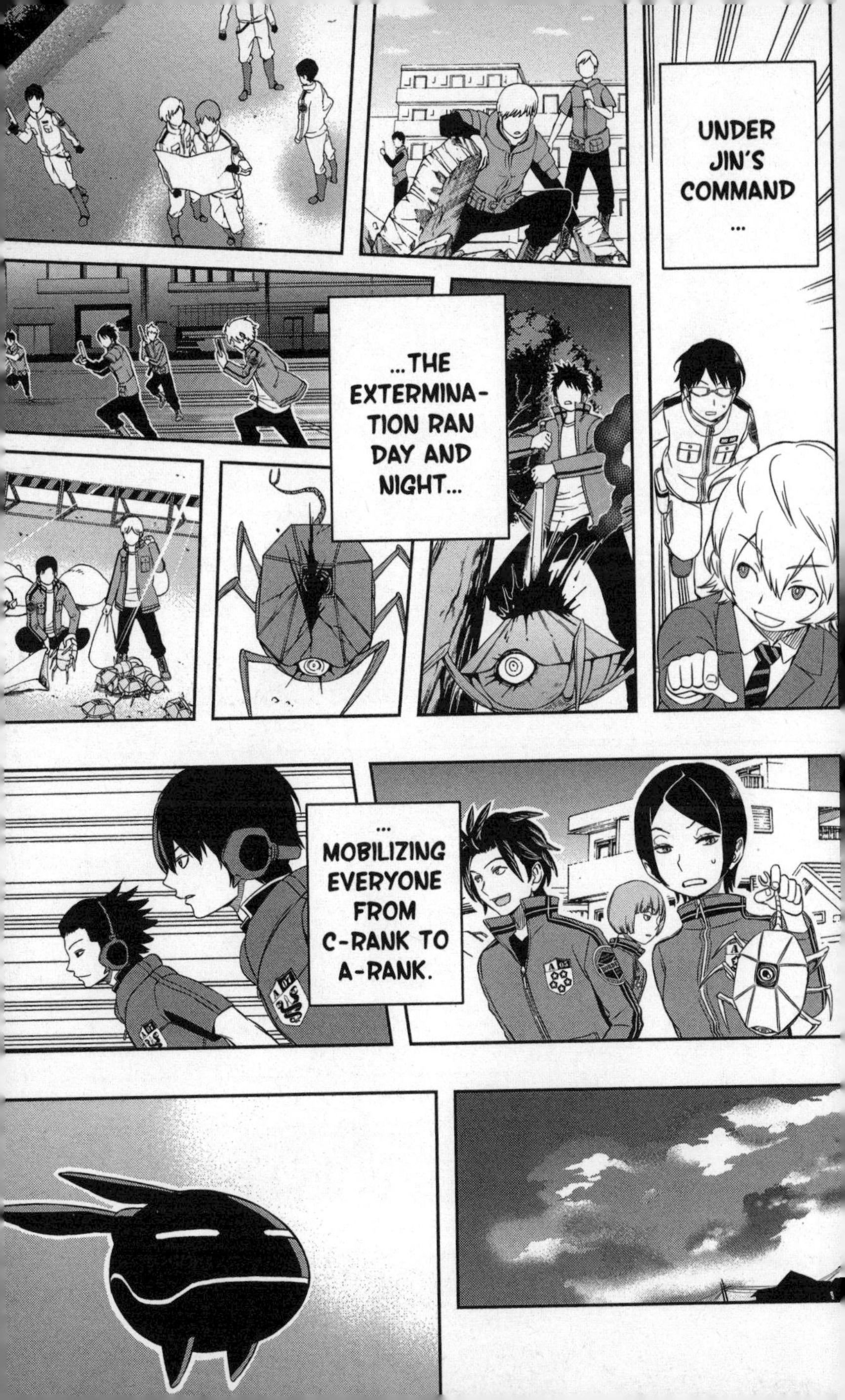
UNDER JIN'S COMMAND ...
...THE EXTERMINATION RAN DAY AND NIGHT...
... MOBILIZING EVERYONE FROM C-RANK TO A-RANK.

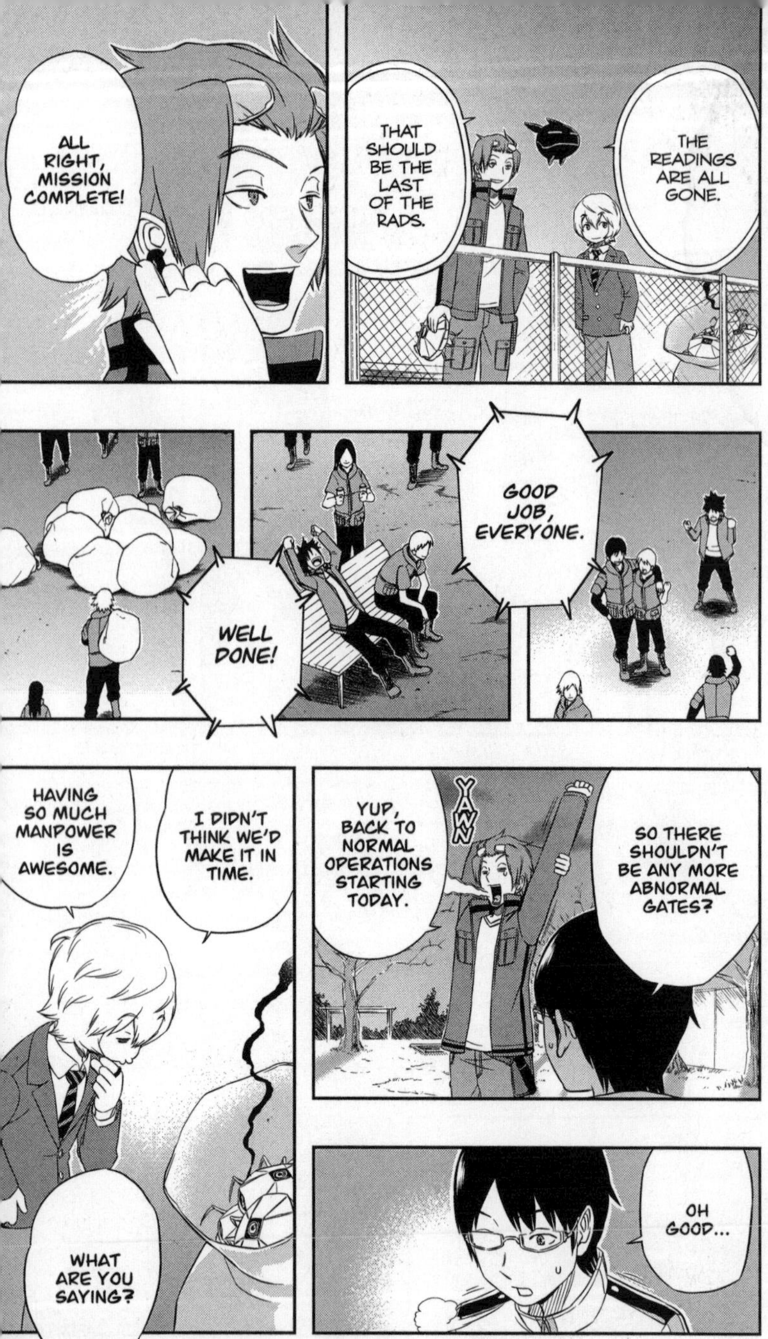
THE READINGS ARE ALL GONE.
THAT SHOULD BE THE LAST OF THE RADS.
ALL RIGHT, MISSION COMPLETE!
GOOD JOB, EVERYONE.
WELL DONE!
SO THERE SHOULDN'T BE ANY MORE ABNORMAL GATES?
YAWN
YUP, BACK TO NORMAL OPERATIONS STARTING TODAY.
OH GOOD...
I DIDN'T THINK WE'D MAKE IT IN TIME.
HAVING SO MUCH MANPOWER IS AWESOME.
WHAT ARE YOU SAYING?

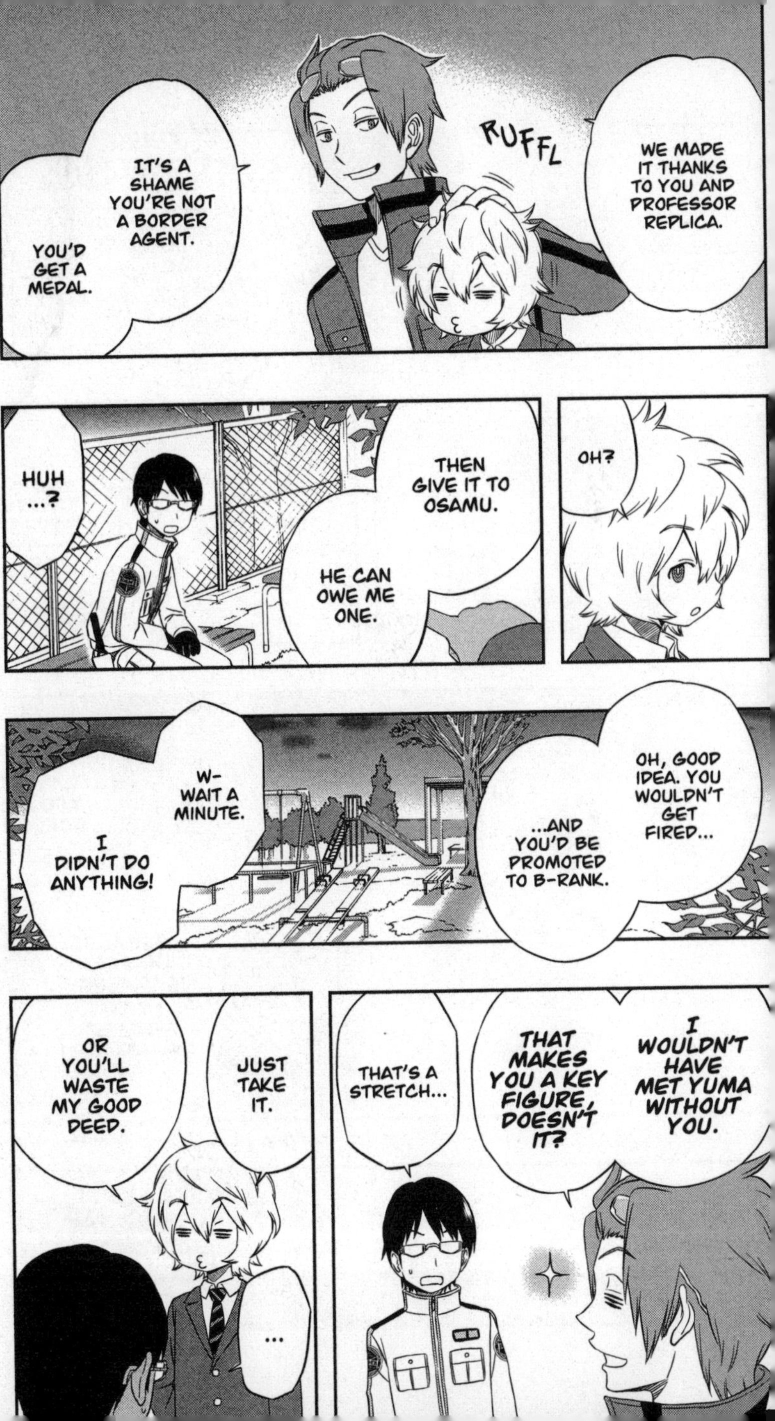
WE MADE IT THANKS TO YOU AND PROFESSOR REPLICA.
RUFFL
IT'S A SHAME YOU'RE NOT A BORDER AGENT.
YOU'D GET A MEDAL.
OH?
THEN GIVE IT TO OSAMU.
HE CAN OWE ME ONE.
HUH ...?
OH, GOOD IDEA. YOU WOULDN'T GET FIRED...
...AND YOU'D BE PROMOTED TO B-RANK.
W- WAIT A MINUTE.
I DIDN'T DO ANYTHING!
I WOULDN'T HAVE MET YUMA WITHOUT YOU.
THAT MAKES YOU A KEY FIGURE, DOESN'T IT?
THAT'S A STRETCH...
JUST TAKE IT.
OR YOU'LL WASTE MY GOOD DEED.
...

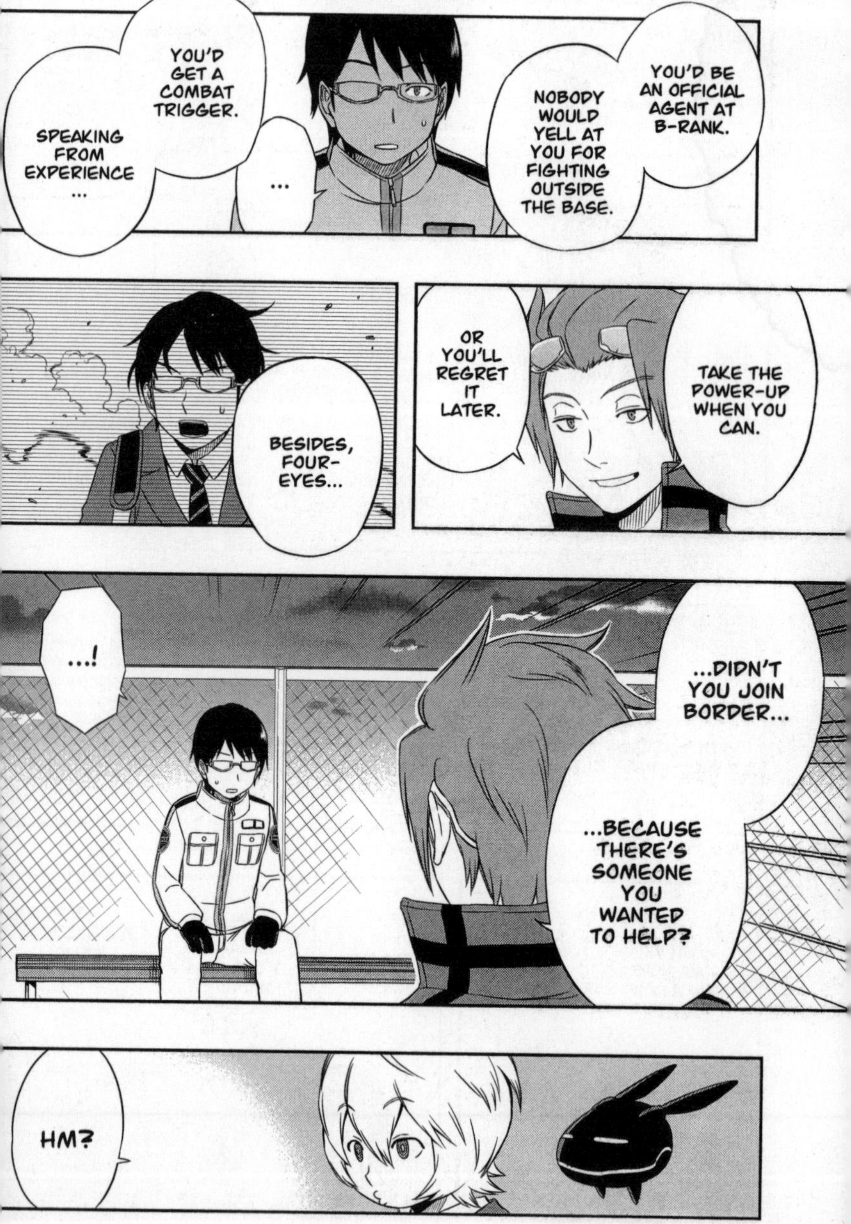
YOU'D BE AN OFFICIAL AGENT AT B-RANK.
NOBODY WOULD YELL AT YOU FOR FIGHTING OUTSIDE THE BASE.
YOU'D GET A COMBAT TRIGGER.
...
SPEAKING FROM EXPERIENCE ...
TAKE THE POWER-UP WHEN YOU CAN.
OR YOU'LL REGRET IT LATER.
BESIDES, FOUR-EYES...
...DIDN'T YOU JOIN BORDER...
...BECAUSE THERE'S SOMEONE YOU WANTED TO HELP?
...!
HM?

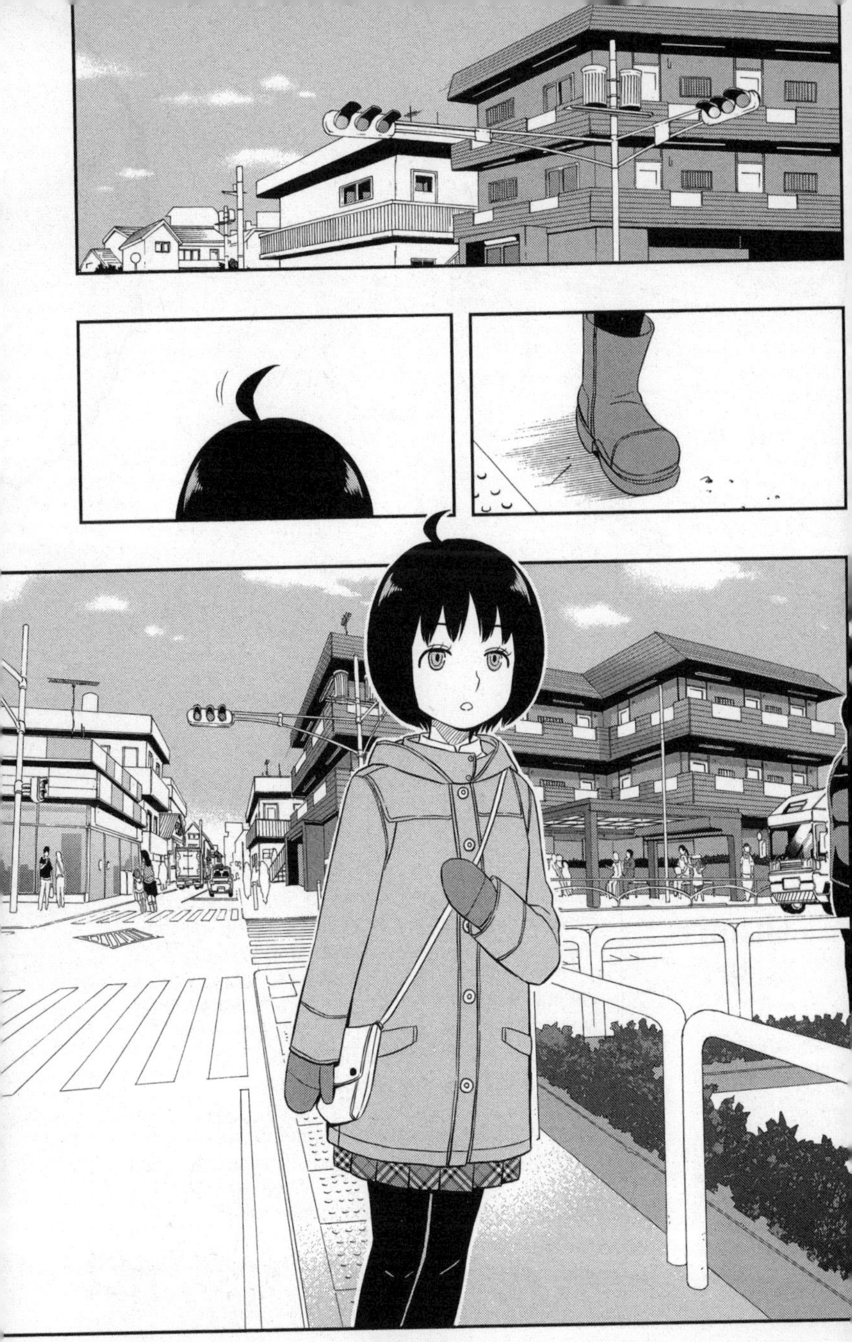

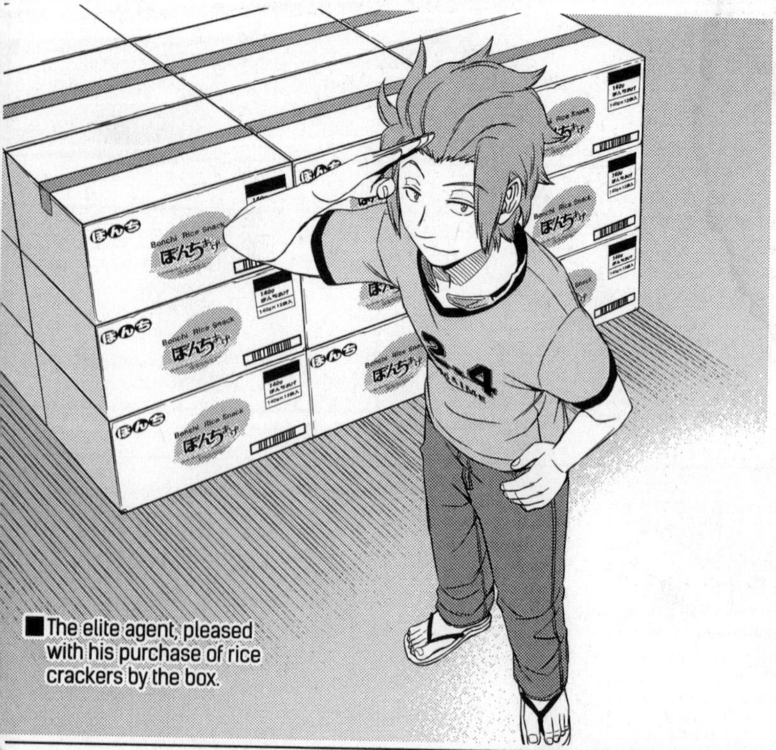
Bonchi Rice Snack

■The elite agent, pleased with his purchase of rice crackers by the box.

## Yuichi Jin

- ■19 years old
- ■Born April 9
- ■Falco, Blood type O
- ■Height: 5'10"
- ■Likes: Bonchi fried rice crackers, girls' butts, pulling strings

Pulled from the one-shot manga *Elite Agent Jin* that became the prototype for *World Trigger*. He was too mature and powerful, so he was converted into a big brother role in *World Trigger*. He's markedly more difficult to draw than the other characters, so it takes way too long to work on the chapters that center around Jin. But they do well in the popularity polls, so he's a high-risk, high-return character.

After I made him eat Bonchi brand rice crackers, the company sent me boxes of them. My assistants and I ate them. Thank you so much. I'll keep drawing them as Jin's favorite. I hope it boosts their sales.

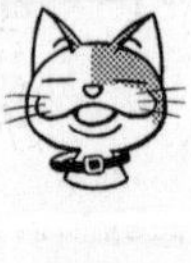

## Chapter 12 Chika Amatori

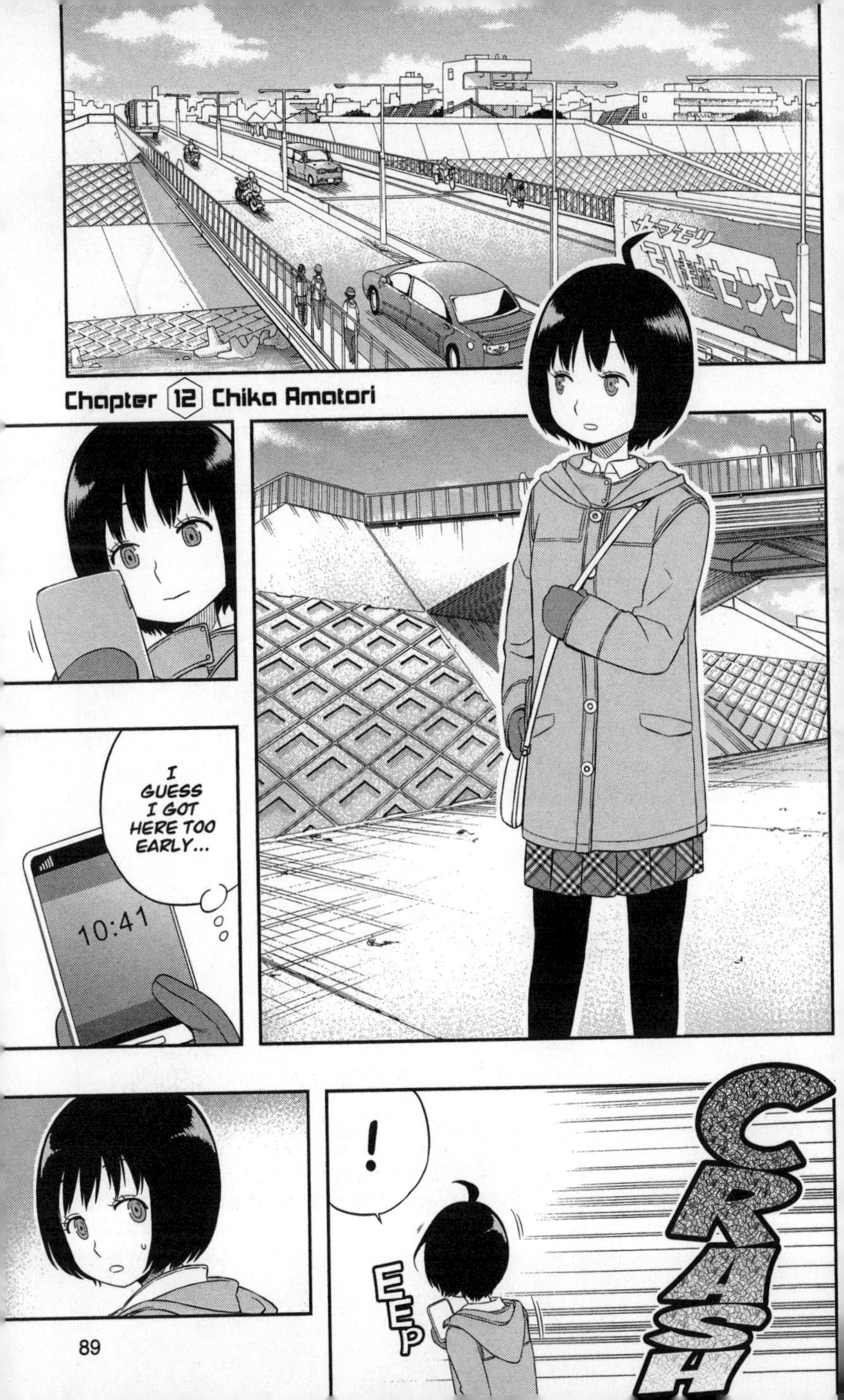

I GUESS I GOT HERE TOO EARLY...
10:41
CRASH
!
EEP

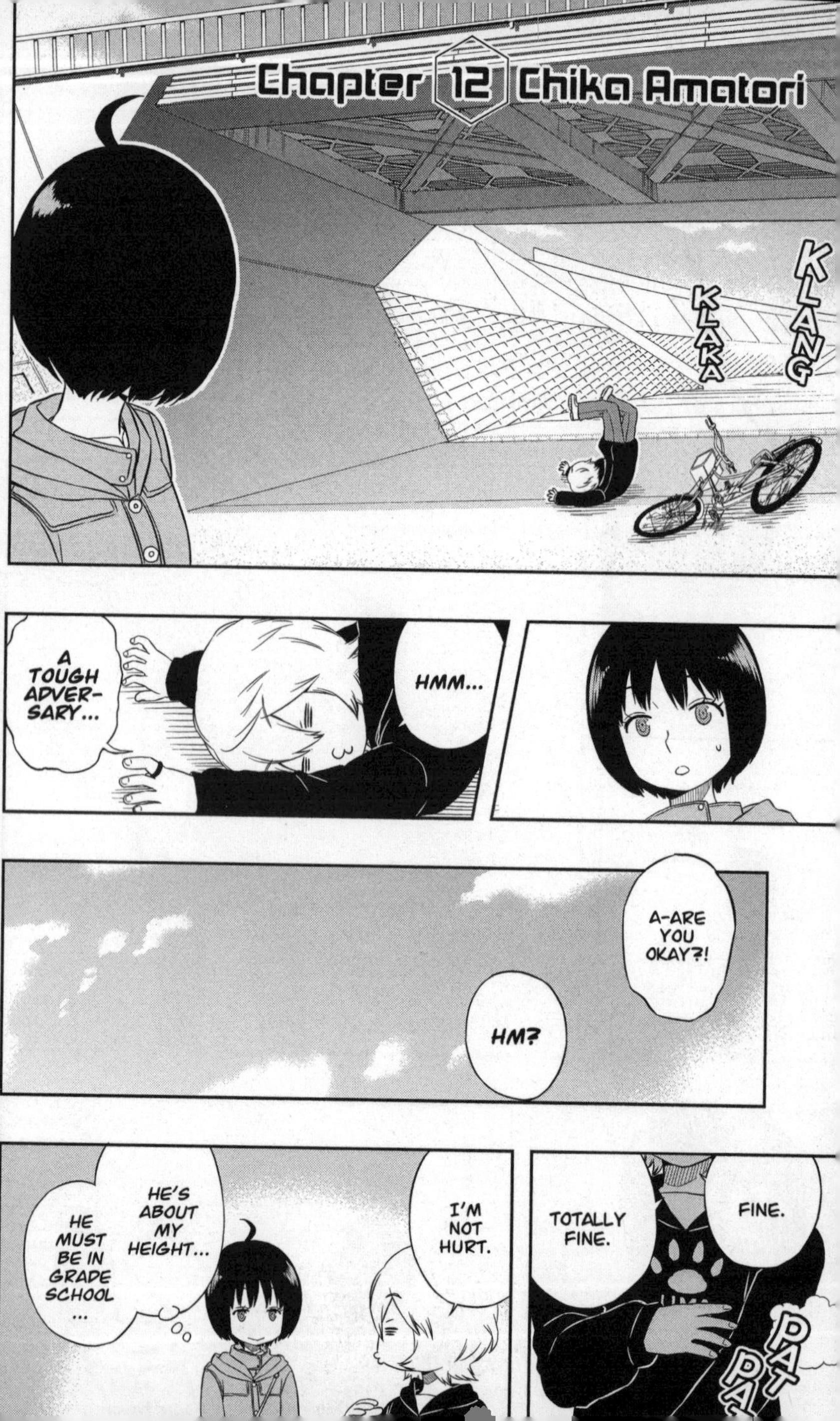
Chapter 12 Chika Amatori
KLANG
KLAKA
HMM...
A TOUGH ADVERSARY...
A-ARE YOU OKAY?!
HM?
FINE.
TOTALLY FINE.
PAT PAT
I'M NOT HURT.
HE'S ABOUT MY HEIGHT...
HE MUST BE IN GRADE SCHOOL ...

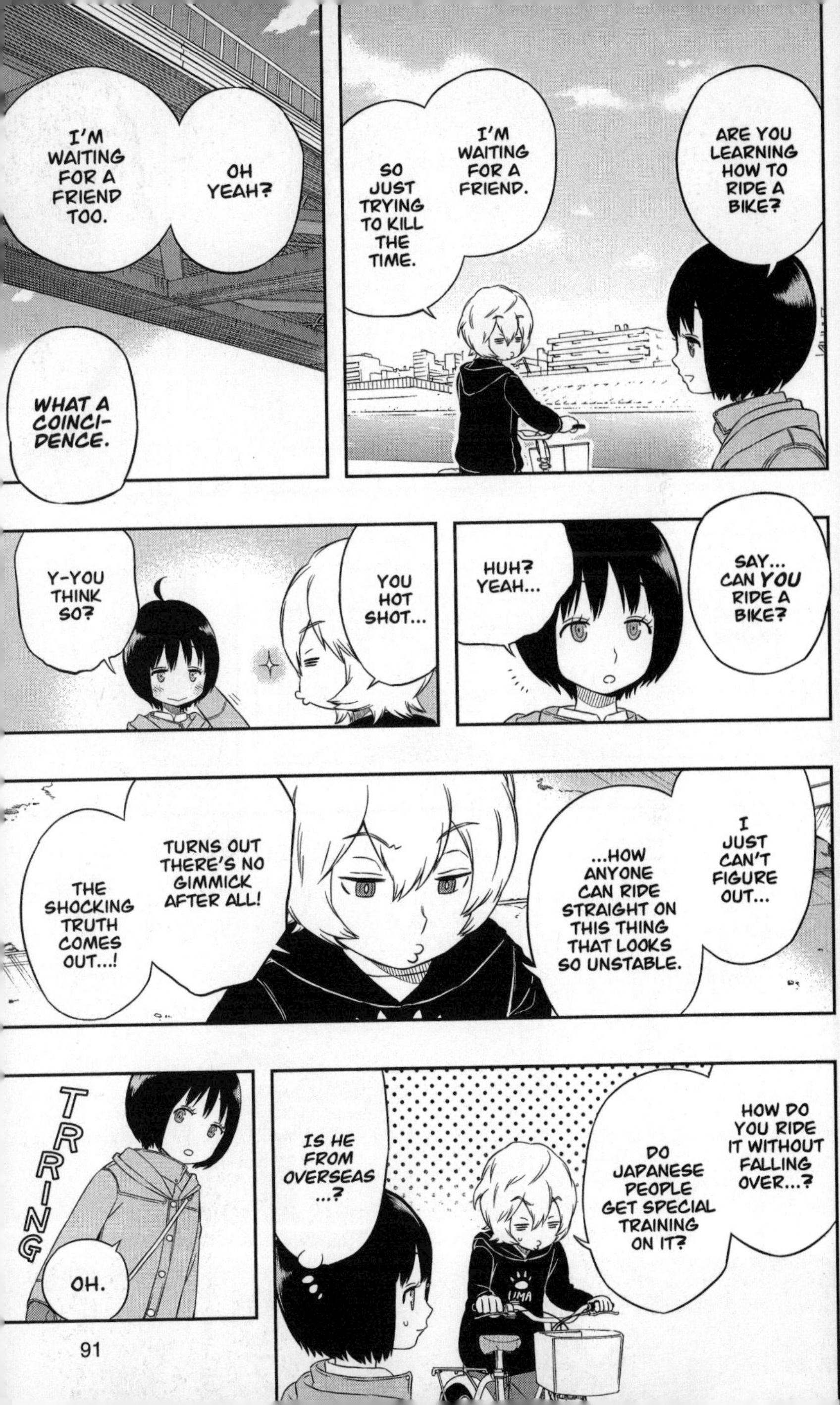
ARE YOU LEARNING HOW TO RIDE A BIKE?
I'M WAITING FOR A FRIEND.
SO JUST TRYING TO KILL THE TIME.
OH YEAH?
I'M WAITING FOR A FRIEND TOO.
WHAT A COINCIDENCE.
SAY... CAN *YOU* RIDE A BIKE?
HUH? YEAH...
YOU HOT SHOT...
Y-YOU THINK SO?
I JUST CAN'T FIGURE OUT...
...HOW ANYONE CAN RIDE STRAIGHT ON THIS THING THAT LOOKS SO UNSTABLE.
TURNS OUT THERE'S NO GIMMICK AFTER ALL!
THE SHOCKING TRUTH COMES OUT...!
HOW DO YOU RIDE IT WITHOUT FALLING OVER...?
DO JAPANESE PEOPLE GET SPECIAL TRAINING ON IT?
IS HE FROM OVERSEAS...?
TRRING
OH.

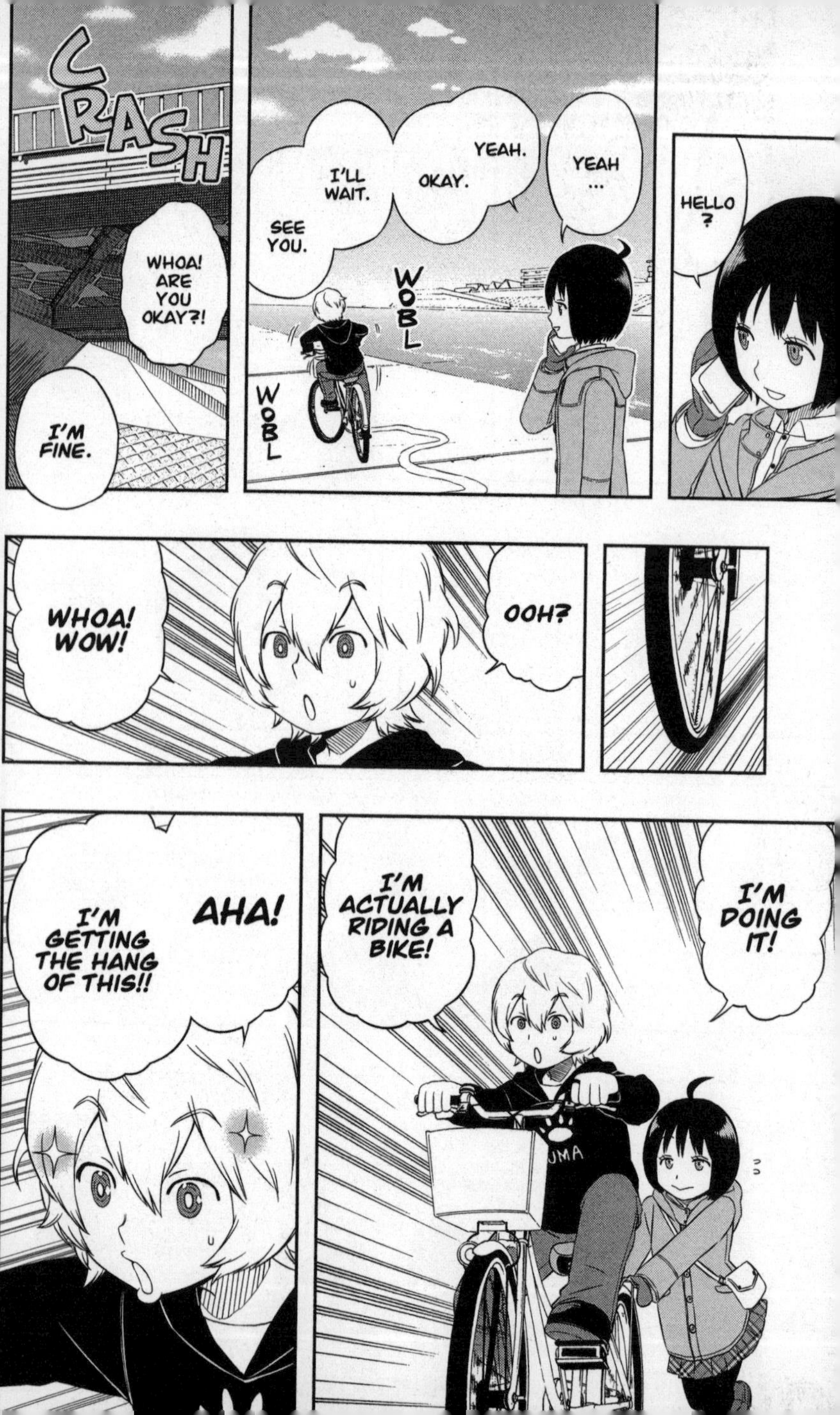
HELLO?
YEAH ...
YEAH. OKAY.
I'LL WAIT. SEE YOU.
WOBL
WOBL
CRASH
WHOA! ARE YOU OKAY?!
I'M FINE.
OOH?
WHOA! WOW!
I'M DOING IT!
I'M ACTUALLY RIDING A BIKE!
AHA!
I'M GETTING THE HANG OF THIS!!

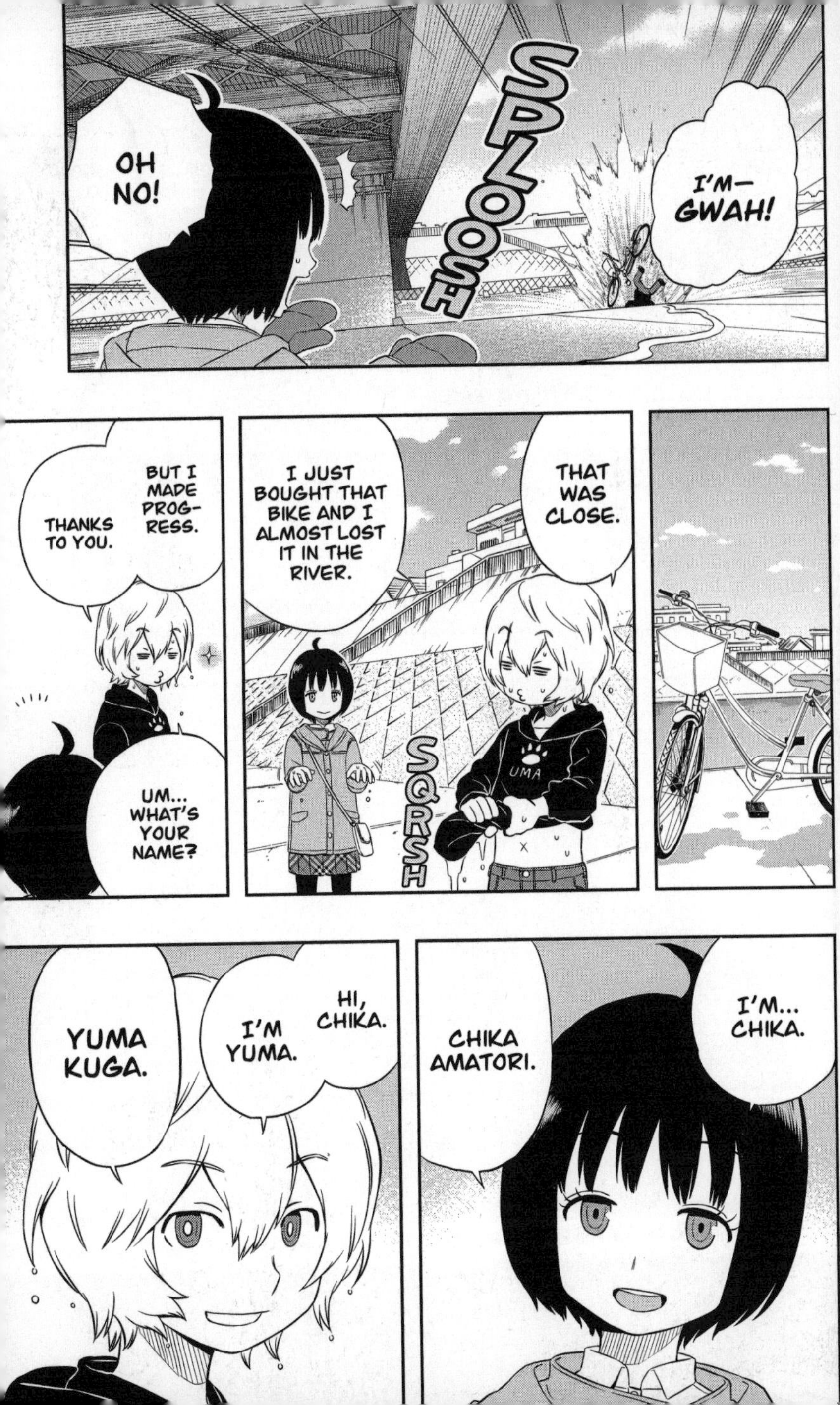
I'M—GWAH!
SPLOOSH
OH NO!
THAT WAS CLOSE.
I JUST BOUGHT THAT BIKE AND I ALMOST LOST IT IN THE RIVER.
SQRSH
BUT I MADE PROG-RESS.
THANKS TO YOU.
UM... WHAT'S YOUR NAME?
I'M... CHIKA.
CHIKA AMATORI.
HI, CHIKA.
I'M YUMA.
YUMA KUGA.

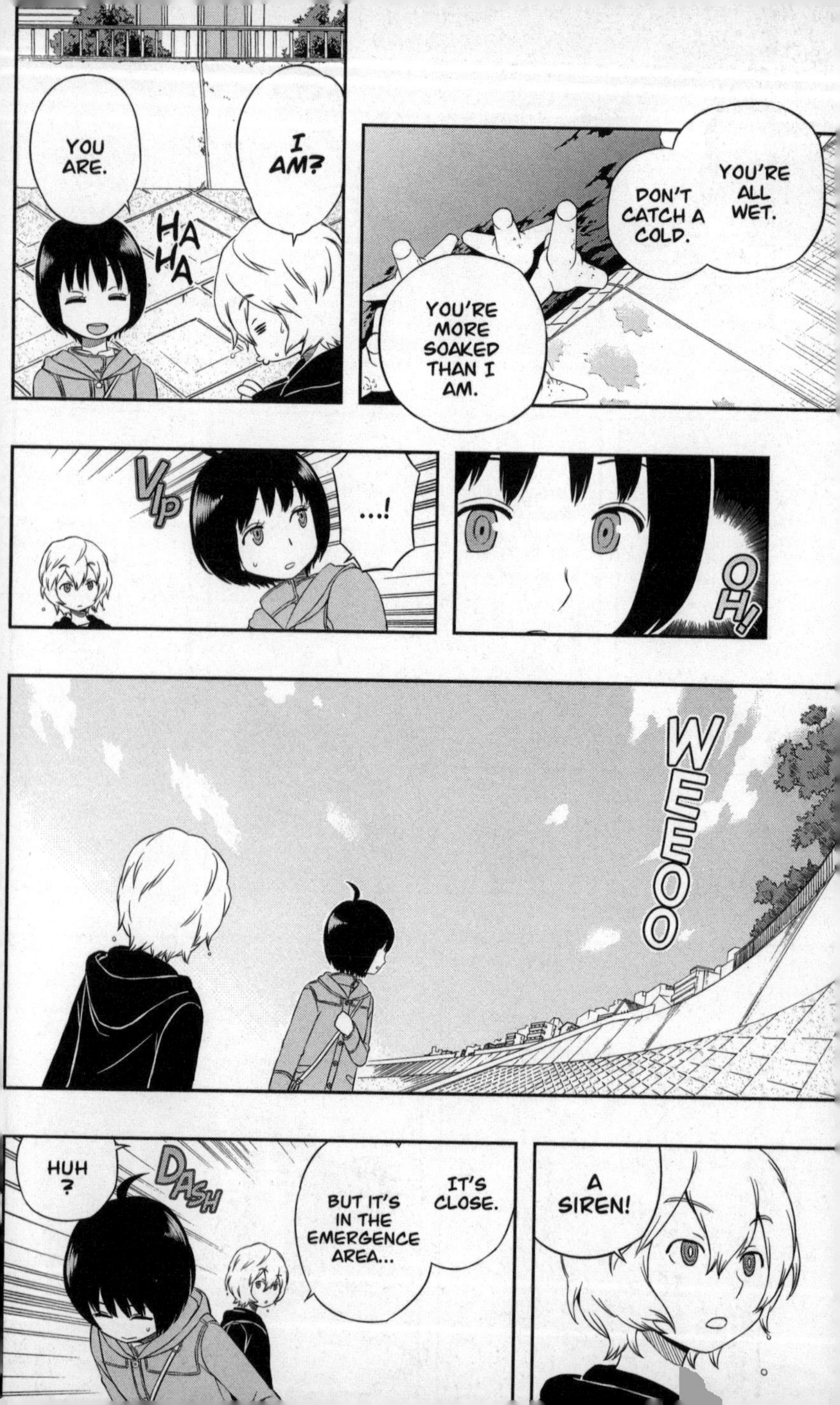
YOU'RE ALL WET.
DON'T CATCH A COLD.
YOU'RE MORE SOAKED THAN I AM.
I AM?
YOU ARE.
HA HA
OH!
...!
VIP
WEEOO
A SIREN!
IT'S CLOSE.
BUT IT'S IN THE EMERGENCE AREA...
HUH?
DASH

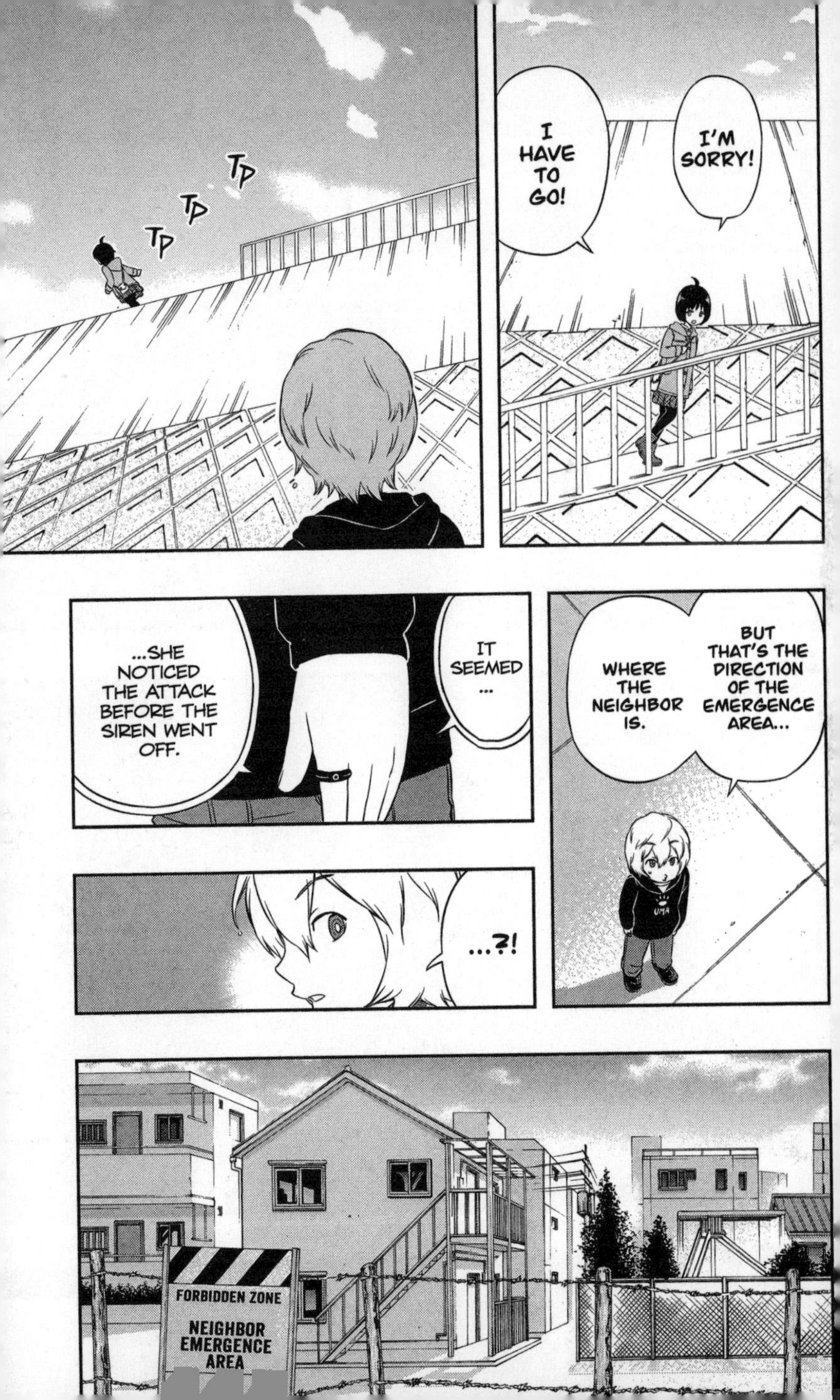
I'M SORRY!
I HAVE TO GO!
TP TP TP
BUT THAT'S THE DIRECTION OF THE EMERGENCE AREA...
WHERE THE NEIGHBOR IS.
IT SEEMED...
...SHE NOTICED THE ATTACK BEFORE THE SIREN WENT OFF.
...?!
FORBIDDEN ZONE
NEIGHBOR EMERGENCE AREA

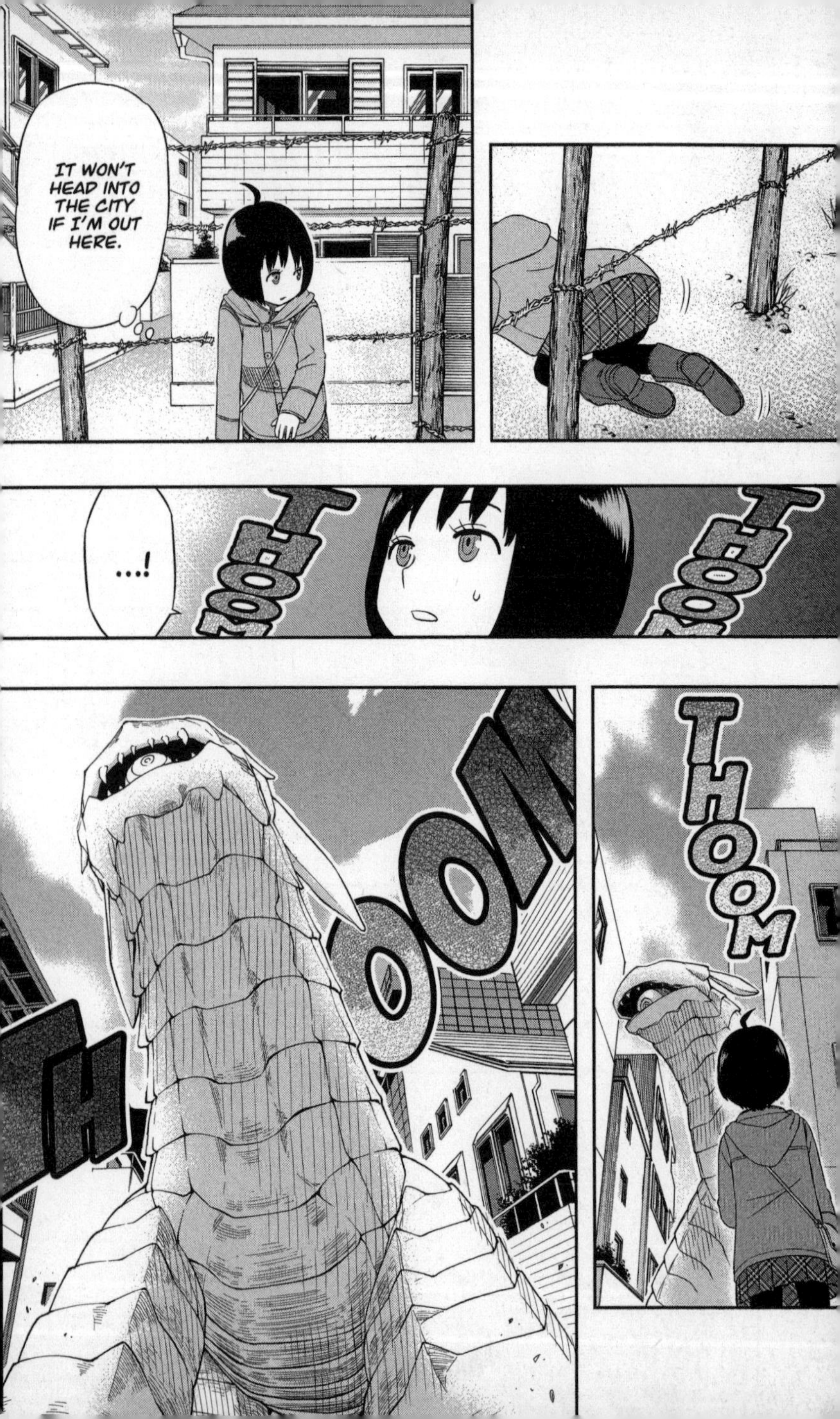
IT WON'T HEAD INTO THE CITY IF I'M OUT HERE.
THOOM
...!
THOOM
THOOM
THOOM

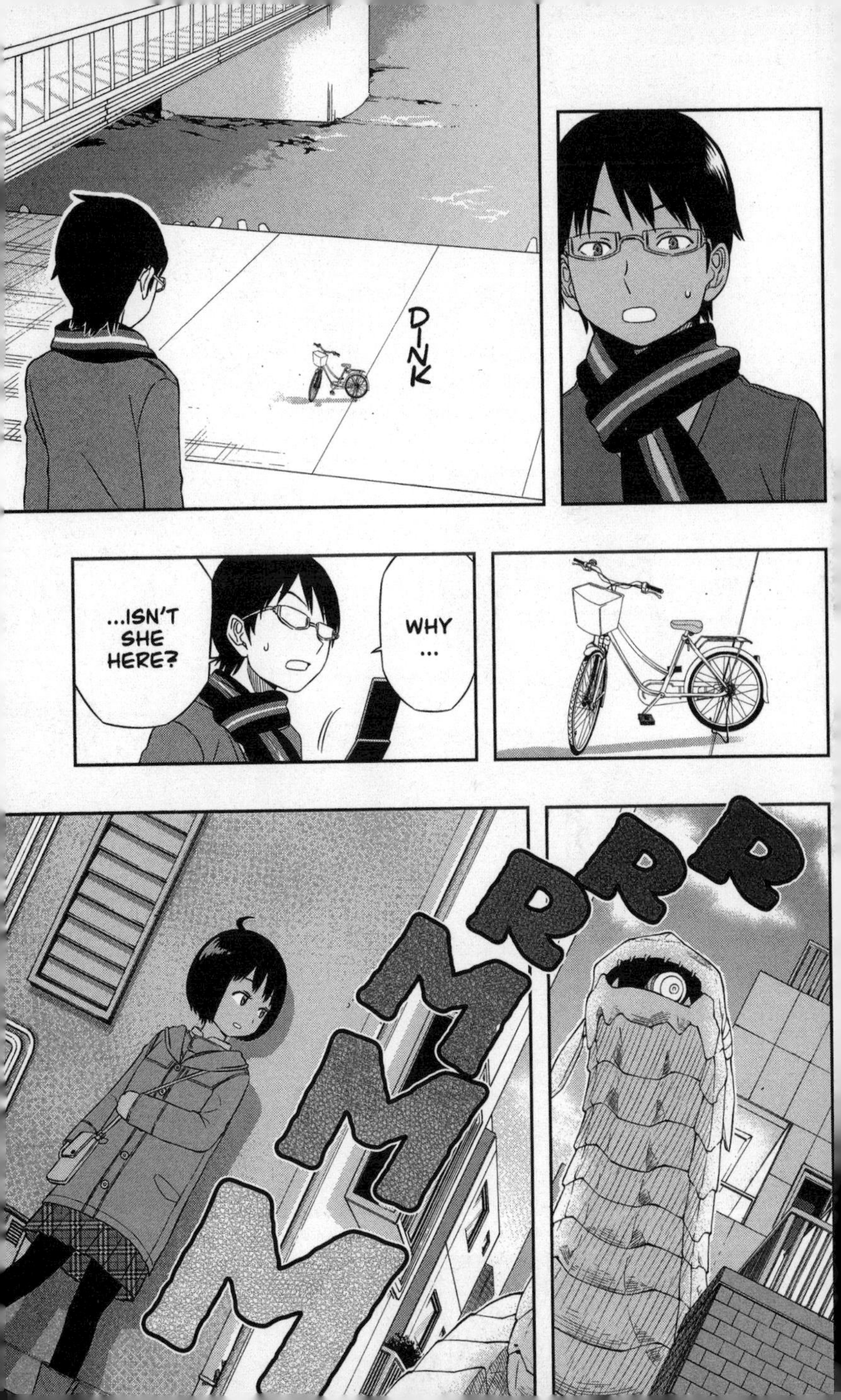
DINK
WHY ...
...ISN'T SHE HERE?
MMMRRR

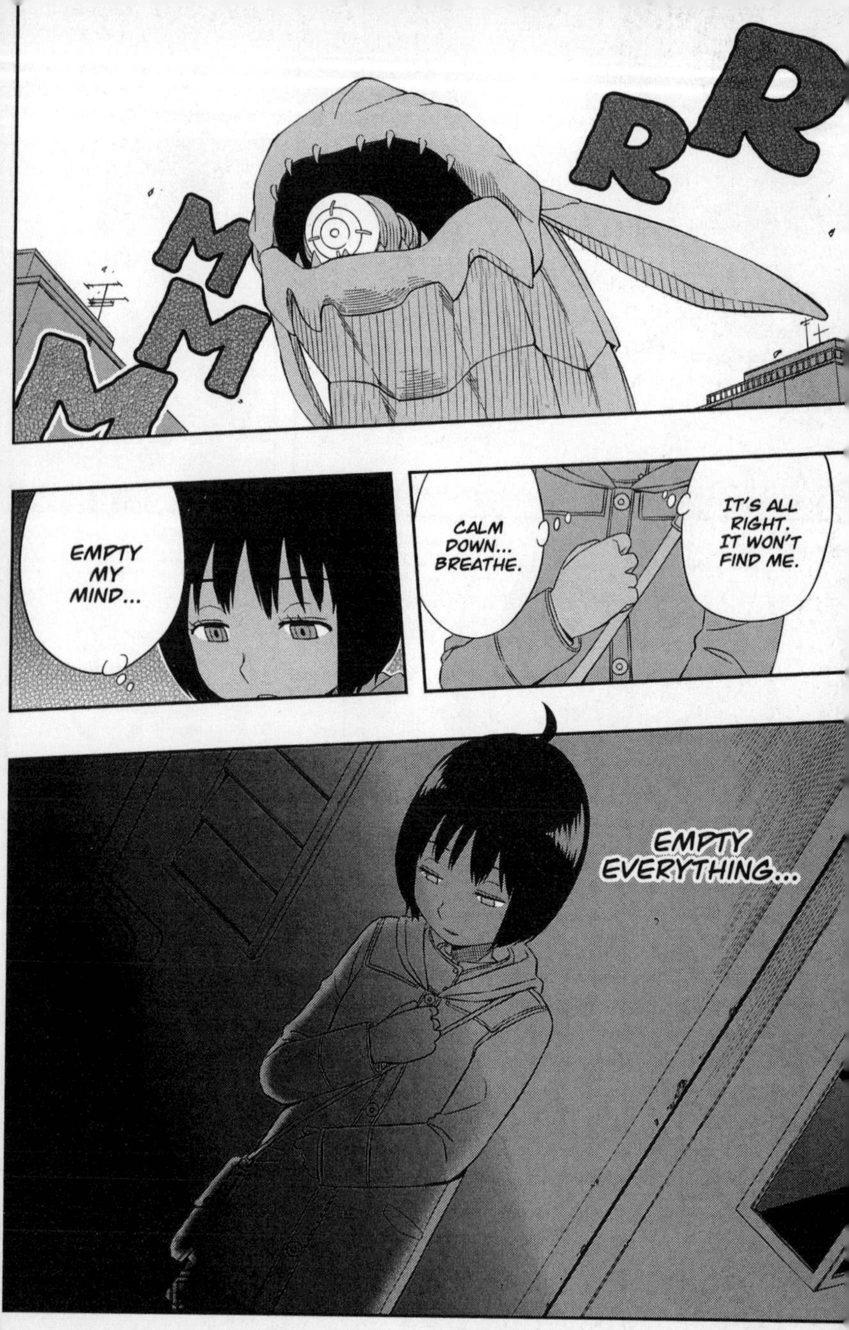
RRMMMM
IT'S ALL RIGHT. IT WON'T FIND ME.
CALM DOWN... BREATHE.
EMPTY MY MIND...
EMPTY EVERYTHING...

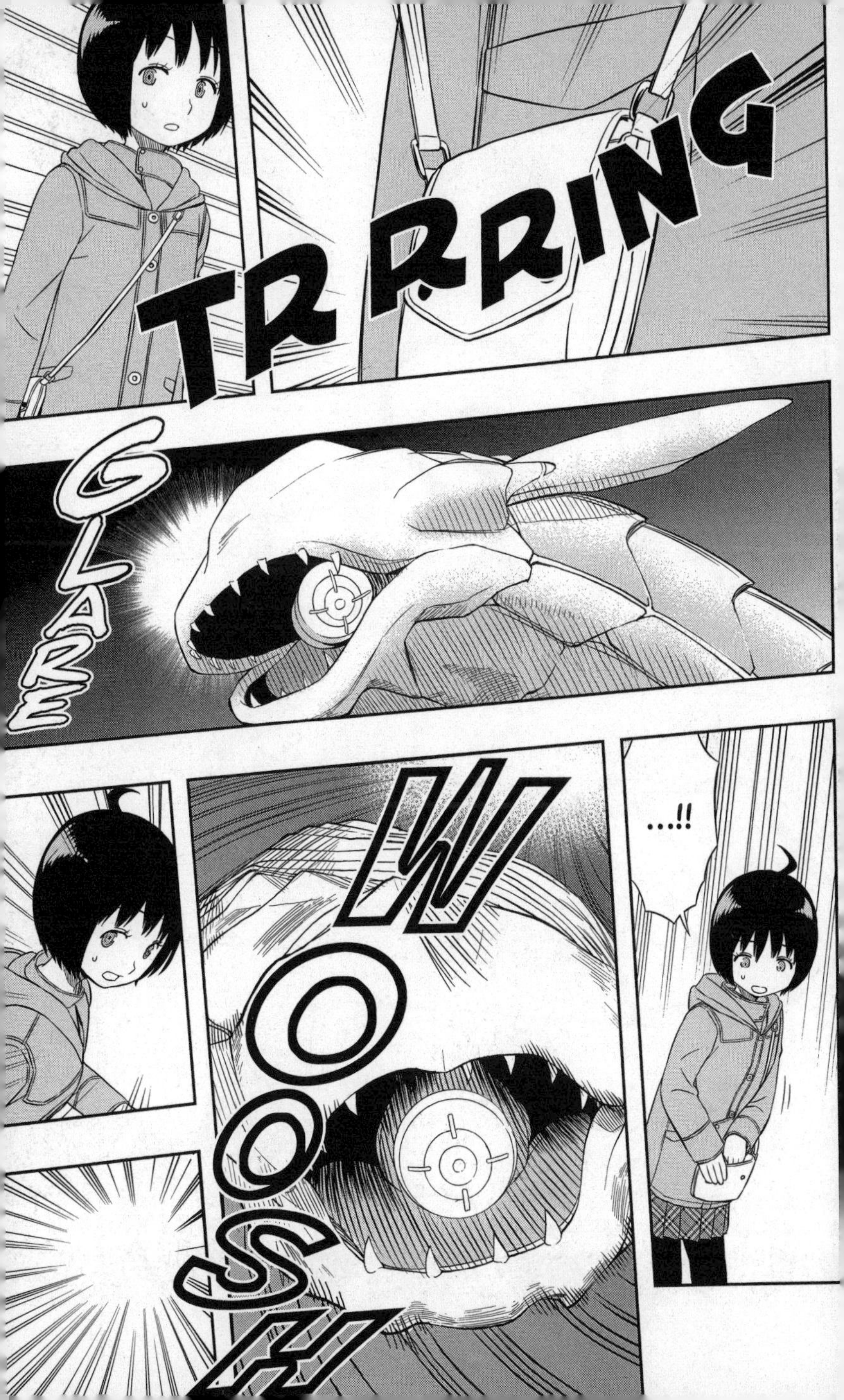
TRRRING
GLARE
...!!
WOOSH

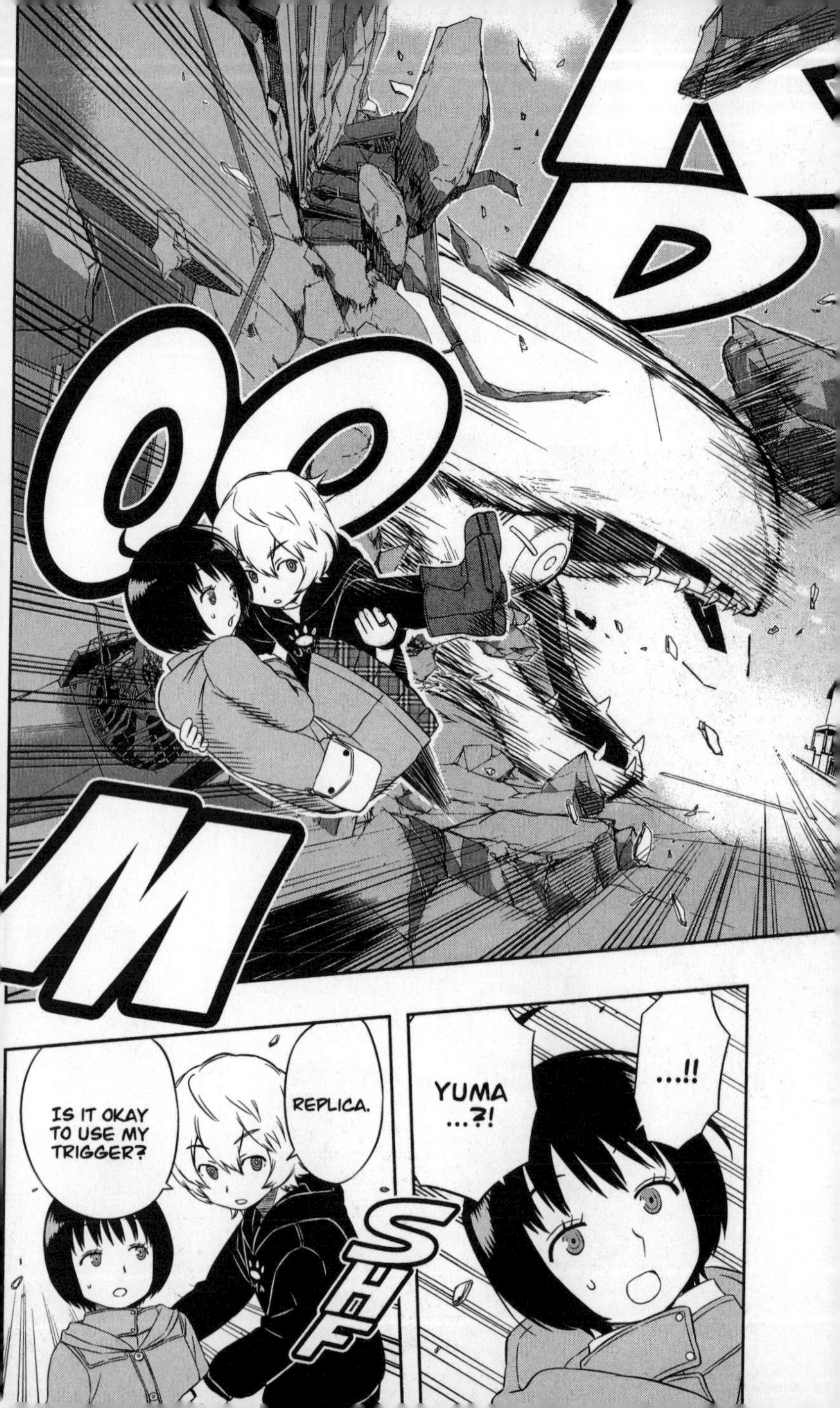
ADOOM
...!!
YUMA ...?!
REPLICA.
IS IT OKAY TO USE MY TRIGGER?
SHF

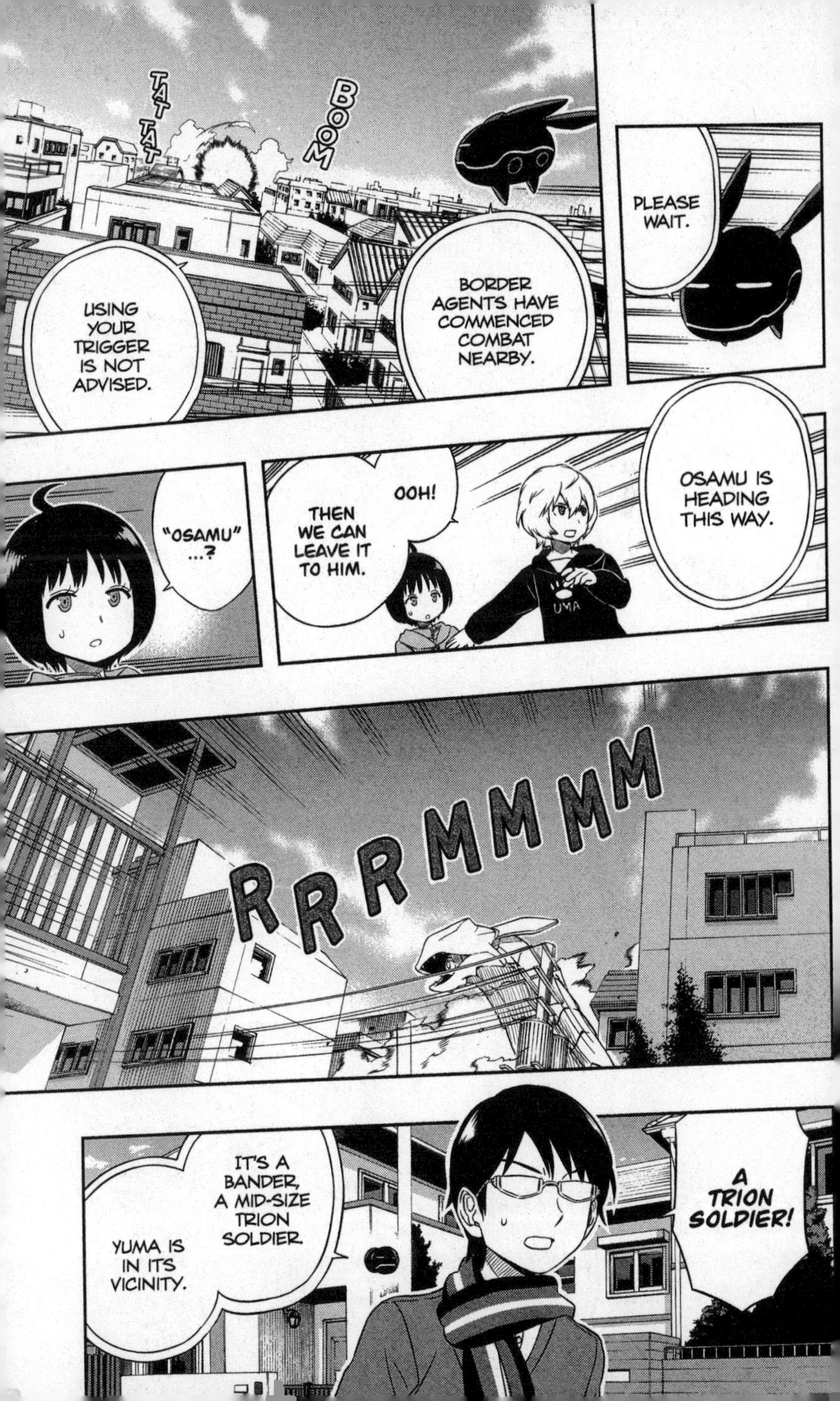
PLEASE WAIT.
BOOM
TAT TAT
BORDER AGENTS HAVE COMMENCED COMBAT NEARBY.
USING YOUR TRIGGER IS NOT ADVISED.
OSAMU IS HEADING THIS WAY.
OOH!
THEN WE CAN LEAVE IT TO HIM.
UMA
"OSAMU" ...?
RRRMMMMM
A TRION SOLDIER!
IT'S A BANDER, A MID-SIZE TRION SOLDIER.
YUMA IS IN ITS VICINITY.

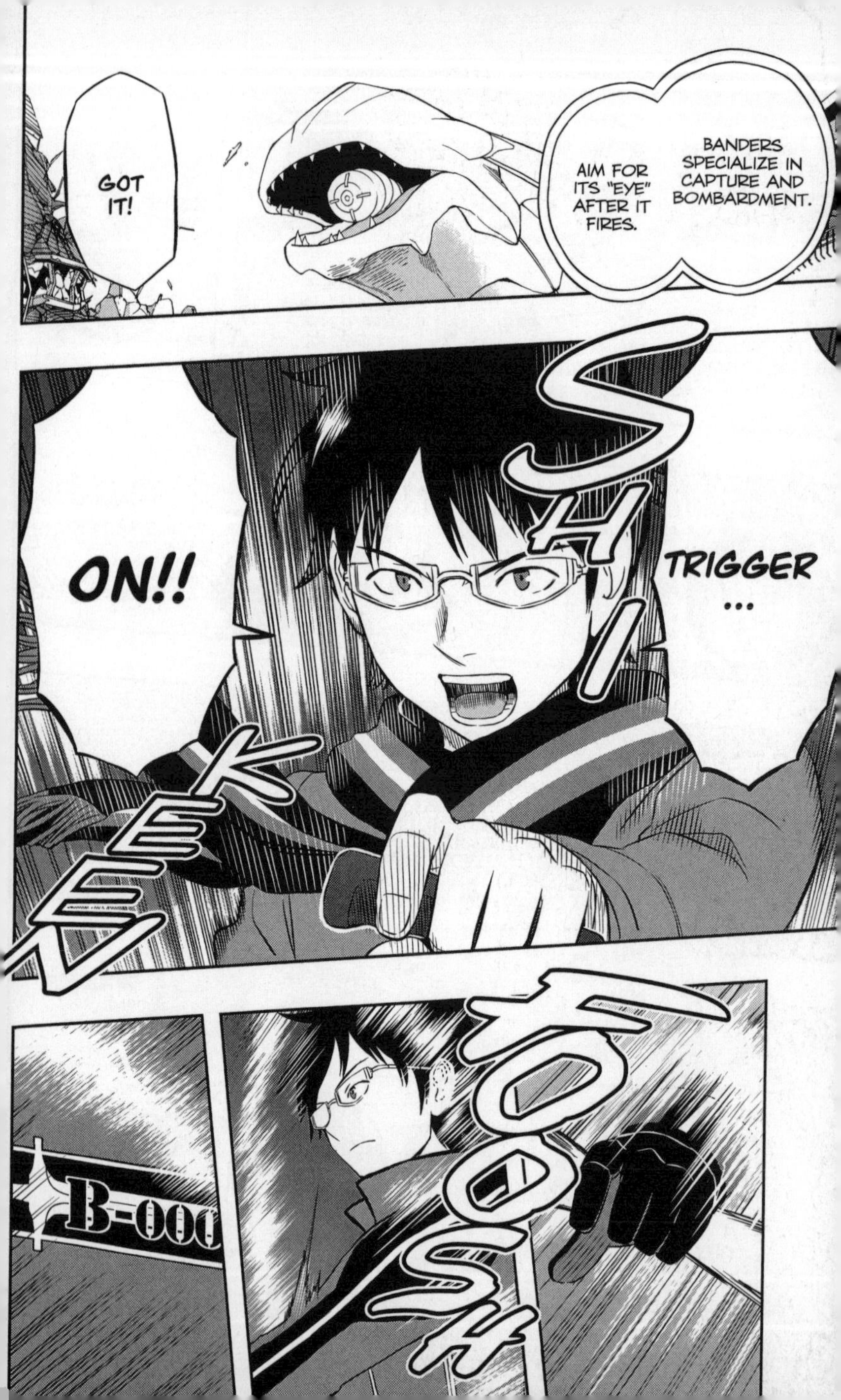

BANDERS SPECIALIZE IN CAPTURE AND BOMBARDMENT.
AIM FOR ITS "EYE" AFTER IT FIRES.
GOT IT!
SHI
TRIGGER ...
ON!!
KEEN
WOOOSH
B-000

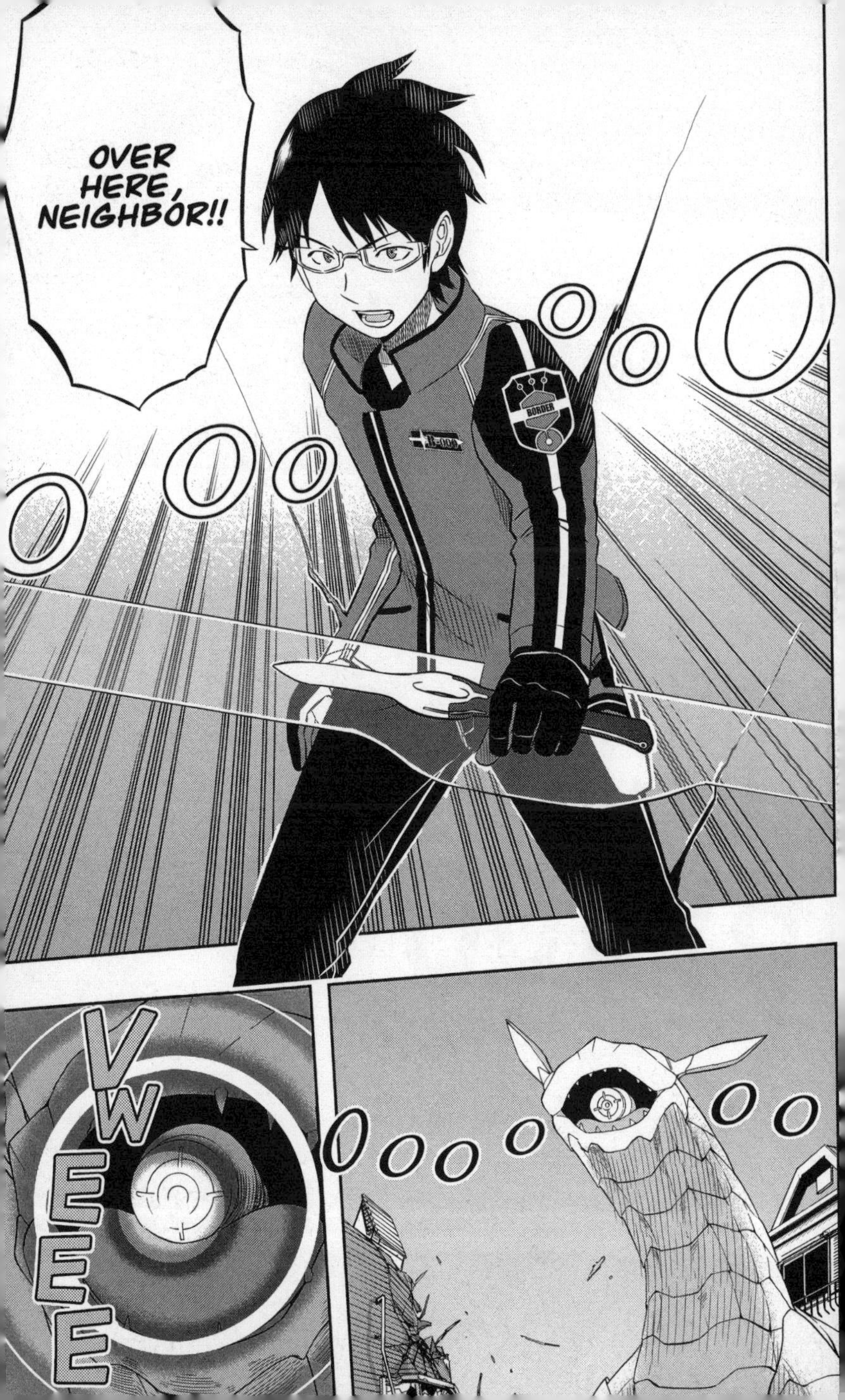
OVER HERE, NEIGHBOR!!
OOOOOOO
OOOOOOOO
VWEEEE

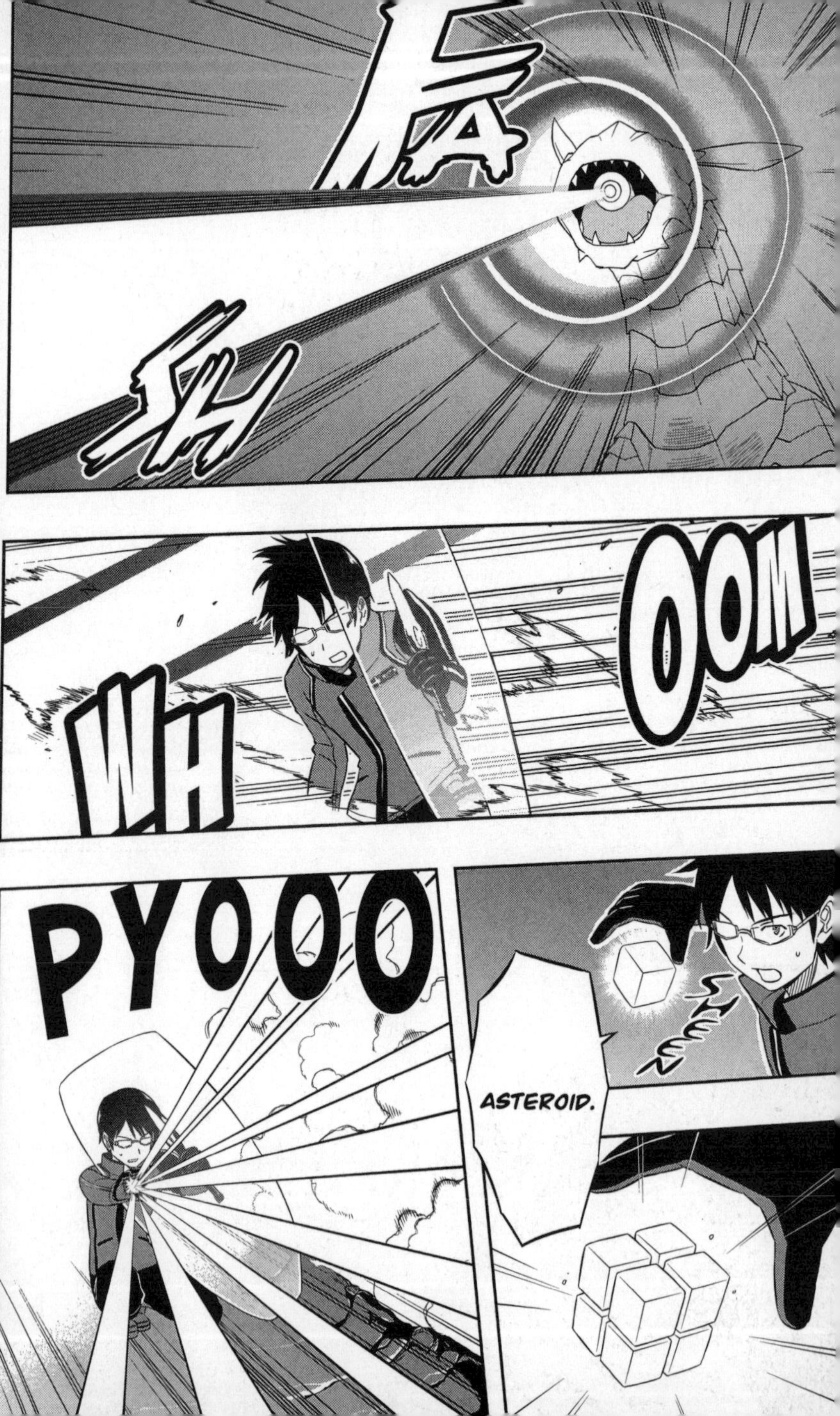
FA
SH
WH
OOM
SHWUN
ASTEROID.
PYOOO

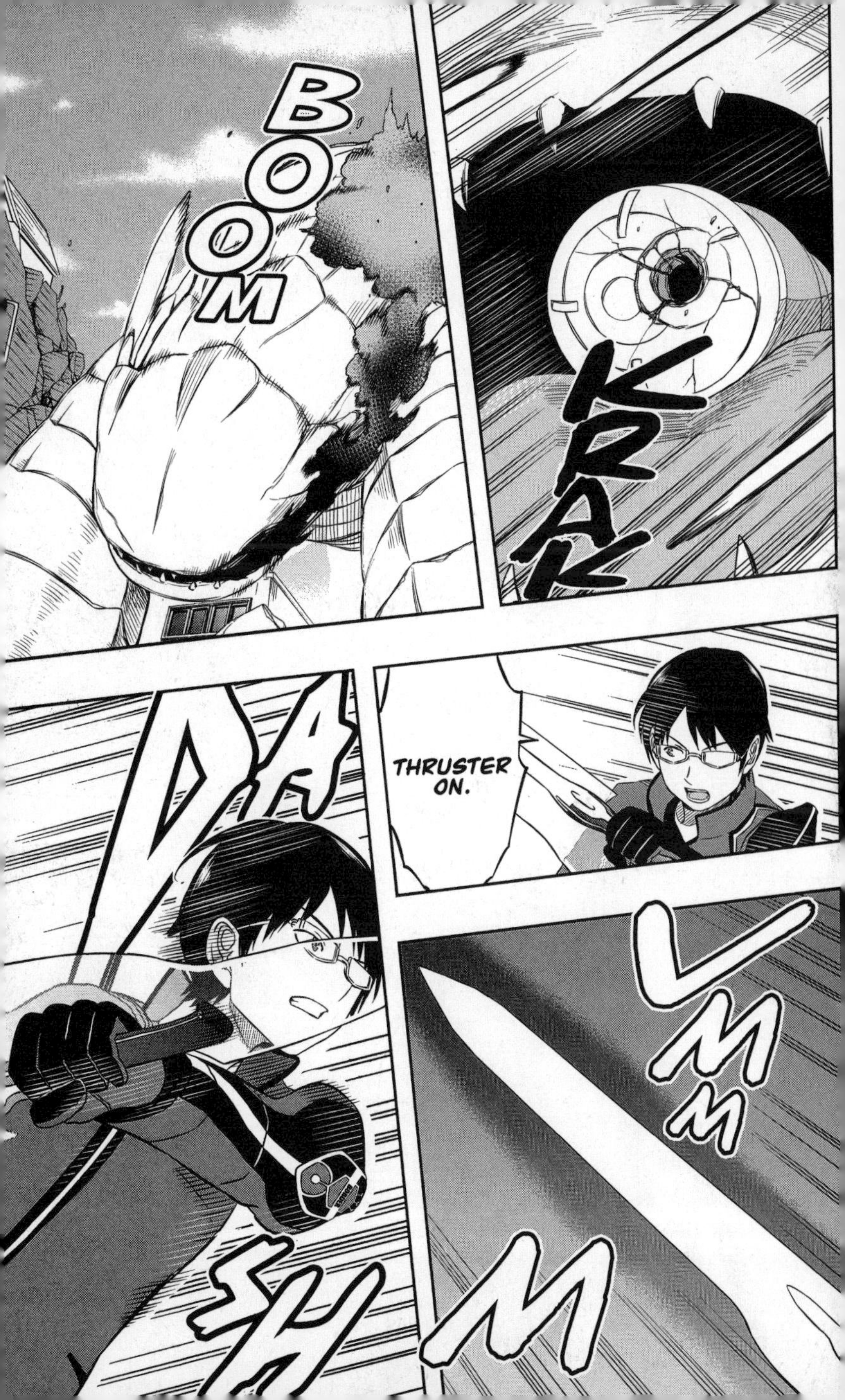
KRAK
BOOM
THRUSTER ON.
VMMM
DASH

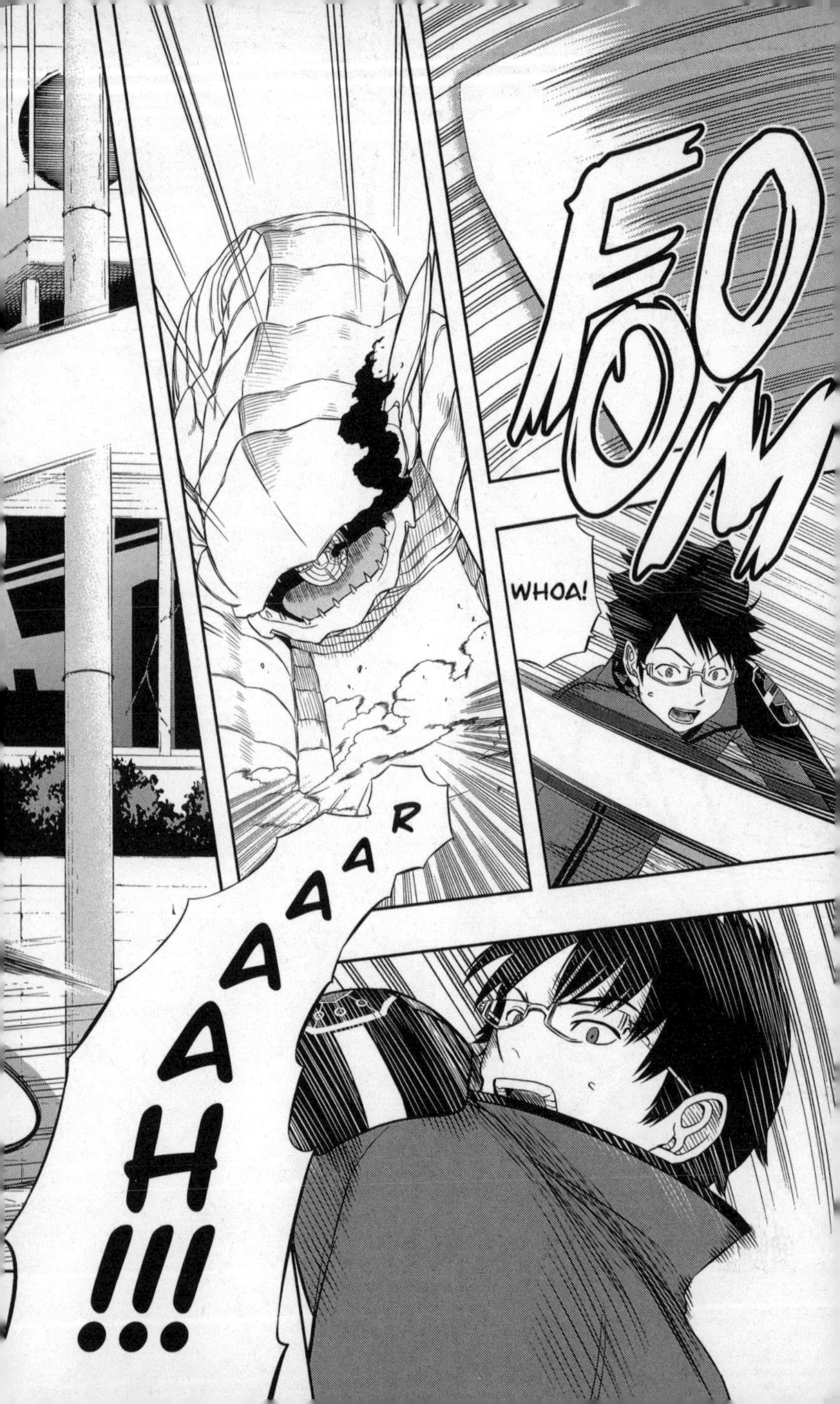
FOOM
WHOA!
AAAAAAR
AH!!!

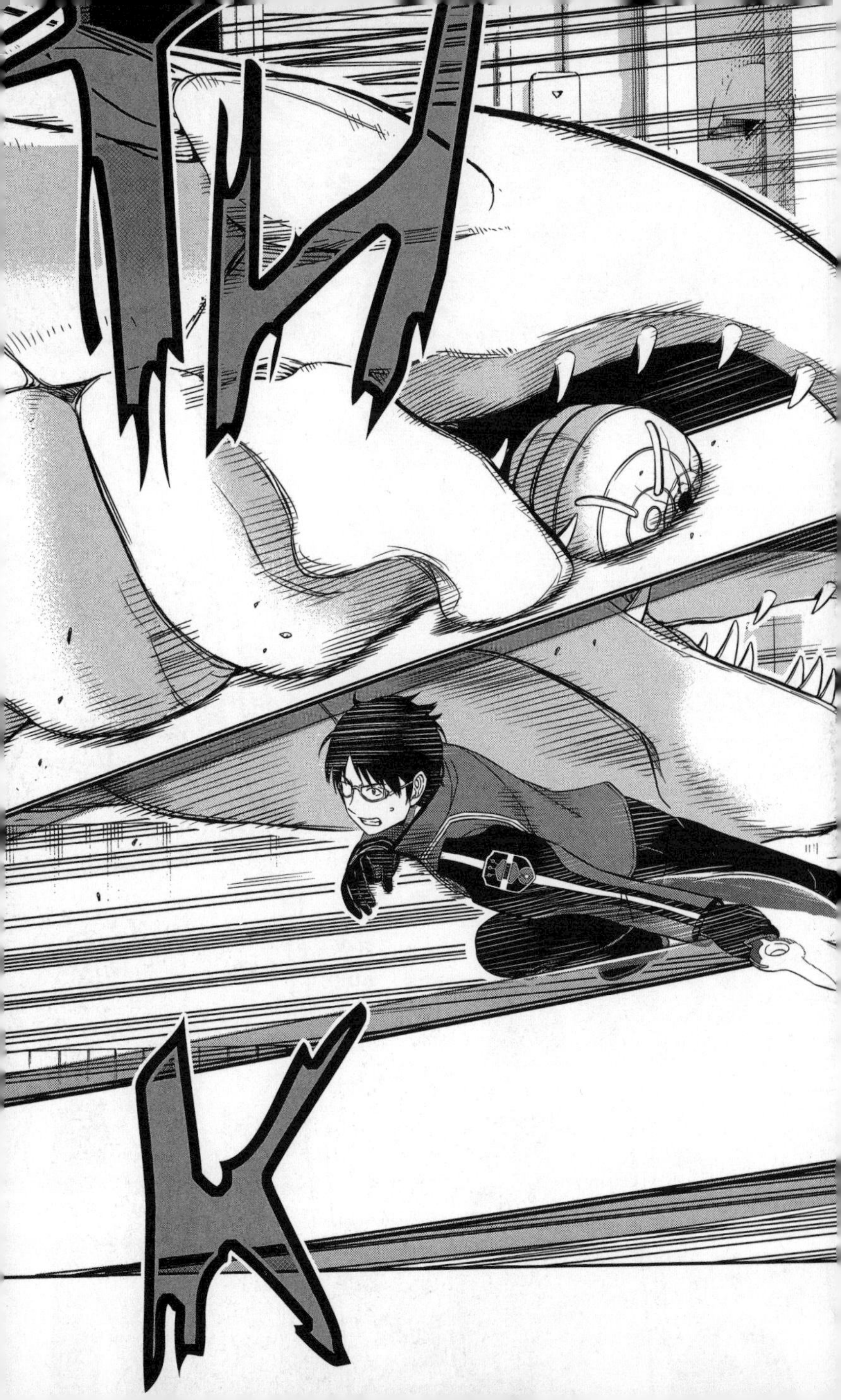

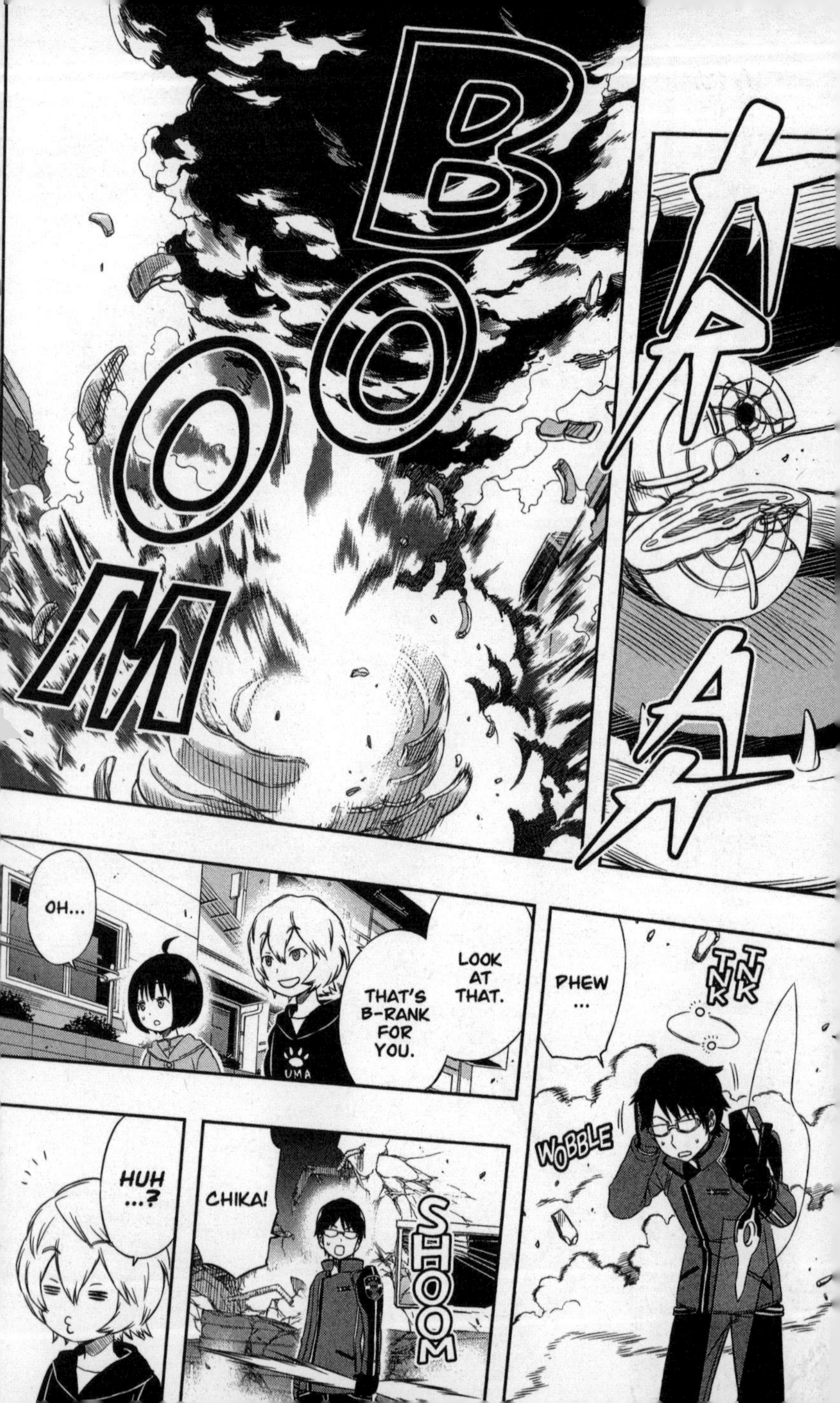
KRAK
BOOOM
PHEW...
TINK TINK
WOBBLE
LOOK AT THAT.
THAT'S B-RANK FOR YOU.
OH...
CHIKA!
SHOOM
HUH...?

READ THIS WAY

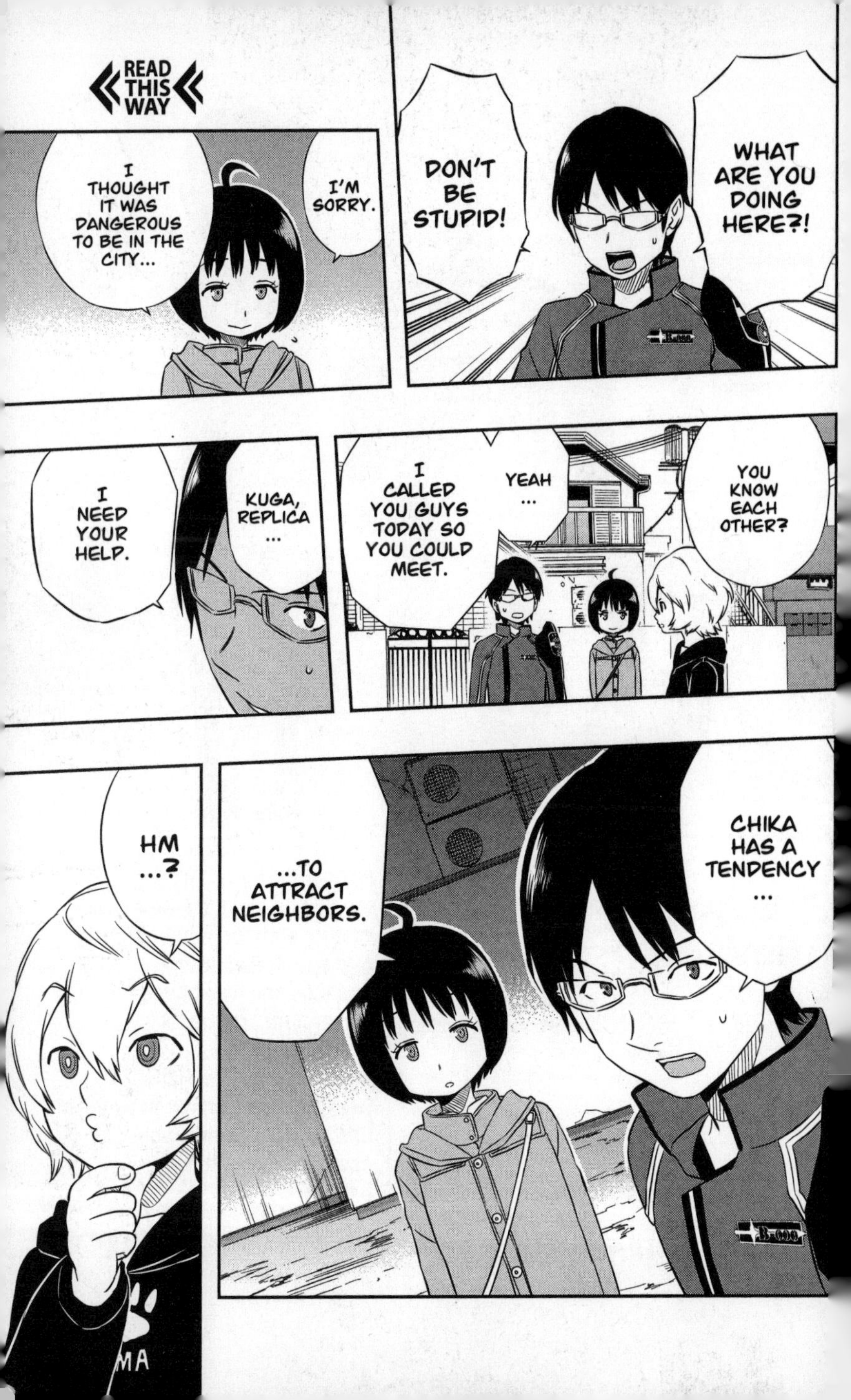
WHAT ARE YOU DOING HERE?!
DON'T BE STUPID!
I'M SORRY.
I THOUGHT IT WAS DANGEROUS TO BE IN THE CITY...
YOU KNOW EACH OTHER?
YEAH ...
I CALLED YOU GUYS TODAY SO YOU COULD MEET.
KUGA, REPLICA ...
I NEED YOUR HELP.
CHIKA HAS A TENDENCY ...
...TO ATTRACT NEIGHBORS.
HM ...?

■ Preliminary sketches (submitted for consideration to the serialization meeting)

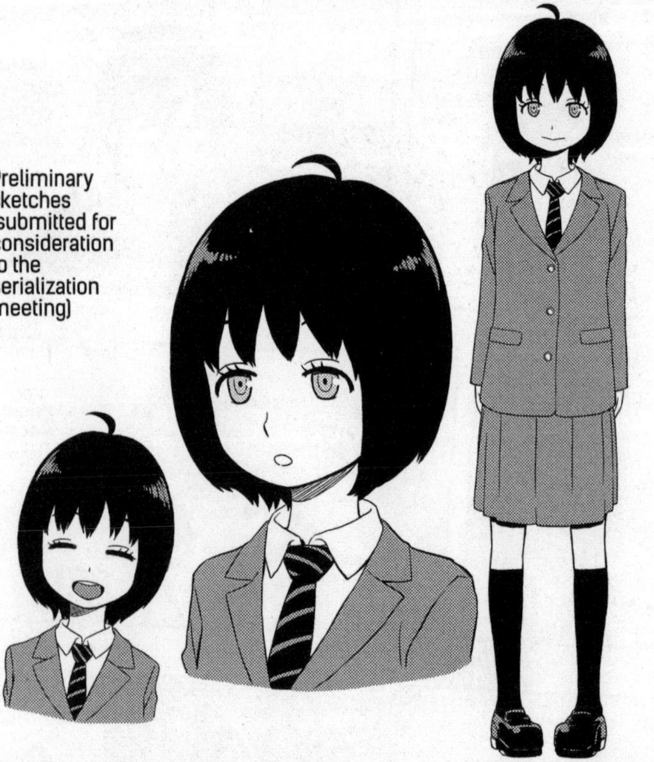

## Chika Amatori

- 13 years old (junior high student)
- Born February 21
- Amphibious, Blood type A
- Height: 4'7"
- Likes: Small animals, kids, white rice, working

Her antenna was still pretty small. She looks a little more mature than the actual Chika. And she looks slimmer because she was based on a character I made for a different one-shot manga who was poor and hard-working. Her name then was Chika Takatori. She's about as easy to draw as Yuma.

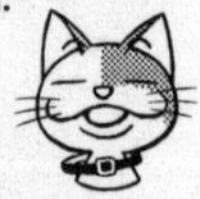

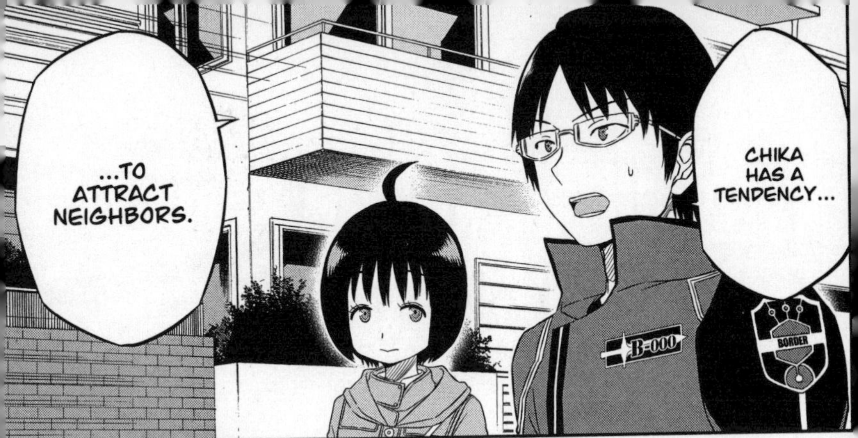
CHIKA HAS A TENDENCY...
...TO ATTRACT NEIGHBORS.
B-000
BORDER

## Chapter 13 Chika Amatori: Part 2

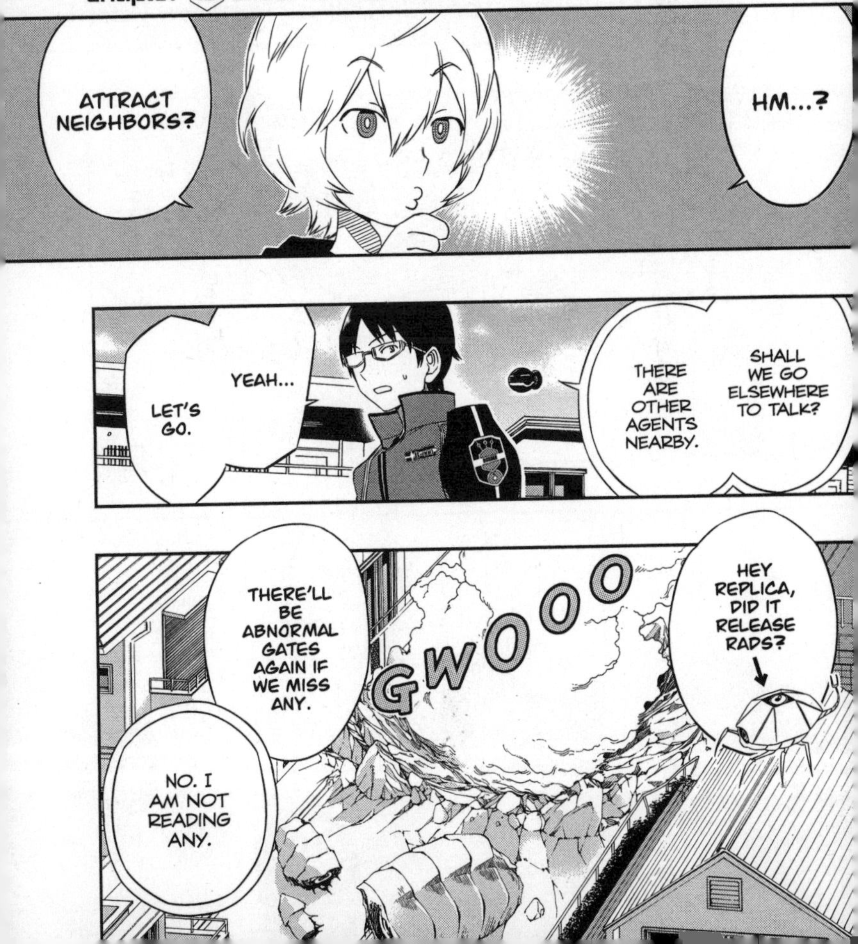
HM...?
ATTRACT NEIGHBORS?
SHALL WE GO ELSEWHERE TO TALK?
THERE ARE OTHER AGENTS NEARBY.
YEAH...
LET'S GO.
HEY REPLICA, DID IT RELEASE RADS?
GWOOOO
THERE'LL BE ABNORMAL GATES AGAIN IF WE MISS ANY.
NO. I AM NOT READING ANY.

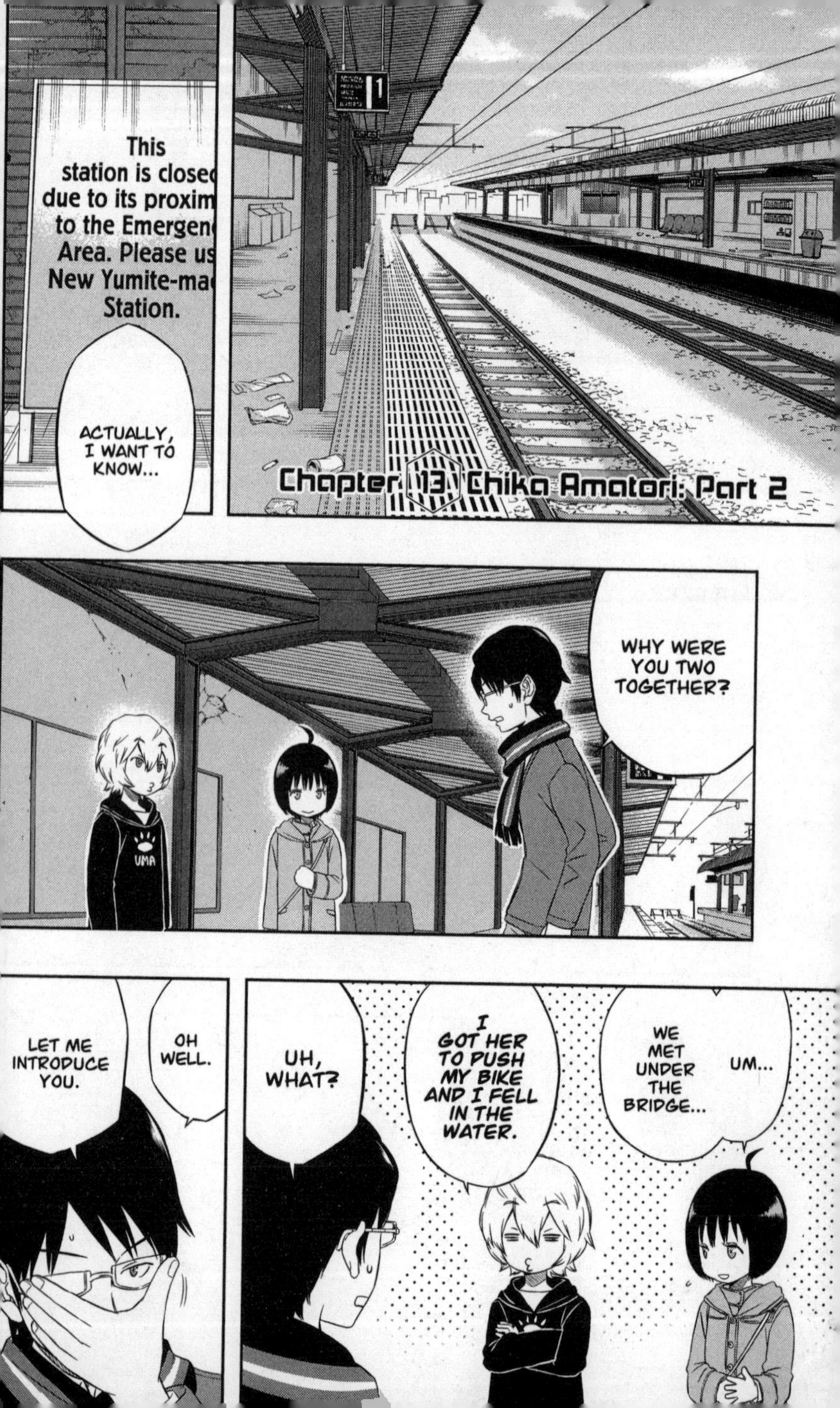
Chapter 13 Chika Amatori: Part 2
This
station is close
due to its proxim
to the Emergen
Area. Please us
New Yumite-ma
Station.
ACTUALLY, I WANT TO KNOW...
WHY WERE YOU TWO TOGETHER?
UM...
WE MET UNDER THE BRIDGE...
I GOT HER TO PUSH MY BIKE AND I FELL IN THE WATER.
UH, WHAT?
OH WELL.
LET ME INTRODUCE YOU.

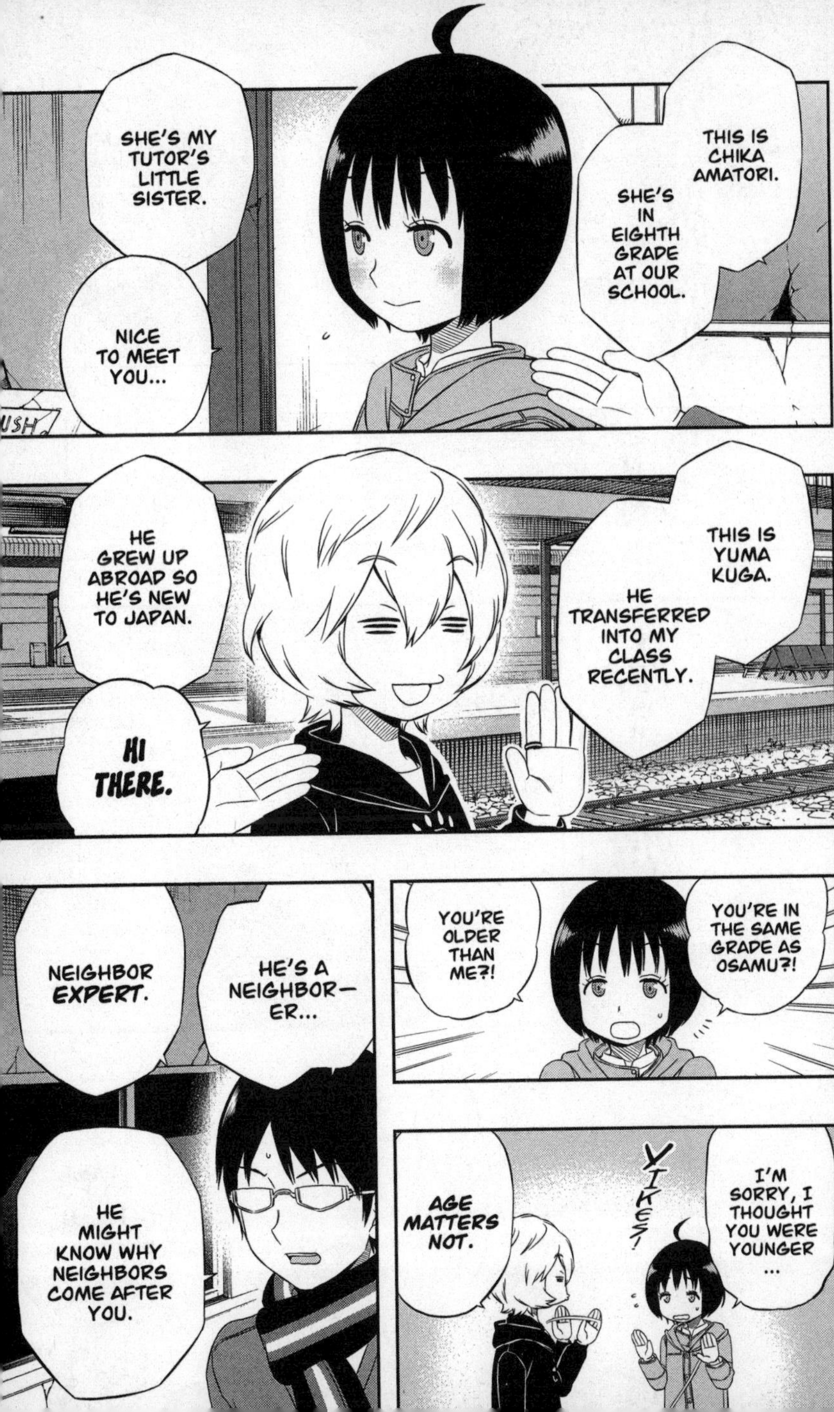
THIS IS CHIKA AMATORI.
SHE'S IN EIGHTH GRADE AT OUR SCHOOL.
SHE'S MY TUTOR'S LITTLE SISTER.
NICE TO MEET YOU...
THIS IS YUMA KUGA.
HE TRANSFERRED INTO MY CLASS RECENTLY.
HE GREW UP ABROAD SO HE'S NEW TO JAPAN.
HI THERE.
YOU'RE IN THE SAME GRADE AS OSAMU?!
YOU'RE OLDER THAN ME?!
I'M SORRY, I THOUGHT YOU WERE YOUNGER ...
YIKES!
AGE MATTERS NOT.
HE'S A NEIGHBOR-ER...
NEIGHBOR EXPERT.
HE MIGHT KNOW WHY NEIGHBORS COME AFTER YOU.

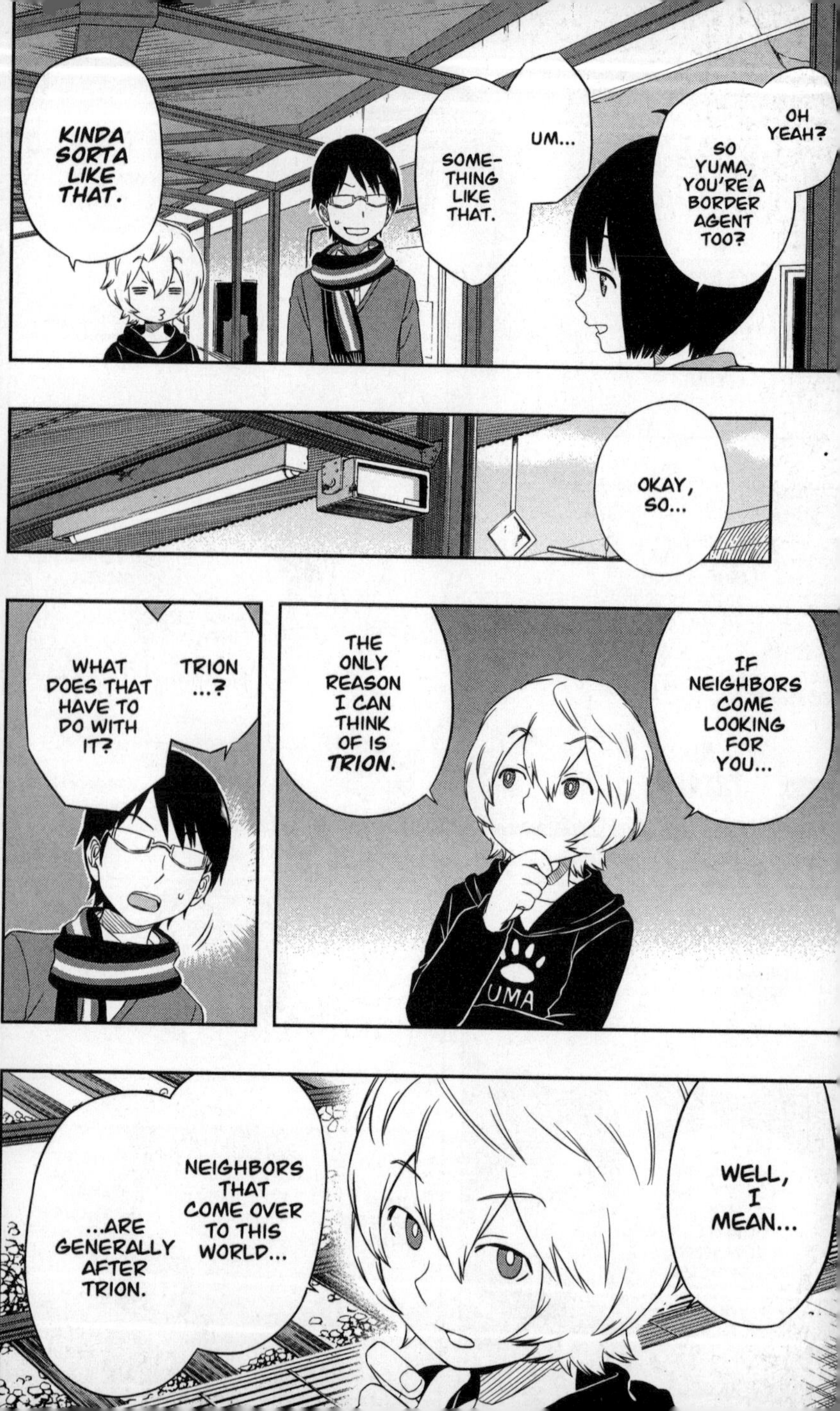
OH YEAH?
SO YUMA, YOU'RE A BORDER AGENT TOO?
UM...
SOMETHING LIKE THAT.
KINDA SORTA LIKE THAT.
OKAY, SO...
IF NEIGHBORS COME LOOKING FOR YOU...
THE ONLY REASON I CAN THINK OF IS TRION.
TRION ...?
WHAT DOES THAT HAVE TO DO WITH IT?
WELL, I MEAN...
NEIGHBORS THAT COME OVER TO THIS WORLD...
...ARE GENERALLY AFTER TRION.

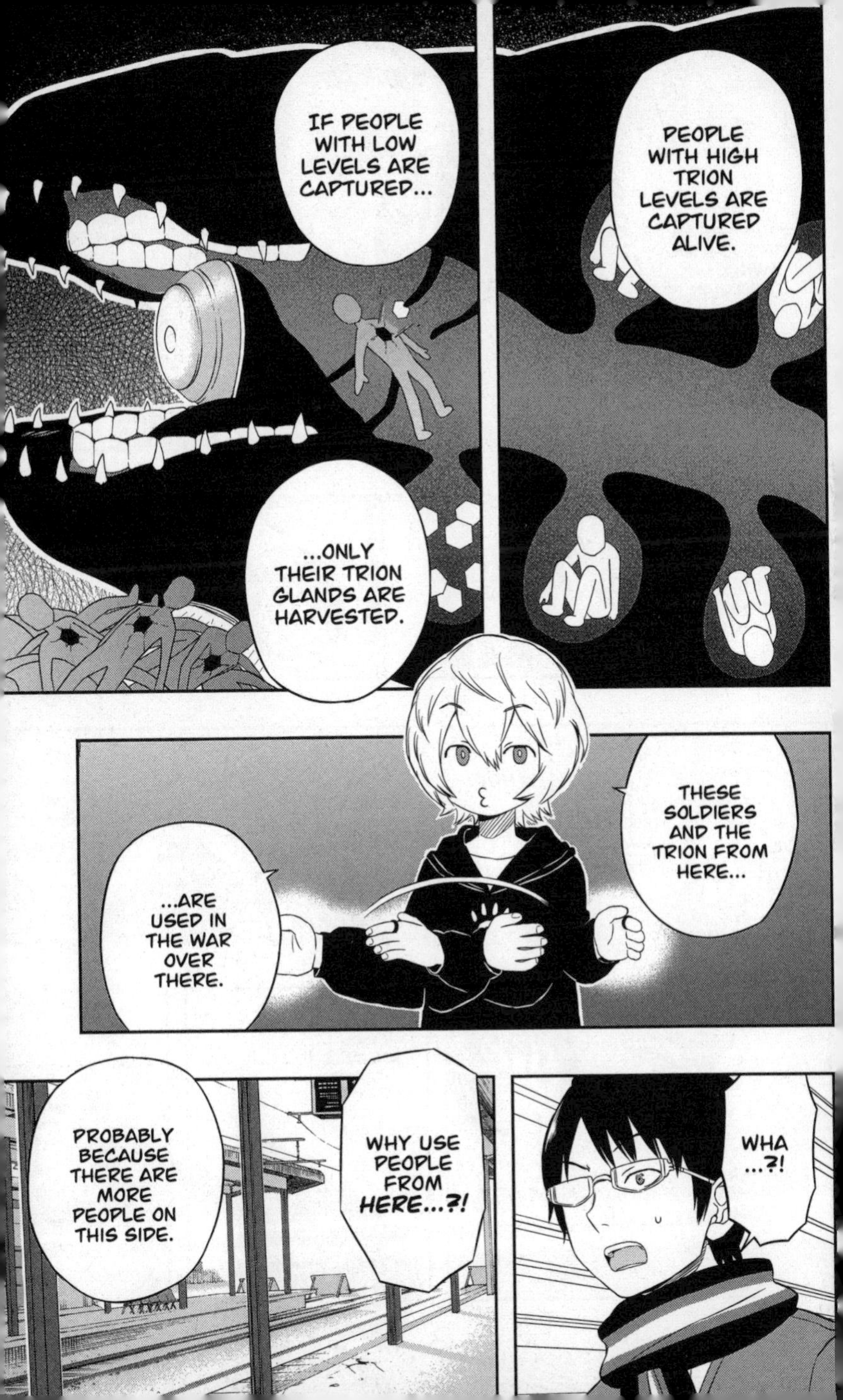
PEOPLE WITH HIGH TRION LEVELS ARE CAPTURED ALIVE.
IF PEOPLE WITH LOW LEVELS ARE CAPTURED...
...ONLY THEIR TRION GLANDS ARE HARVESTED.
THESE SOLDIERS AND THE TRION FROM HERE...
...ARE USED IN THE WAR OVER THERE.
WHA...?!
WHY USE PEOPLE FROM HERE...?!
PROBABLY BECAUSE THERE ARE MORE PEOPLE ON THIS SIDE.

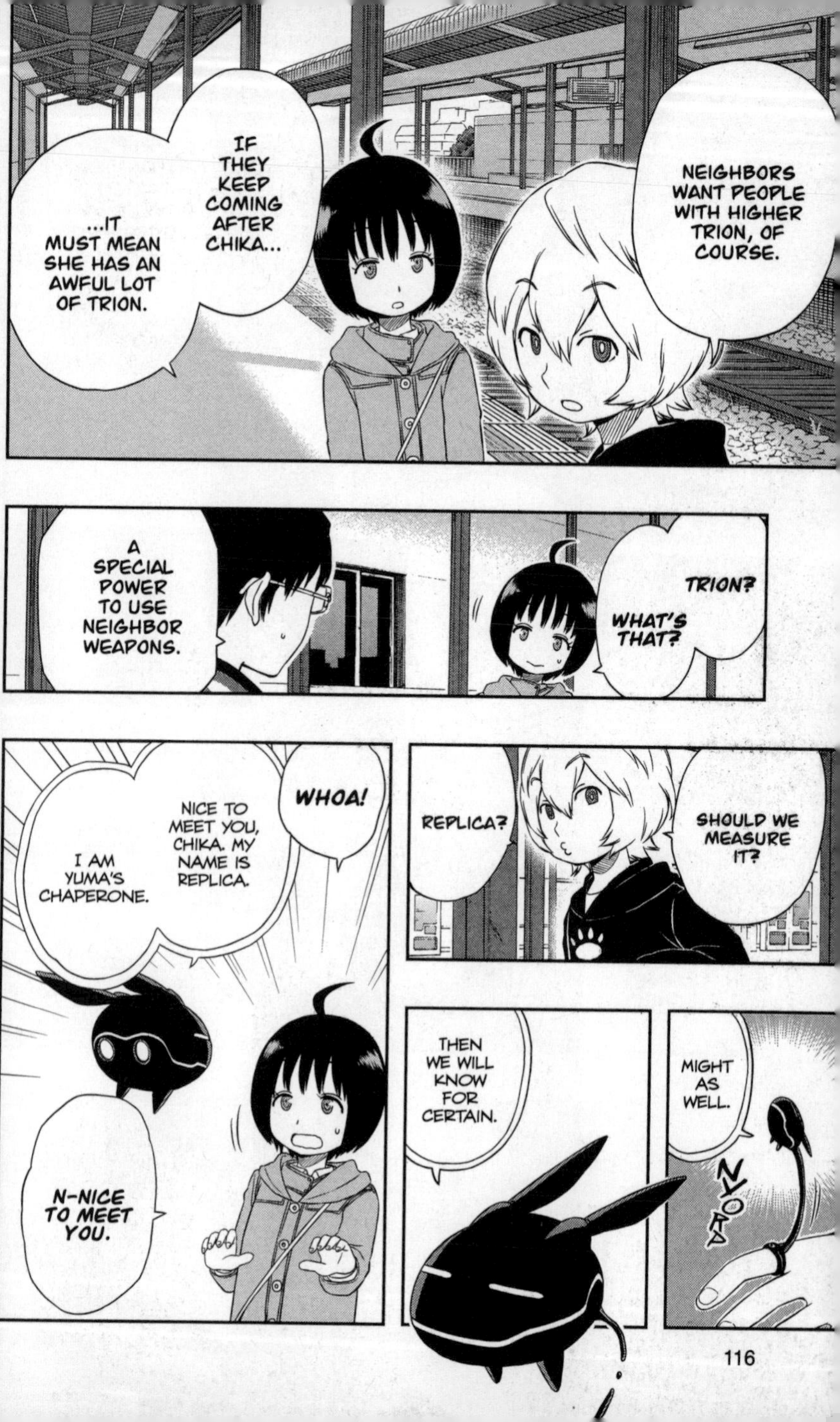

NEIGHBORS WANT PEOPLE WITH HIGHER TRION, OF COURSE.
IF THEY KEEP COMING AFTER CHIKA...
...IT MUST MEAN SHE HAS AN AWFUL LOT OF TRION.
TRION?
WHAT'S THAT?
A SPECIAL POWER TO USE NEIGHBOR WEAPONS.
SHOULD WE MEASURE IT?
REPLICA?
MIGHT AS WELL.
NYORA
THEN WE WILL KNOW FOR CERTAIN.
WHOA!
NICE TO MEET YOU, CHIKA. MY NAME IS REPLICA.
I AM YUMA'S CHAPERONE.
N-NICE TO MEET YOU.

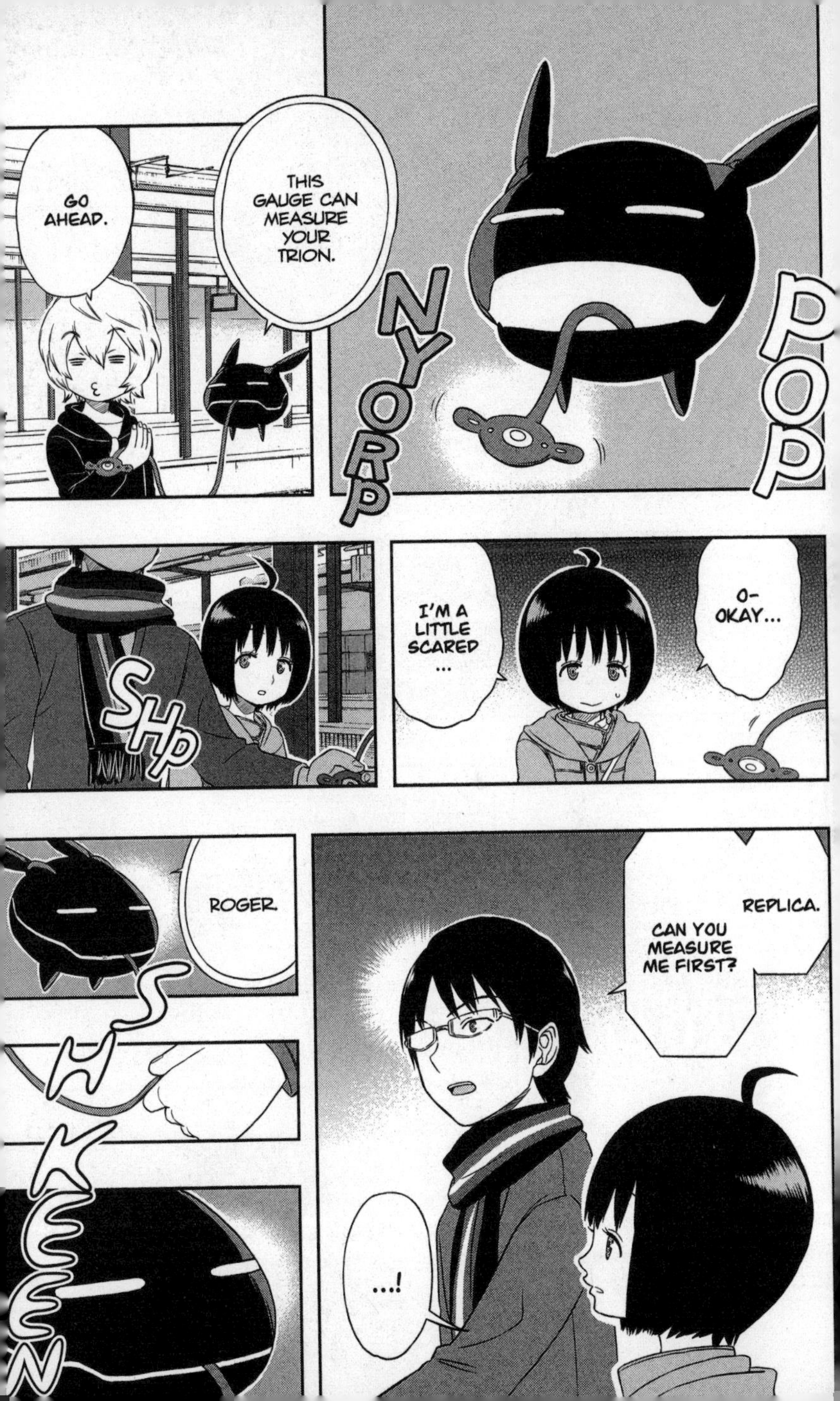
POP
NYORP
THIS GAUGE CAN MEASURE YOUR TRION.
GO AHEAD.
O-OKAY...
I'M A LITTLE SCARED...
SHP
REPLICA.
CAN YOU MEASURE ME FIRST?
...!
ROGER.
SHKEEEN

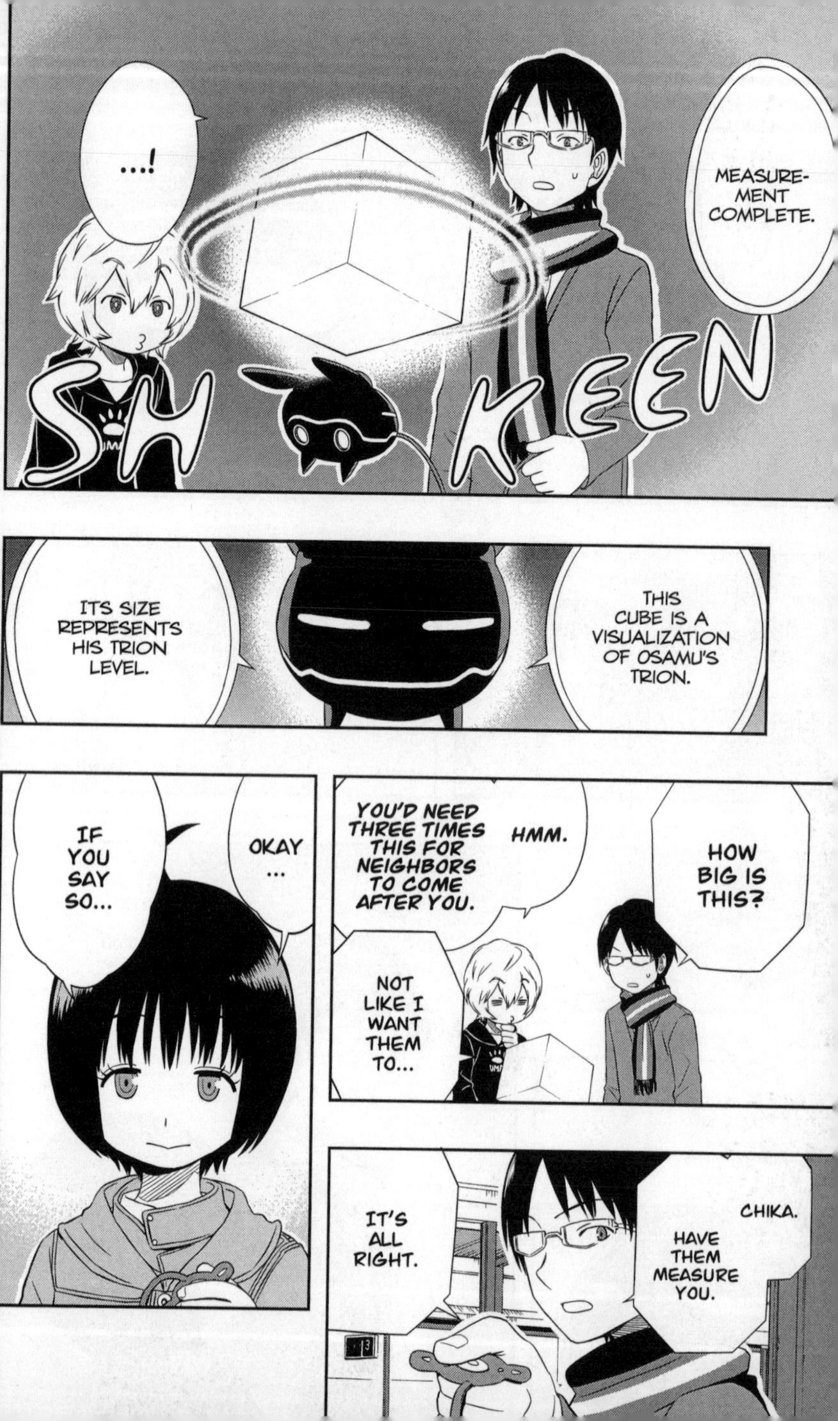
MEASURE-MENT COMPLETE.
...!
SHKEEN
THIS CUBE IS A VISUALIZATION OF OSAMU'S TRION.
ITS SIZE REPRESENTS HIS TRION LEVEL.
HOW BIG IS THIS?
HMM.
YOU'D NEED THREE TIMES THIS FOR NEIGHBORS TO COME AFTER YOU.
NOT LIKE I WANT THEM TO...
CHIKA.
HAVE THEM MEASURE YOU.
IT'S ALL RIGHT.
OKAY...
IF YOU SAY SO...

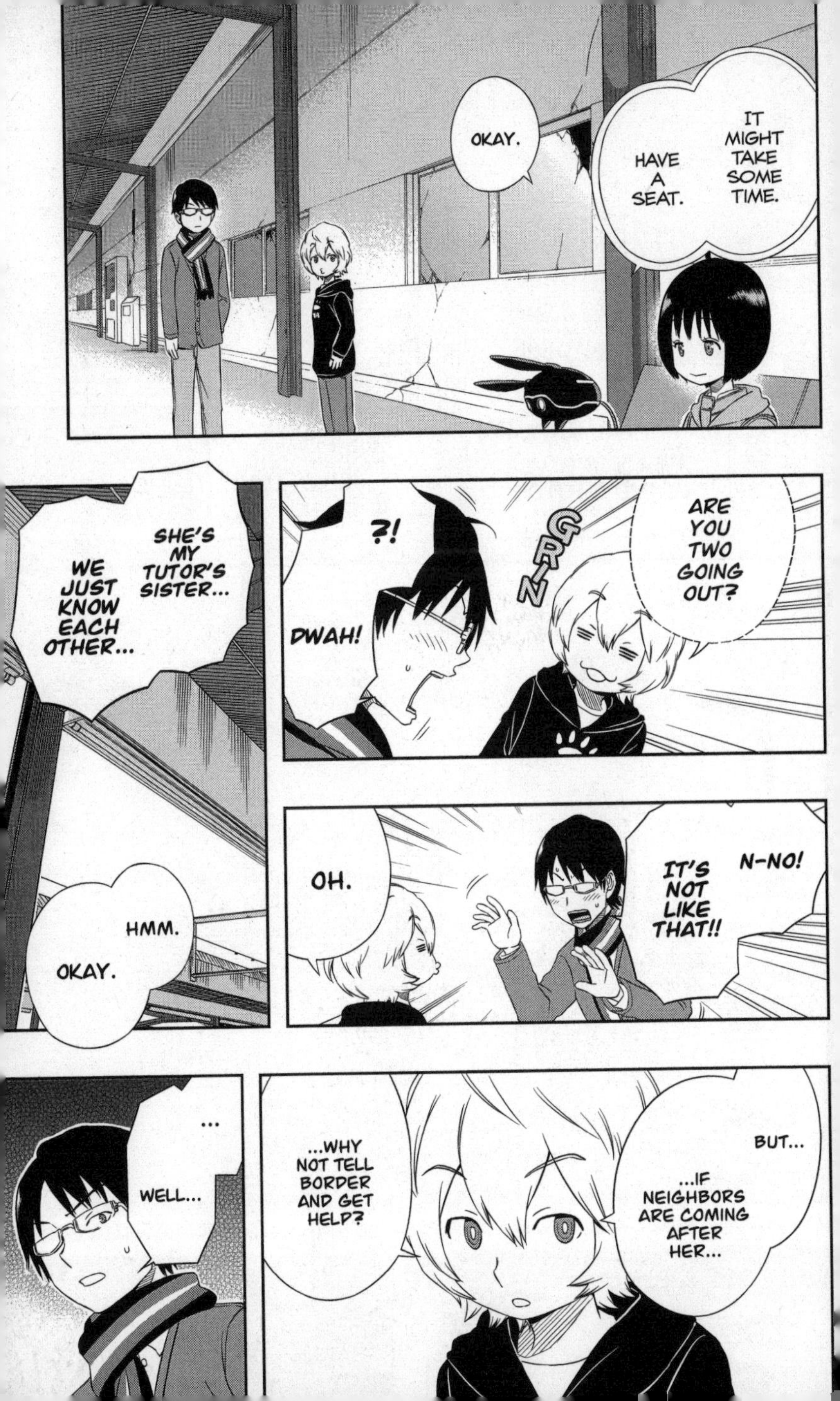
IT MIGHT TAKE SOME TIME.
HAVE A SEAT.
OKAY.
ARE YOU TWO GOING OUT?
GRIN
?!
DWAH!
N-NO!
IT'S NOT LIKE THAT!!
OH.
SHE'S MY TUTOR'S SISTER...
WE JUST KNOW EACH OTHER...
HMM.
OKAY.
BUT...
...IF NEIGHBORS ARE COMING AFTER HER...
...WHY NOT TELL BORDER AND GET HELP?
...
WELL...

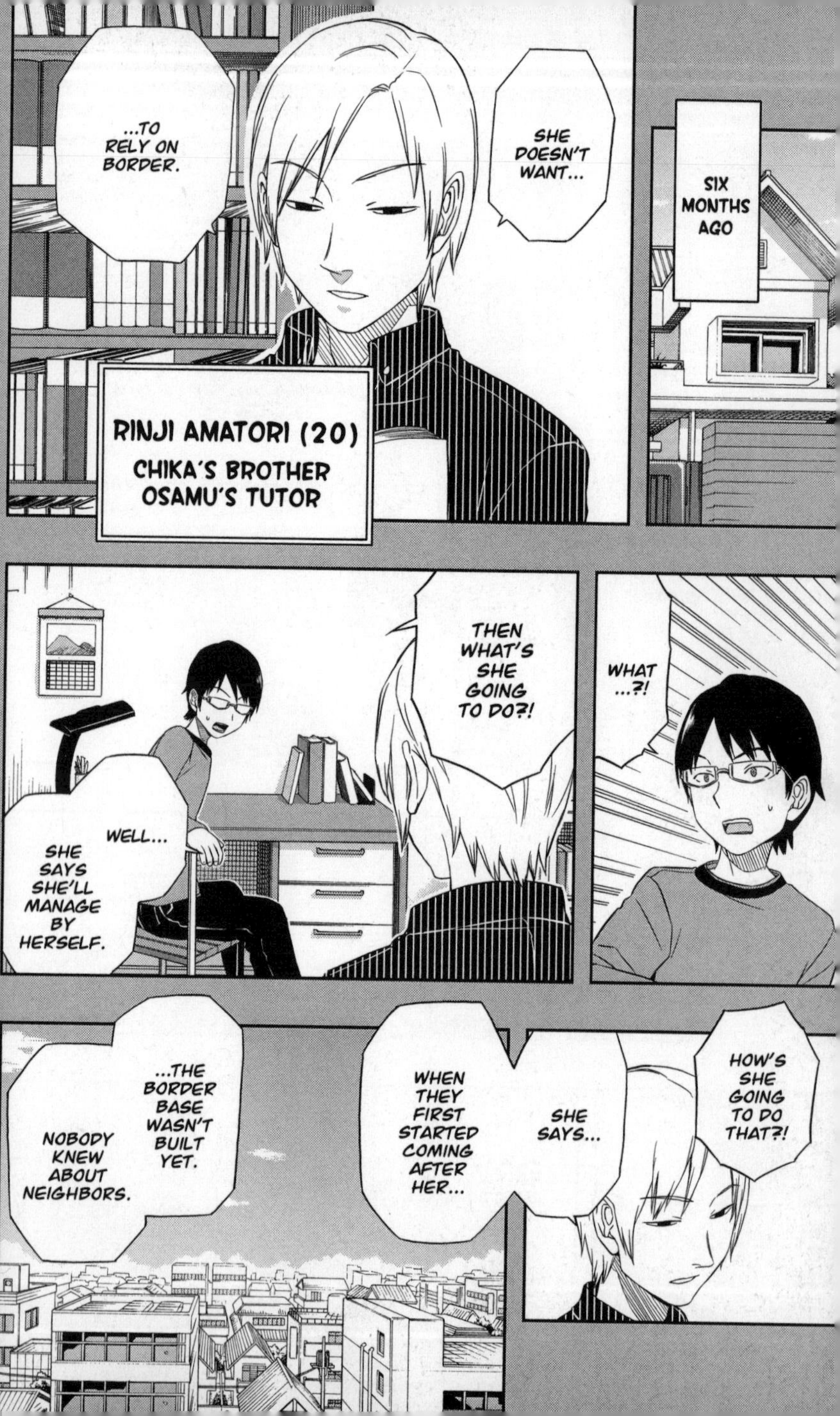
SIX MONTHS AGO
SHE DOESN'T WANT...
...TO RELY ON BORDER.
RINJI AMATORI (20)
CHIKA'S BROTHER
OSAMU'S TUTOR
WHAT ...?!
THEN WHAT'S SHE GOING TO DO?!
WELL...
SHE SAYS SHE'LL MANAGE BY HERSELF.
HOW'S SHE GOING TO DO THAT?!
SHE SAYS...
WHEN THEY FIRST STARTED COMING AFTER HER...
...THE BORDER BASE WASN'T BUILT YET.
NOBODY KNEW ABOUT NEIGHBORS.

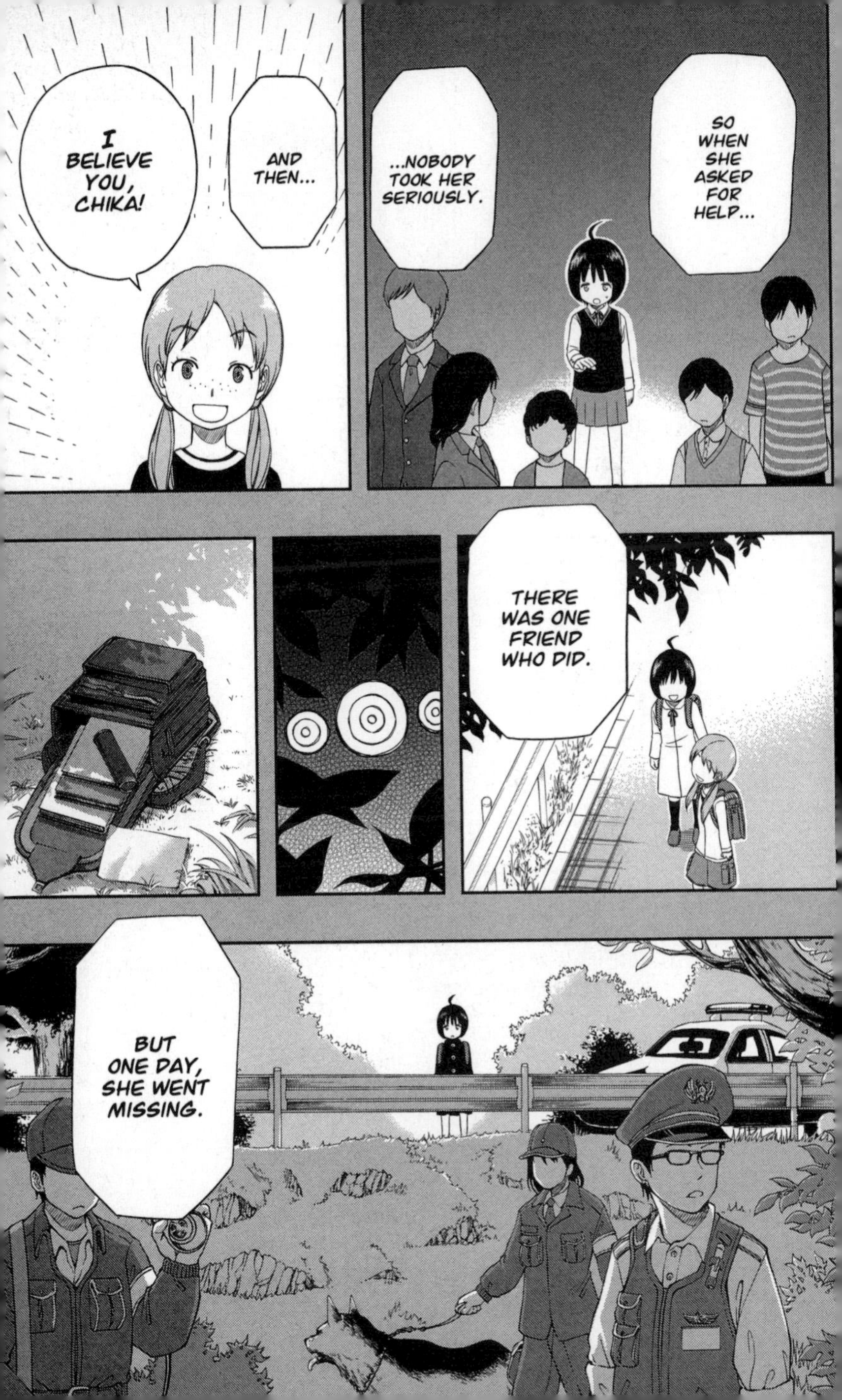
SO WHEN SHE ASKED FOR HELP...
...NOBODY TOOK HER SERIOUSLY.
AND THEN...
I BELIEVE YOU, CHIKA!
THERE WAS ONE FRIEND WHO DID.
BUT ONE DAY, SHE WENT MISSING.

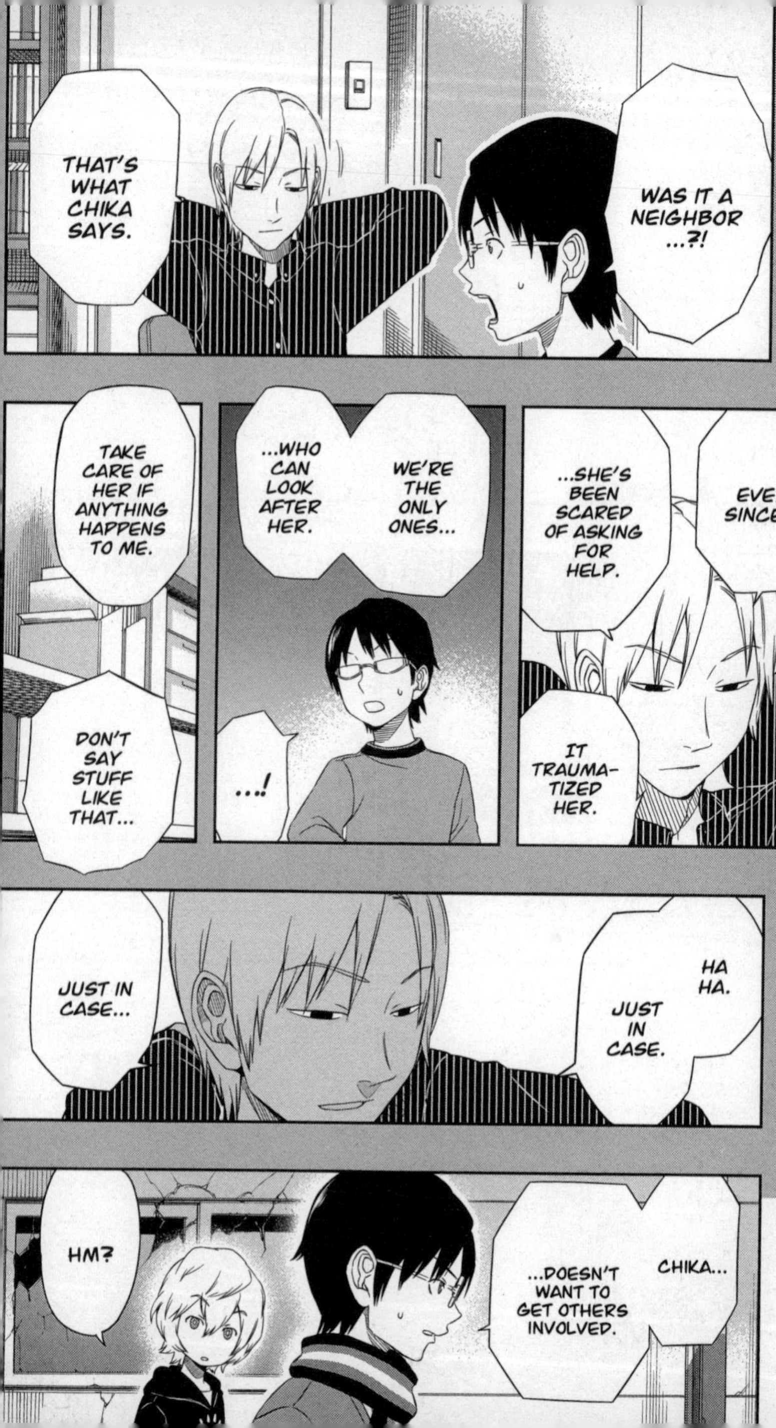
WAS IT A NEIGHBOR ...?!
THAT'S WHAT CHIKA SAYS.
EVER SINCE...
...SHE'S BEEN SCARED OF ASKING FOR HELP.
IT TRAUMA-TIZED HER.
WE'RE THE ONLY ONES...
...WHO CAN LOOK AFTER HER.
...!
TAKE CARE OF HER IF ANYTHING HAPPENS TO ME.
DON'T SAY STUFF LIKE THAT...
HA HA.
JUST IN CASE.
JUST IN CASE...
CHIKA...
...DOESN'T WANT TO GET OTHERS INVOLVED.
HM?

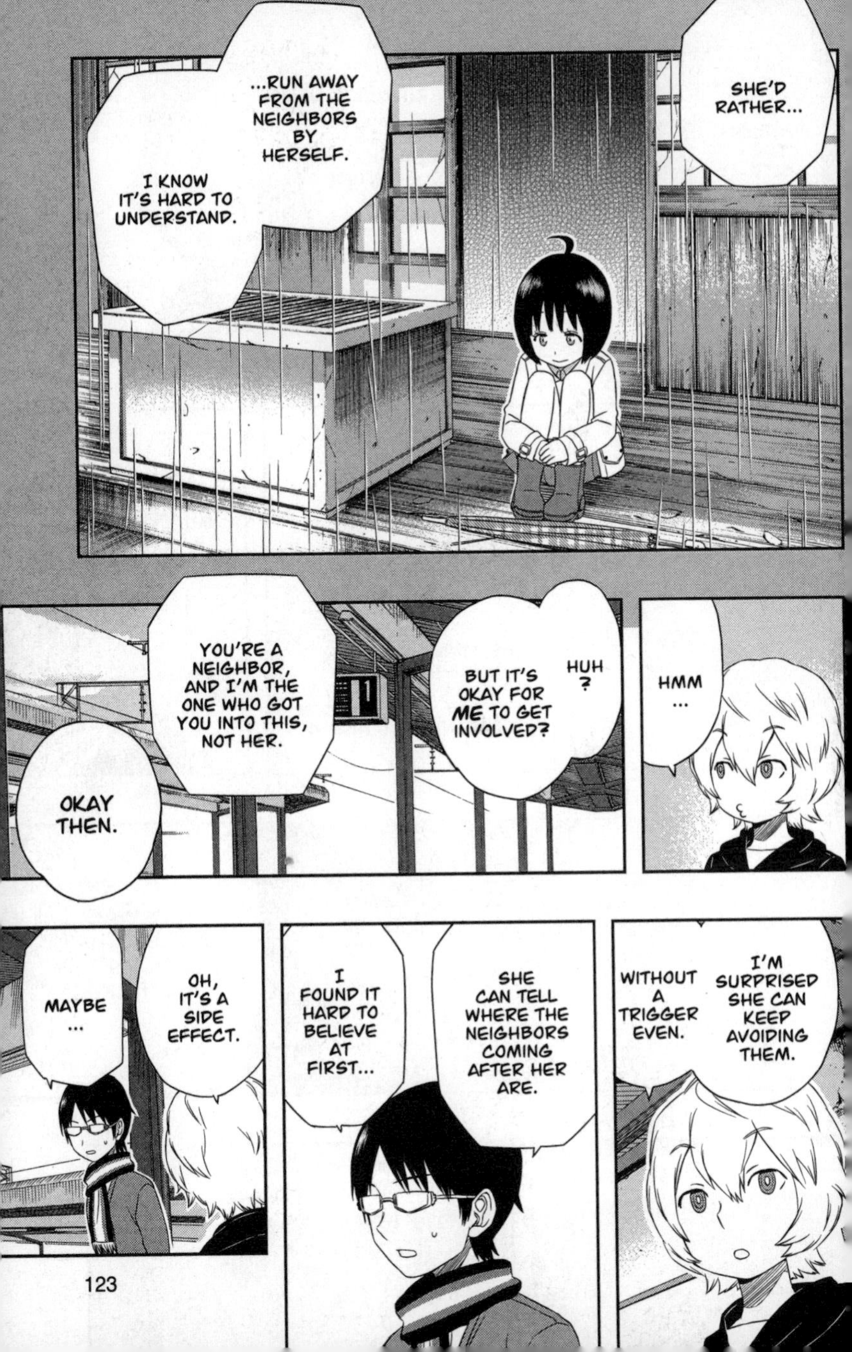
SHE'D RATHER...
...RUN AWAY FROM THE NEIGHBORS BY HERSELF.
I KNOW IT'S HARD TO UNDERSTAND.
HMM ...
HUH?
BUT IT'S OKAY FOR ME TO GET INVOLVED?
YOU'RE A NEIGHBOR, AND I'M THE ONE WHO GOT YOU INTO THIS, NOT HER.
OKAY THEN.
I'M SURPRISED SHE CAN KEEP AVOIDING THEM.
WITHOUT A TRIGGER EVEN.
SHE CAN TELL WHERE THE NEIGHBORS COMING AFTER HER ARE.
I FOUND IT HARD TO BELIEVE AT FIRST...
OH, IT'S A SIDE EFFECT.
MAYBE ...

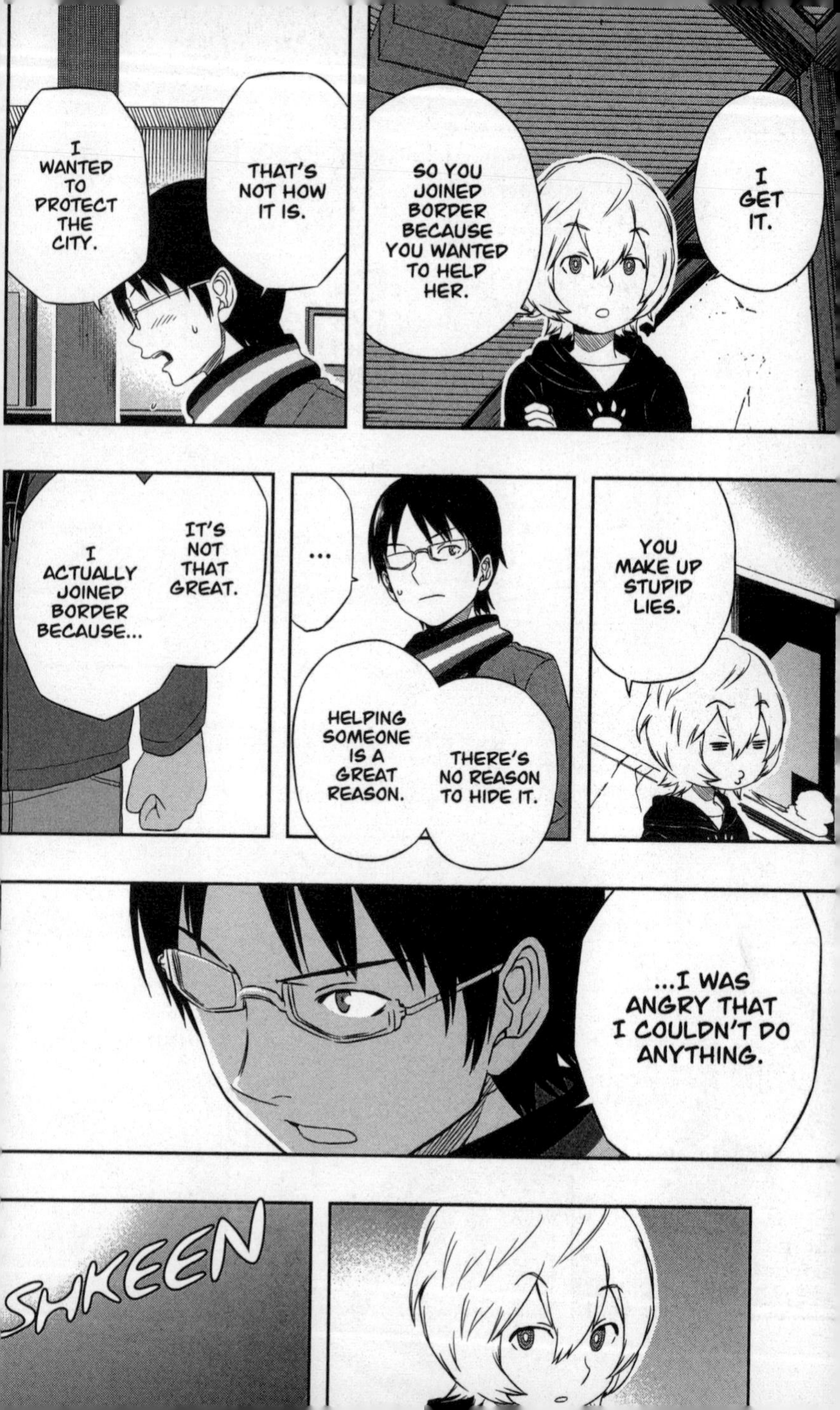
I GET IT.
SO YOU JOINED BORDER BECAUSE YOU WANTED TO HELP HER.
THAT'S NOT HOW IT IS.
I WANTED TO PROTECT THE CITY.
YOU MAKE UP STUPID LIES.
...
THERE'S NO REASON TO HIDE IT.
HELPING SOMEONE IS A GREAT REASON.
IT'S NOT THAT GREAT.
I ACTUALLY JOINED BORDER BECAUSE...
...I WAS ANGRY THAT I COULDN'T DO ANYTHING.
SHKEEN

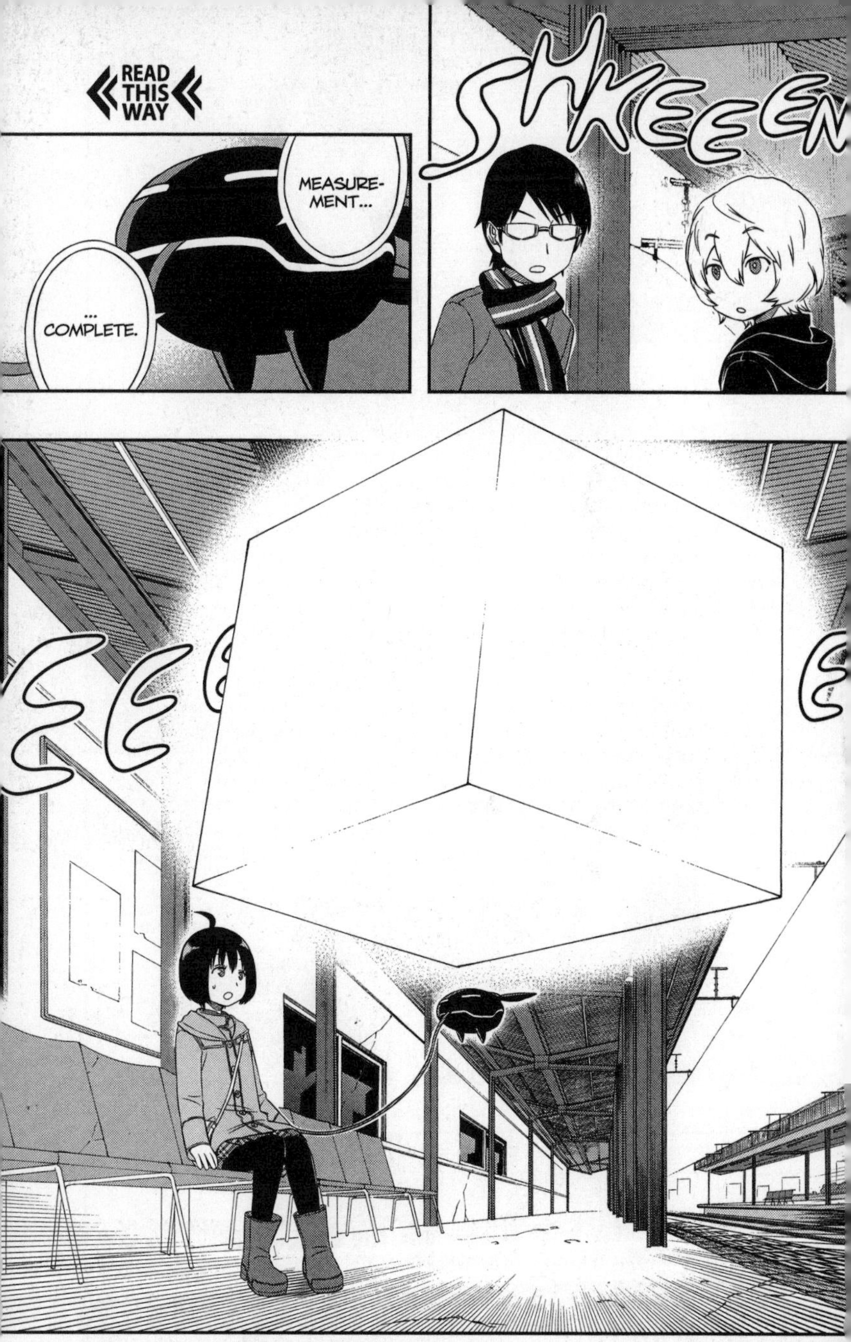
READ THIS WAY
SHKEEEN
MEASUREMENT...
...COMPLETE.

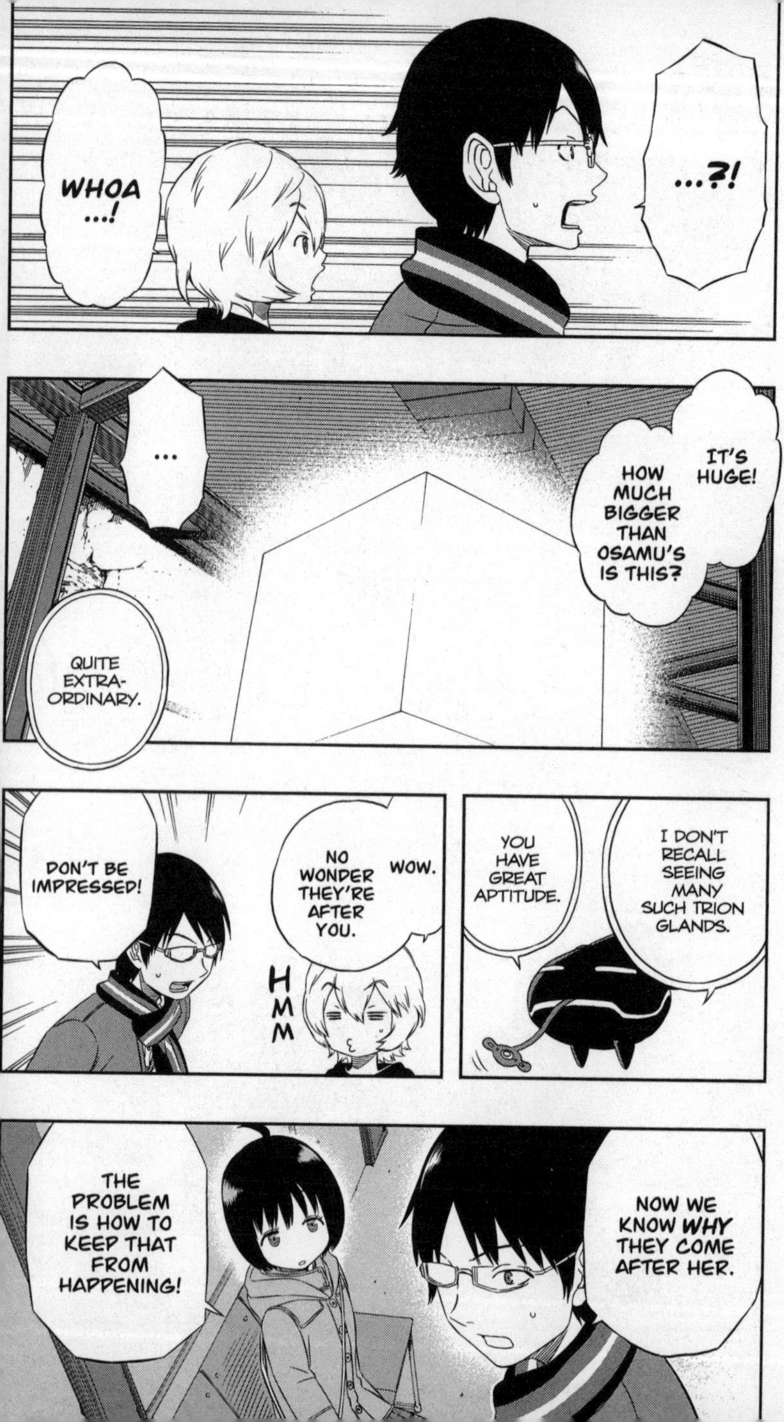
...?!
WHOA ...!
IT'S HUGE!
HOW MUCH BIGGER THAN OSAMU'S IS THIS?
...
QUITE EXTRA-ORDINARY.
I DON'T RECALL SEEING MANY SUCH TRION GLANDS.
YOU HAVE GREAT APTITUDE.
WOW.
NO WONDER THEY'RE AFTER YOU.
HMM
DON'T BE IMPRESSED!
NOW WE KNOW **WHY** THEY COME AFTER HER.
THE PROBLEM IS HOW TO KEEP THAT FROM HAPPENING!

READ THIS WAY

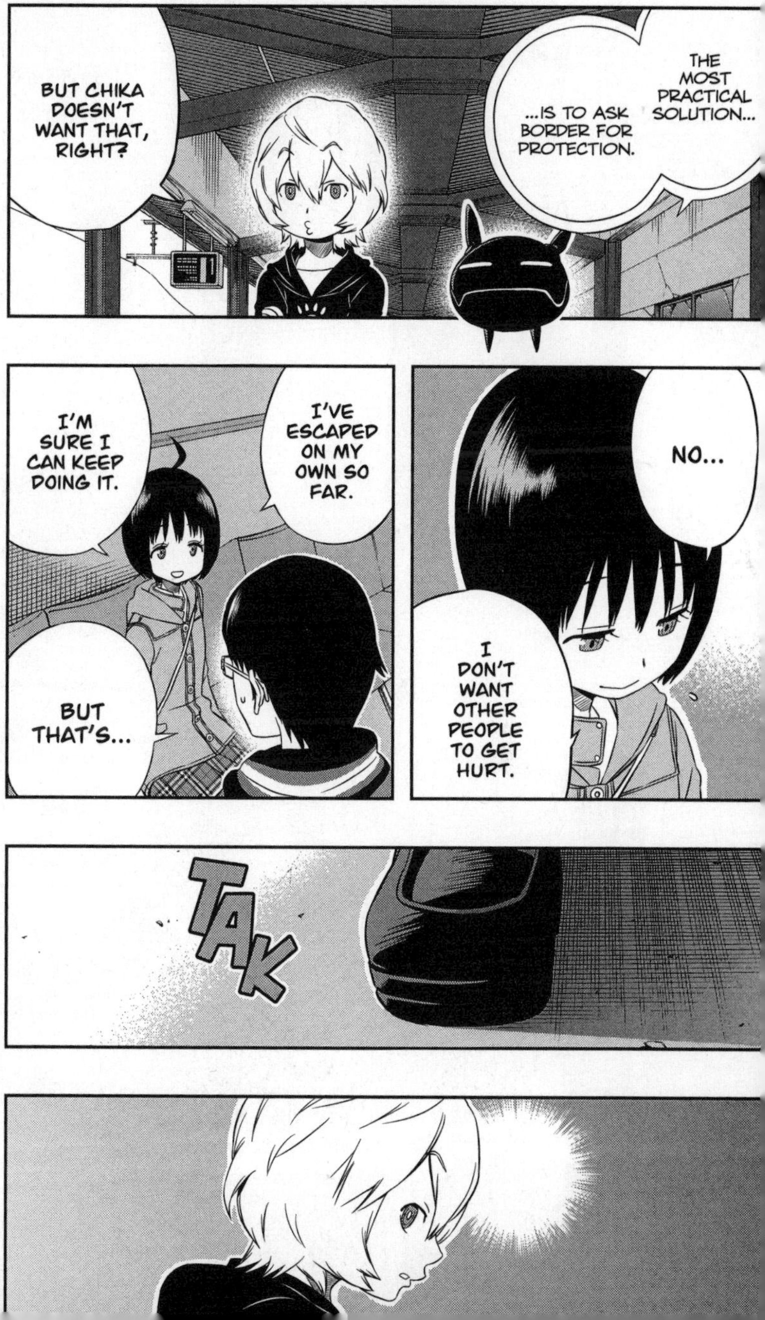
THE MOST PRACTICAL SOLUTION...
...IS TO ASK BORDER FOR PROTECTION.
BUT CHIKA DOESN'T WANT THAT, RIGHT?
NO...
I DON'T WANT OTHER PEOPLE TO GET HURT.
I'VE ESCAPED ON MY OWN SO FAR.
I'M SURE I CAN KEEP DOING IT.
BUT THAT'S...
TAK

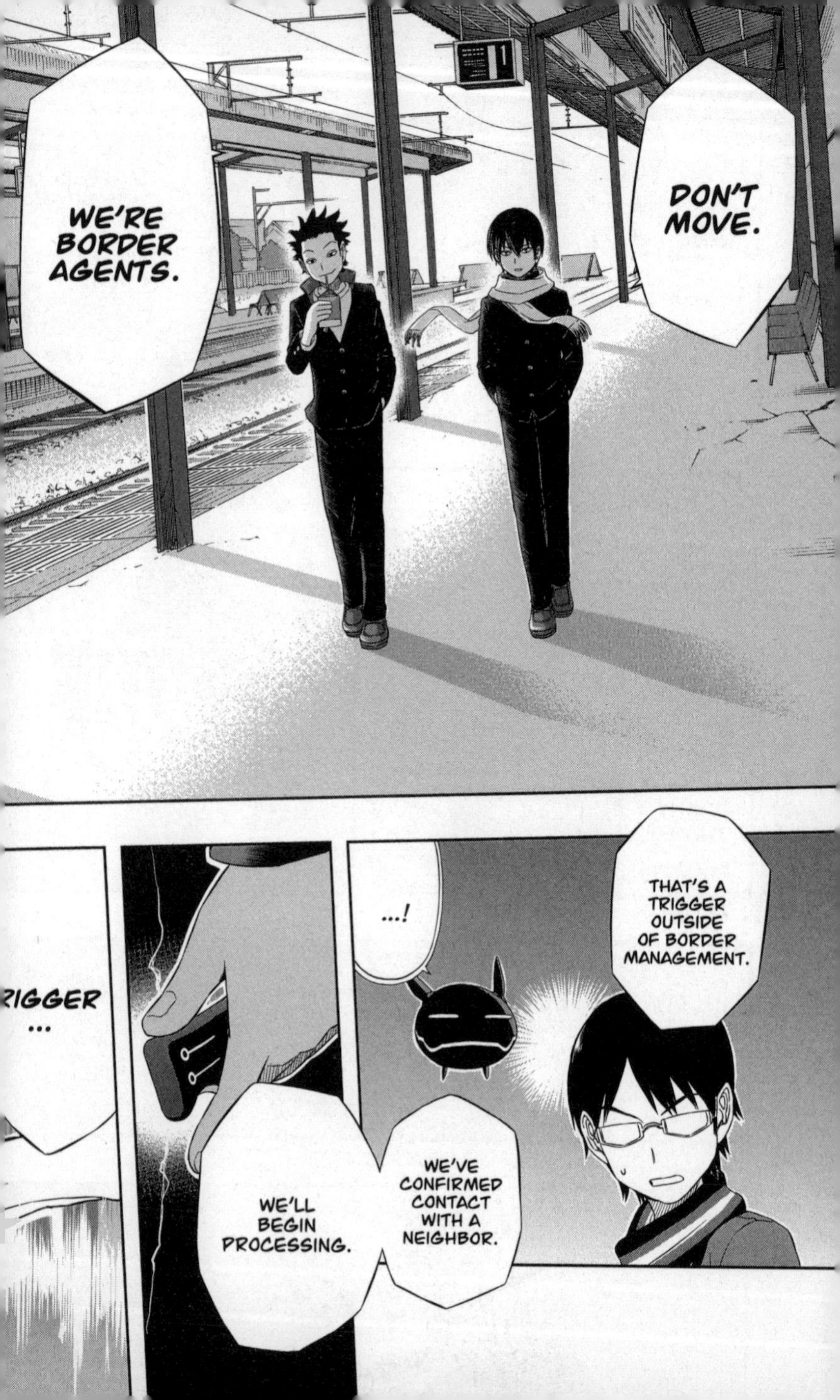
DON'T MOVE.
WE'RE BORDER AGENTS.
THAT'S A TRIGGER OUTSIDE OF BORDER MANAGEMENT.
...!
WE'VE CONFIRMED CONTACT WITH A NEIGHBOR.
WE'LL BEGIN PROCESSING.
RIGGER ...

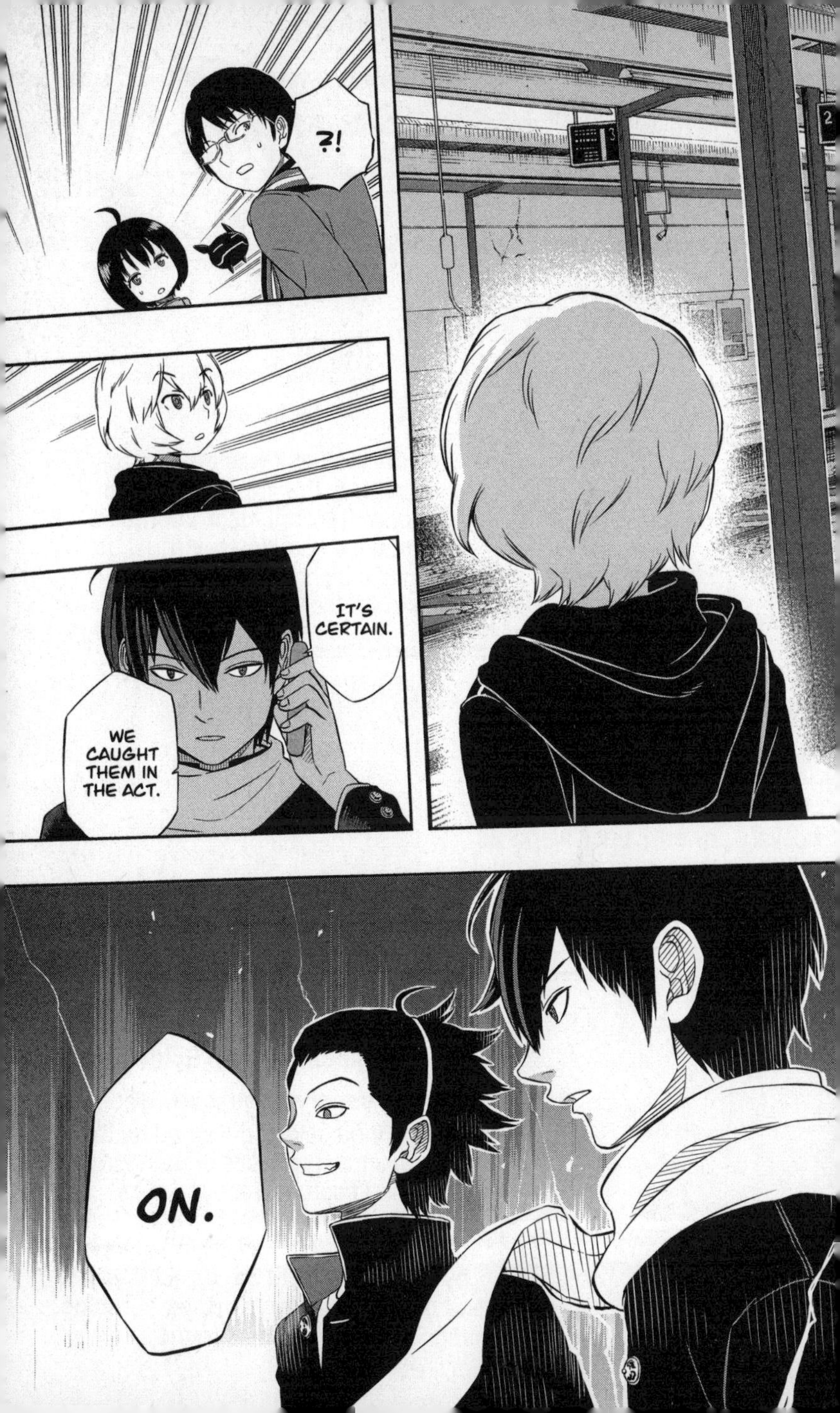
?!
IT'S CERTAIN.
WE CAUGHT THEM IN THE ACT.
ON.

# Trion Soldiers
## Neighbor Minions

### Ilgar
**Bomber Trion Soldier**

The size of an elementary school.

Every inch of it was created for bombing. The annoying part is it goes into self-destruct mode when it's shot down. It must be quite a sight when the whole sky is full of them.

### Rad
**Spying and Scouting Trion Soldier**
The size of a Roomba.

I like the shape. I also like how it's not very powerful but it works its numbers to its advantage. It could be quite a useful tool.

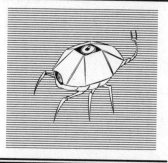

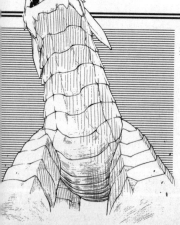

### Bander
**Capturing Trion Soldier**

About the size of a Bamster on a diet.

A tragic Trion soldier designed for the contradictory purposes of bombardment and capture. Because of its looser concept design compared to the Ilgar or Marmod, it got beaten by Osamu. It would be correct to use a whole bunch of them just for bombing. High hopes for the next round.

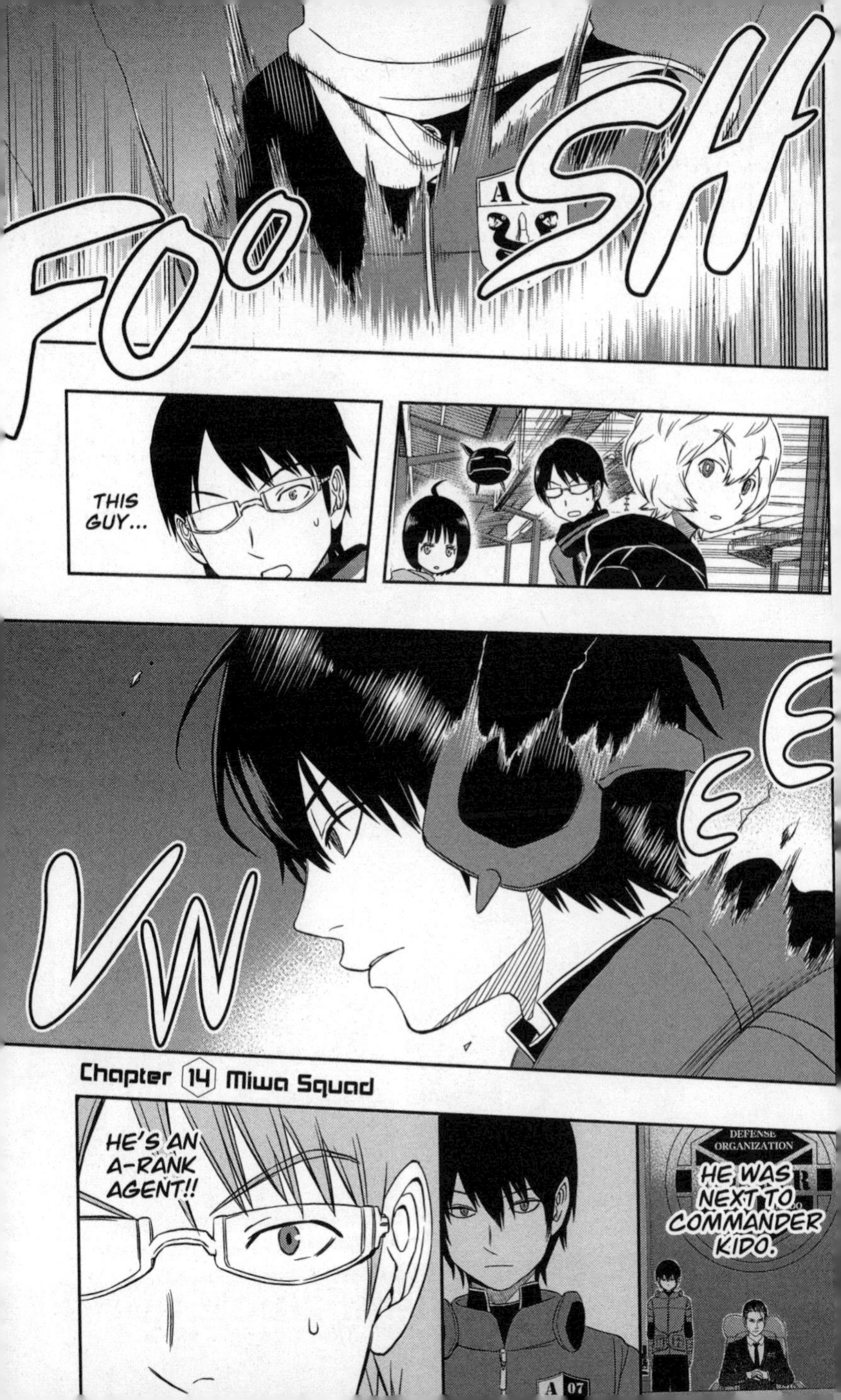
FOOOSH
THIS GUY...
VWEEE
Chapter 14 Miwa Squad
DEFENSE ORGANIZATION
HE WAS NEXT TO COMMANDER KIDO.
HE'S AN A-RANK AGENT!!
A 07

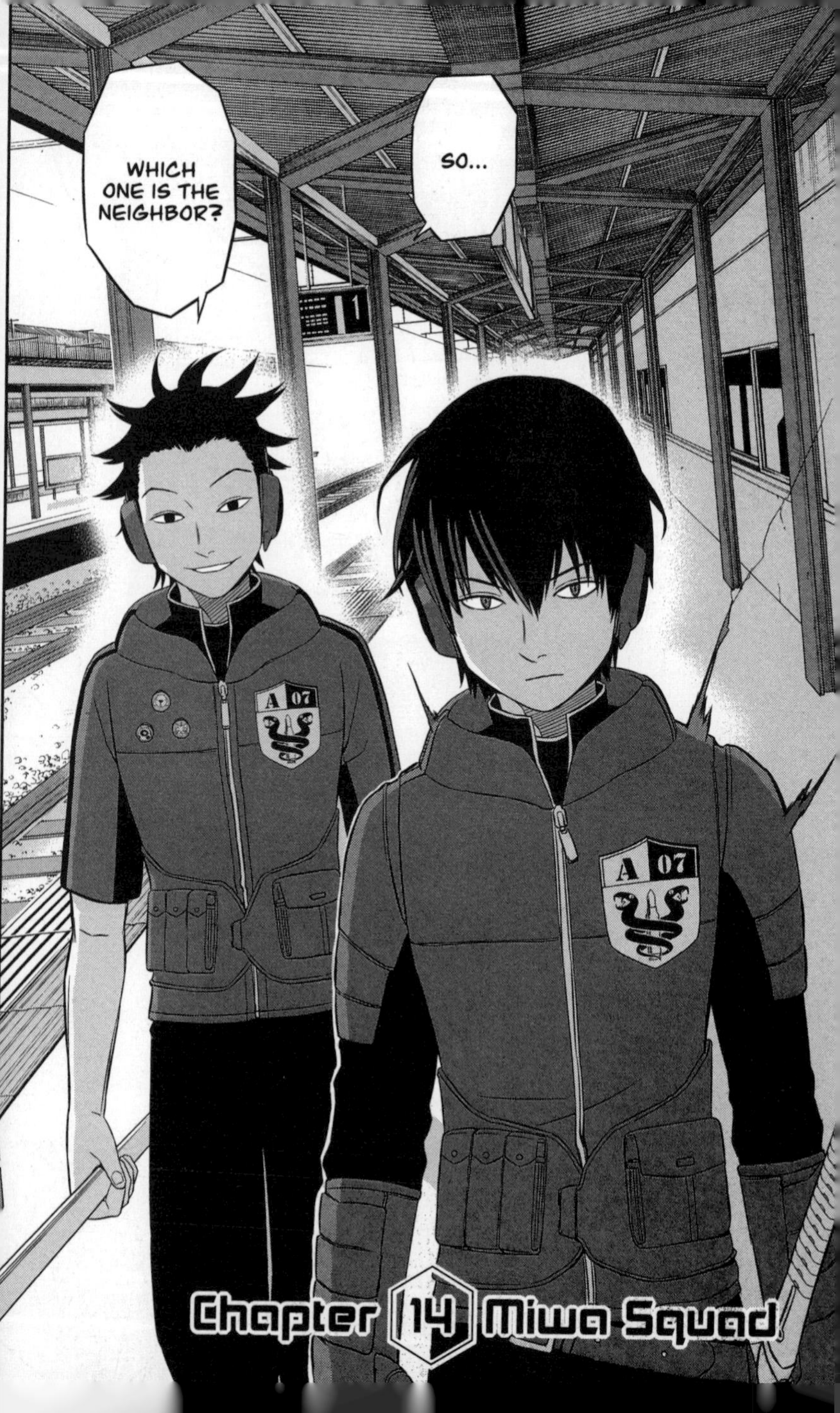
SO...
WHICH ONE IS THE NEIGHBOR?
A 07
A 07
Chapter 14 Miwa Squad

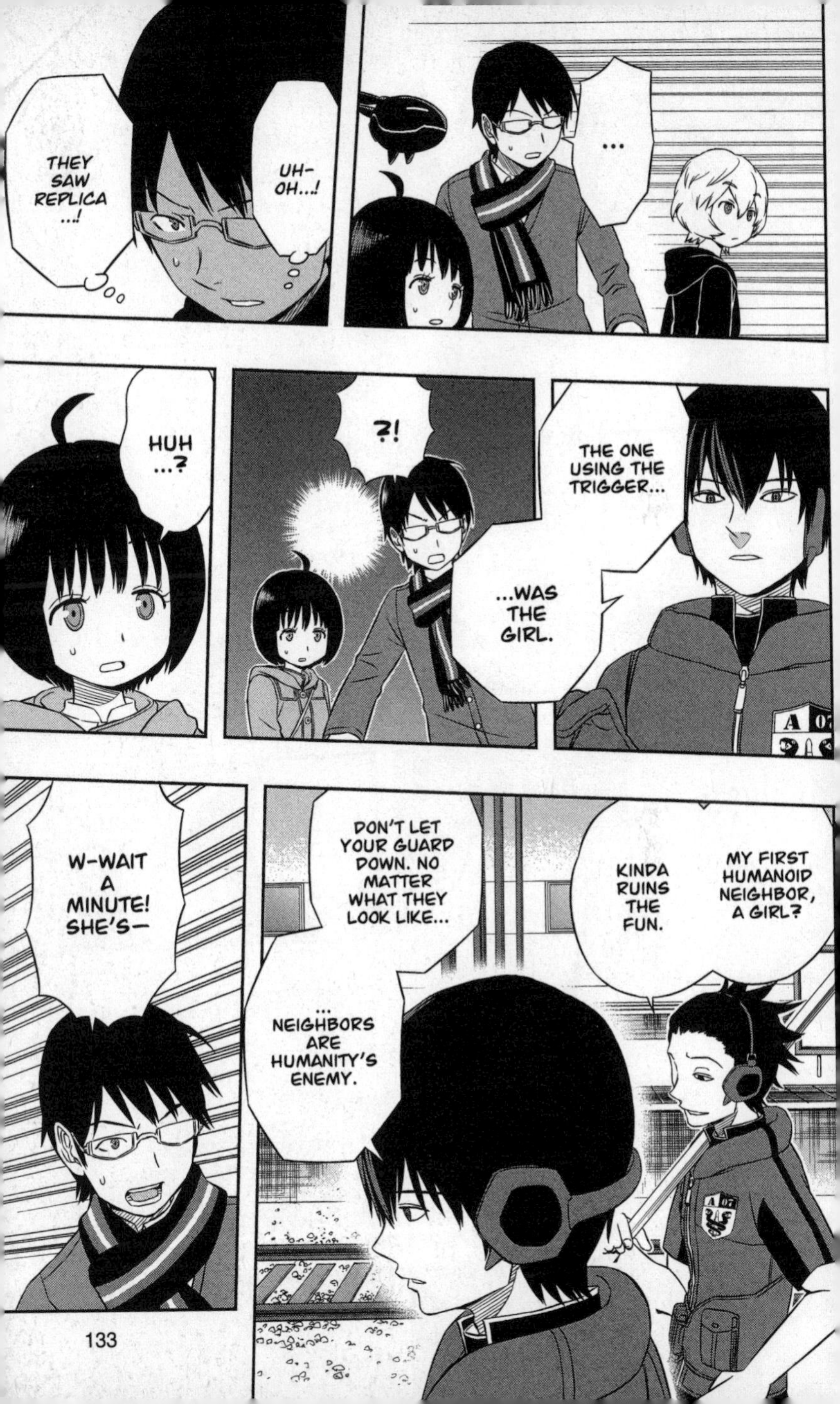
...
UH-OH...!
THEY SAW REPLICA ...!
THE ONE USING THE TRIGGER...
...WAS THE GIRL.
?!
HUH ...?
MY FIRST HUMANOID NEIGHBOR, A GIRL?
KINDA RUINS THE FUN.
DON'T LET YOUR GUARD DOWN. NO MATTER WHAT THEY LOOK LIKE...
... NEIGHBORS ARE HUMANITY'S ENEMY.
W-WAIT A MINUTE! SHE'S—
A 07

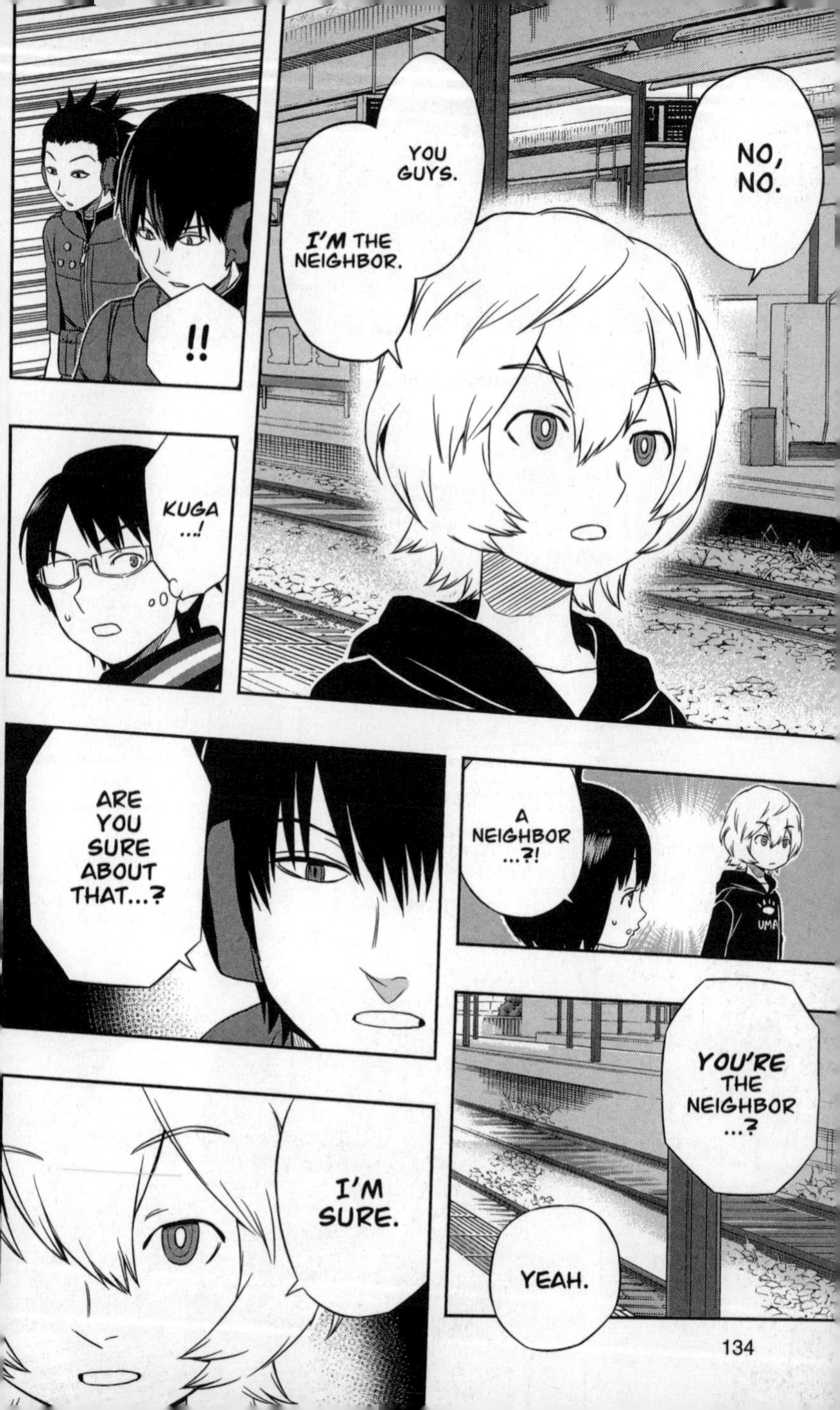
NO, NO.
YOU GUYS.
I'M THE NEIGHBOR.
!!
KUGA ...!
A NEIGHBOR ...?!
ARE YOU SURE ABOUT THAT...?
YOU'RE THE NEIGHBOR ...?
YEAH.
I'M SURE.

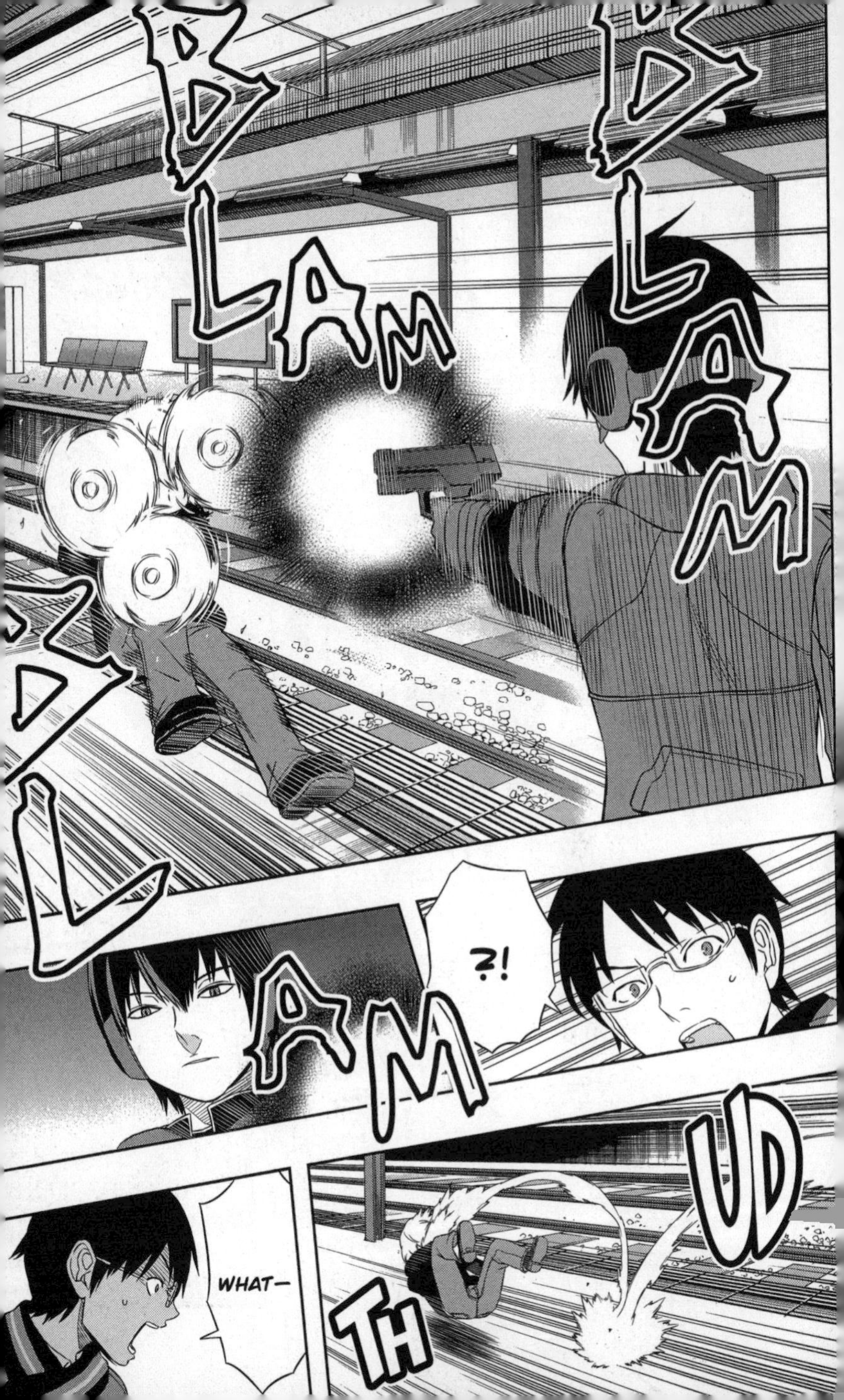

BLAM
BLAM
BLAM
?!
THUD
WHAT—

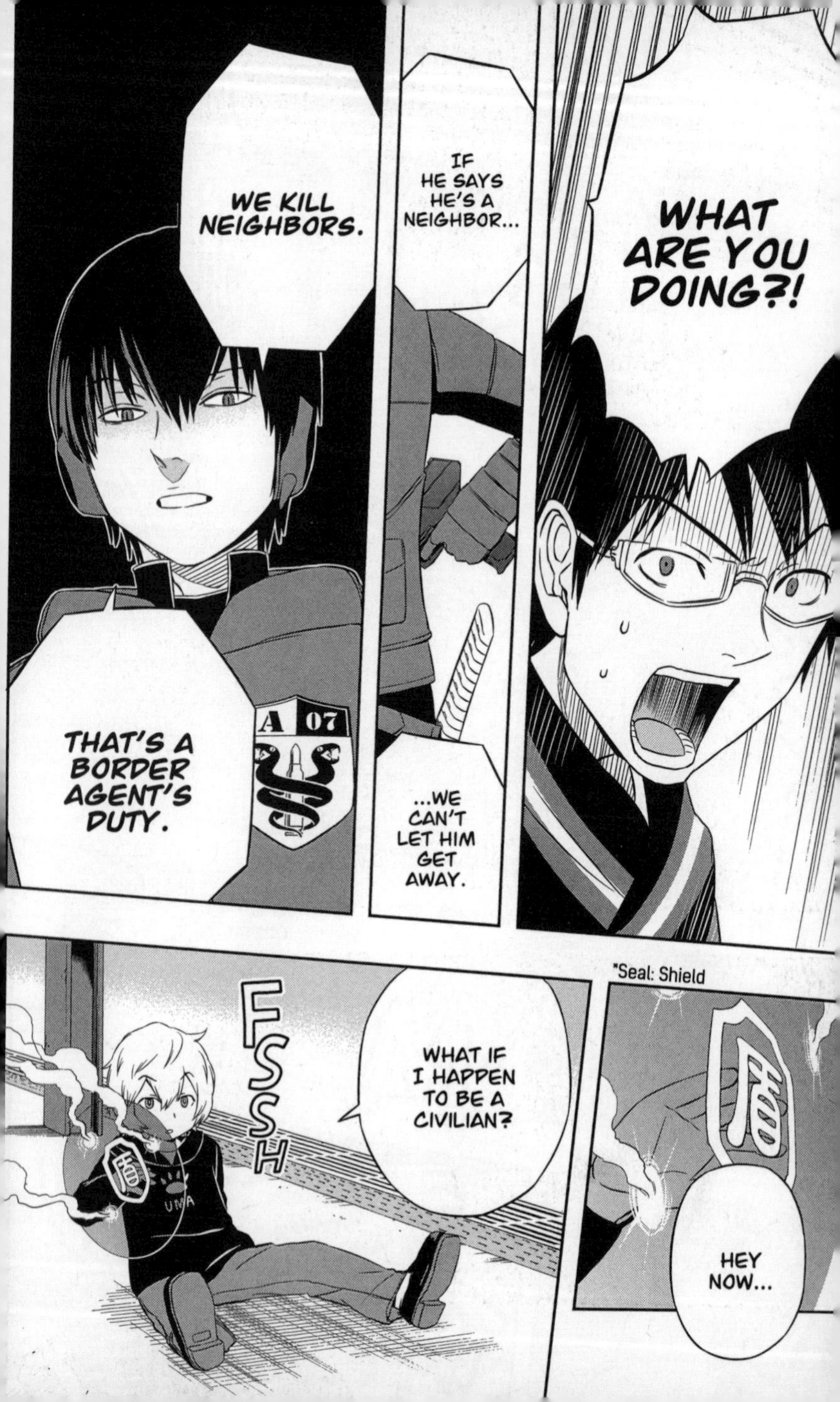
WHAT ARE YOU DOING?!
IF HE SAYS HE'S A NEIGHBOR...
...WE CAN'T LET HIM GET AWAY.
WE KILL NEIGHBORS.
THAT'S A BORDER AGENT'S DUTY.
A 07
*Seal: Shield
HEY NOW...
WHAT IF I HAPPEN TO BE A CIVILIAN?
FSSH
UMA

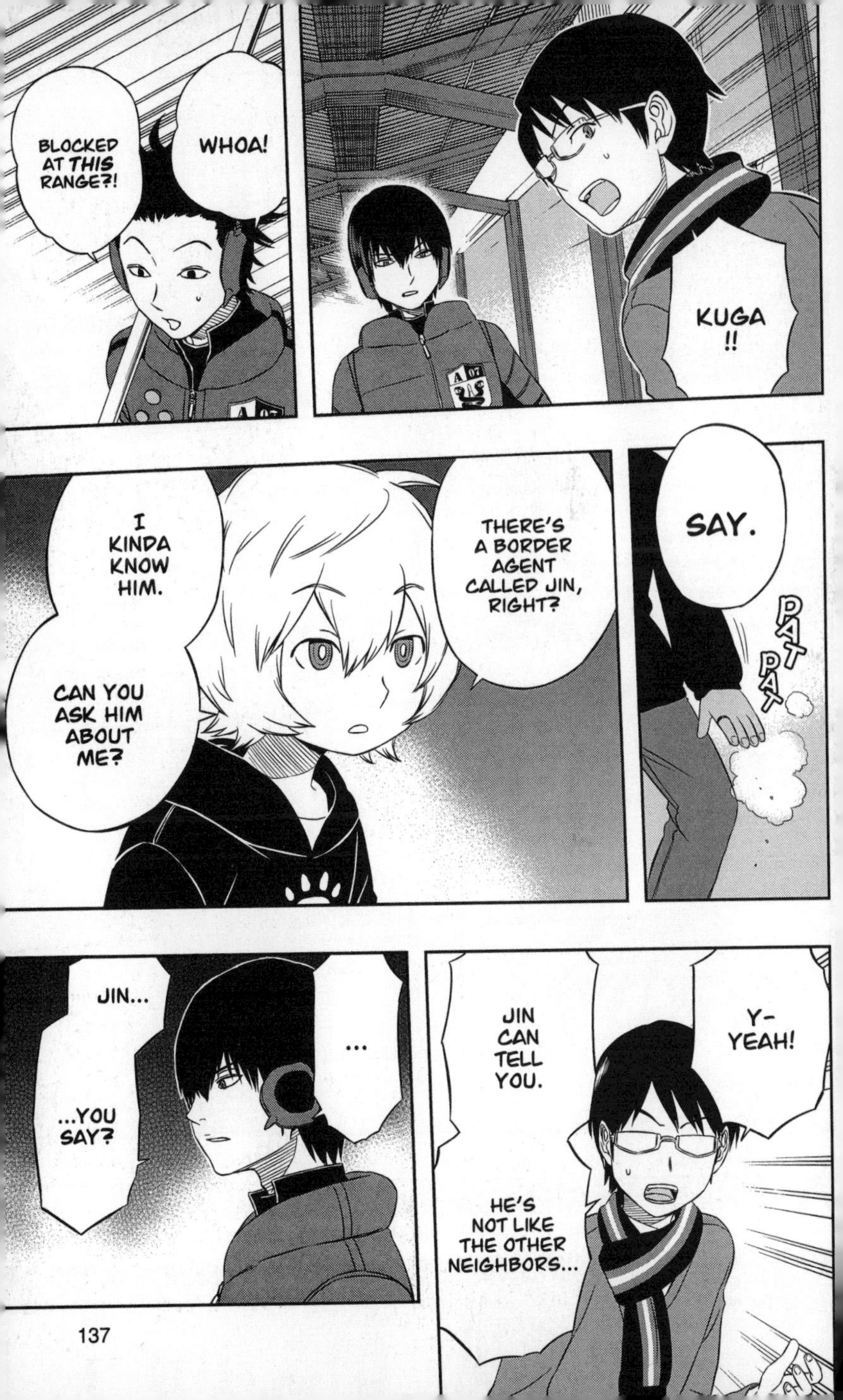
KUGA !!
WHOA!
BLOCKED AT THIS RANGE?!
SAY.
PAT PAT
THERE'S A BORDER AGENT CALLED JIN, RIGHT?
I KINDA KNOW HIM.
CAN YOU ASK HIM ABOUT ME?
Y-YEAH!
JIN CAN TELL YOU.
HE'S NOT LIKE THE OTHER NEIGHBORS...
...
JIN...
...YOU SAY?

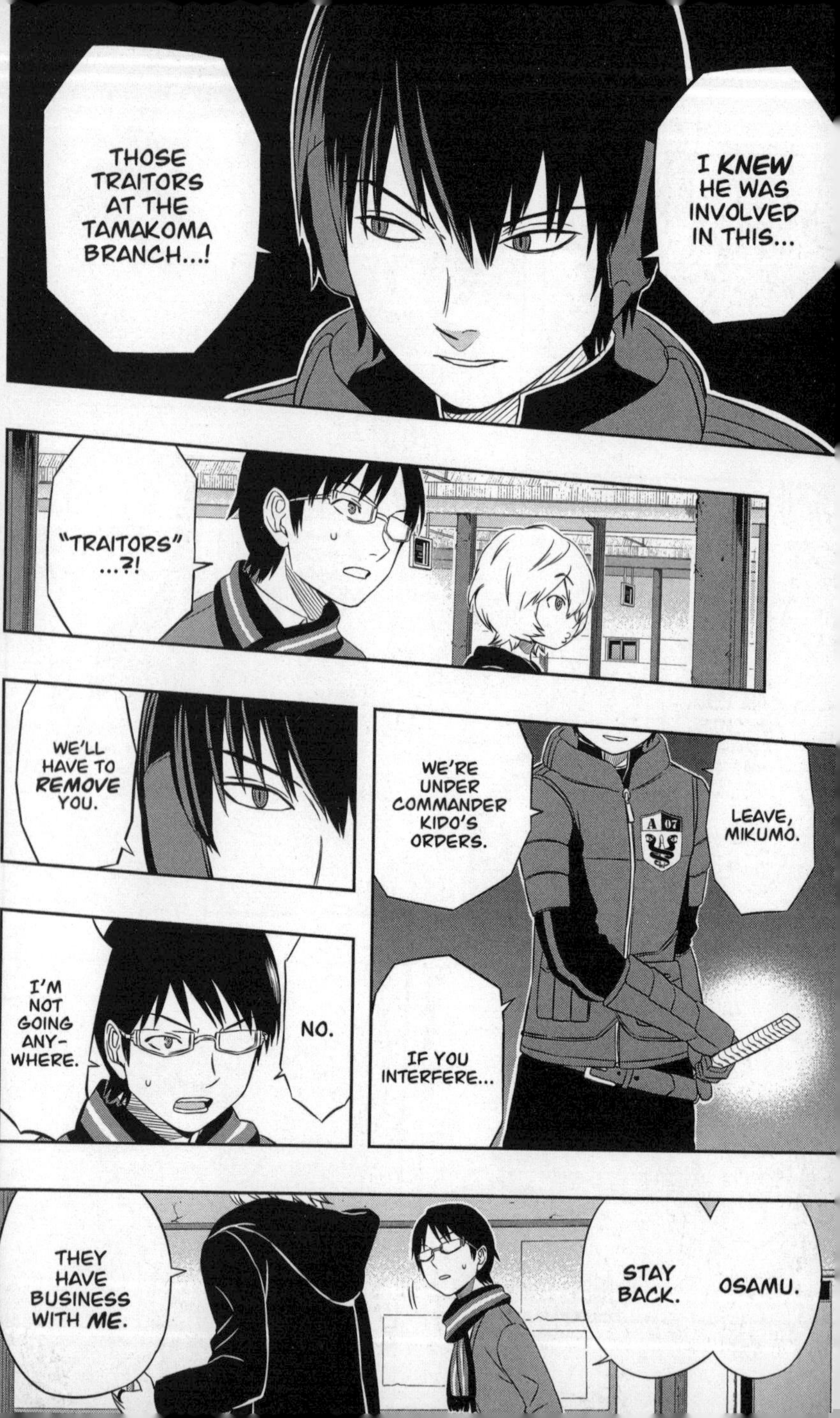

I KNEW HE WAS INVOLVED IN THIS...
THOSE TRAITORS AT THE TAMAKOMA BRANCH...!
"TRAITORS" ...?!
LEAVE, MIKUMO.
WE'RE UNDER COMMANDER KIDO'S ORDERS.
IF YOU INTERFERE...
WE'LL HAVE TO REMOVE YOU.
NO.
I'M NOT GOING ANY-WHERE.
OSAMU.
STAY BACK.
THEY HAVE BUSINESS WITH ME.

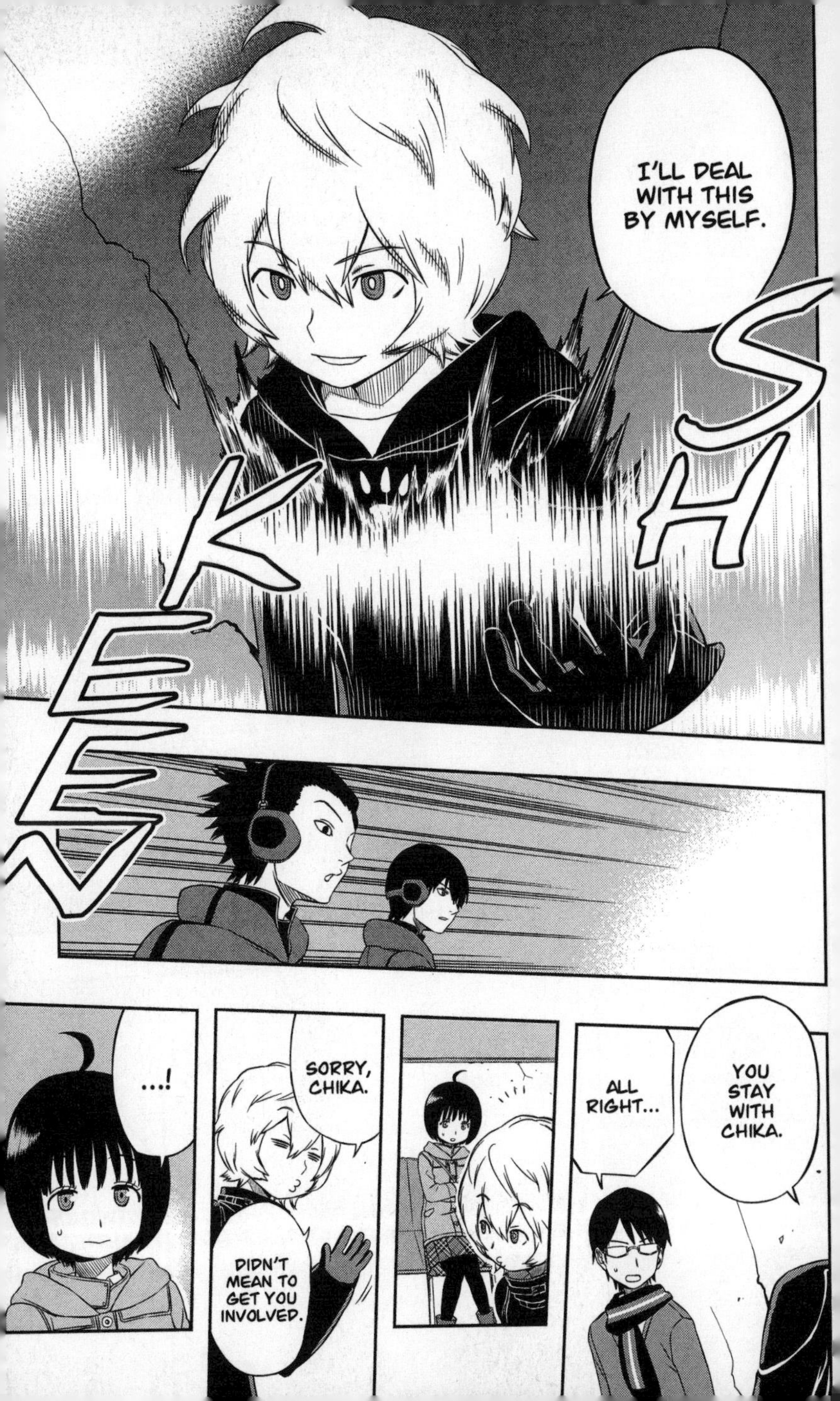
I'LL DEAL WITH THIS BY MYSELF.
SHKEEEN
YOU STAY WITH CHIKA.
ALL RIGHT...
SORRY, CHIKA.
DIDN'T MEAN TO GET YOU INVOLVED.
...!

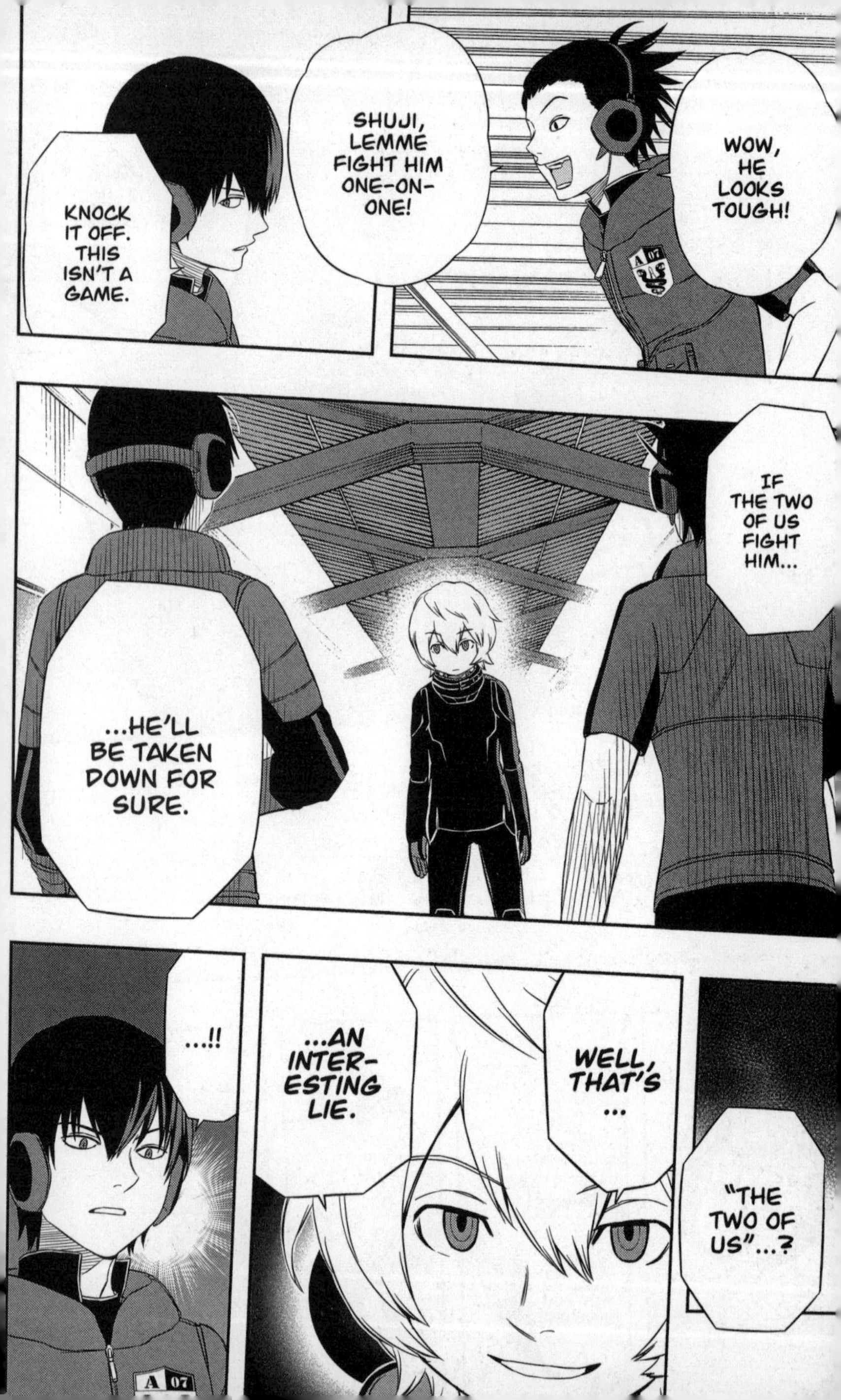
WOW, HE LOOKS TOUGH!
SHUJI, LEMME FIGHT HIM ONE-ON-ONE!
KNOCK IT OFF. THIS ISN'T A GAME.
IF THE TWO OF US FIGHT HIM...
...HE'LL BE TAKEN DOWN FOR SURE.
"THE TWO OF US"...?
WELL, THAT'S ...
...AN INTERESTING LIE.
...!!

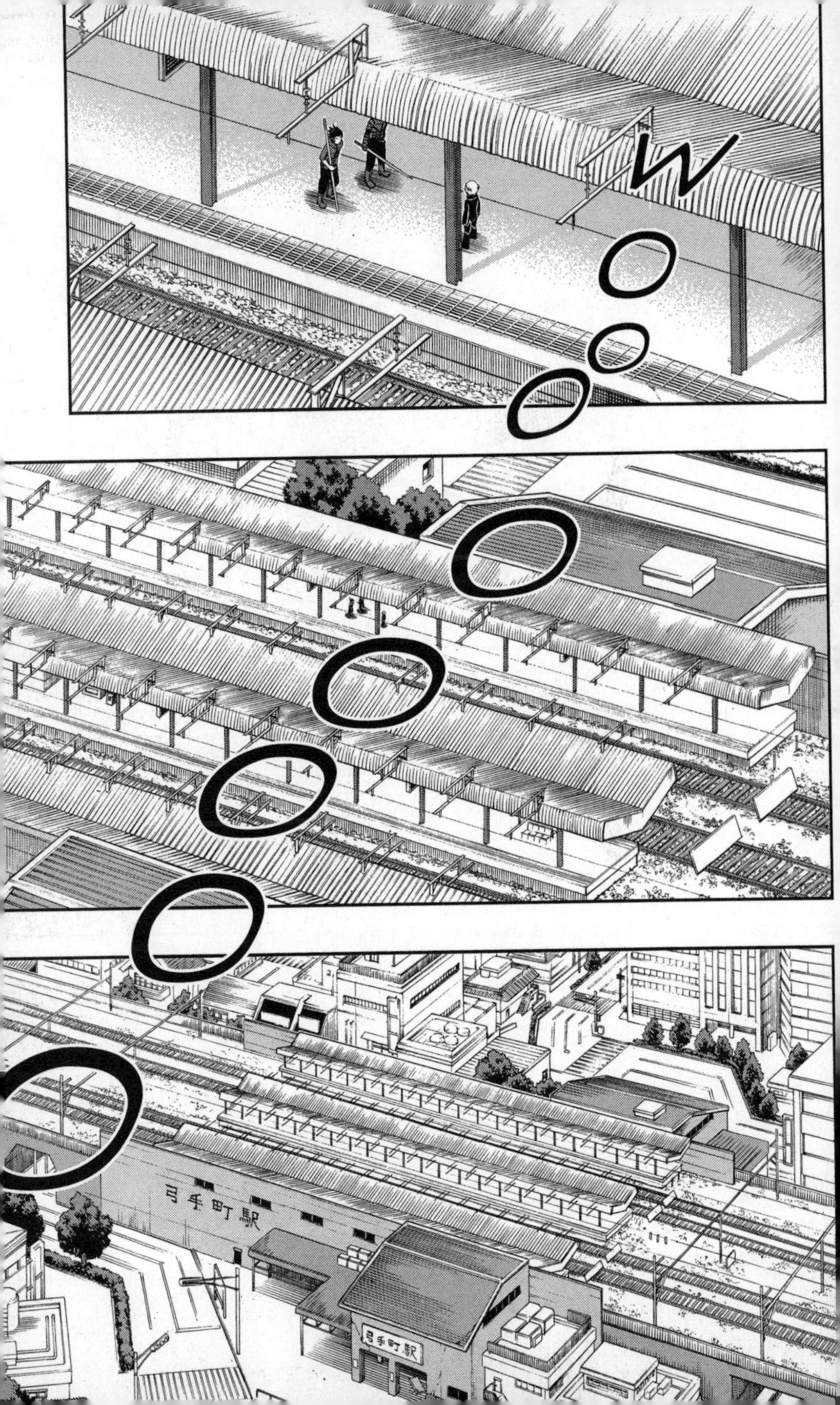
WOOOOOOOO
弓手町駅
弓手町駅

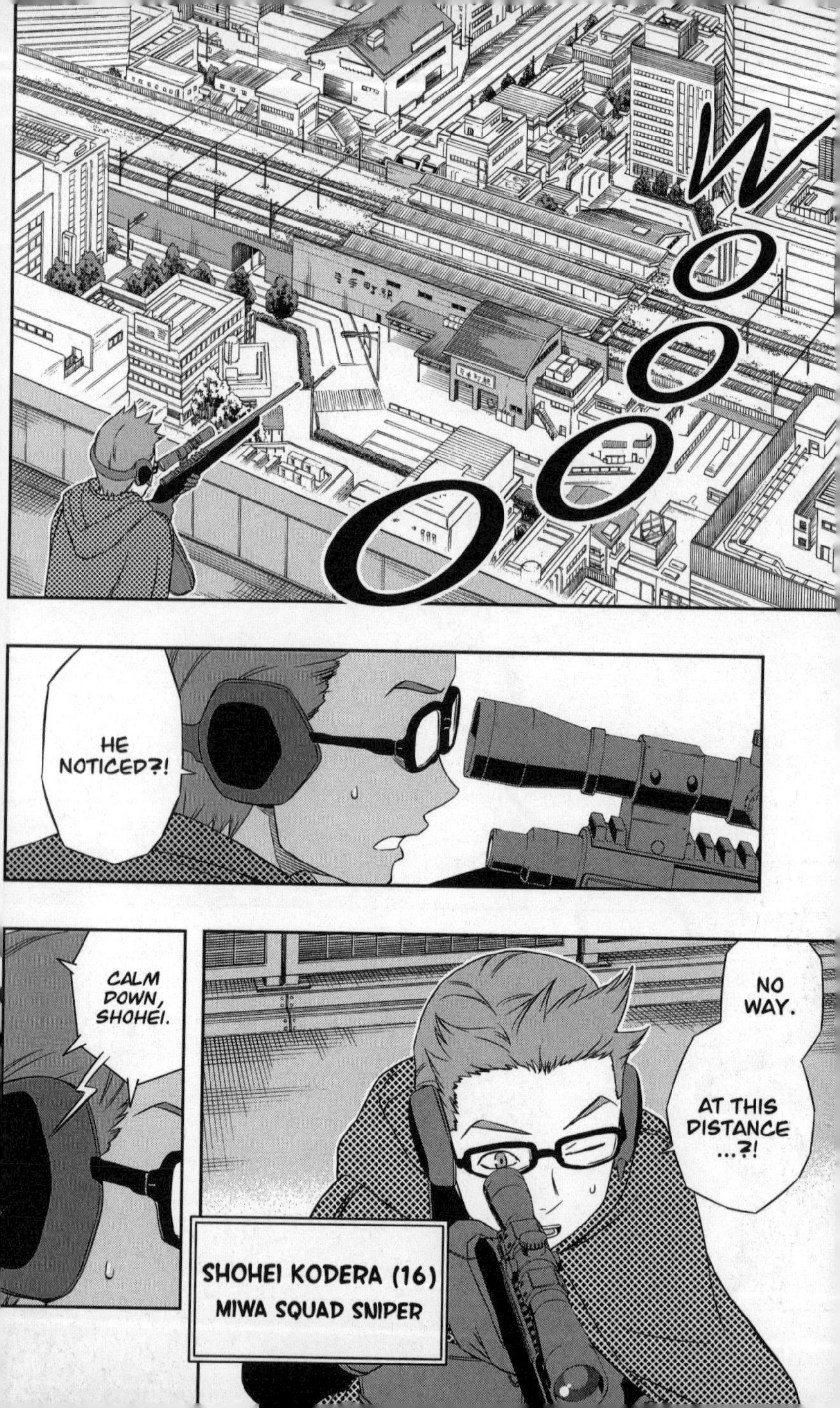
WOOOO
HE NOTICED?!
NO WAY.
AT THIS DISTANCE ...?!
SHOHEI KODERA (16)
MIWA SQUAD SNIPER
CALM DOWN, SHOHEI.

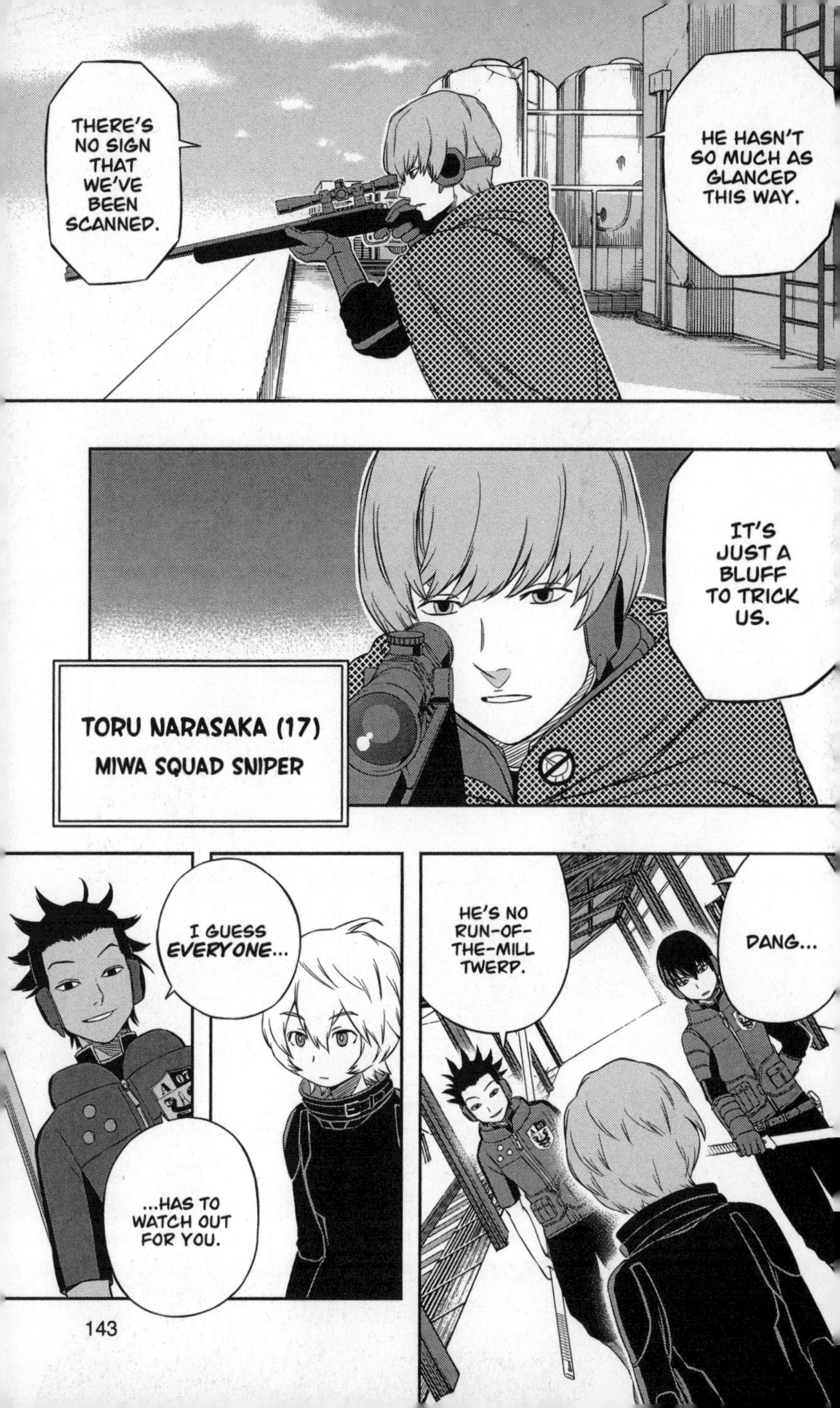
HE HASN'T SO MUCH AS GLANCED THIS WAY.
THERE'S NO SIGN THAT WE'VE BEEN SCANNED.
IT'S JUST A BLUFF TO TRICK US.
TORU NARASAKA (17)
MIWA SQUAD SNIPER
DANG...
HE'S NO RUN-OF-THE-MILL TWERP.
I GUESS EVERYONE...
...HAS TO WATCH OUT FOR YOU.

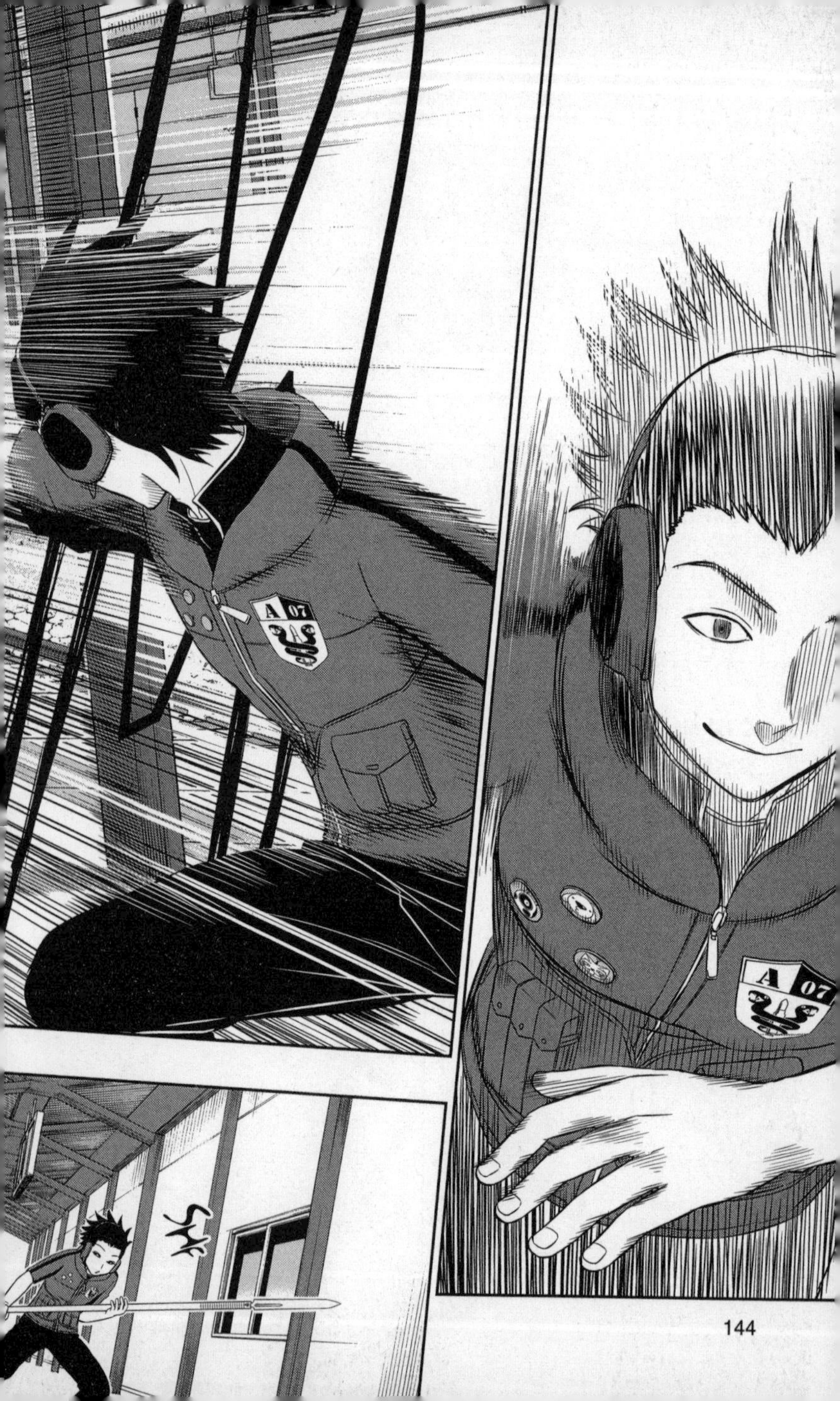

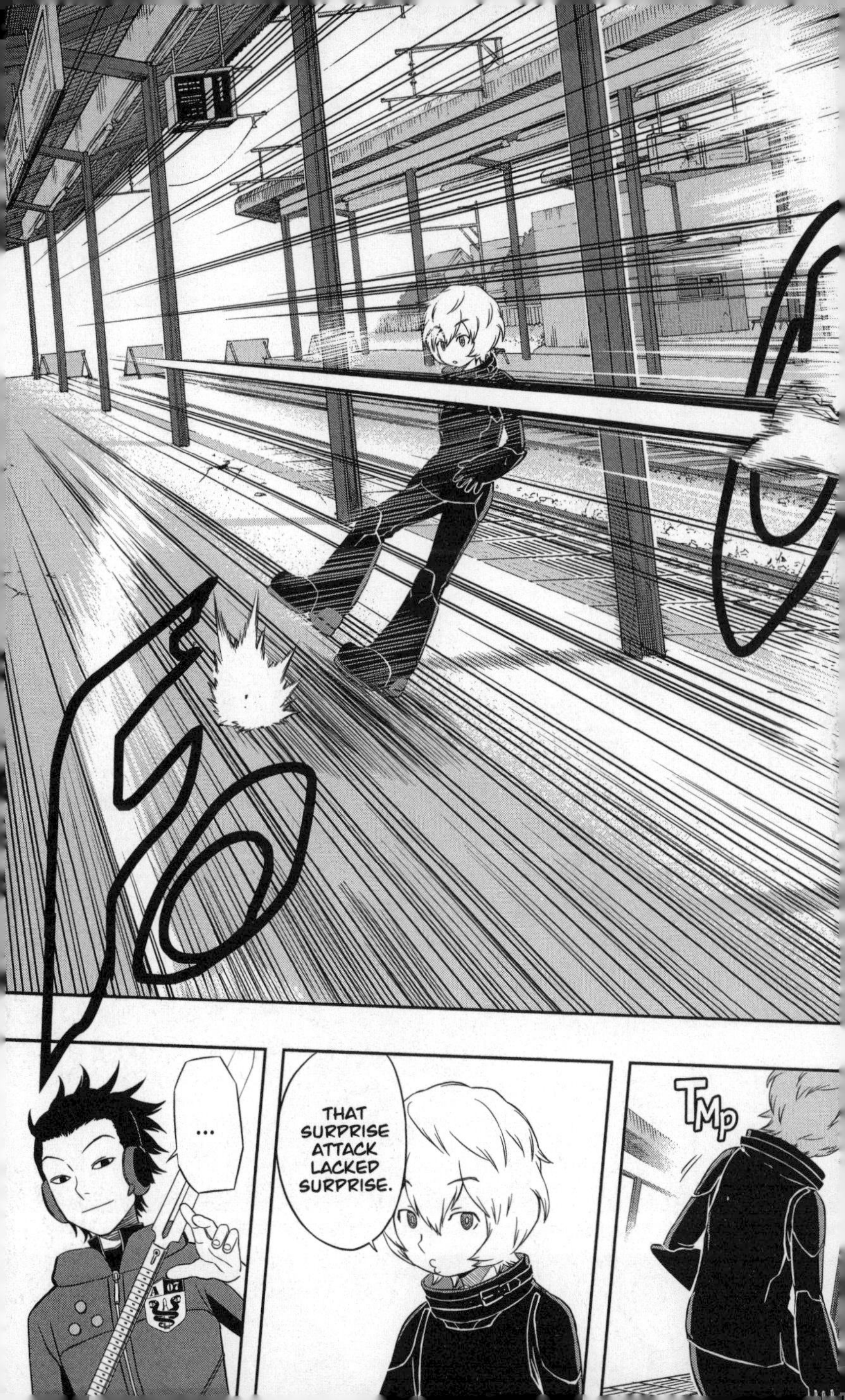
TMP
THAT SURPRISE ATTACK LACKED SURPRISE.
...

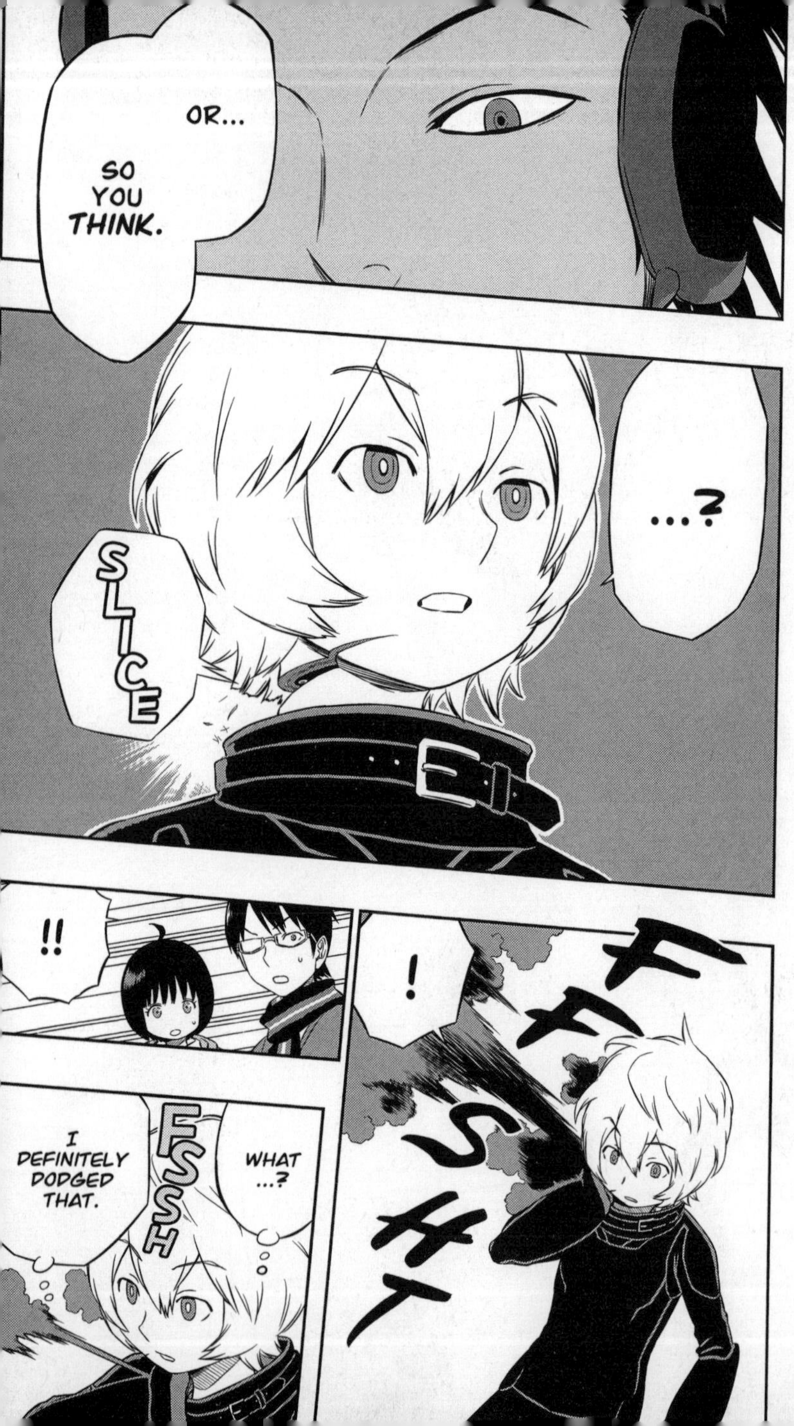
OR...
SO YOU THINK.
...?
SLICE
!
FFSHT
!!
WHAT ...?
FSSH
I DEFINITELY DODGED THAT.

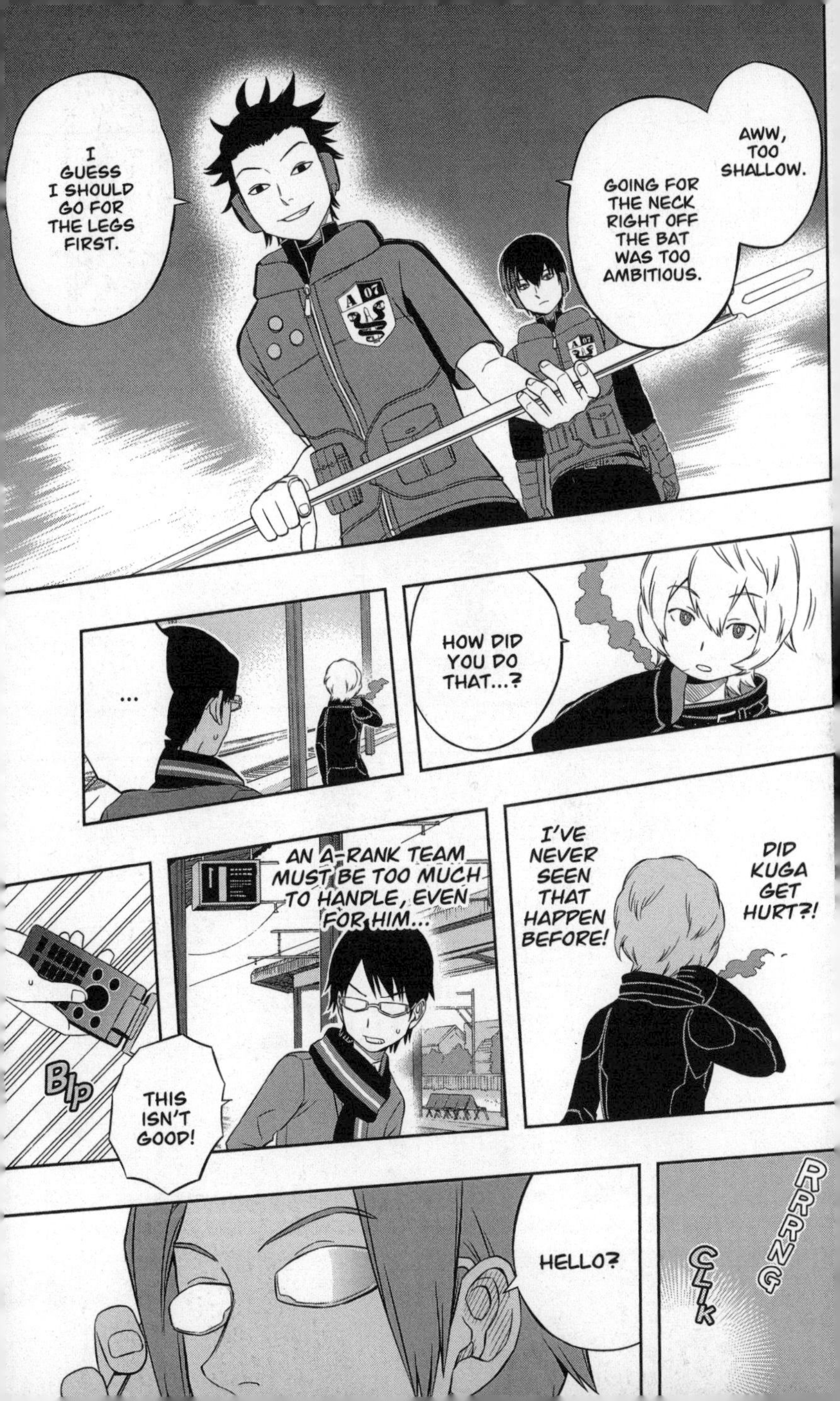
AWW, TOO SHALLOW.
GOING FOR THE NECK RIGHT OFF THE BAT WAS TOO AMBITIOUS.
I GUESS I SHOULD GO FOR THE LEGS FIRST.
HOW DID YOU DO THAT...?
...
DID KUGA GET HURT?!
I'VE NEVER SEEN THAT HAPPEN BEFORE!
AN A-RANK TEAM MUST BE TOO MUCH TO HANDLE, EVEN FOR HIM...
THIS ISN'T GOOD!
BIP
RRRRNG
CLIK
HELLO?

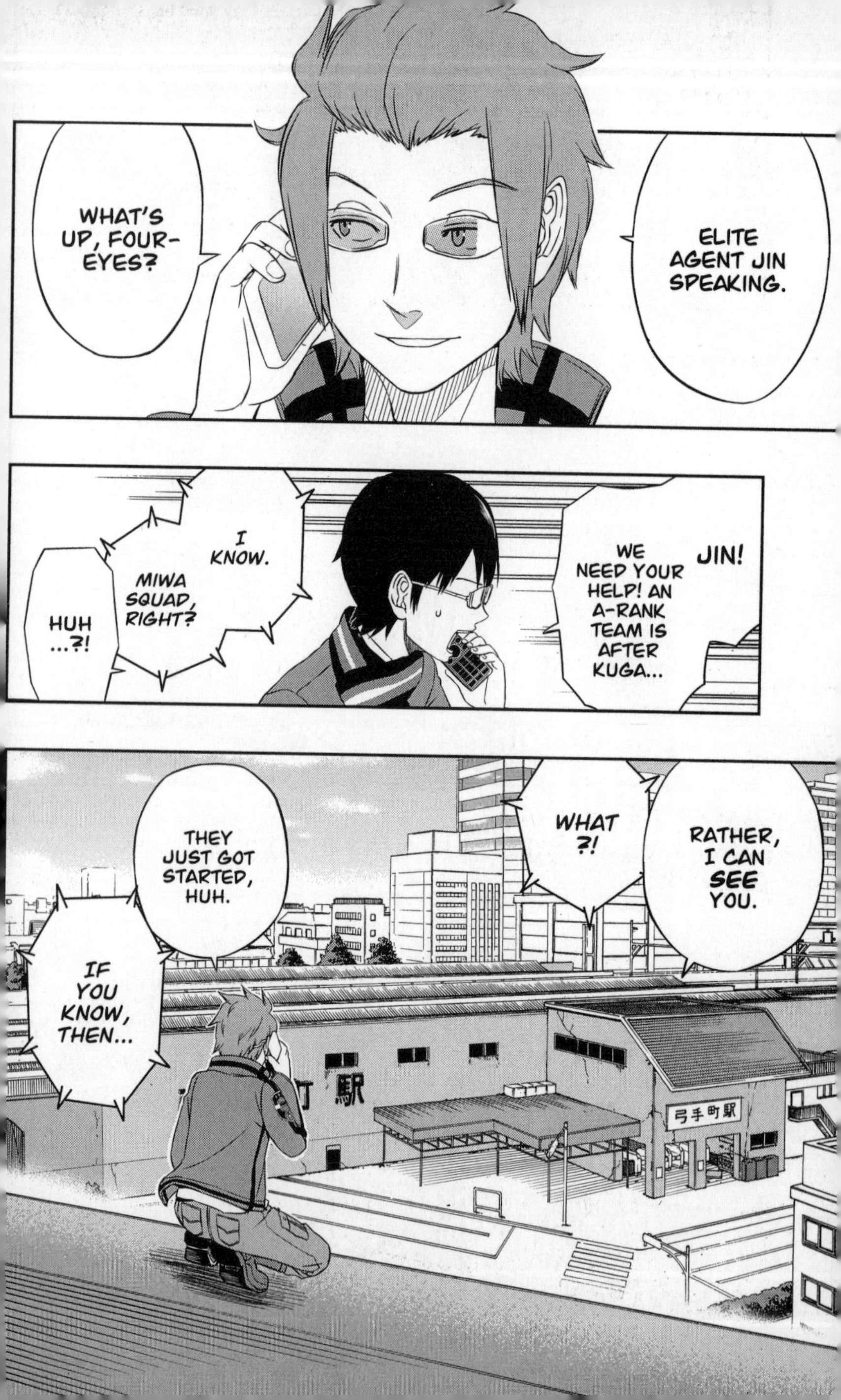
ELITE AGENT JIN SPEAKING.
WHAT'S UP, FOUR-EYES?
JIN!
WE NEED YOUR HELP! AN A-RANK TEAM IS AFTER KUGA...
I KNOW.
MIWA SQUAD, RIGHT?
HUH ...?!
RATHER, I CAN SEE YOU.
WHAT ?!
THEY JUST GOT STARTED, HUH.
IF YOU KNOW, THEN...
弓手町駅

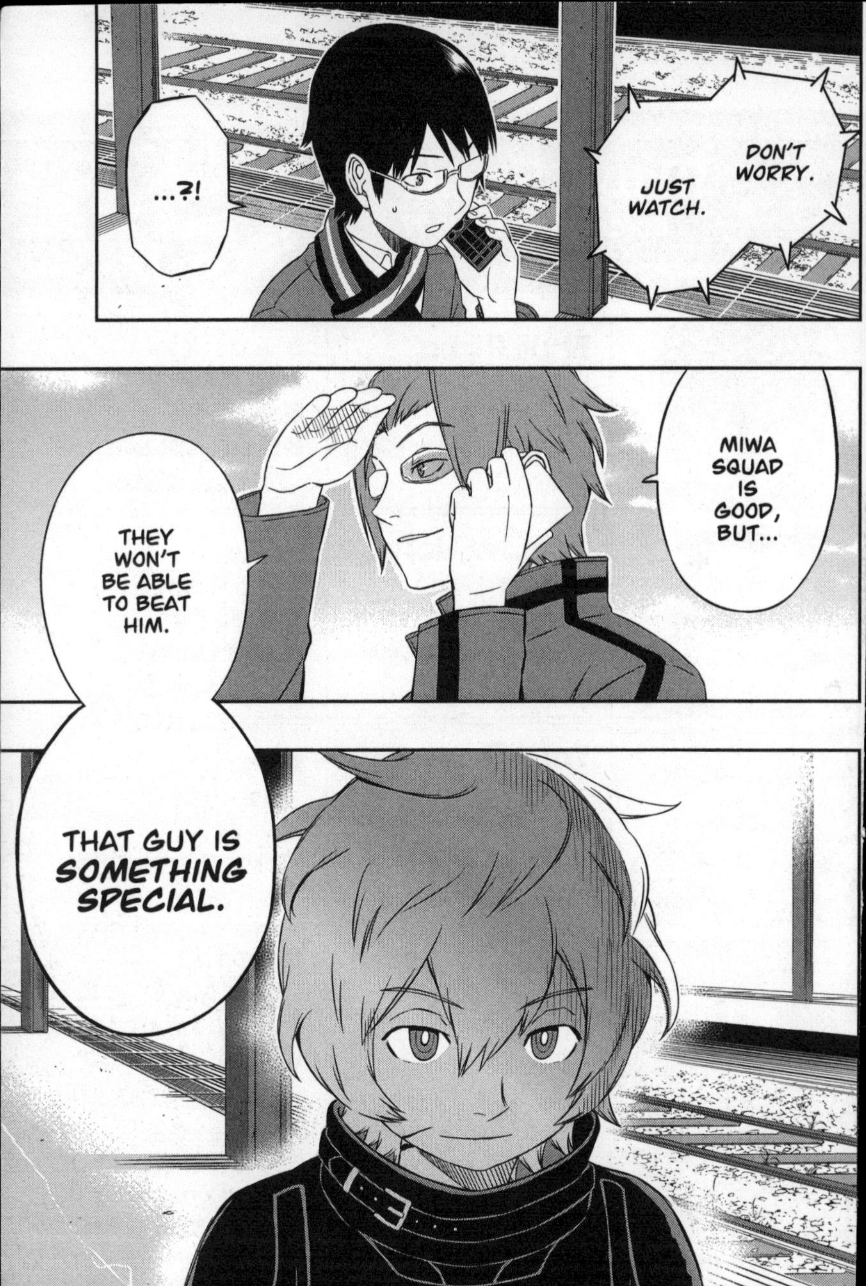
DON'T WORRY. JUST WATCH.
...?!
MIWA SQUAD IS GOOD, BUT...
THEY WON'T BE ABLE TO BEAT HIM.
THAT GUY IS SOMETHING SPECIAL.

# Miwa Squad

**Border HQ A-Rank #7**

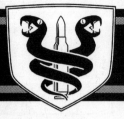

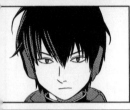

## Shuji Miwa

**Captain, All-Rounder**

■17 years old (high school student)
■Born Oct. 2

■Luna Falcata, Blood type A
■Height: 5'9"
■Likes: Sister, exterminating Neighbors

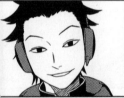

## Yosuke Yoneya

**Attacker**

■17 years old (high school student)
■Born Nov. 29

■Cetacea, Blood type B
■Height: 5'9"
■Likes: Drinks, combat, dogs

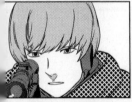

## Toru Narasaka

**Sniper**

■17 years old (high school student)
■Born Sept. 14

■Lupus, Blood type AB
■Height: 5'10"
■Likes: Chocolate, tea

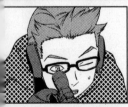

## Shohei Kodera

**Sniper**

■16 years old (high school student)
■Born Nov. 10

■Chronos, Blood type A
■Height: 5'6"
■Likes: Coffee, collecting and analyzing data

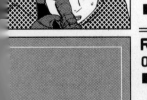

## Ren Tsukimi

**Operator**

■19 years old (college student)
■Born July 25

■Aptenodytes, Blood type AB
■Height: 5'5"
■Likes: Japanese sweets, swimming, fireworks

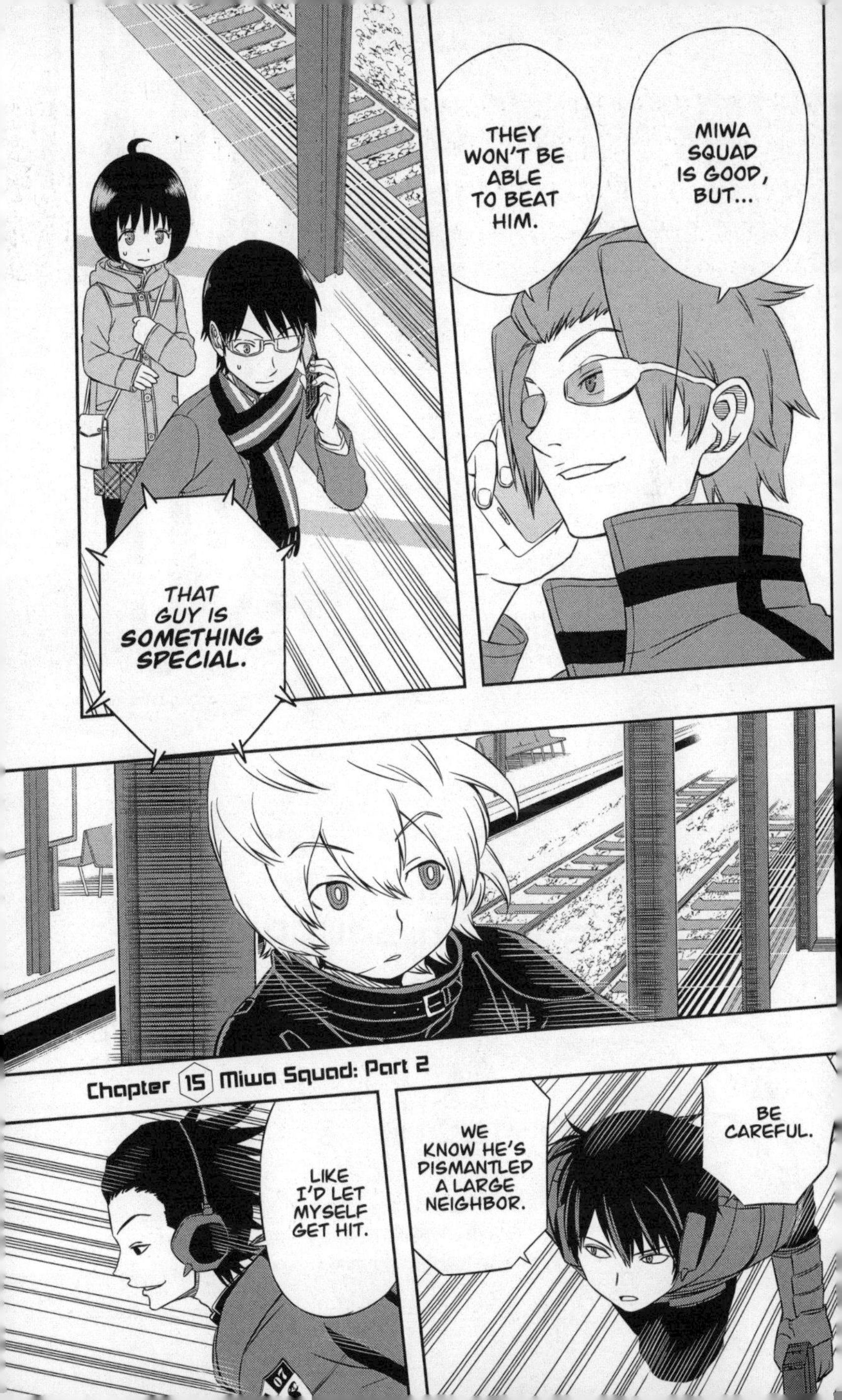
MIWA SQUAD IS GOOD, BUT...
THEY WON'T BE ABLE TO BEAT HIM.
THAT GUY IS SOMETHING SPECIAL.
Chapter 15 Miwa Squad: Part 2
BE CAREFUL.
WE KNOW HE'S DISMANTLED A LARGE NEIGHBOR.
LIKE I'D LET MYSELF GET HIT.

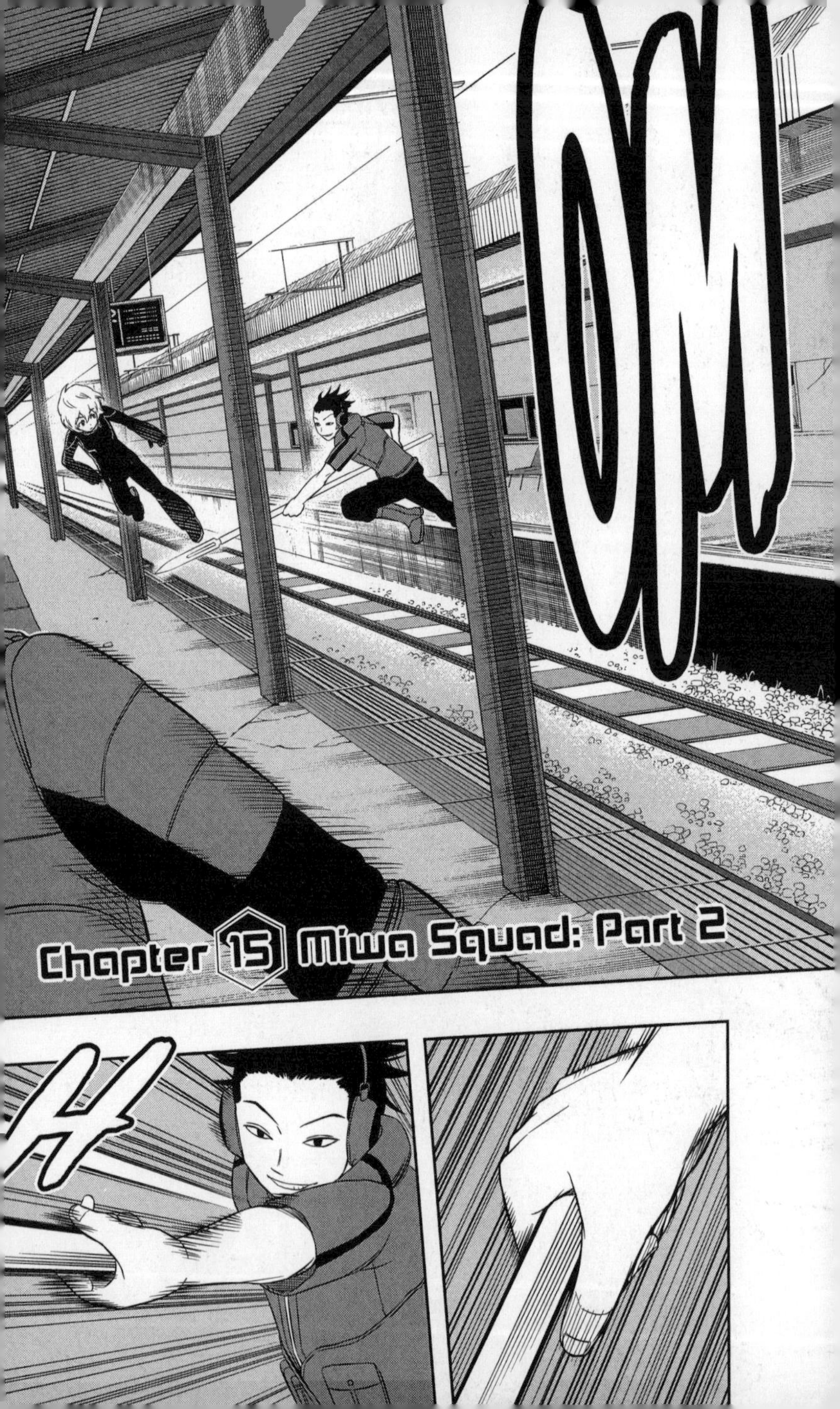
Chapter 15 Miwa Squad: Part 2

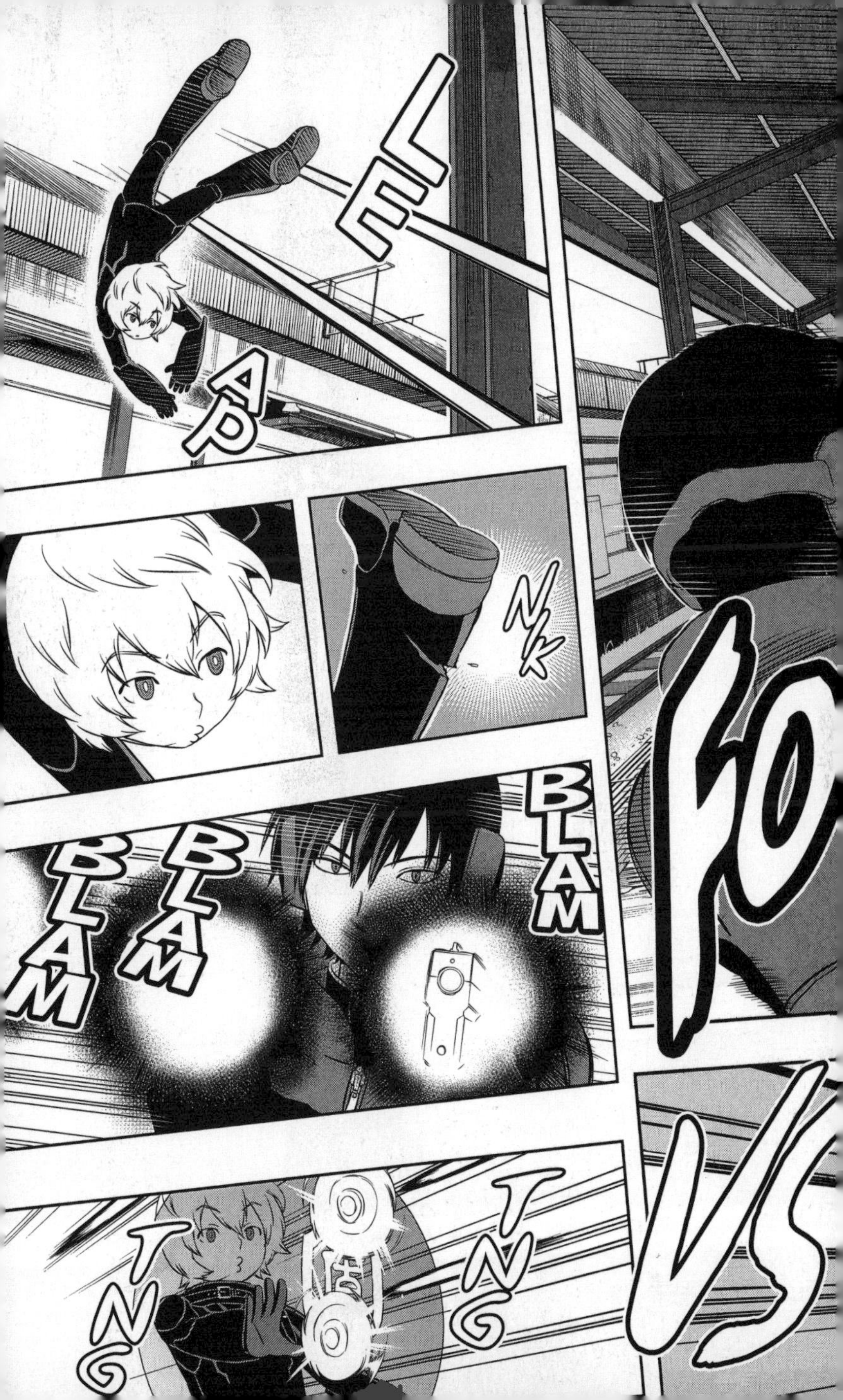

LEAP
NK
BLAM
BLAM
BLAM
TING
TING

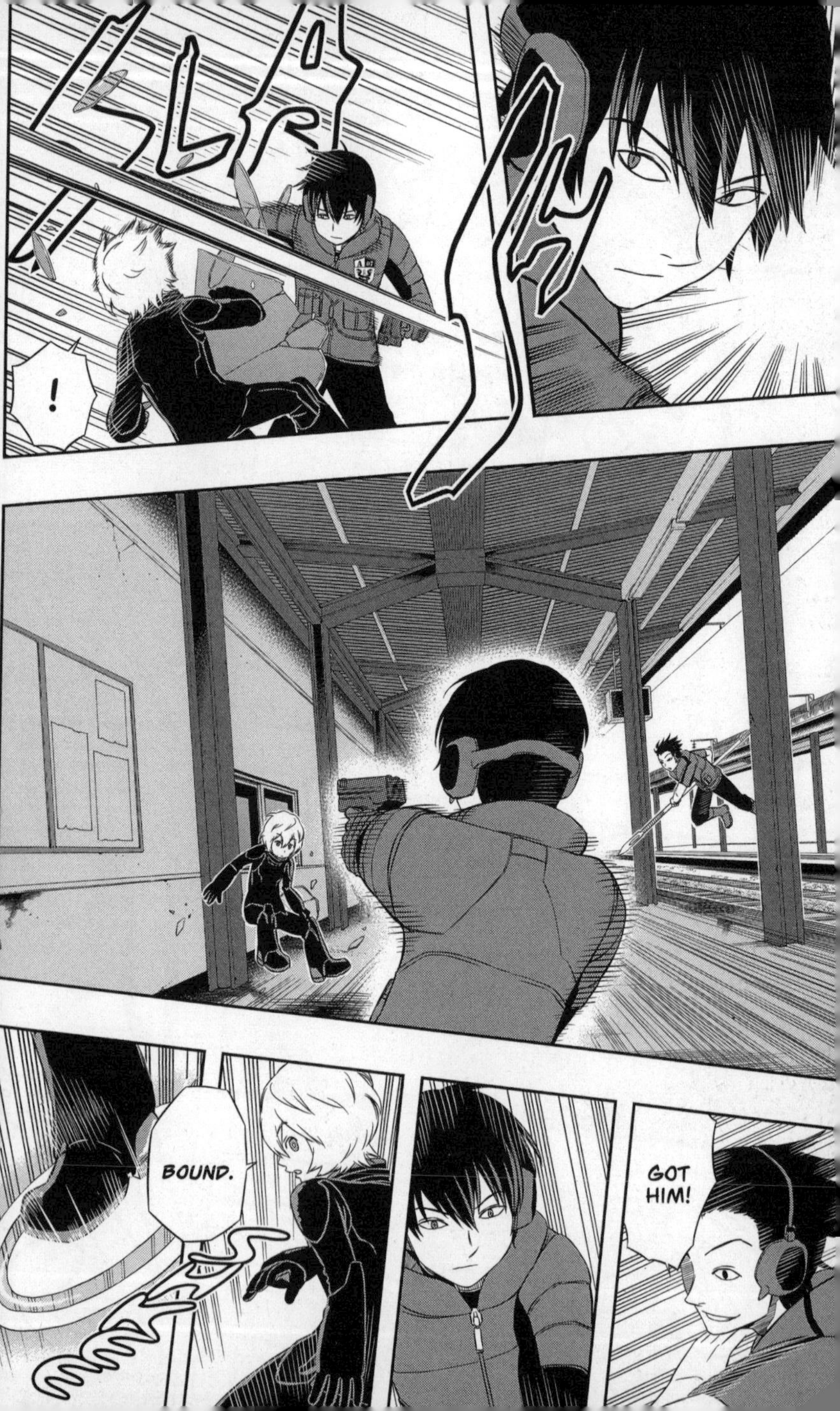
!
GOT HIM!
BOUND.

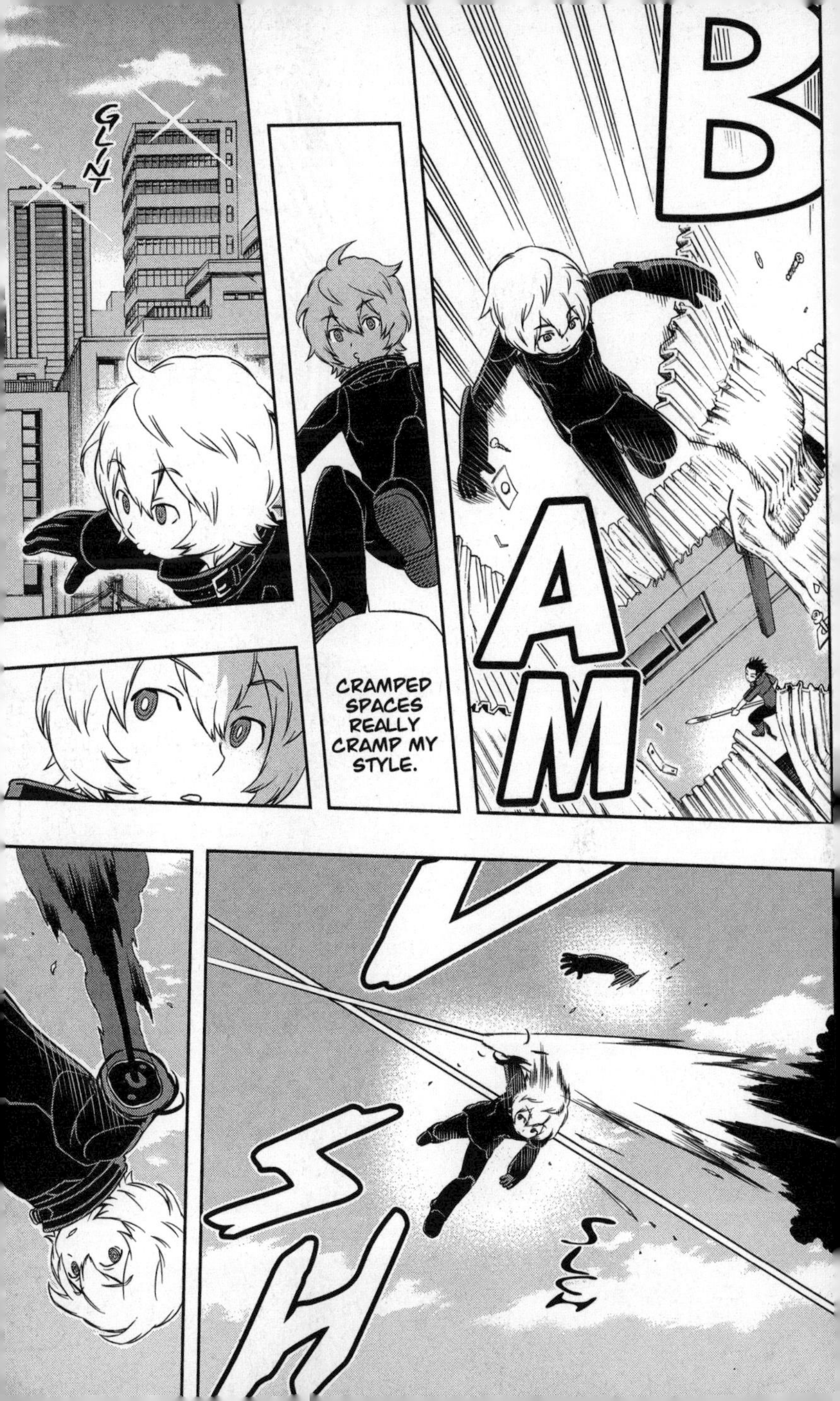
BAM
GLINT
CRAMPED SPACES REALLY CRAMP MY STYLE.

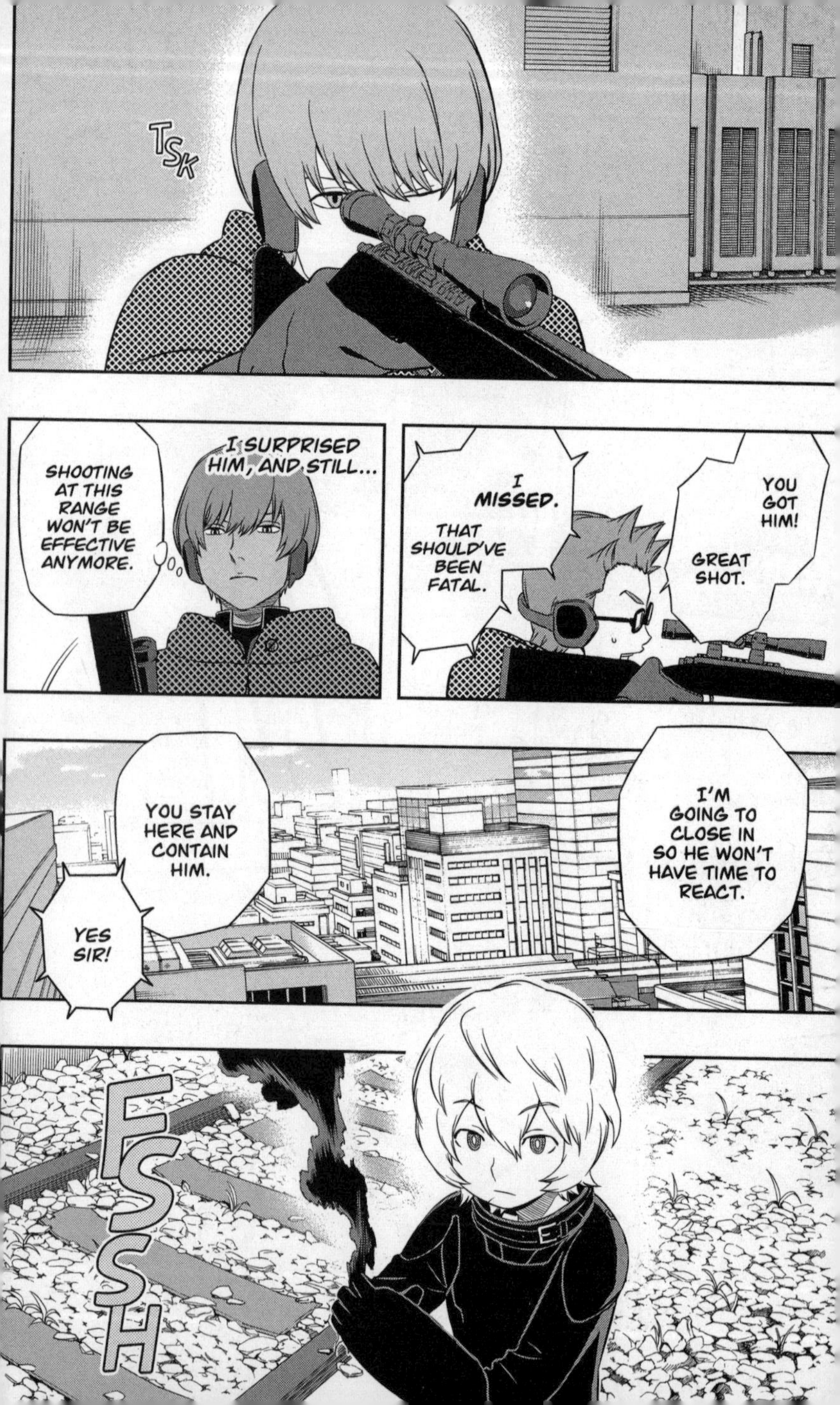
TSK
YOU GOT HIM!
GREAT SHOT.
I MISSED.
THAT SHOULD'VE BEEN FATAL.
I SURPRISED HIM, AND STILL...
SHOOTING AT THIS RANGE WON'T BE EFFECTIVE ANYMORE.
I'M GOING TO CLOSE IN SO HE WON'T HAVE TIME TO REACT.
YOU STAY HERE AND CONTAIN HIM.
YES SIR!
FSSH

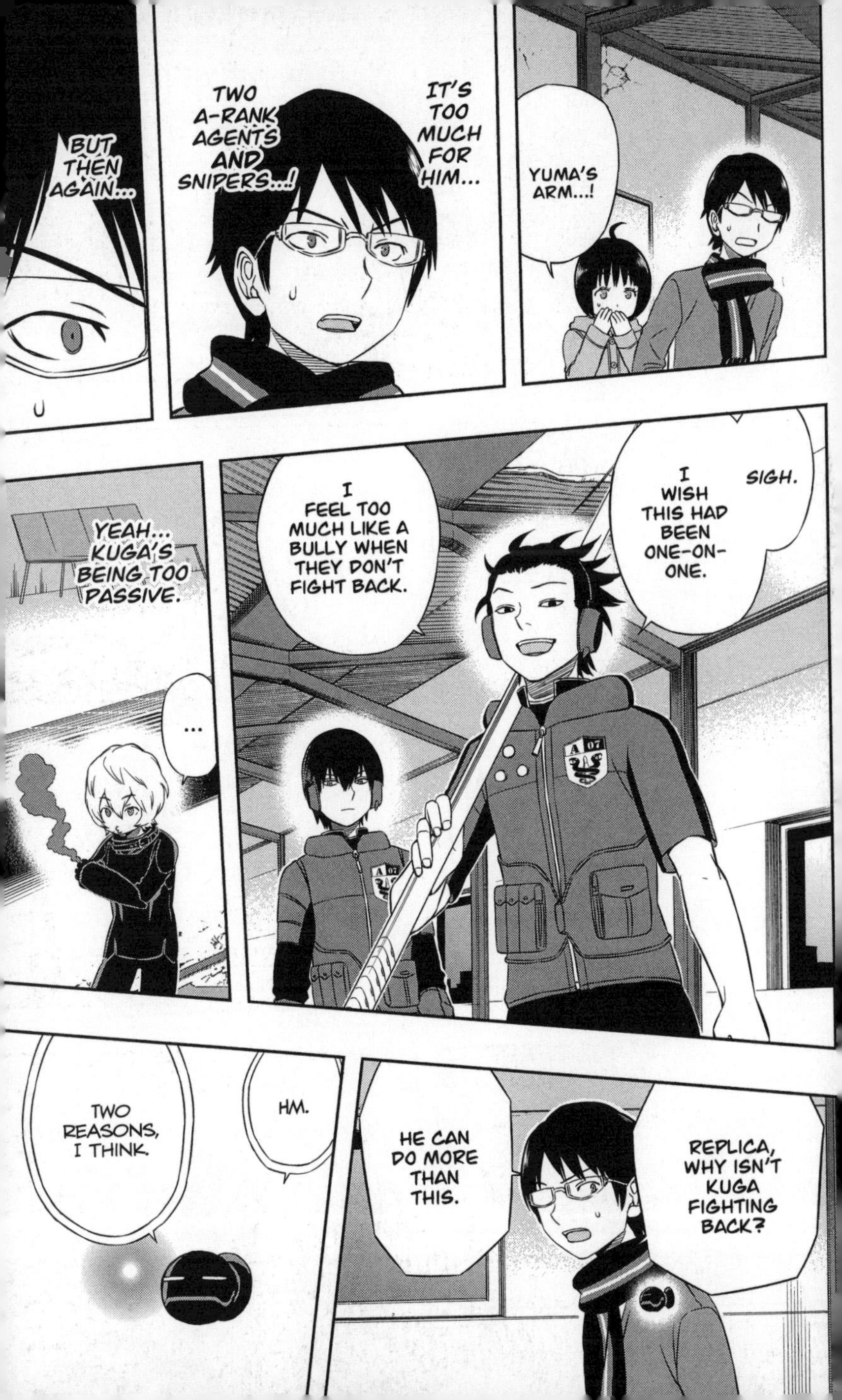
YUMA'S ARM...!
IT'S TOO MUCH FOR HIM...
TWO A-RANK AGENTS AND SNIPERS...!
BUT THEN AGAIN...
SIGH.
I WISH THIS HAD BEEN ONE-ON-ONE.
I FEEL TOO MUCH LIKE A BULLY WHEN THEY DON'T FIGHT BACK.
YEAH... KUGA'S BEING TOO PASSIVE.
...
REPLICA, WHY ISN'T KUGA FIGHTING BACK?
HE CAN DO MORE THAN THIS.
HM.
TWO REASONS, I THINK.

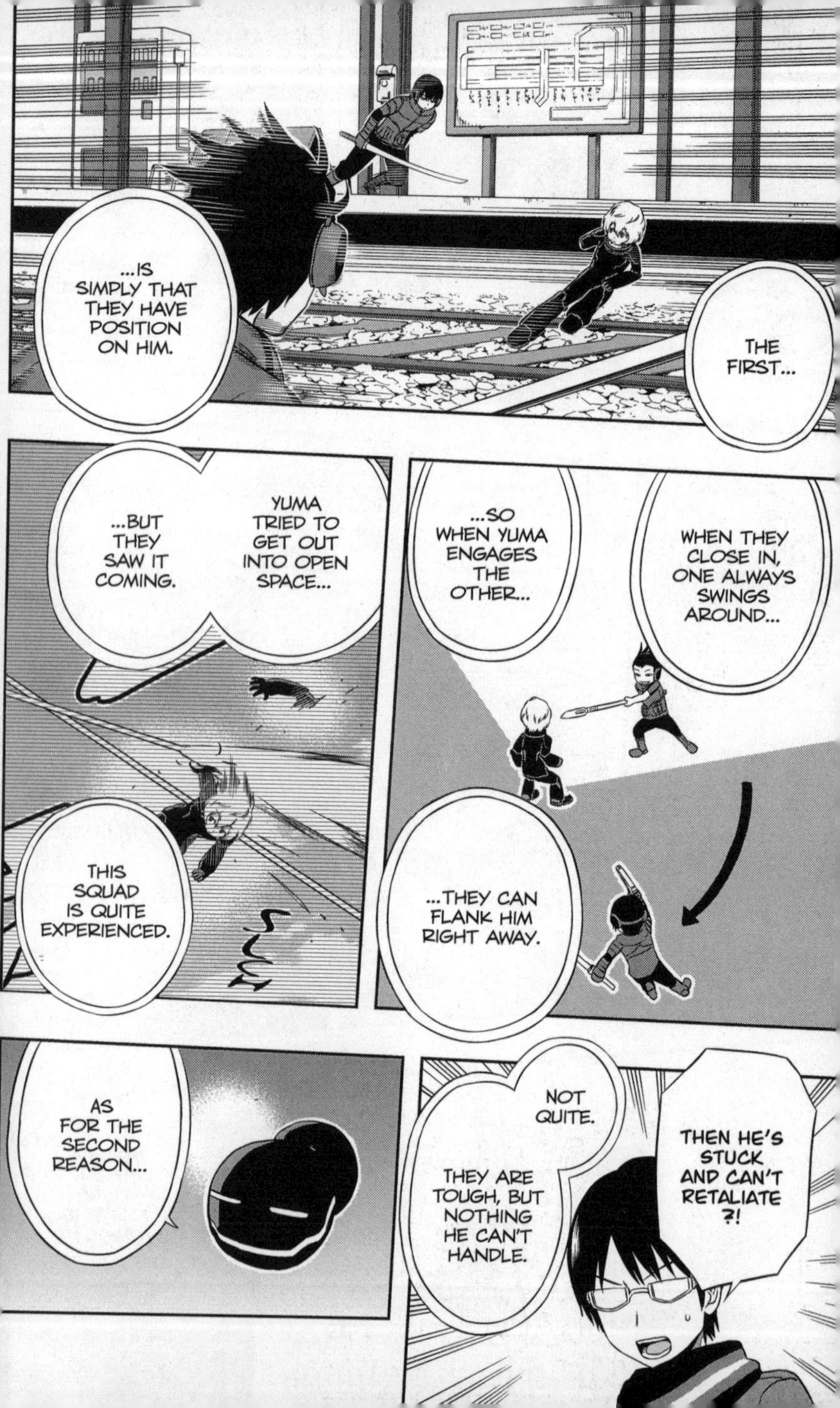
THE FIRST...
...IS SIMPLY THAT THEY HAVE POSITION ON HIM.
WHEN THEY CLOSE IN, ONE ALWAYS SWINGS AROUND...
...SO WHEN YUMA ENGAGES THE OTHER...
...THEY CAN FLANK HIM RIGHT AWAY.
YUMA TRIED TO GET OUT INTO OPEN SPACE...
...BUT THEY SAW IT COMING.
THIS SQUAD IS QUITE EXPERIENCED.
THEN HE'S STUCK AND CAN'T RETALIATE?!
NOT QUITE.
THEY ARE TOUGH, BUT NOTHING HE CAN'T HANDLE.
AS FOR THE SECOND REASON...

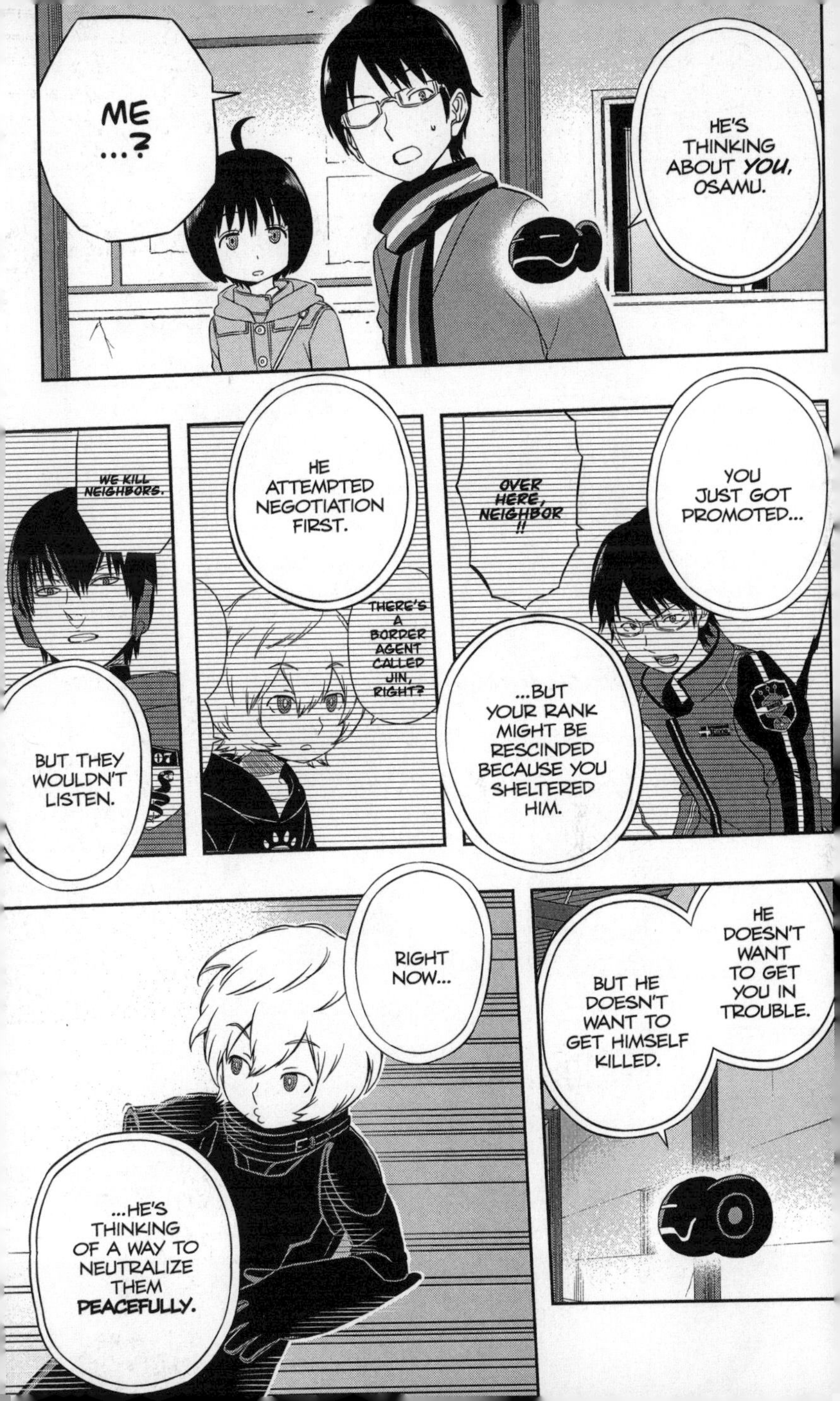

HE'S THINKING ABOUT YOU, OSAMU.
ME ...?
YOU JUST GOT PROMOTED...
OVER HERE, NEIGHBOR!!
...BUT YOUR RANK MIGHT BE RESCINDED BECAUSE YOU SHELTERED HIM.
HE ATTEMPTED NEGOTIATION FIRST.
THERE'S A BORDER AGENT CALLED JIN, RIGHT?
WE KILL NEIGHBORS.
BUT THEY WOULDN'T LISTEN.
HE DOESN'T WANT TO GET YOU IN TROUBLE.
BUT HE DOESN'T WANT TO GET HIMSELF KILLED.
RIGHT NOW...
...HE'S THINKING OF A WAY TO NEUTRALIZE THEM PEACEFULLY.

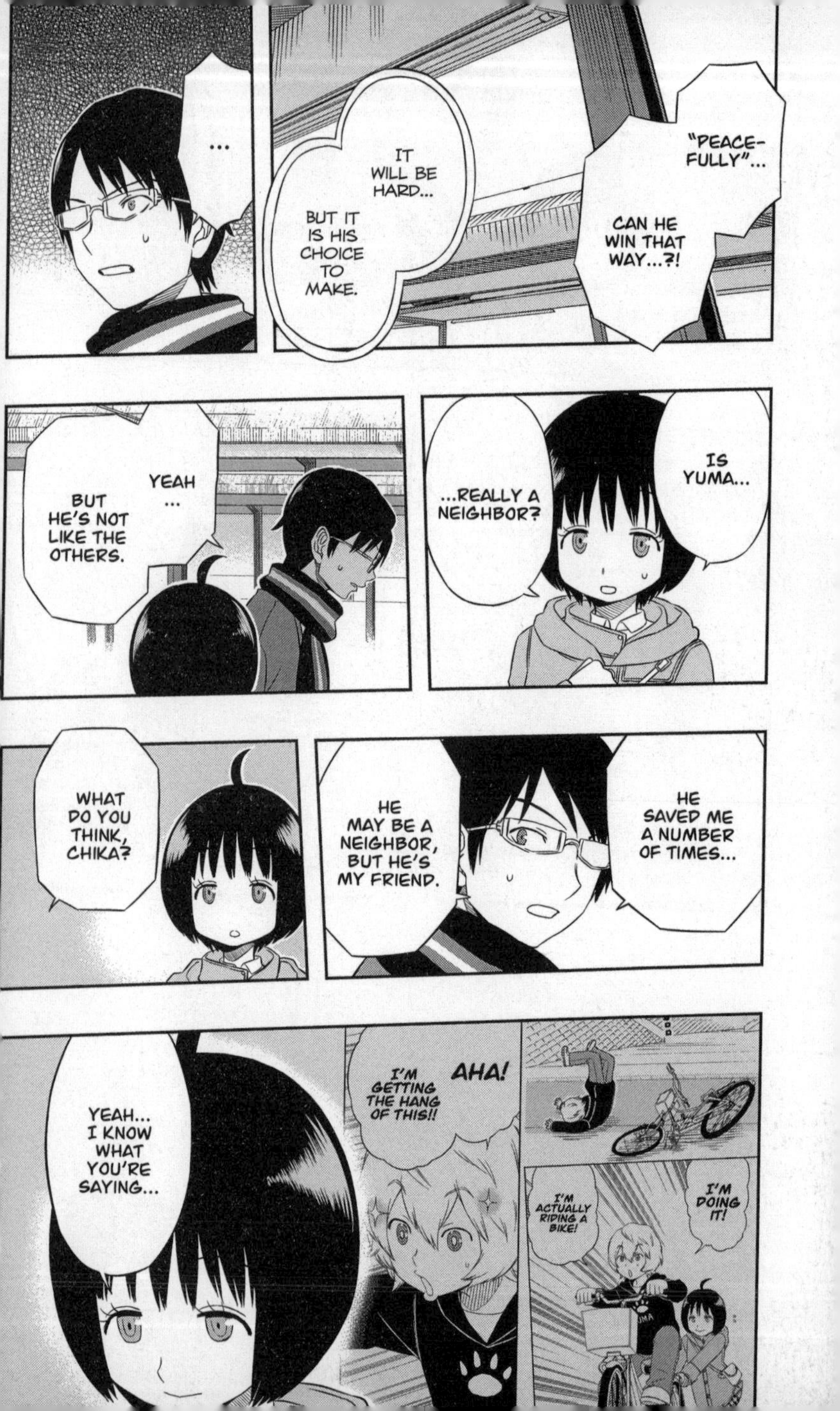
"PEACE-FULLY"...
CAN HE WIN THAT WAY...?!
IT WILL BE HARD...
BUT IT IS HIS CHOICE TO MAKE.
...
IS YUMA...
...REALLY A NEIGHBOR?
YEAH ...
BUT HE'S NOT LIKE THE OTHERS.
HE SAVED ME A NUMBER OF TIMES...
HE MAY BE A NEIGHBOR, BUT HE'S MY FRIEND.
WHAT DO YOU THINK, CHIKA?
I'M DOING IT!
I'M ACTUALLY RIDING A BIKE!
AHA!
I'M GETTING THE HANG OF THIS!!
YEAH... I KNOW WHAT YOU'RE SAYING...

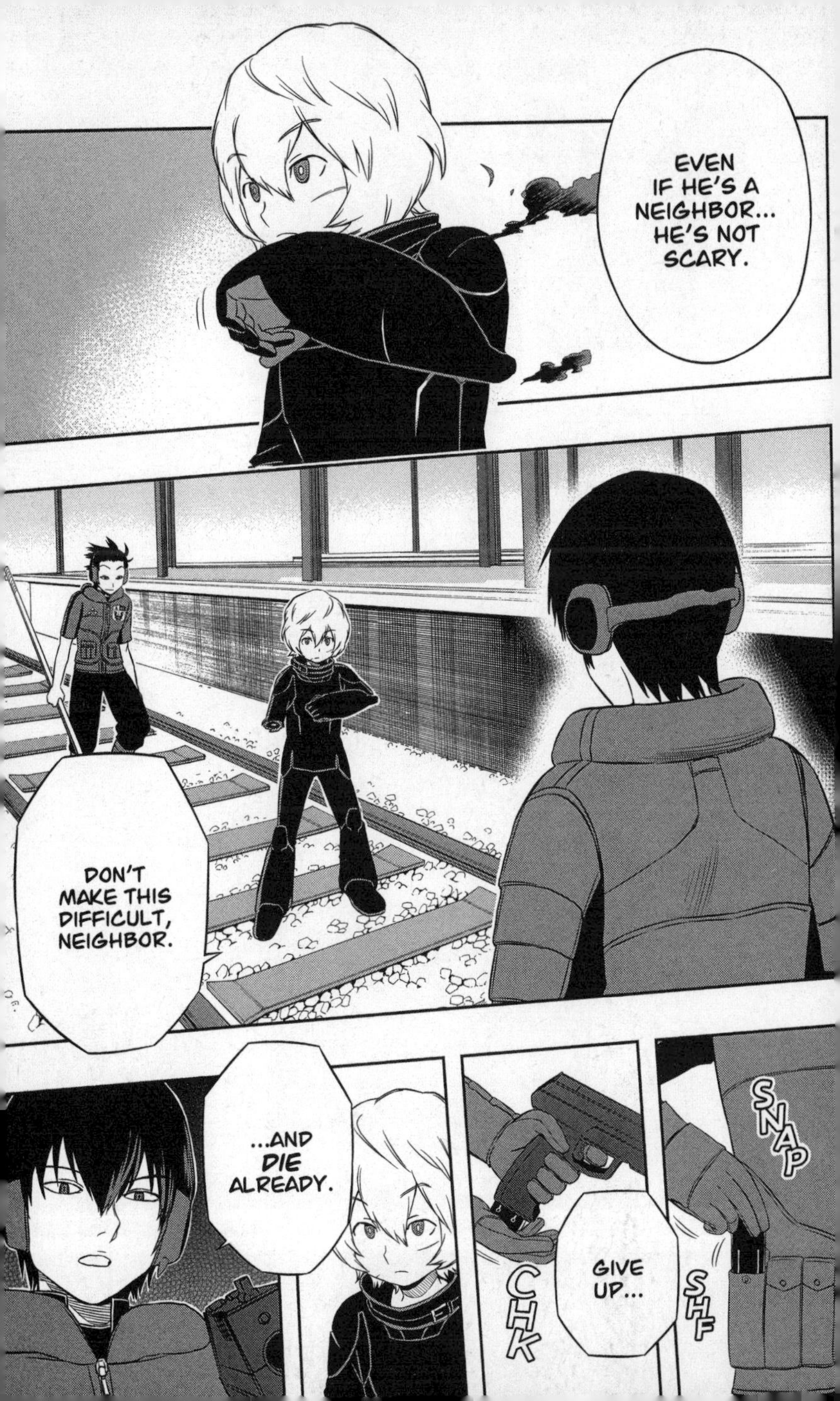
EVEN IF HE'S A NEIGHBOR... HE'S NOT SCARY.
DON'T MAKE THIS DIFFICULT, NEIGHBOR.
SNAP
SHF
GIVE UP...
CHK
...AND DIE ALREADY.

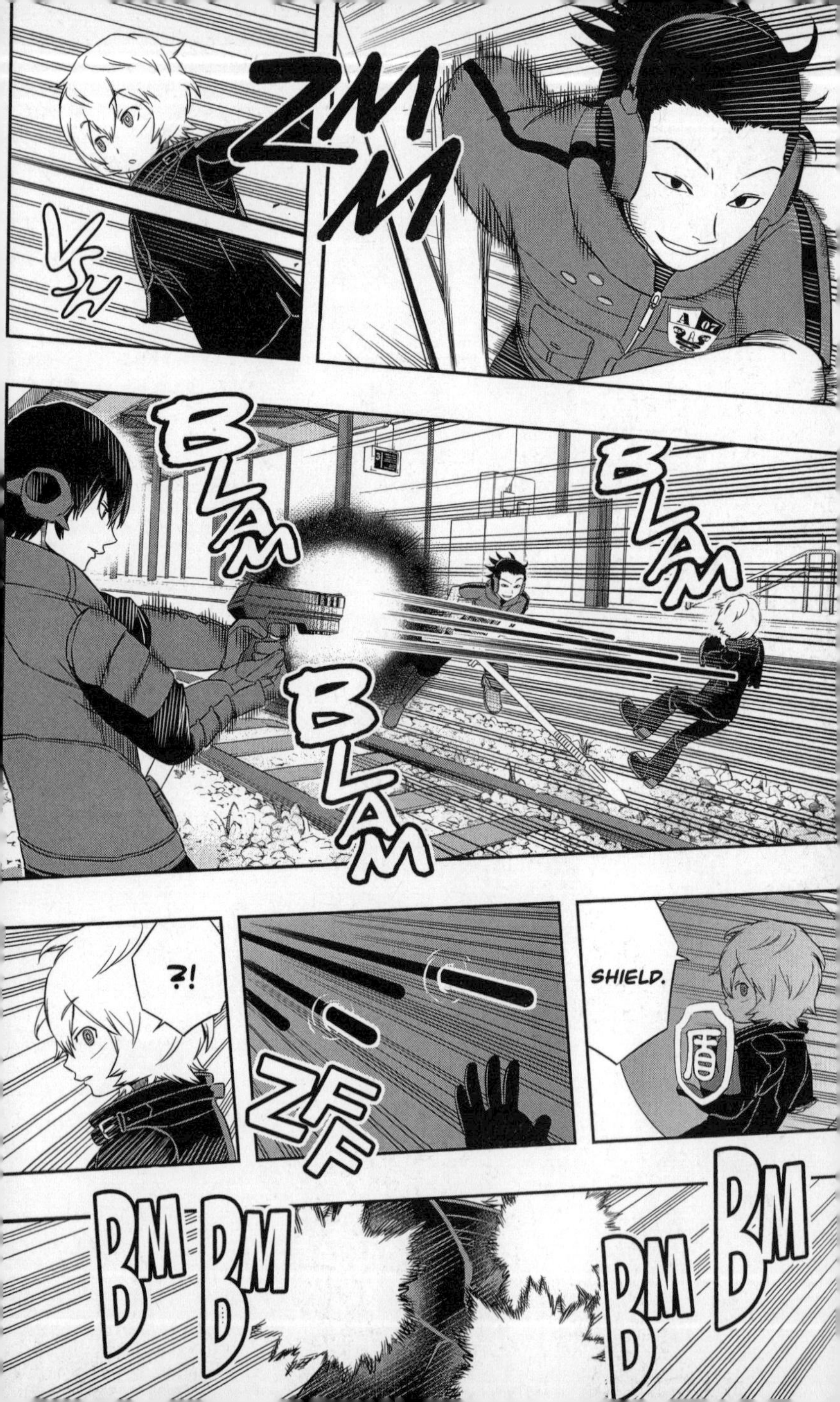
ZMM
VSH
BLAM
BLAM
BLAM
SHIELD.
盾
ZFF
?!
BM BM BM BM

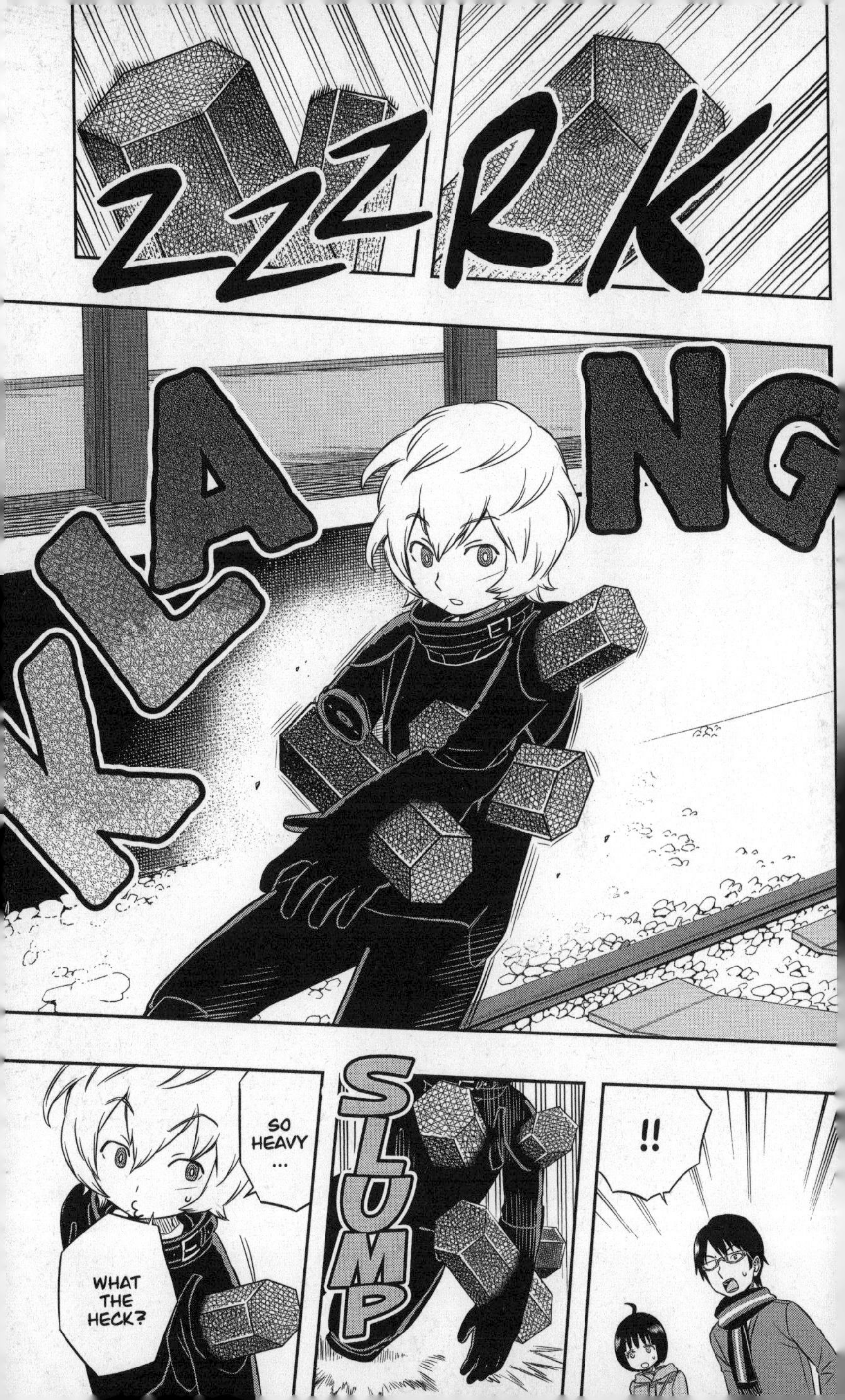
ZZZRK
KLANG
!!
SLUMP
SO HEAVY ...
WHAT THE HECK?

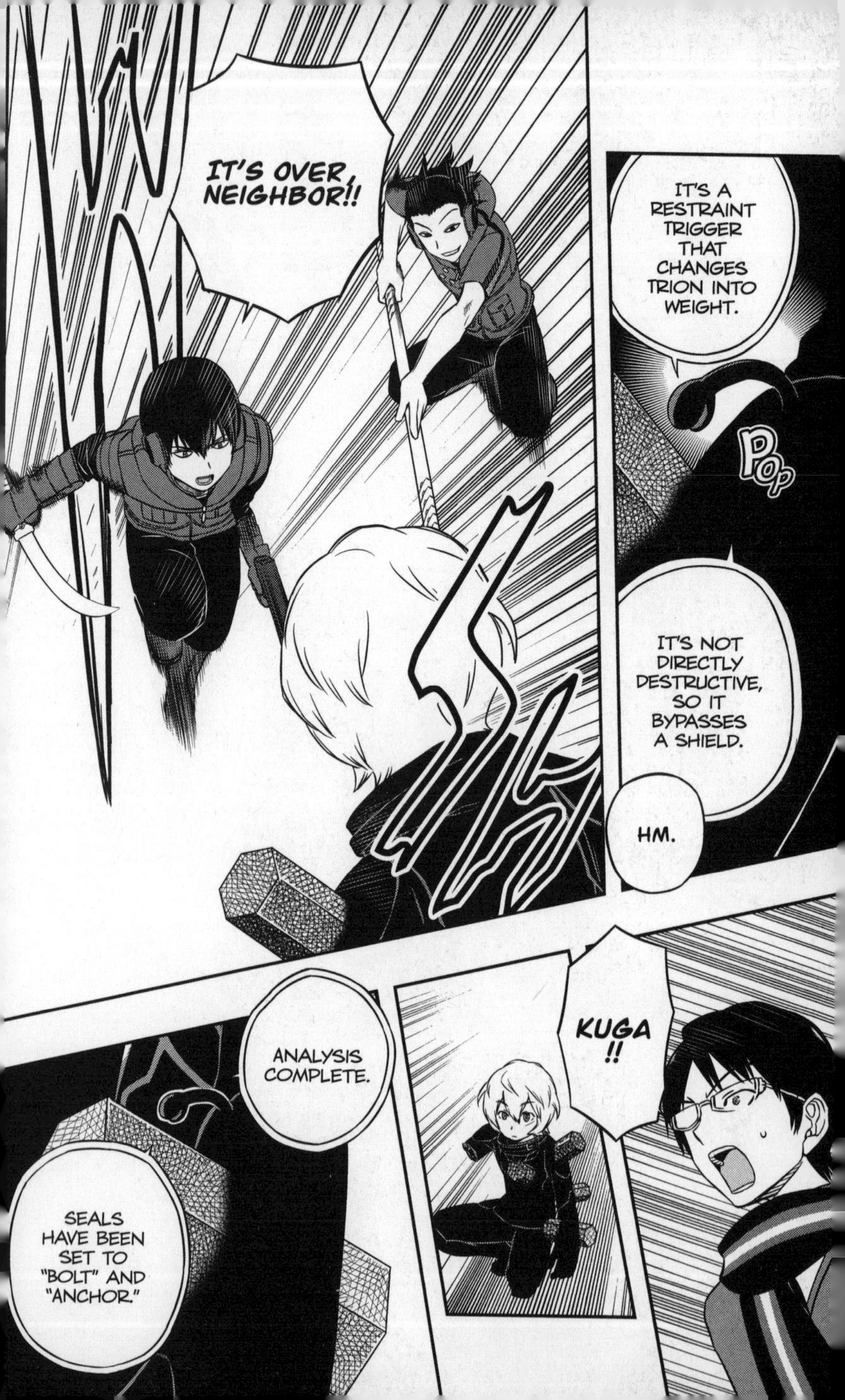
IT'S A RESTRAINT TRIGGER THAT CHANGES TRION INTO WEIGHT.
POP
IT'S NOT DIRECTLY DESTRUCTIVE, SO IT BYPASSES A SHIELD.
HM.
IT'S OVER, NEIGHBOR!!
KUGA!!
ANALYSIS COMPLETE.
SEALS HAVE BEEN SET TO "BOLT" AND "ANCHOR."

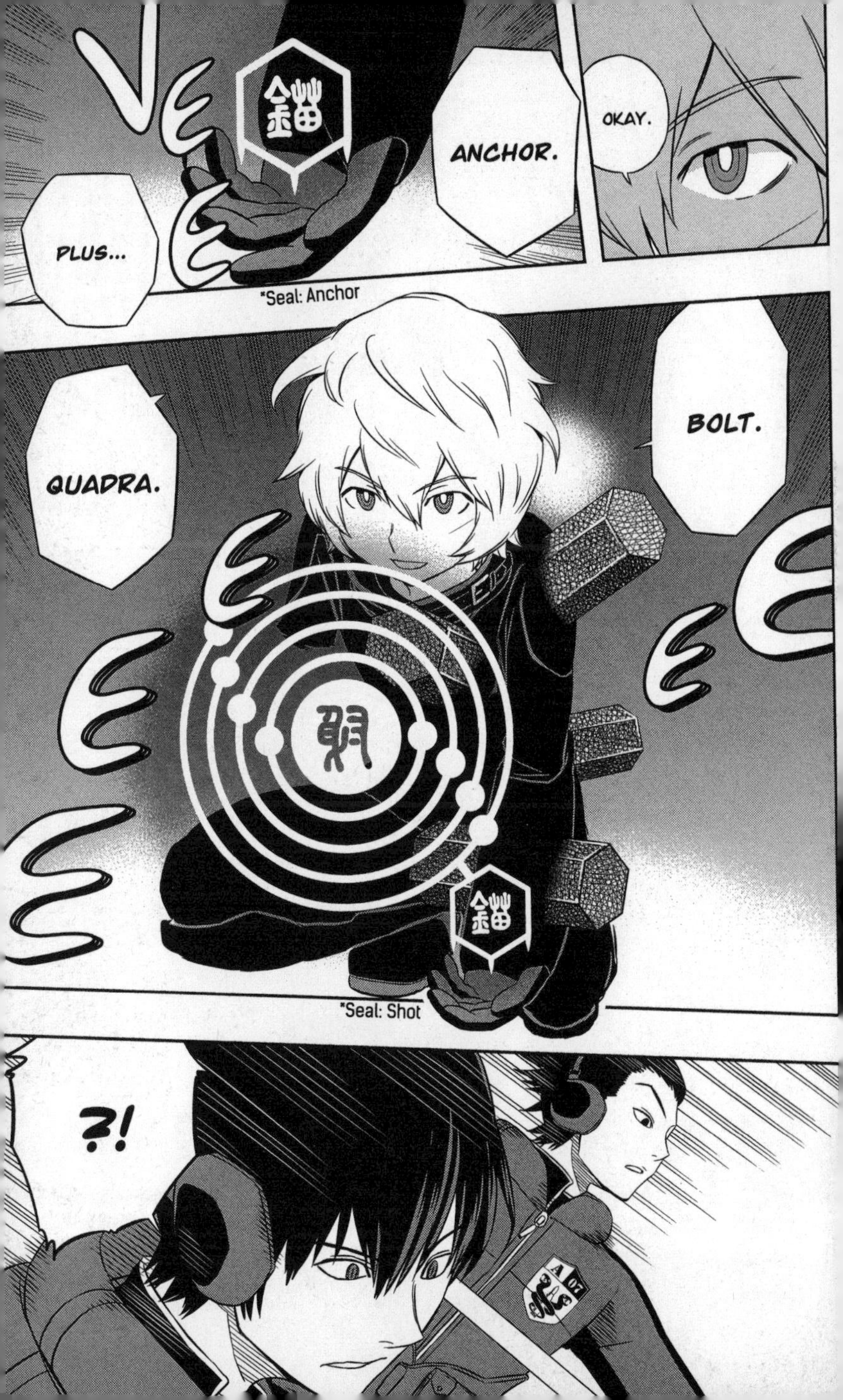
OKAY.
ANCHOR.
PLUS...
*Seal: Anchor
BOLT.
QUADRA.
*Seal: Shot
?!

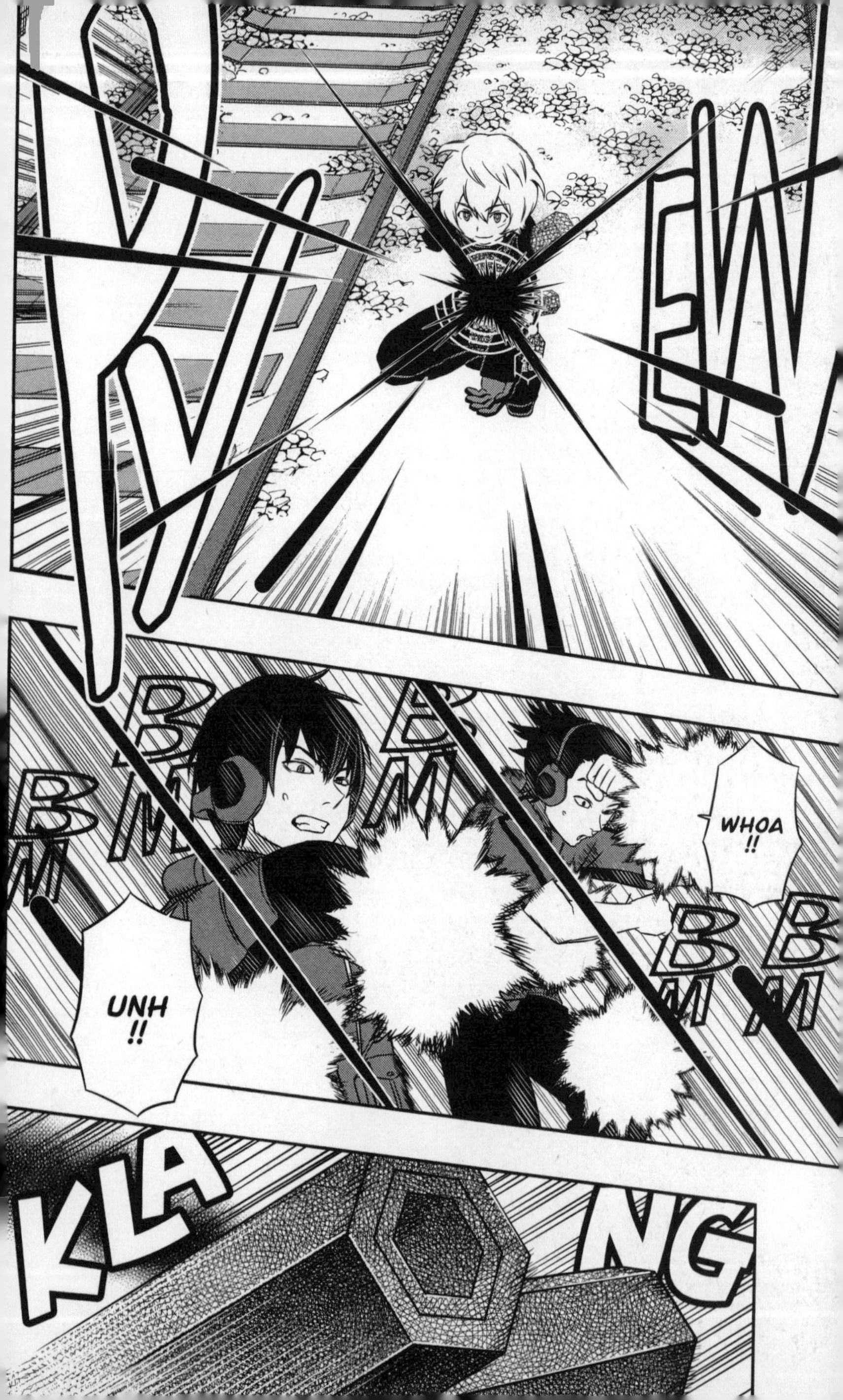
WHOA !!
BMM BMM
BMM BMM
UNH !!
KLANG

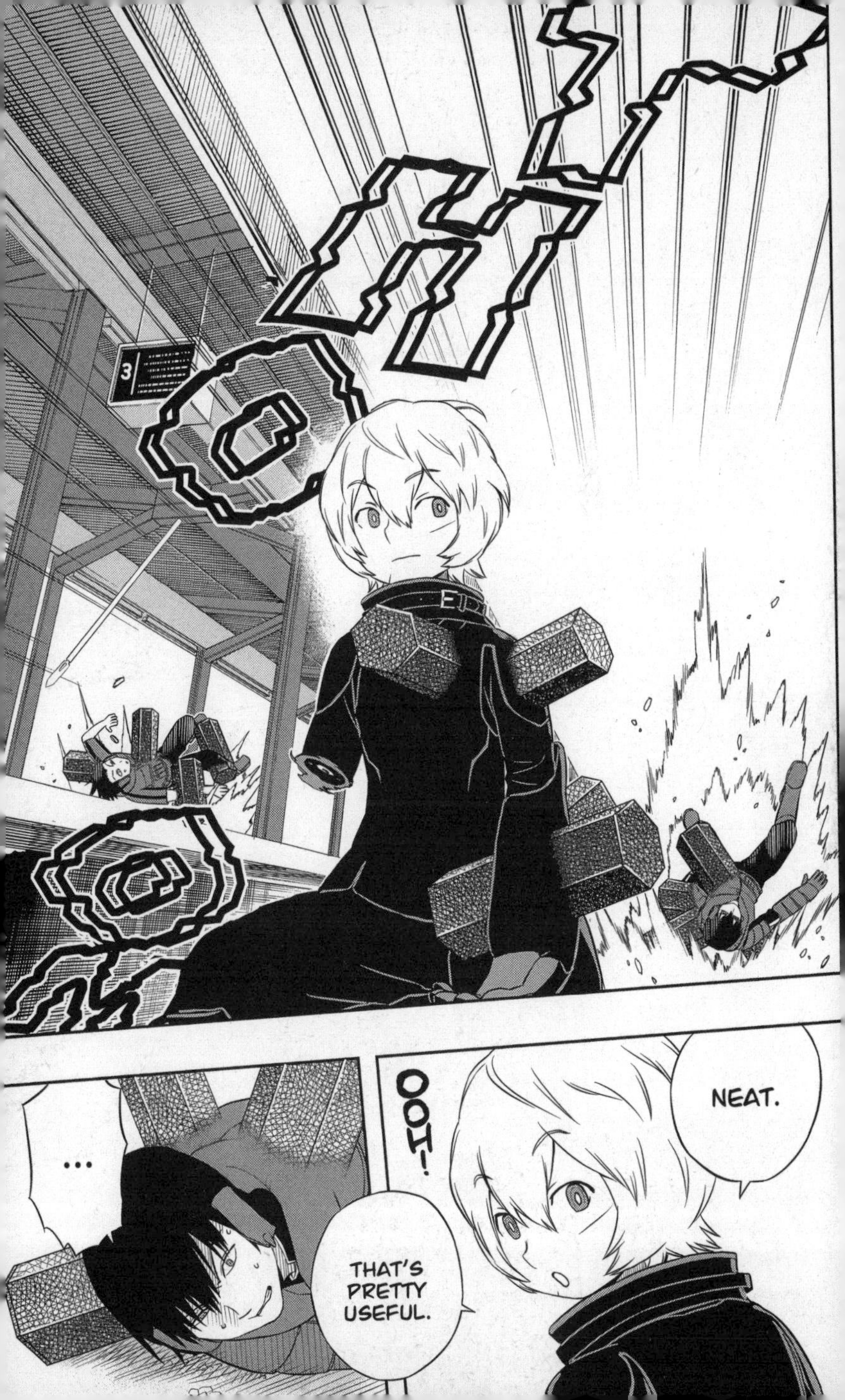
NEAT.
OOH!
THAT'S PRETTY USEFUL.
...

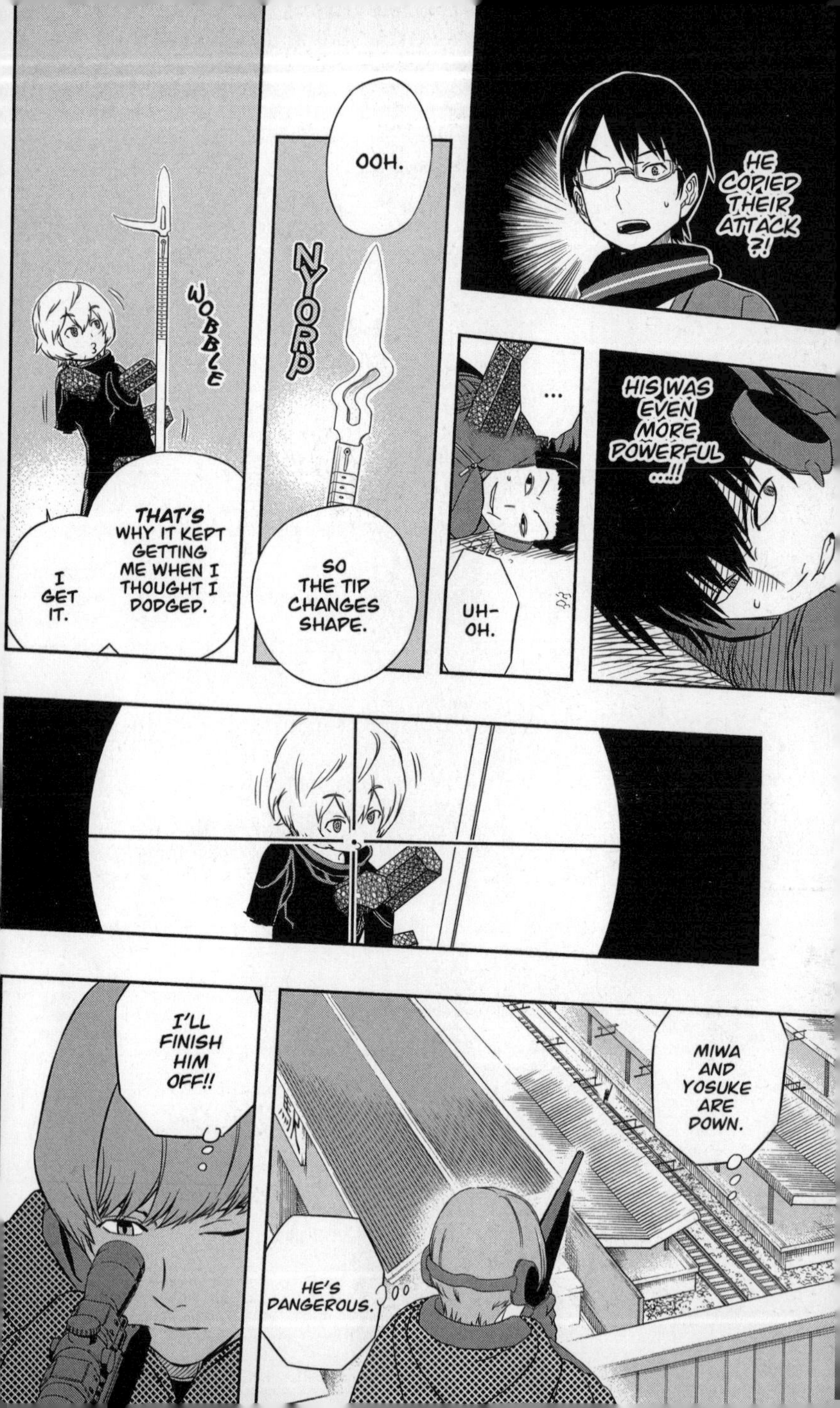
HE COPIED THEIR ATTACK ?!
HIS WAS EVEN MORE POWERFUL ...!!
...
UH-OH.
OOH.
NYORP
SO THE TIP CHANGES SHAPE.
WOBBLE
THAT'S WHY IT KEPT GETTING ME WHEN I THOUGHT I DODGED.
I GET IT.
MIWA AND YOSUKE ARE DOWN.
HE'S DANGEROUS.
I'LL FINISH HIM OFF!!

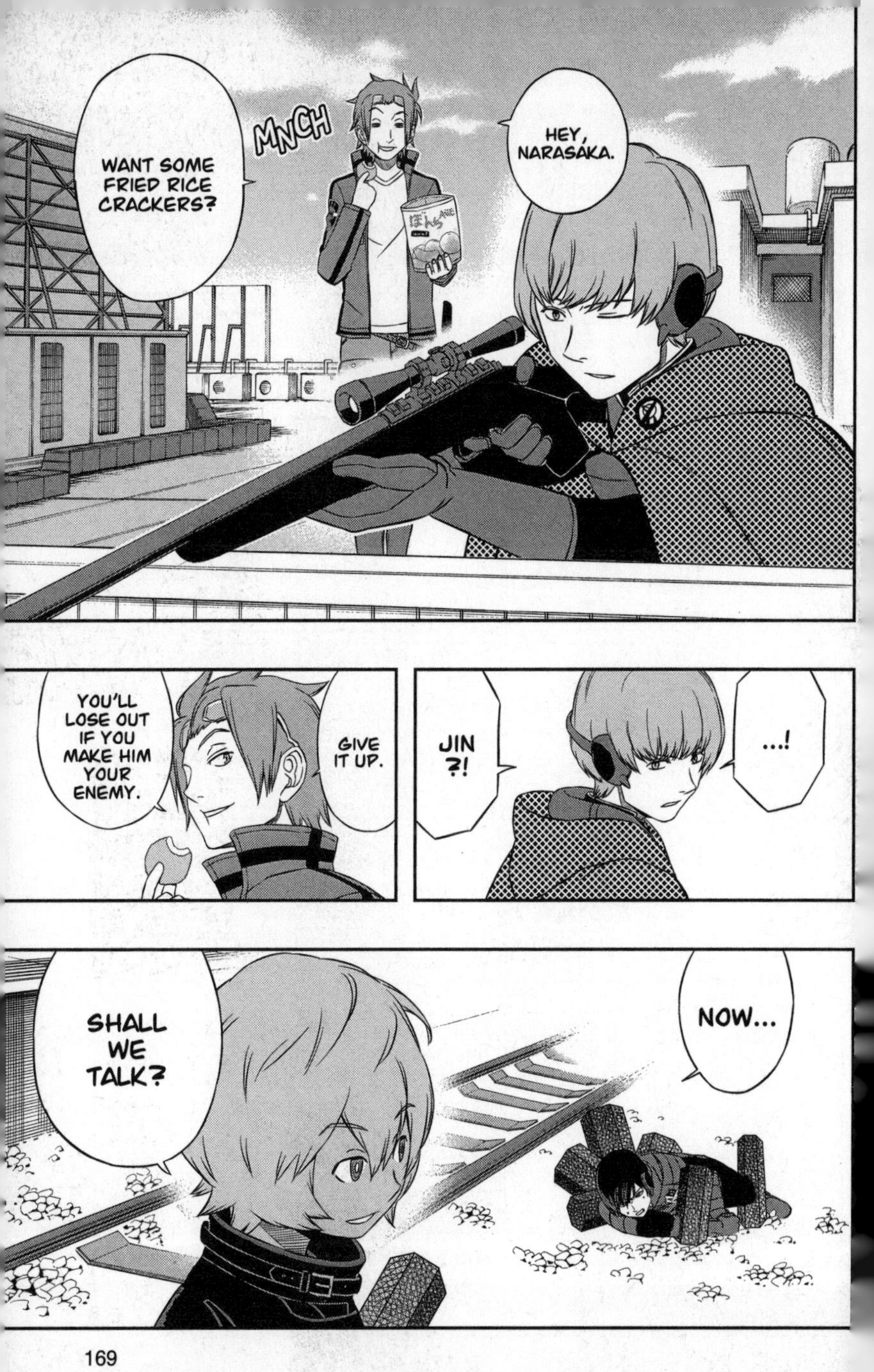
HEY, NARASAKA.
MNCH
WANT SOME FRIED RICE CRACKERS?
...!
JIN ?!
GIVE IT UP.
YOU'LL LOSE OUT IF YOU MAKE HIM YOUR ENEMY.
NOW...
SHALL WE TALK?

# Yuma's Seals

**Because my friend asked, "What do each of the seals do?"**

| | | |
|---|---|---|
| 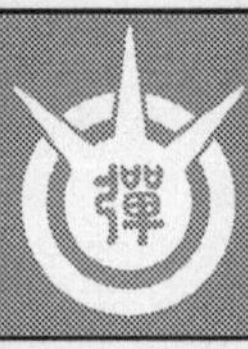弾 | 『弾』<br>BOUND<br>バウンド | Sends things flying, whether it's yourself, others or objects. Can kill humans with its acceleration. Or they might die upon impact. Very dangerous. Using multipliers sends you further. Very, very dangerous. |
| 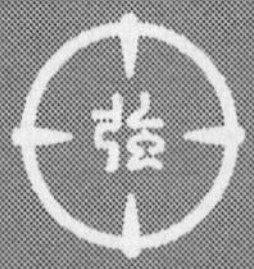強 | 『強』<br>BOOST<br>ブースト | Amplifies the effects of Trion. Can enhance attack strength. Used on the Trion body, it will enhance physical strength. An all-purpose seal to use when you simply want more power. |
| 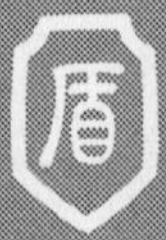盾 | 『盾』<br>SHIELD<br>シールド | Forms a barrier that deflects attacks. It is more powerful if fixed in place, and less effective if carried in hand. Its surface area is increased by using multipliers. Used in conjunction with Boost, it's a good way to increase defense. |
| 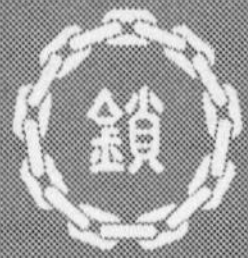鎖 | 『鎖』<br>CHAIN<br>チェイン | Captures the target with a Trion chain. Two or more chains can be connected. By setting a seal on the ground or a wall, it can be used as a trap to restrict the target. Chain durability and range can be increased with multipliers. |
| 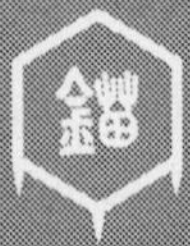錨 | 『錨』<br>ANCHOR<br>アンカー | Copied from Miwa's attack. Changes Trion into a weight to limit the target's mobility. Needs to touch the target directly when not used in conjunction with Bolt. |
| 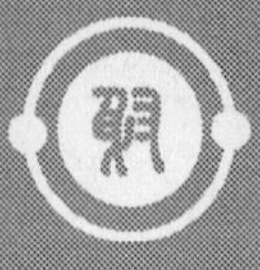射 | 『射』<br>BOLT<br>ボルト | Copied from Miwa's attack. A ranged Trion attack. Used in conjunction with other seals, it can apply that seal's effect to a distant target. Range or number of shots can be increased using a multiplier. |

## Chapter 16 Miwa Squad: Part 3

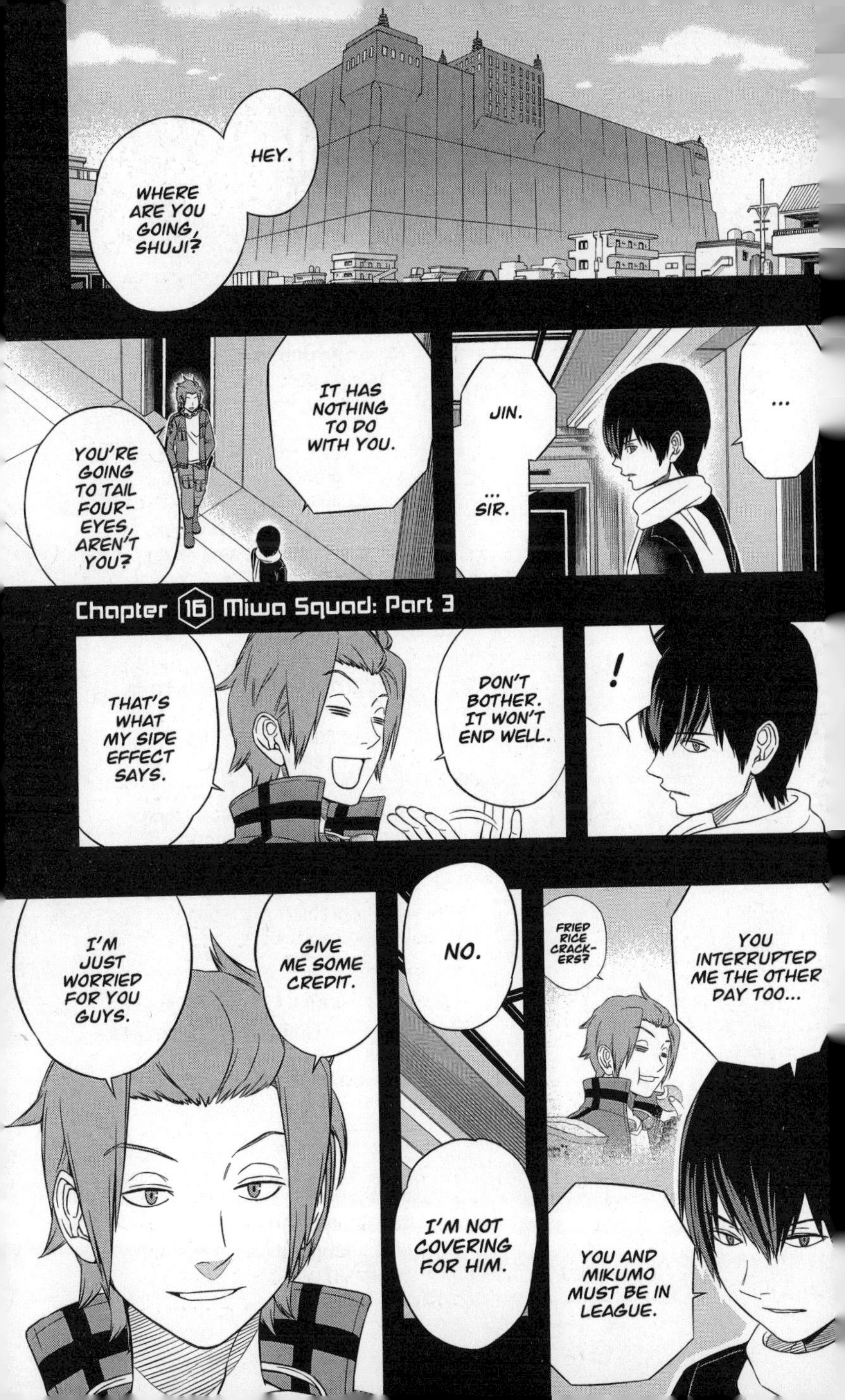
HEY.
WHERE ARE YOU GOING, SHUJI?
...
JIN.
... SIR.
IT HAS NOTHING TO DO WITH YOU.
YOU'RE GOING TO TAIL FOUR-EYES, AREN'T YOU?
!
DON'T BOTHER. IT WON'T END WELL.
THAT'S WHAT MY SIDE EFFECT SAYS.
YOU INTERRUPTED ME THE OTHER DAY TOO...
FRIED RICE CRACKERS?
YOU AND MIKUMO MUST BE IN LEAGUE.
NO.
I'M NOT COVERING FOR HIM.
GIVE ME SOME CREDIT.
I'M JUST WORRIED FOR YOU GUYS.

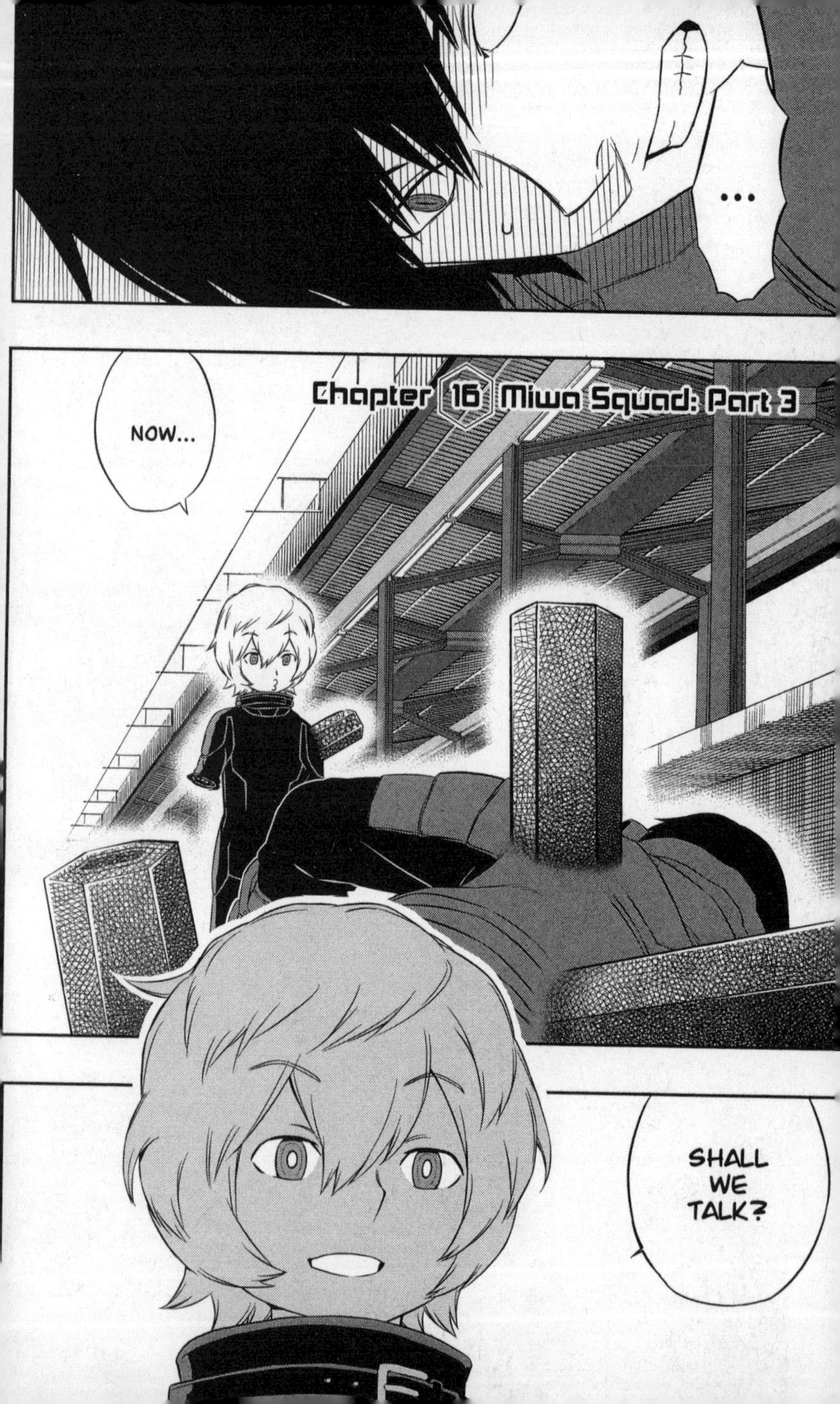
...
Chapter 16 Miwa Squad: Part 3
NOW...
SHALL WE TALK?

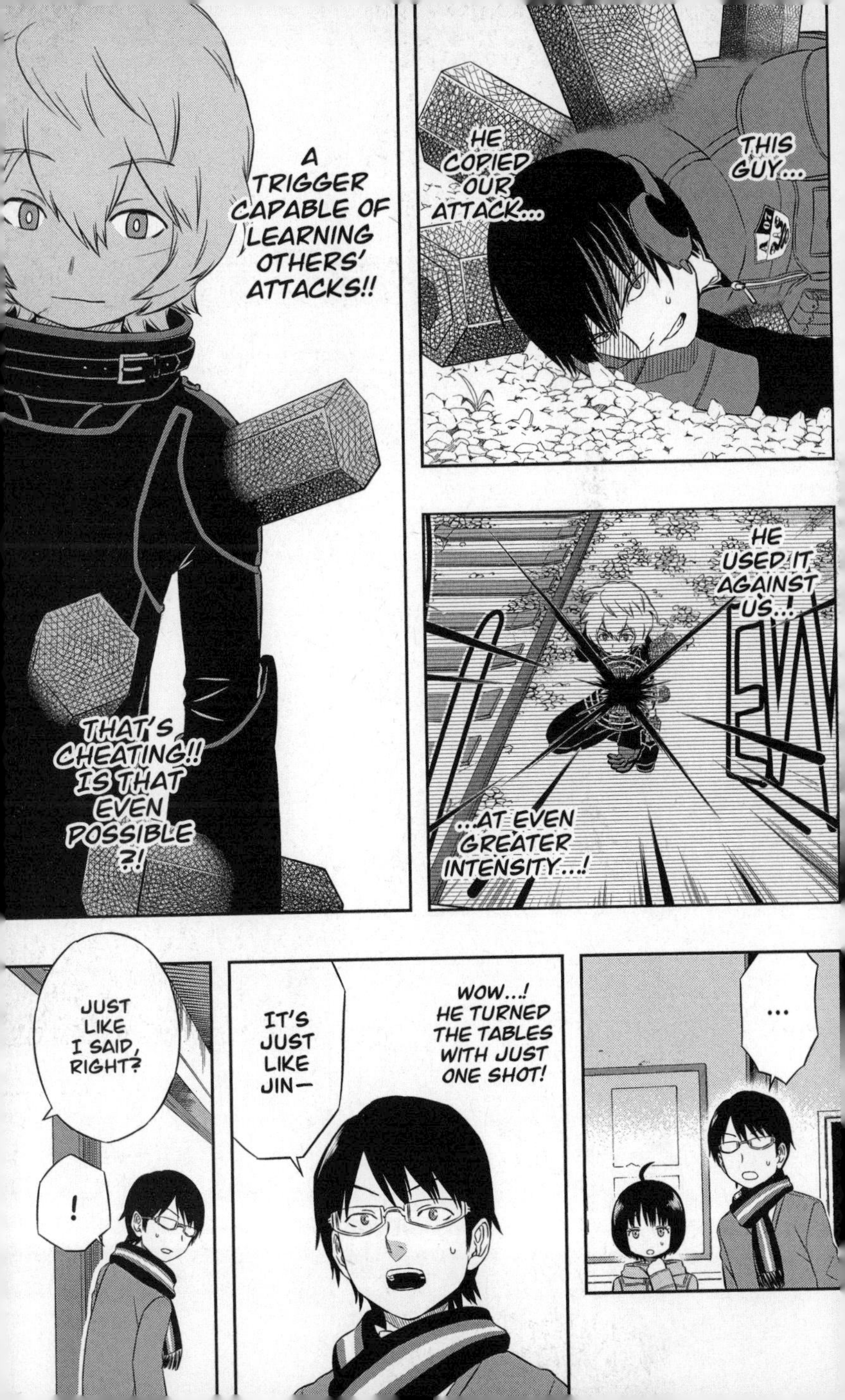
THIS GUY...
HE COPIED OUR ATTACK...
HE USED IT AGAINST US...
...AT EVEN GREATER INTENSITY...!
A TRIGGER CAPABLE OF LEARNING OTHERS' ATTACKS!!
THAT'S CHEATING!! IS THAT EVEN POSSIBLE?!
...
WOW...! HE TURNED THE TABLES WITH JUST ONE SHOT!
IT'S JUST LIKE JIN—
JUST LIKE I SAID, RIGHT?
!

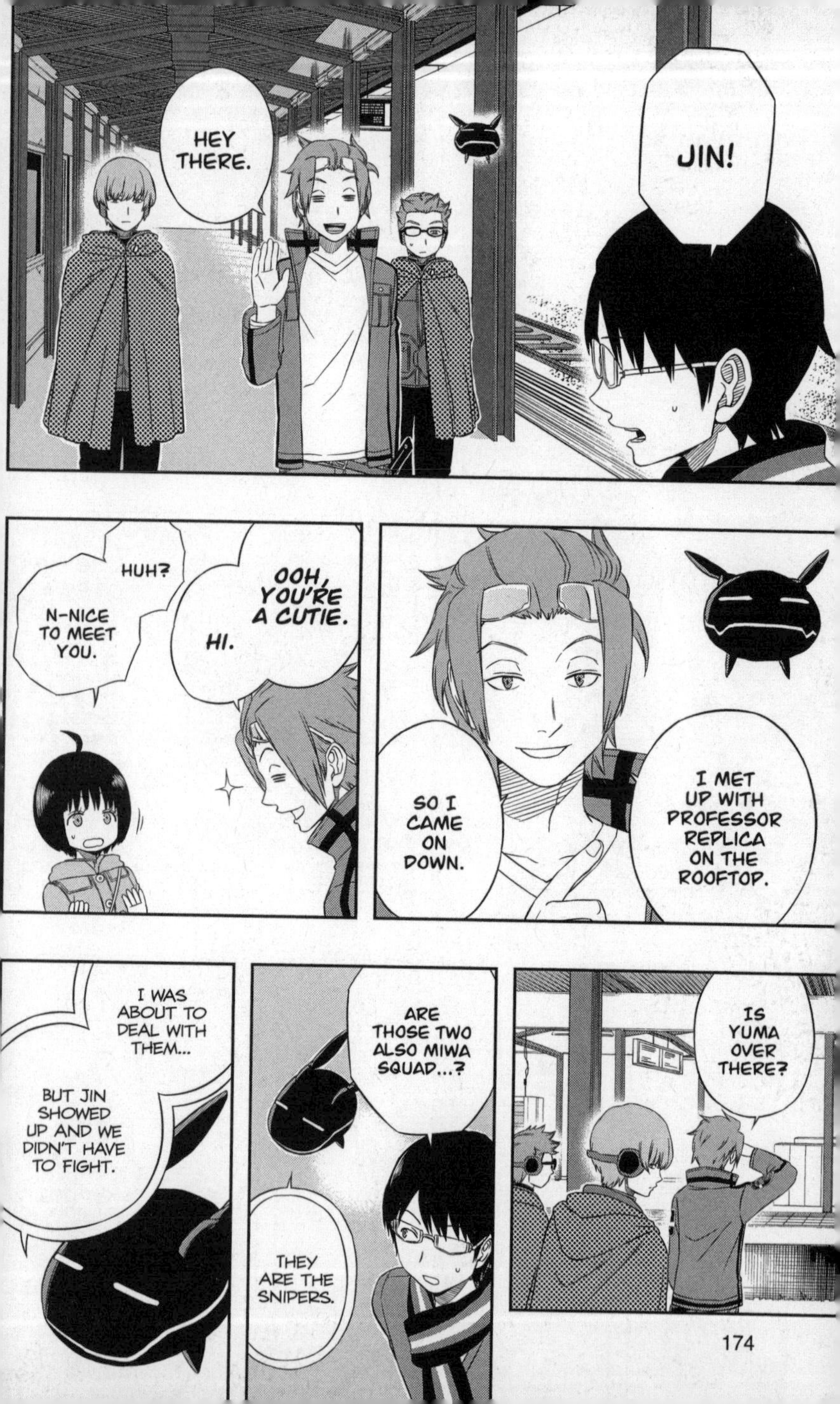
JIN!
HEY THERE.
I MET UP WITH PROFESSOR REPLICA ON THE ROOFTOP.
SO I CAME ON DOWN.
OOH, YOU'RE A CUTIE.
HI.
HUH?
N-NICE TO MEET YOU.
IS YUMA OVER THERE?
ARE THOSE TWO ALSO MIWA SQUAD...?
THEY ARE THE SNIPERS.
I WAS ABOUT TO DEAL WITH THEM...
BUT JIN SHOWED UP AND WE DIDN'T HAVE TO FIGHT.

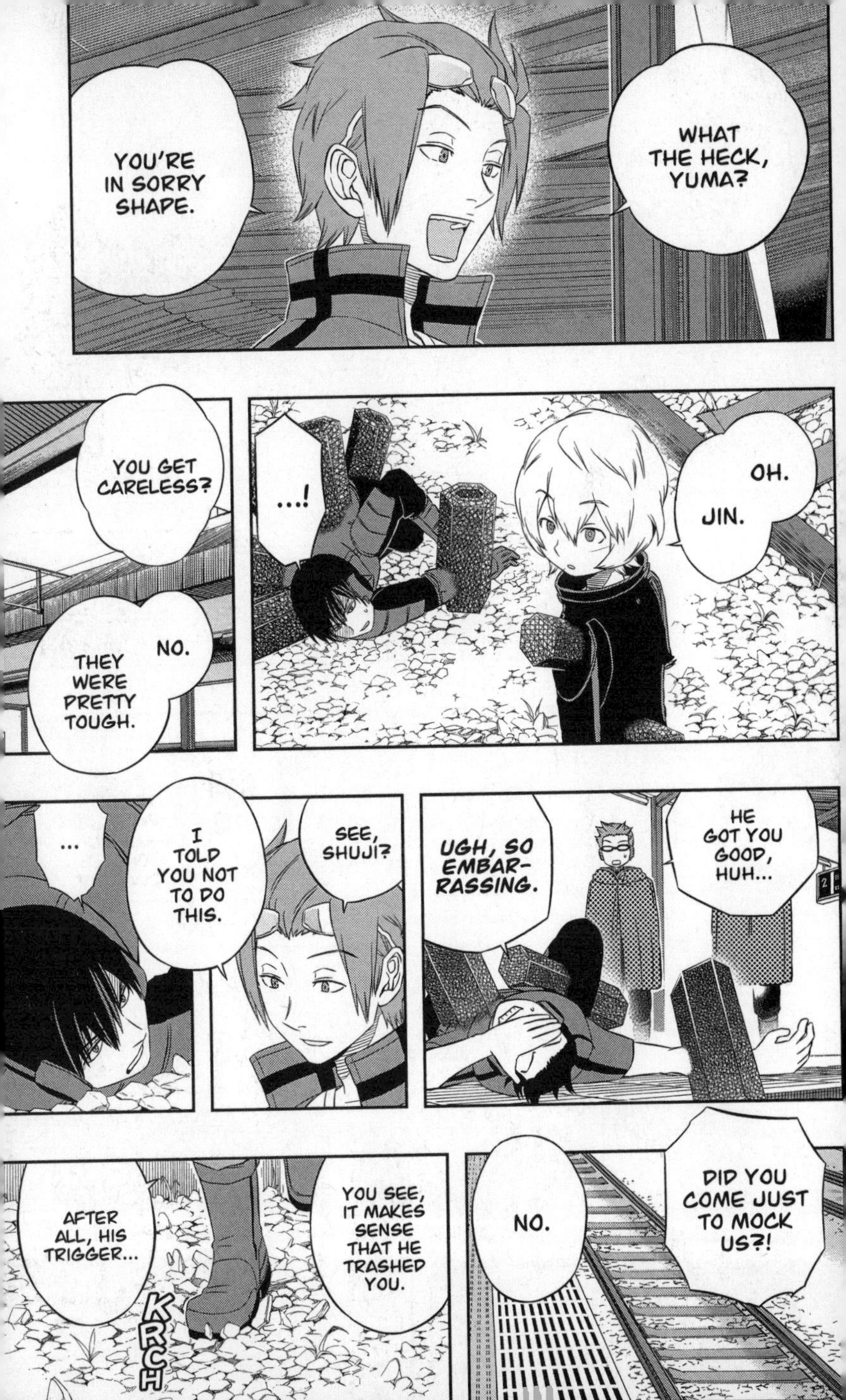
WHAT THE HECK, YUMA?
YOU'RE IN SORRY SHAPE.
OH.
JIN.
...!
YOU GET CARELESS?
NO.
THEY WERE PRETTY TOUGH.
HE GOT YOU GOOD, HUH...
UGH, SO EMBAR-RASSING.
SEE, SHUJI?
I TOLD YOU NOT TO DO THIS.
...
DID YOU COME JUST TO MOCK US?!
NO.
YOU SEE, IT MAKES SENSE THAT HE TRASHED YOU.
AFTER ALL, HIS TRIGGER...
KRCH

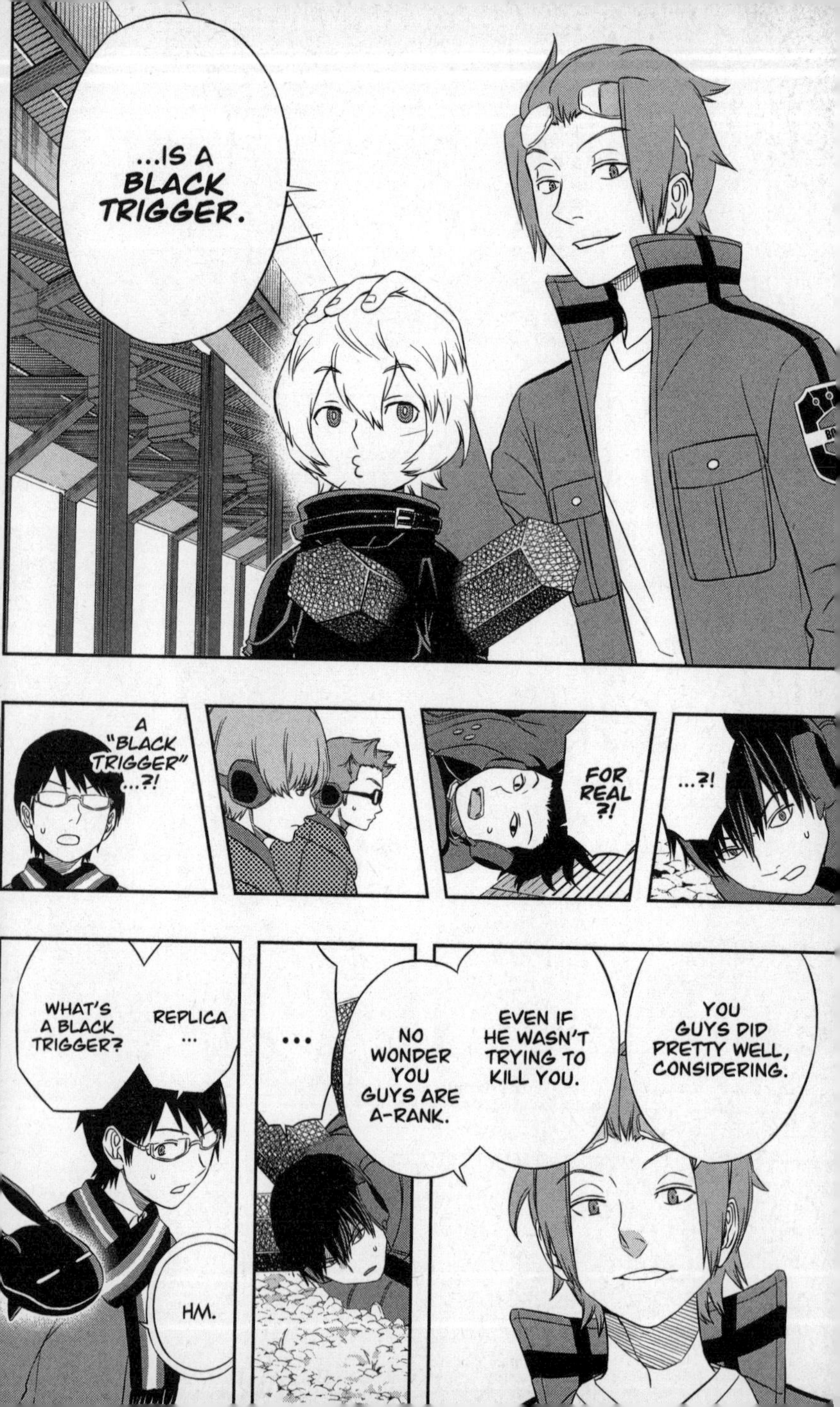
...IS A BLACK TRIGGER.
...?!
FOR REAL ?!
A "BLACK TRIGGER" ...?!
YOU GUYS DID PRETTY WELL, CONSIDERING.
EVEN IF HE WASN'T TRYING TO KILL YOU.
NO WONDER YOU GUYS ARE A-RANK.
...
REPLICA ...
WHAT'S A BLACK TRIGGER?
HM.

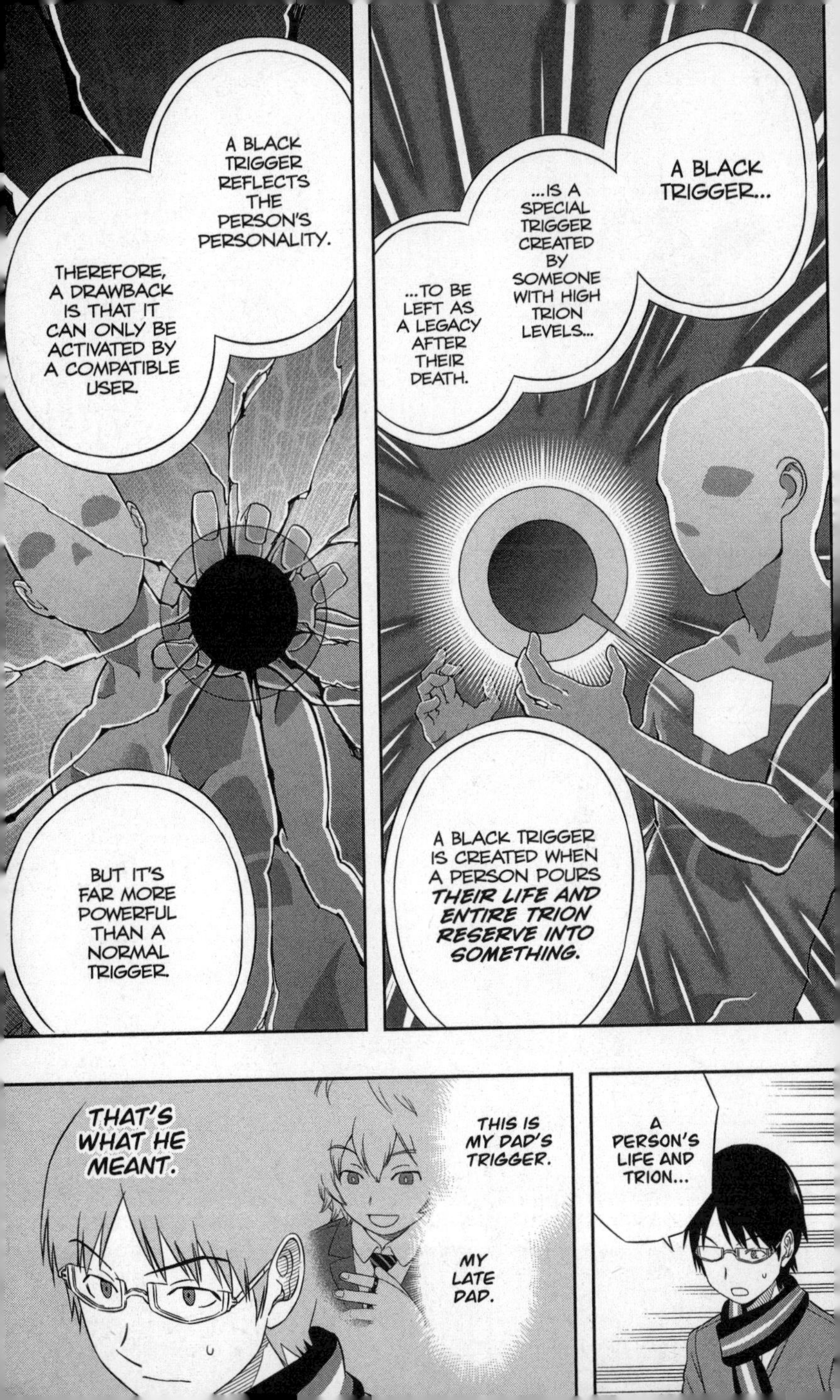
A BLACK TRIGGER...
...IS A SPECIAL TRIGGER CREATED BY SOMEONE WITH HIGH TRION LEVELS...
...TO BE LEFT AS A LEGACY AFTER THEIR DEATH.
A BLACK TRIGGER IS CREATED WHEN A PERSON POURS *THEIR LIFE AND ENTIRE TRION RESERVE INTO SOMETHING.*
A BLACK TRIGGER REFLECTS THE PERSON'S PERSONALITY.
THEREFORE, A DRAWBACK IS THAT IT CAN ONLY BE ACTIVATED BY A COMPATIBLE USER.
BUT IT'S FAR MORE POWERFUL THAN A NORMAL TRIGGER.
A PERSON'S LIFE AND TRION...
THIS IS MY DAD'S TRIGGER.
MY LATE DAD.
*THAT'S WHAT HE MEANT.*

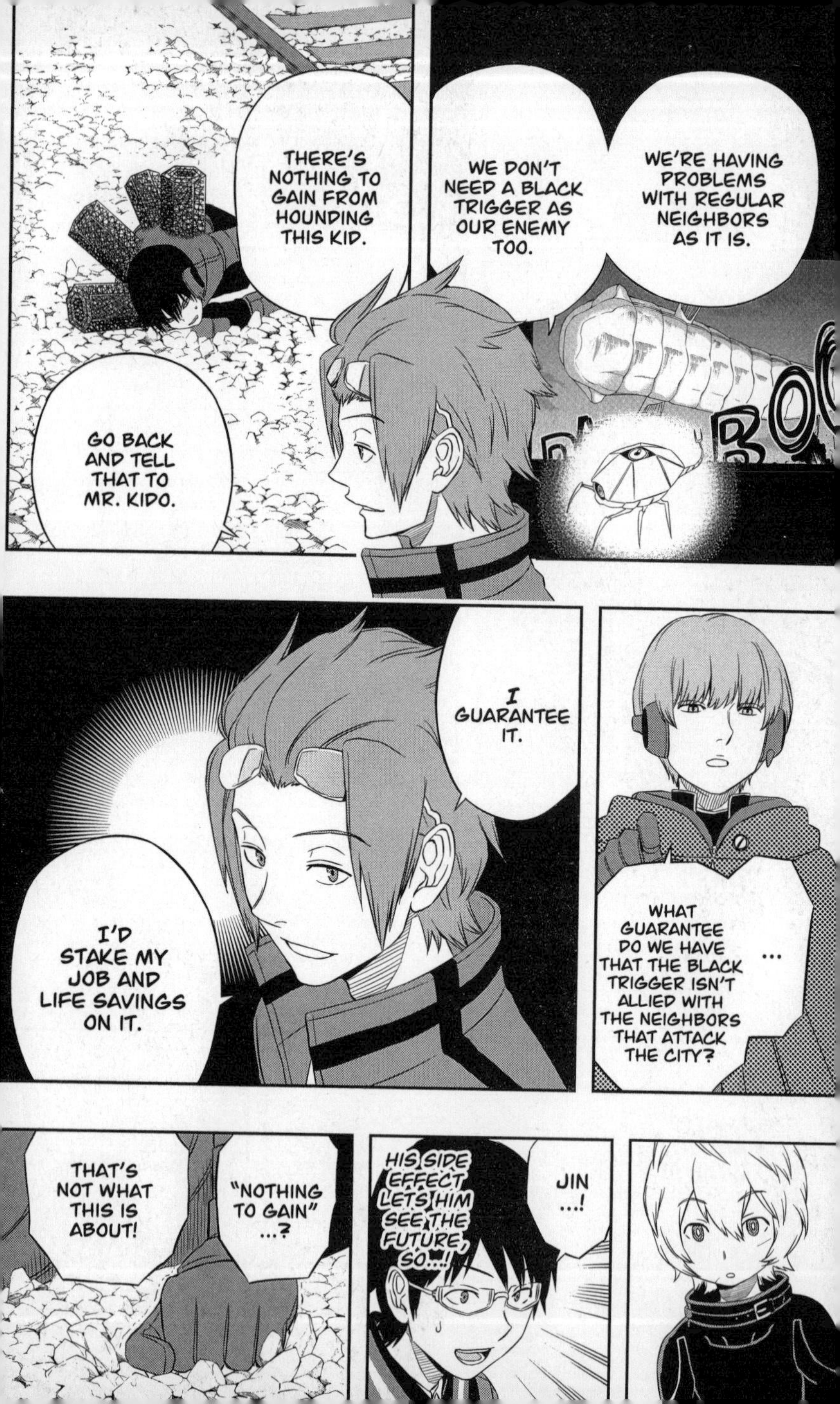
WE'RE HAVING PROBLEMS WITH REGULAR NEIGHBORS AS IT IS.
WE DON'T NEED A BLACK TRIGGER AS OUR ENEMY TOO.
THERE'S NOTHING TO GAIN FROM HOUNDING THIS KID.
GO BACK AND TELL THAT TO MR. KIDO.
WHAT GUARANTEE DO WE HAVE THAT THE BLACK TRIGGER ISN'T ALLIED WITH THE NEIGHBORS THAT ATTACK THE CITY?
...
I GUARANTEE IT.
I'D STAKE MY JOB AND LIFE SAVINGS ON IT.
JIN ...!
HIS SIDE EFFECT LETS HIM SEE THE FUTURE, SO...!
"NOTHING TO GAIN" ...?
THAT'S NOT WHAT THIS IS ABOUT!

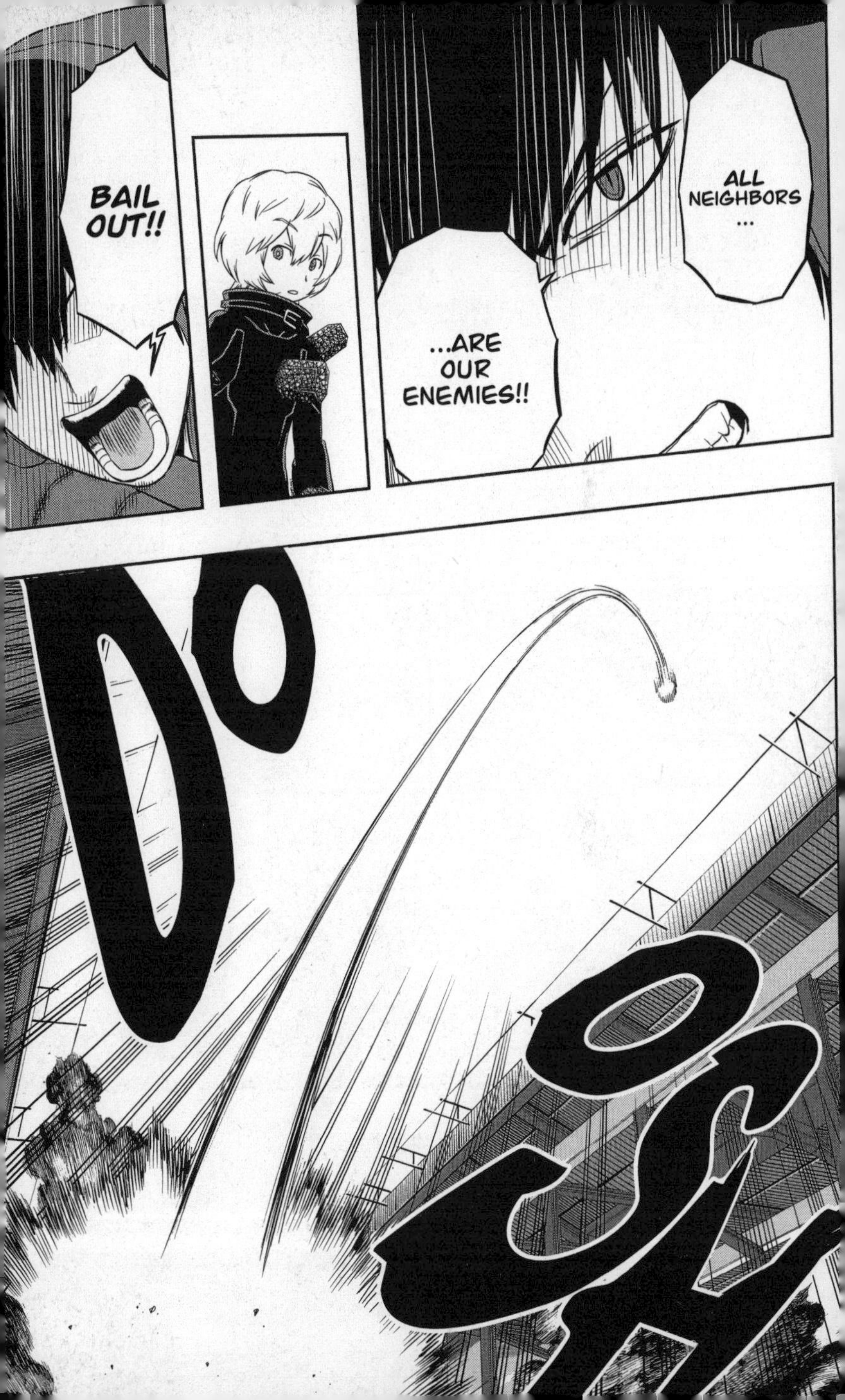
ALL NEIGHBORS ...
...ARE OUR ENEMIES!!
BAIL OUT!!
DOOSH

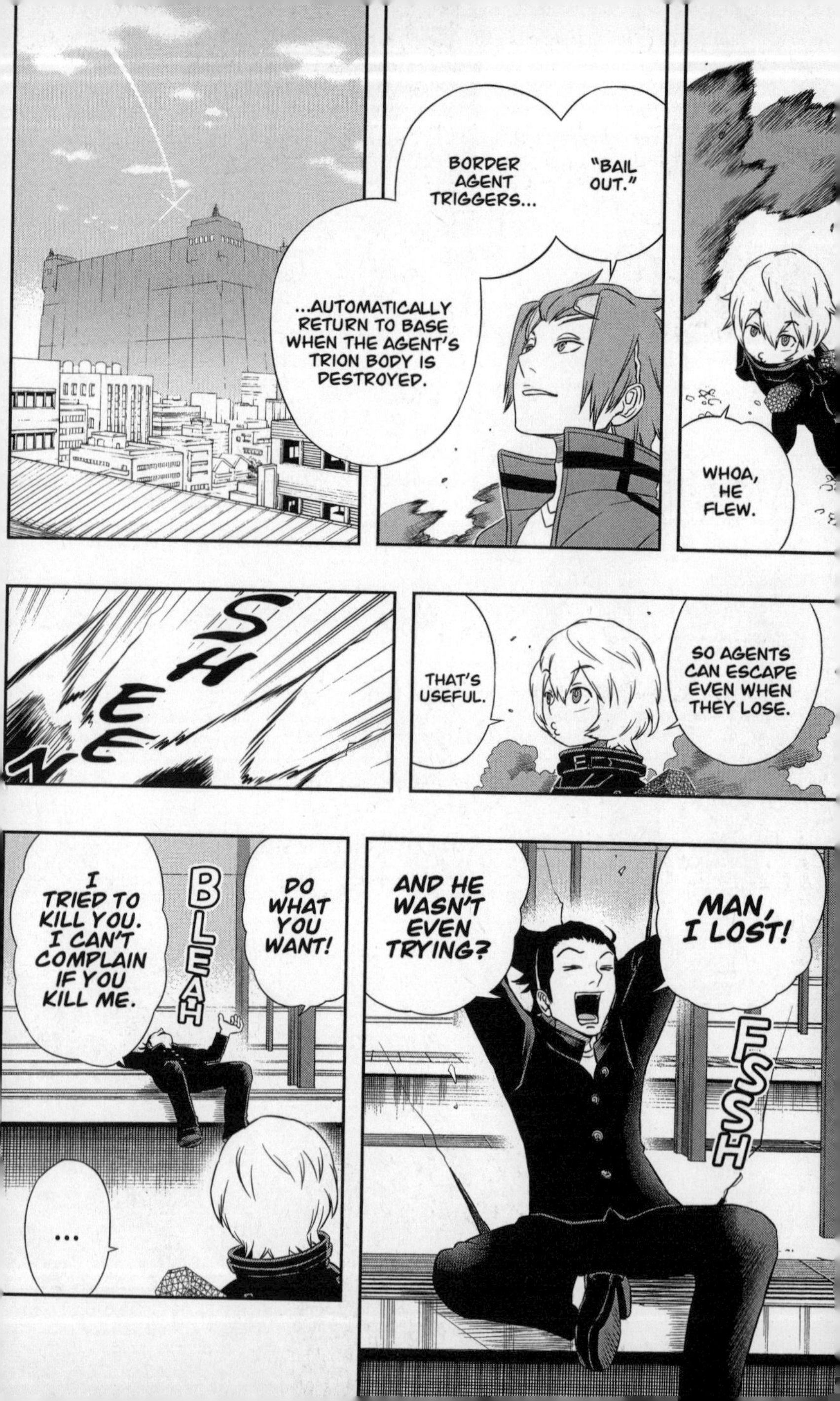
WHOA, HE FLEW.
BORDER AGENT TRIGGERS... "BAIL OUT."
...AUTOMATICALLY RETURN TO BASE WHEN THE AGENT'S TRION BODY IS DESTROYED.
SO AGENTS CAN ESCAPE EVEN WHEN THEY LOSE.
THAT'S USEFUL.
SHEEN
MAN, I LOST!
FSSH
AND HE WASN'T EVEN TRYING?
DO WHAT YOU WANT!
BLEAH
I TRIED TO KILL YOU. I CAN'T COMPLAIN IF YOU KILL ME.
...

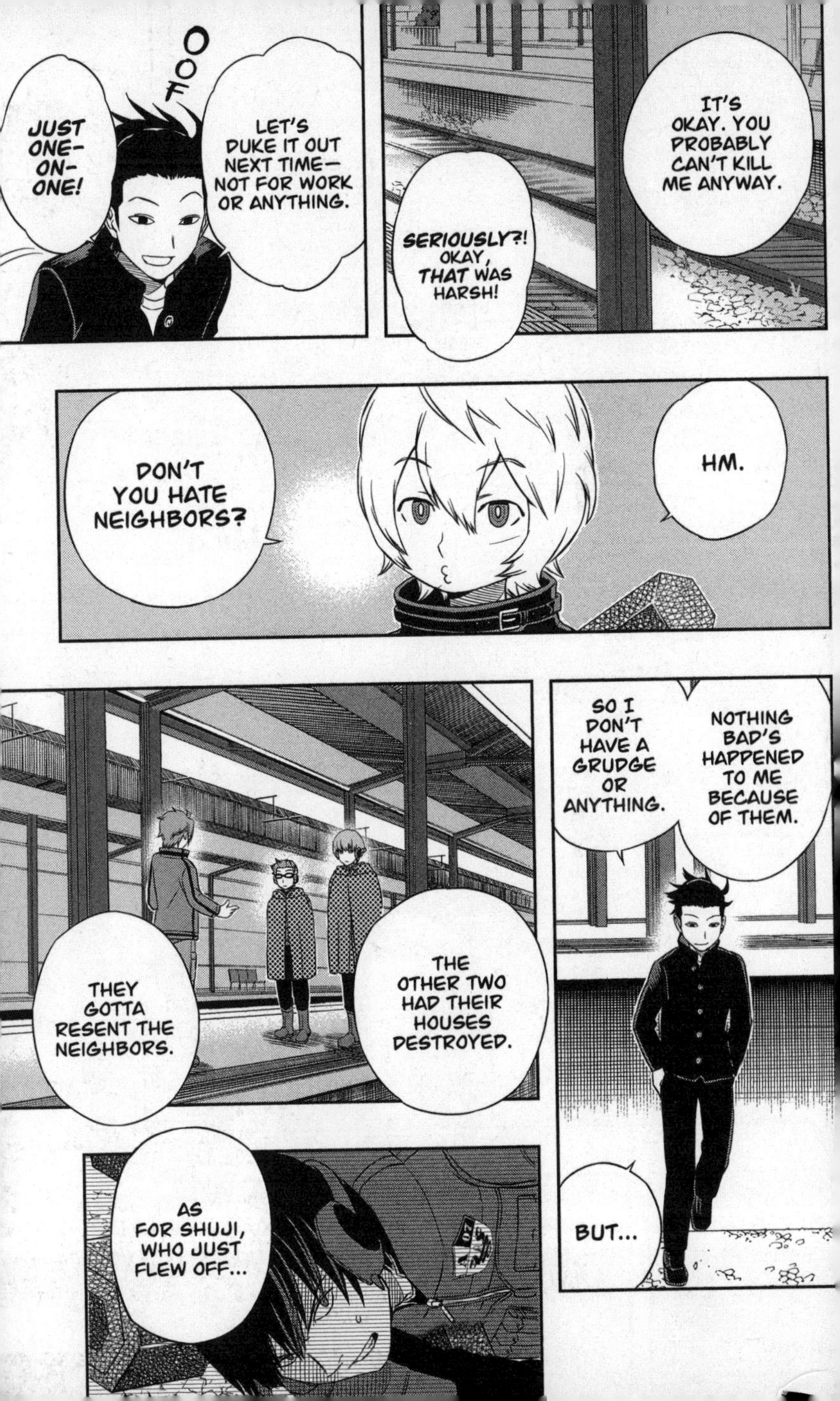
IT'S OKAY. YOU PROBABLY CAN'T KILL ME ANYWAY.
SERIOUSLY?! OKAY, THAT WAS HARSH!
OOF
LET'S DUKE IT OUT NEXT TIME— NOT FOR WORK OR ANYTHING.
JUST ONE-ON-ONE!
HM.
DON'T YOU HATE NEIGHBORS?
NOTHING BAD'S HAPPENED TO ME BECAUSE OF THEM.
SO I DON'T HAVE A GRUDGE OR ANYTHING.
BUT...
THE OTHER TWO HAD THEIR HOUSES DESTROYED.
THEY GOTTA RESENT THE NEIGHBORS.
AS FOR SHUJI, WHO JUST FLEW OFF...

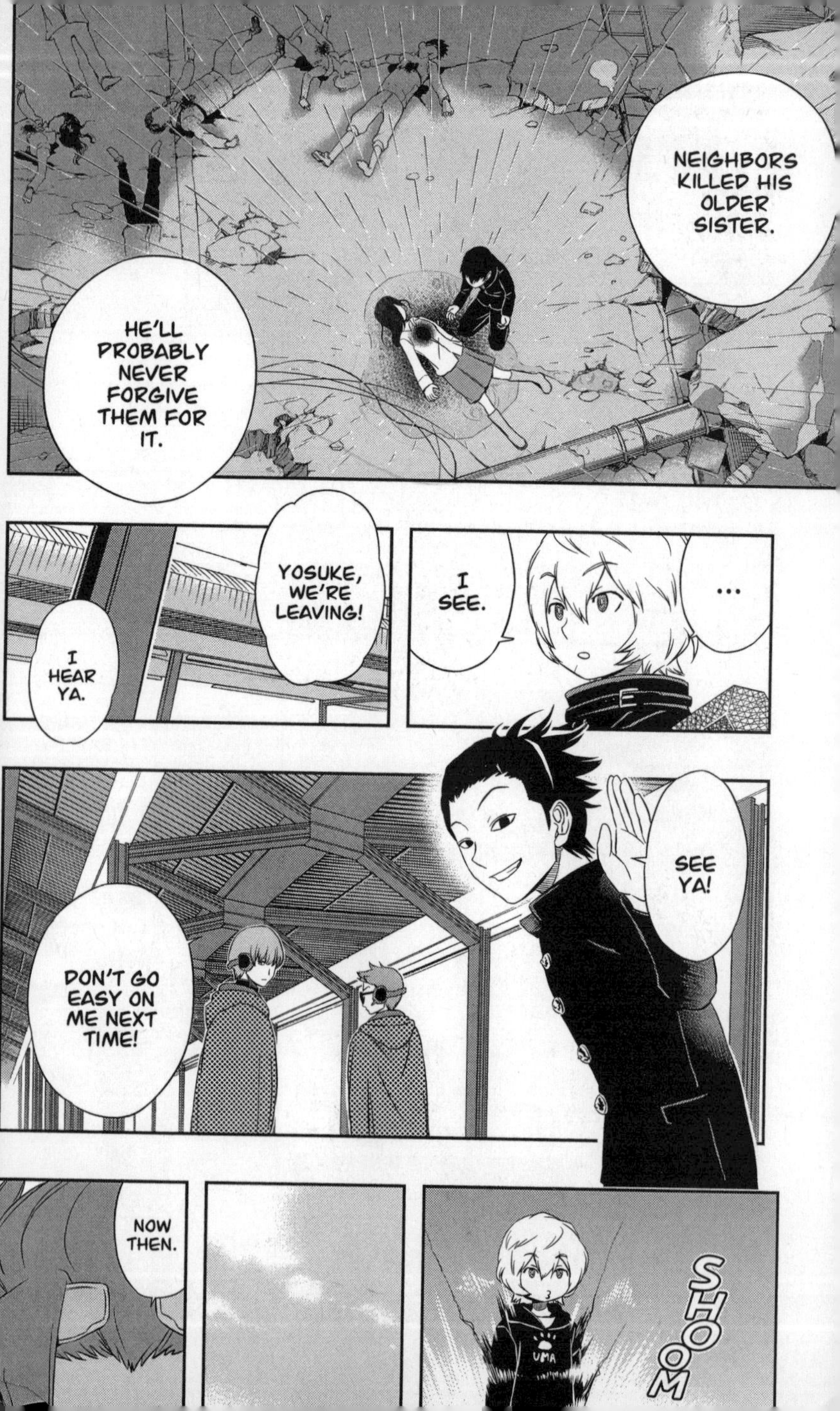
NEIGHBORS KILLED HIS OLDER SISTER.
HE'LL PROBABLY NEVER FORGIVE THEM FOR IT.
...
I SEE.
YOSUKE, WE'RE LEAVING!
I HEAR YA.
SEE YA!
DON'T GO EASY ON ME NEXT TIME!
SHOOM
UMA
NOW THEN.

READ THIS WAY

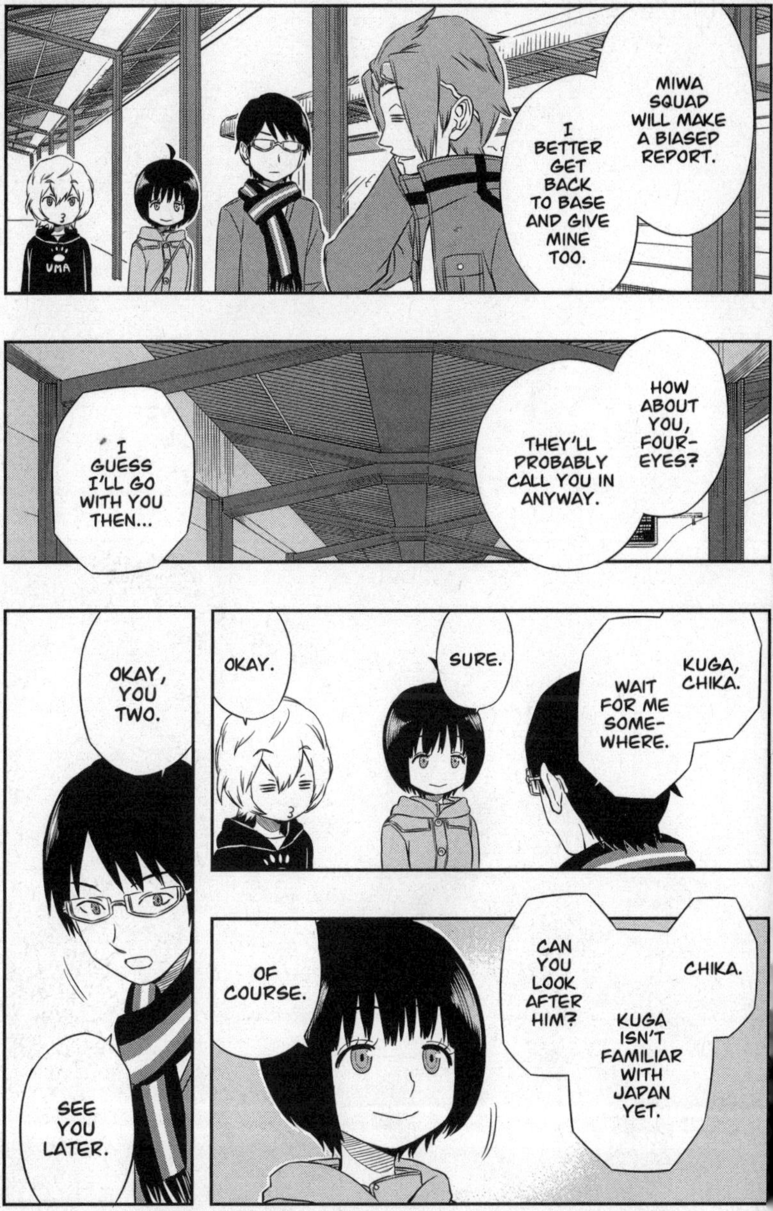
MIWA SQUAD WILL MAKE A BIASED REPORT.
I BETTER GET BACK TO BASE AND GIVE MINE TOO.
HOW ABOUT YOU, FOUR-EYES?
THEY'LL PROBABLY CALL YOU IN ANYWAY.
I GUESS I'LL GO WITH YOU THEN...
KUGA, CHIKA.
WAIT FOR ME SOME-WHERE.
SURE.
OKAY.
CHIKA.
KUGA ISN'T FAMILIAR WITH JAPAN YET.
CAN YOU LOOK AFTER HIM?
OF COURSE.
OKAY, YOU TWO.
SEE YOU LATER.

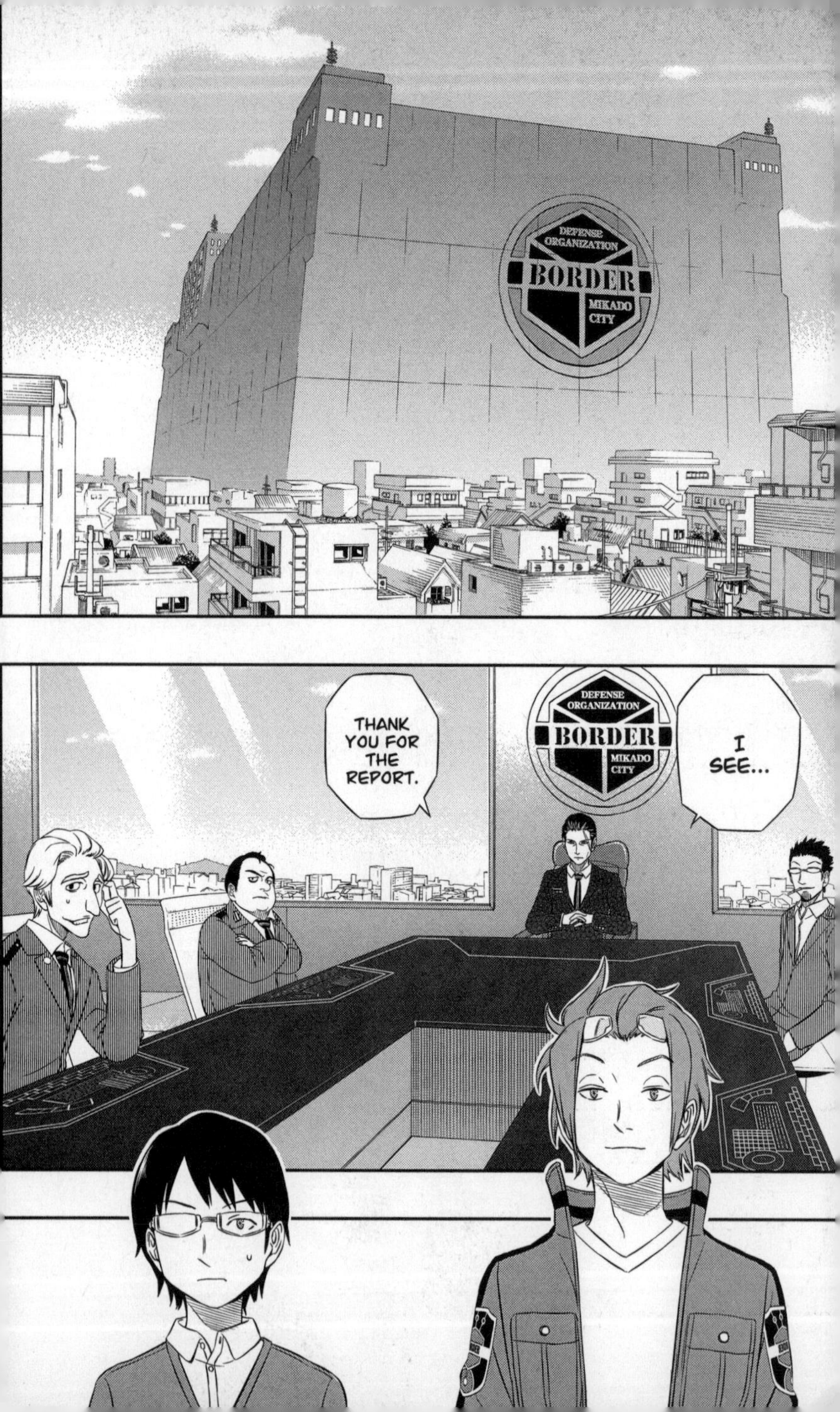
DEFENSE ORGANIZATION BORDER MIKADO CITY
I SEE...
THANK YOU FOR THE REPORT.

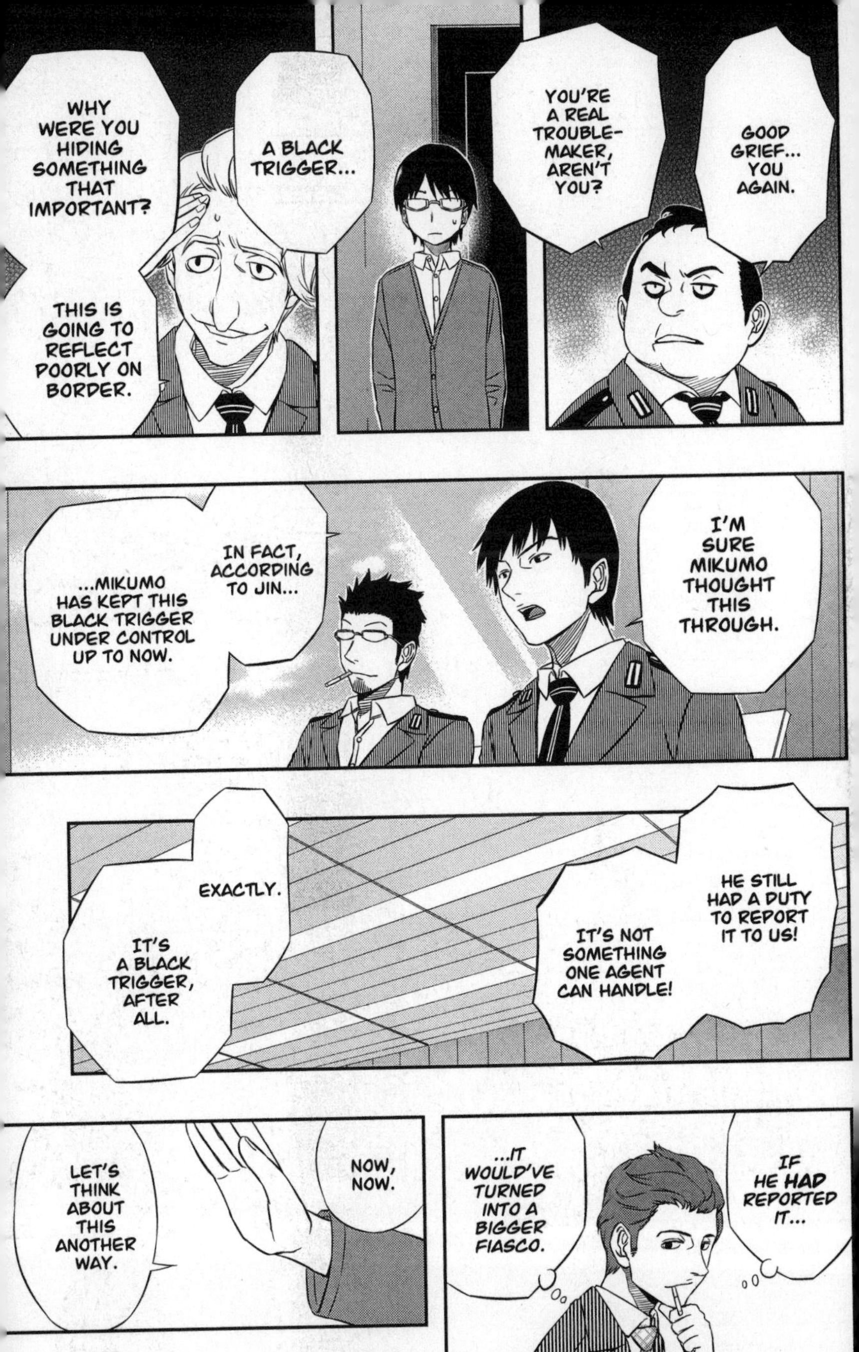
GOOD GRIEF... YOU AGAIN.
YOU'RE A REAL TROUBLE-MAKER, AREN'T YOU?
A BLACK TRIGGER...
WHY WERE YOU HIDING SOMETHING THAT IMPORTANT?
THIS IS GOING TO REFLECT POORLY ON BORDER.
I'M SURE MIKUMO THOUGHT THIS THROUGH.
IN FACT, ACCORDING TO JIN...
...MIKUMO HAS KEPT THIS BLACK TRIGGER UNDER CONTROL UP TO NOW.
HE STILL HAD A DUTY TO REPORT IT TO US!
IT'S NOT SOMETHING ONE AGENT CAN HANDLE!
EXACTLY.
IT'S A BLACK TRIGGER, AFTER ALL.
IF HE HAD REPORTED IT...
...IT WOULD'VE TURNED INTO A BIGGER FIASCO.
NOW, NOW.
LET'S THINK ABOUT THIS ANOTHER WAY.

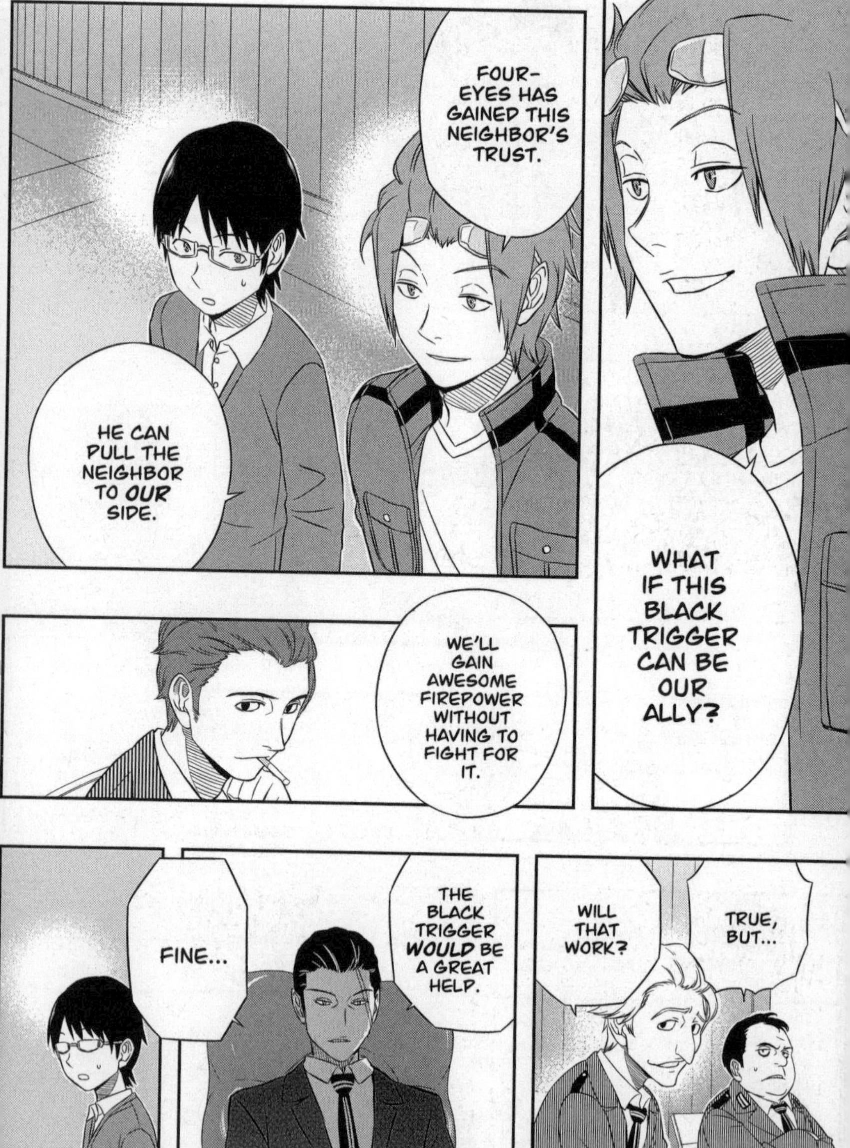
WHAT IF THIS BLACK TRIGGER CAN BE OUR ALLY?
FOUR-EYES HAS GAINED THIS NEIGHBOR'S TRUST.
HE CAN PULL THE NEIGHBOR TO *OUR* SIDE.
WE'LL GAIN AWESOME FIREPOWER WITHOUT HAVING TO FIGHT FOR IT.
TRUE, BUT...
WILL THAT WORK?
THE BLACK TRIGGER *WOULD* BE A GREAT HELP.
FINE...

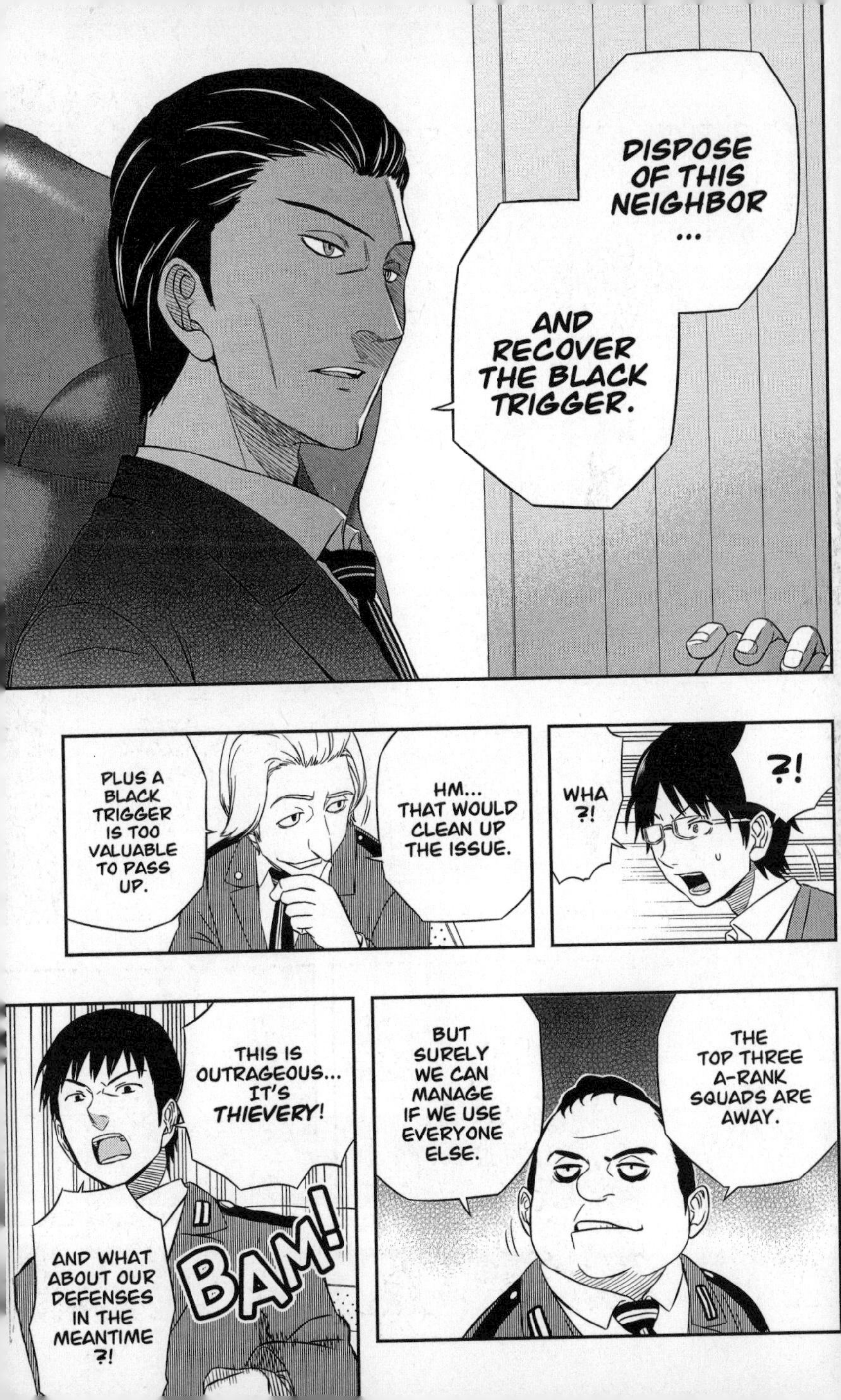
DISPOSE OF THIS NEIGHBOR...
AND RECOVER THE BLACK TRIGGER.
?!
WHA ?!
HM... THAT WOULD CLEAN UP THE ISSUE.
PLUS A BLACK TRIGGER IS TOO VALUABLE TO PASS UP.
THE TOP THREE A-RANK SQUADS ARE AWAY.
BUT SURELY WE CAN MANAGE IF WE USE EVERYONE ELSE.
THIS IS OUTRAGEOUS... IT'S THIEVERY!
BAM!
AND WHAT ABOUT OUR DEFENSES IN THE MEANTIME ?!

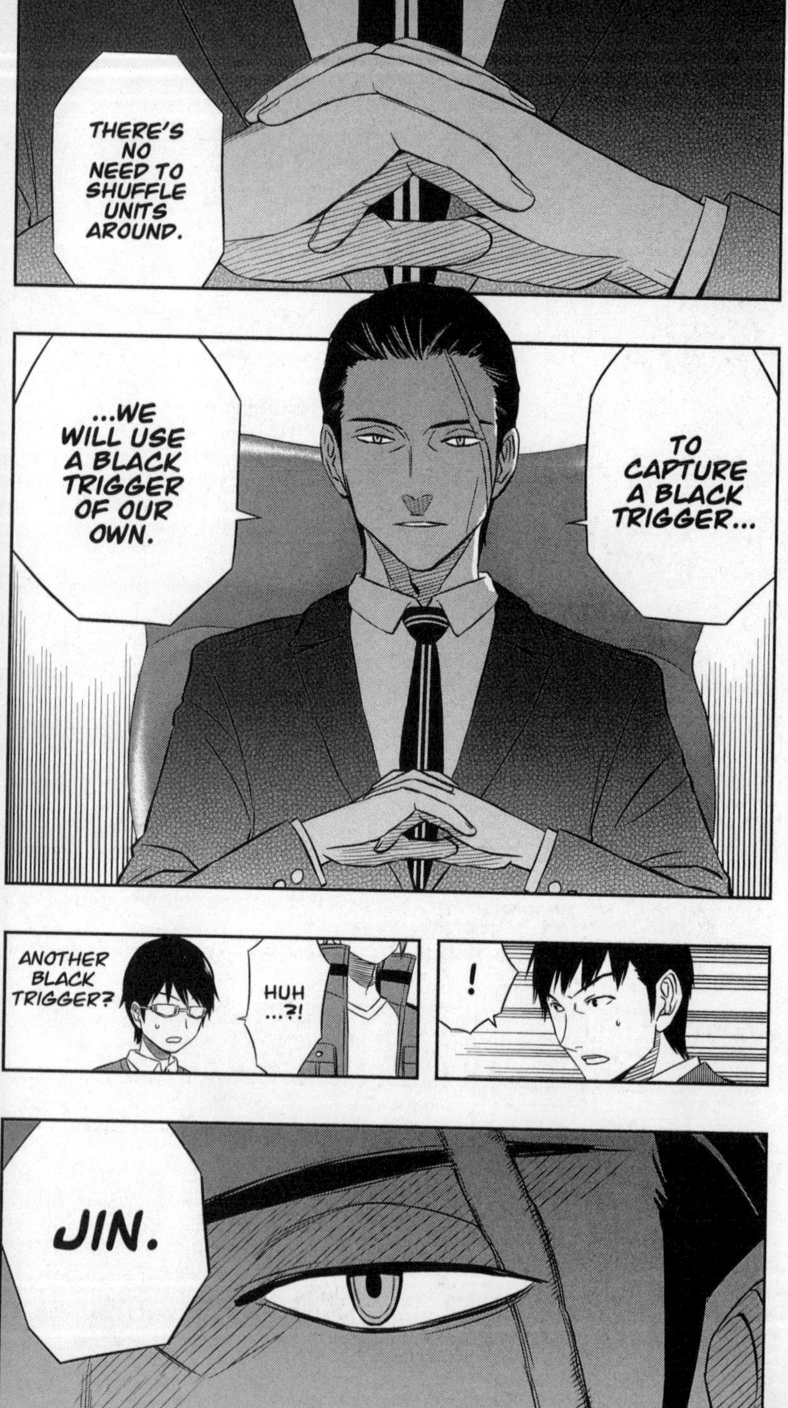
THERE'S NO NEED TO SHUFFLE UNITS AROUND.
TO CAPTURE A BLACK TRIGGER...
...WE WILL USE A BLACK TRIGGER OF OUR OWN.
!
HUH ...?!
ANOTHER BLACK TRIGGER?
JIN.

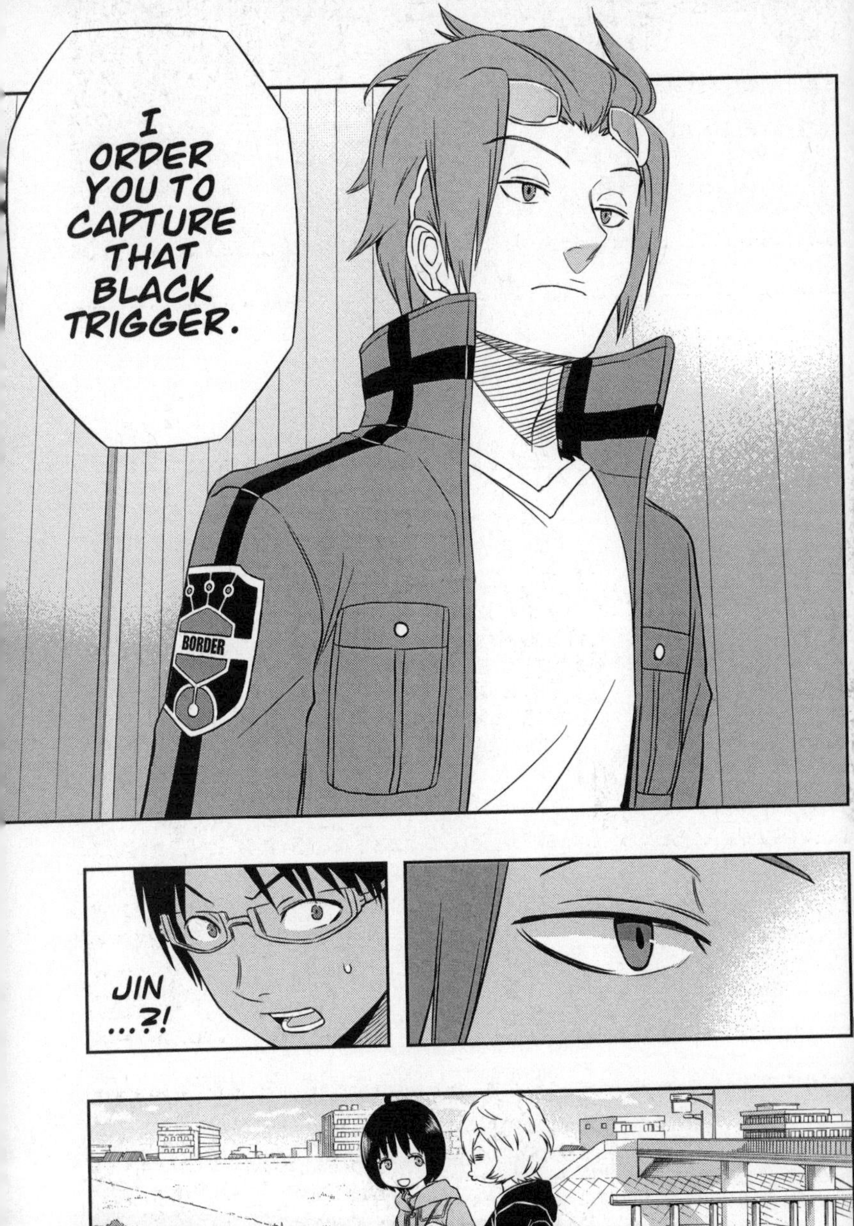
I ORDER YOU TO CAPTURE THAT BLACK TRIGGER.
BORDER
JIN ...?!

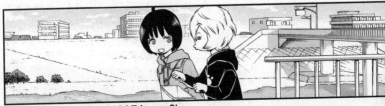

To Be Continued In **World Trigger** 3!

# WORLD TRIGGER

## Bonus Character Pages

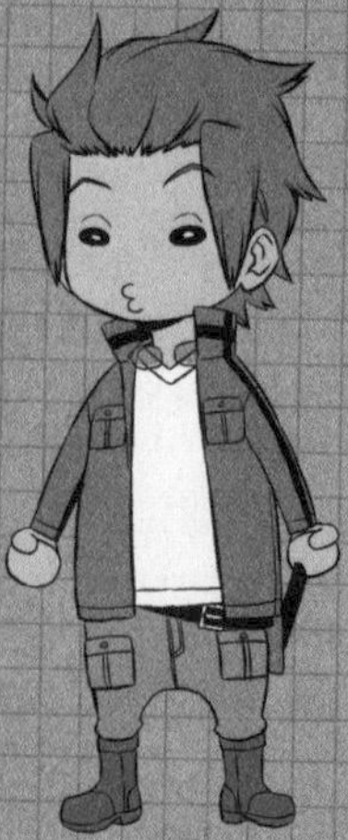

### JIN

**The Bonchi Rice Cracker Diet**

He's an elite agent of sexual harassment, using his Side Effect to pick out women who'll better tolerate his advances. Speaking of advances, he moves the plot along really well, but he's so convenient that it's a problem. He has the same silhouette as Arashiyama, so it's rumored that one of them will get an afro or a mohawk at his next power-up.

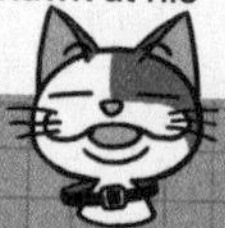

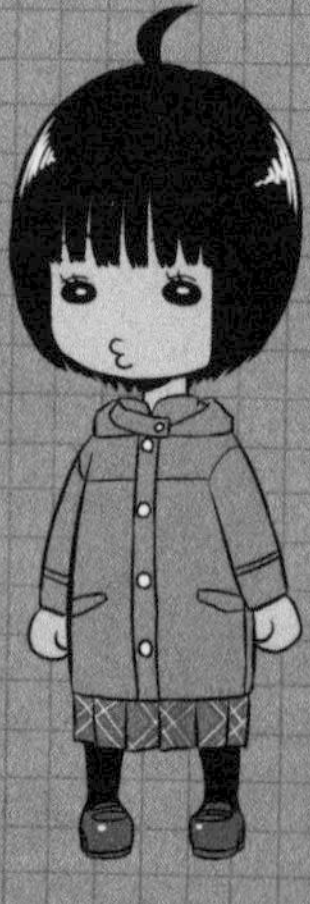

### CHIKA

**Neighbor Magnet**

A quiet character with a tough-luck past—one of the character types I'm not good at. But she shows some backbone in the next volume, so it gets easier. People say she's slowly getting smaller while her hair antenna is getting bigger, so it's possible her antenna is absorbing her body.

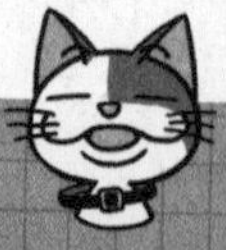

# MIWA
## A-Rank Sister Complex [The Serious One]

A guy with a sister complex who's popular with female readers. He's always angry, but his forehead is covered by hair, so it's hard to draw a convincing angry face. Not a very functional design. I'd like to give him a haircut one of these days.

# YONEYA
## A-Rank Short Sleeves [Or so you think.]

He's always had lifeless eyes, but I kinda like him. I'm glad a lot of people noticed his buttons. He's actually a cousin of Shiori, who appears in volume 3. Unfortunately, his family doesn't run a rice store, unlike what his name implies.

# NARASAKA
## A-Rank Mushroom Cut [Sniper]

He appears to be a relative of a mushroom, but he's actually in the bamboo family. My assistants and editor think he's really skilled for some reason, even though he hasn't done much. Do people judge a book by its cover after all?

# KODERA
## A-Rank Glasses [Glasses]

He's A-Rank but always breaking out in a cold sweat. He is always behind the team, even though lower-ranked agents grumble about him. He's a glasses-wearing character who's often surprised. Since that's the same as Osamu's role, it's rumored that the one who loses at the high jump will have to turn into a delinquent or reveal that he's gay.

# YOU'RE READING THE WRONG WAY!

*World Trigger* reads from right to left, starting in the upper-right corner. Japanese is read from right to left, meaning that action, sound effects, and word-balloon order are completely reversed from the English order.

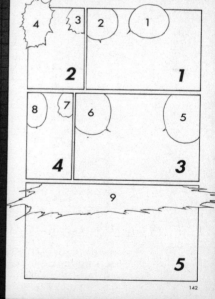

142